Revolutionary State-Making in Dar es Salaam

Tracing Dar es Salaam's rise and fall as an epicentre of Third World revolution, George Roberts explores the connections between the global Cold War, African liberation struggles, and Tanzania's efforts to build a socialist state. Instead of understanding decolonisation through a national lens, he locates the intersection of these dynamics in a globally connected city in East Africa. *Revolutionary State-Making in Dar es Salaam* introduces a vibrant cast of politicians, guerrilla leaders, diplomats, journalists, and intellectuals whose trajectories collided in the city. In its cosmopolitan and rumour-filled hotel bars, embassy receptions, and newspaper offices, they grappled with challenges of remaking a world after empire. Yet Dar es Salaam's role on the frontline of the African revolution and its provocative stance towards global geopolitics came at considerable cost. Roberts explains how Tanzania's strident anti-imperialism ultimately drove an authoritarian turn in its socialist project and tighter control over the city's public sphere. This title is also available as Open Access on Cambridge Core.

George Roberts is Lecturer in Modern African History at King's College London, where his research focuses on the international history of decolonisation in Eastern Africa. He was previously a Junior Research Fellow at Trinity College, University of Cambridge. He was awarded PhD by the University of Warwick in 2016, which was shortlisted for the Audrey Richards Prize for the best doctoral thesis in African Studies by the African Studies Association of the UK in 2018.

African Studies Series

The African Studies series, founded in 1968, is a prestigious series of monographs, general surveys, and textbooks on Africa covering history, political science, anthropology, economics, and ecological and environmental issues. The series seeks to publish work by senior scholars as well as the best new research.

Editorial Board
David Anderson, *The University of Warwick*
Carolyn Brown, *Rutgers University, New Jersey*
Christopher Clapham, *University of Cambridge*
Richard Roberts, *Stanford University, California*
Leonardo A. Villalón, *University of Florida*

Other titles in the series are listed at the back of the book.

Revolutionary State-Making in Dar es Salaam

African Liberation and the Global Cold War, 1961–1974

GEORGE ROBERTS
King's College London

CAMBRIDGE
UNIVERSITY PRESS

University Printing House, Cambridge CB2 8BS, United Kingdom

One Liberty Plaza, 20th Floor, New York, NY 10006, USA

477 Williamstown Road, Port Melbourne, VIC 3207, Australia

314–321, 3rd Floor, Plot 3, Splendor Forum, Jasola District Centre, New Delhi – 110025, India

103 Penang Road, #05–06/07, Visioncrest Commercial, Singapore 238467

Cambridge University Press & Assessment is part of the University of Cambridge.

It furthers the University's mission by disseminating knowledge in the pursuit of education, learning, and research at the highest international levels of excellence.

www.cambridge.org
Information on this title: www.cambridge.org/9781009281652
DOI: 10.1017/9781009281621

© George Roberts 2022

Reissued as Open Access, 2022

This work is in copyright. It is subject to statutory exceptions and to the provisions of relevant licensing agreements; with the exception of the Creative Commons version the link for which is provided below, no reproduction of any part of this work may take place without the written permission of Cambridge University Press.

An online version of this work is published at doi.org/10.1017/9781009281621 under a Creative Commons Open Access license CC-BY-NC-ND 4.0 which permits re-use, distribution and reproduction in any medium for non-commercial purposes providing appropriate credit to the original work is given. You may not distribute derivative works without permission. To view a copy of this license, visit https://creativecommons.org/licenses/by-nc-nd/4.0

All versions of this work may contain content reproduced under license from third parties. Permission to reproduce this third-party content must be obtained from these third-parties directly.

When citing this work, please include a reference to the DOI 10.1017/9781009281621

First published 2022

A catalogue record for this publication is available from the British Library.

ISBN 978-1-009-28165-2 Paperback

Cambridge University Press has no responsibility for the persistence or accuracy of URLs for external or third-party internet websites referred to in this publication and does not guarantee that any content on such websites is, or will remain, accurate or appropriate.

Contents

List of Maps	page vi
Acknowledgements	vii
List of Abbreviations	xii
Introduction	1
1 The Making of a Cold War City in Eastern Africa	26
2 Revisiting the Politics of the Arusha Declaration	66
3 Dilemmas of Non-Alignment: Tanzania and the German Cold War	100
4 The Assassination of Eduardo Mondlane: Mozambican Revolutionaries in Dar es Salaam	135
5 Tanzania's '68: Cold War Interventions, Youth Protest, and Global Anti-Imperialism	173
6 Decolonising the Media: Press and Politics in Revolutionary Dar es Salaam	203
7 *Mwongozo*: The African Revolution, Reloaded	237
Conclusion	273
Bibliography	288
Index	317

Maps

1.1 Tanzania and its neighbours, circa 1968   *page* xv
1.2 Central Dar es Salaam, circa 1968   xvi

Acknowledgements

This book has taken me to many places, but it started life as a doctoral thesis at the University of Warwick. As my supervisors, David Anderson and Dan Branch were prepared to offer a wide-eyed twenty-something a lengthy tether to roam the archives in pursuit of Dar es Salaam's revolutionaries. I am grateful for all their help during my PhD and then in navigating the academic world beyond the thesis. Special thanks are also due to Emma Hunter, who introduced me to East African history as an undergraduate and has supported me on many occasions since. Across the Atlantic, James Brennan has been an unfailing ally throughout the book's development. He's shared all sorts of archive files, read multiple drafts, pointed me in surprising directions, and filled the smallest niches in my knowledge. This work would have been far poorer without his input and I can only hope I've returned his generosity as best I can.

I have many debts in Tanzania. I started my PhD in the company of Max Chuhila, who has remained a crucial source of encouragement and friendship ever since. He and his colleagues at the History Department of the University of Dar es Salaam (UDSM) have always provided a welcoming host academic community on my visits to Tanzania. I am grateful to all of those who took time to share their memories with me and put me in contact with other eyewitnesses to Dar es Salaam's revolutionary politics. Several have sadly since passed away. In particular I would like to thank Ian Bryceson, Salim Msoma, Juma Mwapachu, and Mohamed Said, as well as Muhammad Yussuf at the Zanzibar Institute for Research and Public Policy. I enjoyed talking with Mejah Mbuya, whose enthusiasm for Dar es Salaam's revolutionary heritage is unparalleled. The city street plan in this book is his work as much as mine. On several visits to Dar es Salaam, Natalie Smith was a very welcoming host and even more generous friend. Hanifa and her family provided a home-from-home while I studied Swahili in Iringa. I learned much from talking contemporary

Tanzanian politics with then doctoral researchers Michaela Collord, Cyrielle Maingraud-Martinaud, and Dan Paget. I would also like to thank Peter Bofin, Blandina Giblin, James Giblin, Allison Goforth, and Julie Santella for their help and friendship in all sorts of ways while in Tanzania. Research in the country would not have been possible without the support of the Commission of Science and Technology and Oswald Masebo at UDSM. I am thankful to the staff at the Tanzanian National Archives in Dar es Salaam, the National Records Centre in Dodoma, the basement room of the National Library, and the team led by Dr Kassim Mohamed at the East Africana Collection at UDSM.

Writing global and international history is a necessarily collective enterprise. I am extremely grateful for having colleagues who have shared documents, suggested archival collections, answered highly specific questions, and bounced ideas back and forth. In London, I have spent many long afternoons drinking chai and talking East African history with Ahmed Rajab, who has been a constant source of enthusiasm for this project. For feedback on various parts of the manuscript, I am indebted to Emily Bridger, Kate Bruce-Lockhart, Eric Burton, Sebastian Gehrig, Sacha Hepburn, Ismay Milford, Gerard McCann, and Simon Stevens. Miles Larmer was an exacting but generous doctoral examiner, and this book is much stronger for his comments. John Iliffe, who taught History at the University of Dar es Salaam during the years covered here, read the whole dissertation in astonishingly quick time, and provided cogent feedback as I began to revise it into the book. The final version was produced amid the disruption of the coronavirus pandemic and I am grateful to colleagues and librarians who answered calls to provide materials at short notice. In addition to those already mentioned, I would particularly like to acknowledge the help of Emily Callaci, Chambi Chachage, Kevin Donovan, Dan Hodgkinson, Trevor Grundy, Julia Held, Zoe LeBlanc, Andrew Ivaska, Sebabatso Manoeli, Jamie Miller, Graham Mytton, Anna Ross, Jodie Yuzhou Sun, and Natalia Telepneva.

Research for this book would not have been possible without the guidance of my language teachers, from secondary school to my doctoral studies. I am especially grateful for the sympathetic help afforded to me by archivists who put up with my efforts in German, Portuguese, and Swahili. In Warsaw, Paweł Pujszo interpreted and translated with great patience at the archives of the Polish Foreign Ministry. In Lisbon, Filipa Lima Félix transcribed a Portuguese-language documentary film. Pranjali Srivastava helped with preliminary research at the Indian National Archives in Delhi, which prompted me to submit a request for the digitalisation of relevant files there. On a slightly different linguistic note, I am indebted to John Hargreaves for teaching me about the power of English. In turn, I have been fortunate to have taught classes of engaging undergraduates, especially on my 'Africa and the Cold War' course at Warwick. Their questions, comments, and energy helped to shape this work.

The journey from PhD to this present book took place while I was a Junior Research Fellow at Trinity College, Cambridge. John Lonsdale, another former member of the History Department in Dar es Salaam, has been a staunch supporter of my work as my mentor. I am grateful for the friendship of a community of early career historians in Cambridge, especially Arthur Asseraf, Cécile Feza Bushidi, Merve Fejzula, Nicki Kindersley, Emma Stone Mackinnon, Hannah Shepherd, and Partha Pratim Shil. Julienne Obadia helped me keep my head down in our coffee shop working sessions. There are a number of people whom I have not (yet) met in person, but who were instrumental in shaping these pages as the book neared completion. Maria Marsh and Atifa Jiwa at Cambridge University Press guided the project towards publication. Four reviewers provided incisive comments on the manuscript, which helped me to sharpen the overall argument. The brilliant Kate Blackmer designed and produced the maps of East Africa and Dar es Salaam, accommodating even the most arcane requests for fine-tuning. The cover photograph comes courtesy of Salim Amin and the team at the Camerapix archives in Nairobi.

This research was supported by a doctoral scholarship from the Arts and Humanities Research Council and travel funding from the Royal Historical Society, the Society for the History of American Foreign Relations, the Lyndon Baines Johnson President Library, the Gerald R. Ford Presidential Library, the German History Society, and the Society for the Study of French History. I am grateful to Taylor & Francis for granting permission to use material that forms the basis of Chapter 4, which was published in an earlier form as 'The Assassination of Eduardo Mondlane: FRELIMO, Tanzania, and the Politics of Exile in Dar es Salaam', in *Cold War History*, 17 (2017), 1–19.

Perhaps my greatest thanks are due to those people who haven't read any of the words which follow in this book, but whose friendship and warmth have sustained me as I've written them. I couldn't have a more supportive group of friends, who came together at university over a decade ago and have kept close even as we are now scattered around the world. Despite being an exceptionally talented bunch of people, none of them take themselves too seriously; their humour and self-deprecation have been a welcome reassurance away from academic life. Over the last few years, Anna's love, advice, and encouragement have kept me on track as I completed this book. Now that this is done, I look forward to new adventures together. Finally, I would like to thank my family for all their support along the way. As a child, my parents taught me the importance of self-respect and of saying 'thank you'. It's therefore only fitting that I end these acknowledgements by expressing my deepest gratitude to them.

This title is part of the Cambridge University Press *Flip it Open* Open Access Books program and has been "flipped" from a traditional book to an Open Access book through the program.

Flip it Open sells books through regular channels, treating them at the outset in the same way as any other book; they are part of our library collections for Cambridge Core, and sell as hardbacks and ebooks. The one crucial difference is that we make an upfront commitment that when each of these books meets a set revenue threshold we make them available to everyone Open Access via Cambridge Core.

This paperback edition has been released as part of our Open Access commitment and we would like to use this as an opportunity to thank the libraries and other buyers who have helped us flip this and the other titles in the program to Open Access.

To see the full list of libraries that we know have contributed to *Flip it Open*, as well as the other titles in the program please visit www.cambridge.org/fio-acknowledgements

Abbreviations

ADN	Allgemeiner Deutscher Nachrichtendienst (General German News Agency) – *GDR*
ANC	African National Congress – *South Africa*
ASP	Afro-Shirazi Party – *Zanzibar*
BBC	British Broadcasting Corporation
CCM	Chama cha Mapinduzi (Party of the Revolution) – *Tanzania*
CDU	Christlich Demokratische Union (Christian Democratic Union) – *FRG*
CIA	Central Intelligence Agency – *USA*
CID	Criminal Investigation Department – *Tanzania*
COREMO	Comité Revolucionário de Moçambique (Mozambique Revolutionary Committee)
EAC	East African Community
EAF	East African Federation
FCO	Foreign and Commonwealth Office – *UK*
FRELIMO	Frente de Libertação de Moçambique (Mozambique Liberation Front)
FRG	Federal Republic of Germany
GDR	German Democratic Republic
IPI	International Press Institute
KGB	Komitet gosudarstvennoy bezopasnosti (Committee for State Security) – *Soviet Union*
MAE	Ministère des affaires étrangères (Ministry of Foreign Affairs) – *France*
MAE-DAL	Direction Afrique Levant, MAE (Africa and Middle East Division) – *France*
MAE-DAM	Direction Afrique Malgache, MAE (Africa and Madagascar Division) – *France*
MfAA	Ministerium für Auswärtige Angelegenheiten (Ministry for Foreign Affairs) – *GDR*

MfS	Ministerium für Staatsicherheit (Ministry for State Security, 'Stasi') – *GDR*
MNE	Ministério dos Negócios Estrangeiros (Ministry of Foreign Affairs) – *Portugal*
MOLINACO	Mouvement de Libération Nationale des Comores (National Liberation Movement of Comoros)
MSZ	Ministerstwa Spraw Zagranicznych (Ministry of Foreign Affairs) – *Poland*
NATO	North Atlantic Treaty Organization
NEC	TANU National Executive Committee
NUTA	National Union of Tanganyika Workers
NWICO	New World Information and Communications Order
OAU	Organisation of African Unity
PAC	Pan-Africanist Congress of Azania – *South Africa*
PAFMECA	Pan-African Freedom Movement of Eastern and Central Africa
PAIGC	Partido Africano da Independência da Guiné e Cabo Verde (African Party for the Independence of Guinea and Cape Verde)
PAYM	Pan-African Youth Movement
PDP	Panafrican Democratic Party – *Malawi*
PIDE	Polícia Internacional e do Defesa do Estado (International and State Defence Police) – *Portugal*
RTD	Radio Tanzania Dar es Salaam
SCCIM	Serviços de Centralização e Coordenação de Moçambique (Services for the Centralisation and Coordination of Information for Mozambique) – *Portugal*
SHIHATA	Shirika la Habari la Tanzania (News Agency of Tanzania)
SPD	Sozialdemocratische Partei Deutschlands (Social Democratic Party of Germany) – *FRG*
STC	State Trading Corporation – *Tanzania*
SWAPO	South West Africa People's Organisation – *Namibia*
TANU	Tanganyika African National Union
TAZARA	Tanzania-Zambia Railway Authority
TBC	Tanganyika Broadcasting Corporation
TPDF	Tanzania People's Defence Force
TYL	TANU Youth League

UDI	Unilateral Declaration of Independence
UDSM	University of Dar es Salaam
UN	United Nations
USARF	University Students' African Revolutionary Front – *Tanzania*
ZANU	Zimbabwe African National Union
ZAPU	Zimbabwe African People's Union
ZNP	Zanzibar Nationalist Party
ZPPP	Zanzibar and Pemba People's Party

Map 1.1 Tanzania and its neighbours, circa 1968. Map by Kate Blackmer.

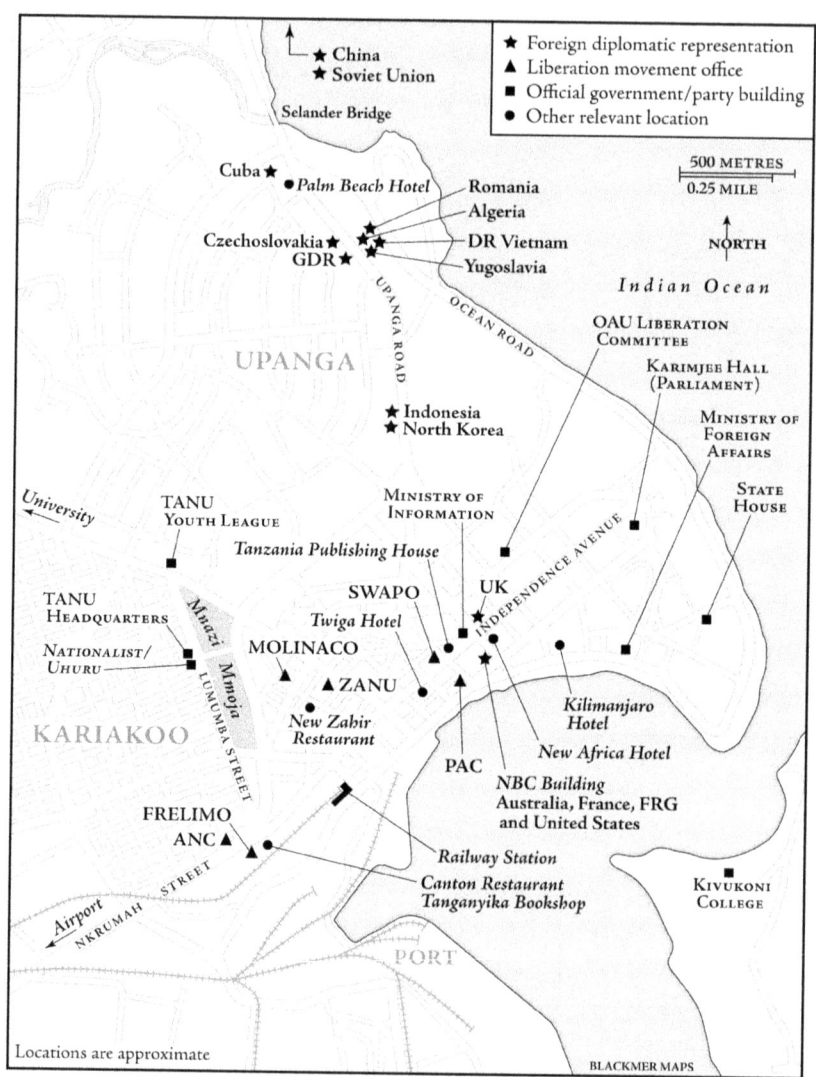

Map 1.2 Central Dar es Salaam, circa 1968. Map by Kate Blackmer, incorporating research by George Roberts and Mejah Mbuya of Afriroots, with assistance from Natalie Smith.

Introduction

Today, Nkrumah Street offers little hint of its illustrious past. Beginning by Dar es Salaam's old railway station, it leads south out of the city centre. Its shabby art deco façades and shaded colonnades exude a certain charm, but nothing more to attract the attention of the casual passer-by. Yet Nkrumah Street and its environs were once the heartbeat of revolutionary Africa. In the 1960s, these same buildings were emblazoned with an alphabet soup of signs: ANC, PAC, SWAPO, ZANU, ZAPU, FRELIMO. The occupiers of these offices were guests of the Tanzanian government. They were unusual guests: exiles from the white minority ruled territories of southern Africa. They were also sometimes troublesome guests, as we will see. By day, the liberation movement leaders organised anticolonial struggles and canvassed for support. By night, the revolutionaries gravitated towards Dar es Salaam's upmarket hotels, where they were regular fixtures at the terrace bars of the Kilimanjaro and New Africa.

The rest of the world took notice. Journalists crowded into press conferences as guerrilla leaders gave updates on their wars of liberation. Cold War diplomats looked for snippets of valuable intelligence and sought to turn the revolutionaries' ears. Despite its peripheral place in the global economy, Dar es Salaam became host to an array of foreign embassies of all geopolitical stripes. One American described the city as 'a real United Nations, as much as the UN Plaza in New York. No-one is riding particularly high, and everyone watches everyone else – civilly, for the most part.'[1] Dar es Salaam became a propaganda battlefield. Chinese booksellers pushed volumes of Marx, Lenin, and Mao. East and West German diplomats engaged in clandestine attempts to besmirch their rivals via the local press or anonymous pamphlets. This revolutionary vibe attracted radical

---

[1] Pickering to State Dept, 2 July 1969, NARA, RG 59, CFPF 1967–69, Box 2515, POL 15–1 TANZAN.

academics from around the world to the city's university. Meanwhile, Tanzania's postcolonial elite attempted to build a non-aligned 'African socialist' state, rejecting the Cold War poles of capitalism and communism to stake out their own ideological path to modernity.

For some, Dar es Salaam was a city of hope and dreams. A Namibian exile recalled his excitement at the revolutionary possibilities present in this mecca of liberation. 'We had heard much talk about Dar es Salaam while still in Namibia', he wrote. 'It became every Namibian's dream to one day see Dar es Salaam.'[2] The city's lecture halls and newspaper columns buzzed with calls for socialist nation-building that looked to China, Cuba, and Vietnam for inspiration. For others, particularly in the West, the city was a dangerous staging ground for communist penetration – 'a pistol pointing at the heart of African troubles', as one British journalist put it.[3] The Tanzanian government's approach sat somewhere in between. It was without question among the most committed African supporters of the continued struggle against colonialism. The country's first president, Julius Nyerere, spoke powerfully of shining a torch from Mount Kilimanjaro to provide a beacon of hope across the unliberated territories of the continent. But these commitments were tempered with anxieties about their consequences. Nyerere's government feared the destabilising effect of these external forces on the country's politics, especially given the scant respect for Third World sovereignty exhibited by the superpowers and the white minority regimes. 'Vigilance' became a national watchword. The Tanzanian state decried the subversion of its employees and the propaganda wars fought out by foreign powers in Dar es Salaam. In a word which captured his anxiety about the dangerous consequences of loose political gossip, Nyerere dubbed the capital 'Rumourville'.

This book explains how Dar es Salaam became a hive of revolutionary activity in Africa. It examines the politics of Cold War rivalries, African liberation movements, and socialist state-building in a Third World state. These dynamics were thoroughly enmeshed. This created opportunities for furthering political ambition and interests but posed obstacles to their successful pursuit. From cabinet ministers and parliamentarians to journalists and guerrilla leaders, Dar es Salaam's

[2] Helao Shityuwete, *Never Follow the Wolf: The Autobiography of a Namibian Freedom Fighter* (London: Kliptown, 1990), 93–94.
[3] Ronald Payne, 'Russians and Chinese Use Tanzania as Arms Centre', *Sunday Telegraph*, 21 March 1965, 1–2.

African elites brokered relationships with outside powers and projected their own ideological agendas into the Cold War world. At the same time, this book argues that the challenges which these transnational connections posed to Tanzania's fragile sovereignty were a significant factor in the shutting down of political space in the country. It approaches these developments through a multilateral and multiarchival study of revolutionary state-making in Dar es Salaam.

Revolutionary Cities, Cold War Cities

The rise of 'global' and 'transnational' approaches to history has profoundly altered the way in which we think about the longue durée process of decolonisation in Africa. Breaking with nationalist narratives, these new histories have shown how struggles against imperialism and postcolonial state-making projects were shaped by the movement of people, texts, and ideas. Although these approaches have helped us to move beyond the containers of empire and nation-state, they come with their own potential pitfalls. Tracing transnational dynamics reveals a world in motion, but also brings teleological dangers in following individuals and ideas across the globe while disconnecting them from the physical spaces which they occupied along the way. As Tim Harper reminds us, 'rather than solely looking for connections – as the pursuit of the transnational seems to impel us constantly – it is equally important to recreate the neighbourhood itself'.[4] In this light, this book joins a growing number of works which explore the potential for cities to serve as a geographic lens for writing political histories which ground global and transnational dynamics in local contexts.

The Dar es Salaam of the 1960s and 1970s took its place in a long genealogy of globally connected revolutionary cities. Their rise and fall were shaped by the processes of colonisation and decolonisation, underpinned by technological and infrastructural change. During the high tide of European colonialism around the turn of the twentieth century, global networks linked imperial peripheries with metropolitan capitals to turn growing cities into incubators of new forms of political

---

[4] Tim Harper, 'Singapore, 1915, and the Birth of the Asian Underground', in Tim Harper and Sunil Amrith (eds.), *Sites of Asian Interaction: Ideas, Networks, and Mobility* (Delhi: Cambridge University Press, 2014), 33.

dissent. In East Asia, the late nineteenth-century communications revolution in marine transport, the telegraph, and the rise of the press gave rise to politicised, multicultural colonial publics.[5] These same infrastructural transformations turned cities as distant as New York and Beirut into sites of radical and anarchist activity.[6] In early twentieth-century London and Paris, interactions between imperial subjects encouraged the formation of anticolonial nationalisms, black internationalism, and nascent Third World solidarities.[7]

The double helix formed by the twin dynamics of decolonisation and the Cold War sustained these older cosmopolitan nodes, while also creating new urban centres of vibrant revolutionary activity. As the colonial world became the Third World, cities that lay on the fault lines of international geopolitics and anti-imperial struggles became hives of intellectual and political activity. Another revolution in global communications, particularly the expansion of air travel, facilitated intercontinental movement between urban centres. Rangoon briefly established itself as a pivotal city in the coordination of socialist organisation across Asia and Africa.[8] Hong Kong functioned as a grey zone in the Cold War in East Asia, through which capital was channelled between communist China and the West, as well as a base for superpower intelligence operations.[9] Having been an outpost of espionage during the Second World War, Mexico City became a key Cold War battleground in Central America.[10] These 'Cold War cities' were not just the site of diplomatic

---

[5] Harper and Amrith (eds.), *Sites of Asian Interaction*; Su Lin Lewis, *Cities in Motion: Urban Life and Cosmopolitanism in Southeast Asia, 1920–1940* (Cambridge: Cambridge University Press, 2016).

[6] Tom Goyens, *Beer and Revolution: The German Anarchist Movement in New York City, 1880–1914* (Urbana: University of Illinois Press, 2007); Ilham Khuri-Makdisi, *The Eastern Mediterranean and the Making of Global Radicalism, 1860–1914* (Berkeley: University of California Press, 2010).

[7] Jennifer Anne Boittin, *Colonial Metropolis: The Urban Grounds of Anti-Imperialism and Feminism in Interwar Paris* (Lincoln: University of Nebraska Press, 2010); Michael Goebel, *Anti-Imperial Metropolis: Interwar Paris and the Seeds of Third World Nationalism* (New York: Cambridge University Press, 2015); Marc Matera, *Black London: The Imperial Metropolis and Decolonization in the Twentieth Century* (Berkeley: University of California Press, 2015).

[8] Su Lin Lewis, 'Asian Socialism and the Forgotten Architects of Post-Colonial Freedom, 1952–1956', *Journal of World History*, 30 (2019), 55–88.

[9] Priscilla Roberts and John M. Carroll (eds.), *Hong Kong in the Cold War* (Hong Kong: Hong Kong University Press, 2016).

[10] Renata Keller, *Mexico's Cold War: Cuba, the United States, and the Legacy of the Mexican Revolution* (New York: Cambridge University Press, 2015);

and intelligence activity. Rather, their radical politics were driven by interventions and claim-making from beyond the state. For example, Saigon became a centre not just for American military organisation, but challenges to the South Vietnamese state from students, religious leaders, and other urban opposition movements.[11] In South America, a peripatetic mixture of intellectuals and revolutionaries migrated from one city to another – Montevideo to Santiago to Buenos Aires – as a chain of coups brought to power military regimes that cracked down on the left.[12]

In independent Africa, radical governments turned their capitals into continental centres for revolutionary thinking, organisation, and mobilisation. Situated at a geographic and ideological crossroads between Europe, Africa, and the Middle East, Cairo was the first of these cosmopolitan cities to emerge. The city's strategic location and Gamal Abdel Nasser's presence at the forefront of the pan-African and pan-Arab movements attracted aspiring political figures from across the region.[13] In Ghana, Kwame Nkrumah's government seized the torch of African liberation. Accra drew anticolonial leaders from across Africa and the diaspora to major conferences and provided institutional support for the continent's liberation movements as they began to organise armed struggles.[14] In Algiers, groups advocating for a diverse range of radical and emancipatory causes, such as Palestinian independence, Brazilian democracy, and Black Power, operated missions alongside revolutionaries from southern Africa.[15]

Eric Zolov, *The Last Good Neighbor: Mexico in the Global Sixties* (Durham, NC: Duke University Press, 2020).

[11] Heather Marie Stur, *Saigon at War: South Vietnam and the Global Sixties* (Cambridge: Cambridge University Press, 2020).

[12] Aldo Marchesi, *Latin America's Radical Left: Rebellion and Cold War in the Global 1960s*, trans. Laura Pérez Carrara (New York: Cambridge University Press, 2018).

[13] Zoe LeBlanc, 'Circulating Anti-Colonial Cairo: Decolonizing News Media and the Making of the Third World in Egypt, 1952–78', PhD diss. (Vanderbilt University, 2019).

[14] Meredith Terretta, 'Cameroonian Nationalists Go Global: From Forest *Maquis* to a Pan-African Accra', *Journal of African History*, 51 (2010), 189–212; Jeffrey S. Ahlman, 'Road to Ghana: Nkrumah, Southern Africa, and the Eclipse of a Decolonizing Africa', *Kronos*, 37 (2011), 23–40; Matteo Grilli, *Nkrumaism and African Nationalism: Ghana's Pan-African Foreign Policy in the Age of Decolonization* (Cham: Palgrave Macmillan, 2017).

[15] Jeffrey James Byrne, *Mecca of Revolution: Algeria, Decolonization, and the Third World Order* (Oxford: Oxford University Press, 2015); Elaine

If Algiers was, to cite two recent book titles, a 'mecca of revolution' and 'Third World capital', then Dar es Salaam became a similar entrepôt of anticolonial liberation south of the Sahara. Even before Tanganyika attained independence in 1961, the city had developed a reputation as a meeting place for the region's political movements. Independence, as well as Dar es Salaam's location on the 'frontline' in the fight against minority rule, quickened the pace of this influx of exiles and refugees. To an even greater extent than Algiers, Dar es Salaam was also a contact zone in which this revolutionary politics was enwrapped in local state-making practices, as the ruling Tanganyika African National Union (TANU) attempted to construct an African socialist society. By the mid-1960s, Cairo, Accra, Algiers, and Dar es Salaam were Africa's major urban sites of anticolonial mobilisation. They were part of a global network which spanned the former metropolitan centres, the capitals of the communist world, and other revolutionary cities across the Third World. This urban anticolonial archipelago was held together by a mobile cast of politicians, intellectuals, and other activists who possessed the means to obtain an air ticket. They were tracked by the agents – declared and undeclared – of the superpowers, their allies, and the white minority states.

The Cold War was a global conflict, entwined with the longue durée process of decolonisation. Across the Third World, the superpowers promoted their ideological models of modernity, proffered aid packages, intervened in liberation struggles, and became entangled in the civil and regional wars which often followed.[16] Away from these zones

---

Mokhtefi, Algiers, *Third World Capital: Freedom Fighters, Revolutionaries, Black Panthers* (London: Verso, 2018).

[16] The key foundational text is Odd Arne Westad, *The Global Cold War: Third World Interventions and the Making of Our Times* (Cambridge: Cambridge University Press, 2005). On the Cold War in Africa, see for example Piero Gleijeses, *Conflicting Missions: Havana, Washington and Africa, 1959–1976* (Chapel Hill: University of North Carolina Press, 2002); Piero Gleijeses, *Visions of Freedom: Havana, Washington, Pretoria and the Struggle for Southern Africa, 1976–1991* (Chapel Hill: University of North Carolina Press, 2013); Sergey Mazov, *A Distant Front in the Cold War: The USSR in West Africa and the Congo, 1956–1964* (Washington, DC: Woodrow Wilson Center Press, 2010); Lise Namikas, *Battleground Africa: Cold War in the Congo, 1961–1965* (Washington, DC: Woodrow Wilson Center Press, 2013); Nancy Mitchell, *Jimmy Carter in Africa: Race and the Cold War* (Washington, DC: Woodrow Wilson Center Press, 2016); Radoslav A. Yordanov, *The Soviet Union and the Horn of Africa During the Cold War* (Lanham, MD: Lexington, 2016).

of hot conflict, African capitals became sites of ideological competition and information gathering. After Tanganyika became independent, the Cold War powers and their allies rushed to set up embassies in Dar es Salaam. The Soviet Union and China sized up the credentials of guerrilla leaders and sought to influence the direction of Tanzanian socialism. The United States, forever on the defensive against a local stream of accusations of neo-imperialism, attempted to counter these communist advances. Among these bigger beasts of the Cold War, a host of smaller states pursued their own agendas. East Germany and West Germany turned Dar es Salaam into their own Cold War battlefield, as Chapter 3 shows. This politics was not solely the preserve of accredited diplomats. It was practised by a host of intermediaries, including news agency correspondents and journalists, who built transnational connections with local powerbrokers.

The Cold War powers descended on Dar es Salaam in such numbers because of the presence of the anticolonial movements in the city. At their offices, hotel bars, and embassy receptions, the revolutionaries made use of the grey diplomatic spaces which existed in Dar es Salaam to seek aid and arms from the superpowers. Like their comrades elsewhere in the Third World, African guerrilla movements became key actors in the local political scene which they encountered in Dar es Salaam.[17] Their activities were influenced by Tanzanians who occupied powerful gatekeeping roles in the state apparatus. Just as Christian Williams has shown in the case of training camps in inland Tanzania, exile was an experience characterised by tension as much as unity.[18] Whereas the guerrilla rank-and-file and other refugees experienced the austerity of camp life, in Dar es Salaam their leaders fraternised with diplomats and journalists from across the Cold War world in the capital's upmarket hotels. These encounters were vital in mobilising international support for the liberation struggles, but they could also open up divisions within movements, as shown by the case of the assassination of Mozambique's Eduardo Mondlane in Chapter 4.

---

[17] Paul Thomas Chamberlin, *The Global Offensive: The United States, the Palestine Liberation Organization, and the Making of the Post-Cold War World* (Oxford: Oxford University Press, 2012).

[18] Christian Williams, *National Liberation in Post-Colonial Southern Africa: An Ethnographic History of SWAPO's Exile Camps* (Cambridge: Cambridge University Press, 2015).

Africa's 'Cold War cities' were the product not just of a vibrant political cosmopolitanism, but also of the geopolitical anxieties of the era. The states inherited by Africa's first generation of post-independence leaders were mostly fragile constructions. The dramatic events in Congo reminded Africa's elites of the precarious nature of their authority. The fate of Patrice Lumumba, murdered in 1961 by his Katangese enemies with the aid of American intelligence and Belgian mining interests, cast a long shadow. The 'hidden hand' of the CIA or its communist counterparts seemed to lurk around every corner. The spate of coups which took place across the continent provided further cause for alarm. The consequence was the emergence of what Priya Lal has dubbed a 'Cold War political culture', which left its mark on both the conceptualisation and implementation of socialism in Tanzania.[19] Official discourse was replete with fears of foreign subversion and an incantation for citizens to remain vigilant at all times. Nyerere himself was aware that this was verging on paranoia. 'It is perfectly true that many of us in Africa are in danger of getting a phobia about foreign plots and of attributing to foreign machinations all the evils we suffer from', he admitted. But, at the same time, 'no intelligent and knowledgeable person would deny that outside forces do take advantage of African division for their own benefit'.[20] It was this Cold War political culture that also provided the justification for the increasingly authoritarian approach of the Tanzanian state in the enforcement of socialism into the 1970s.

The Cold War became inscribed into the urban politics of Dar es Salaam. The Tanzanian government developed an obsession with the subversive activities of rumourmongers and foreign spies in Dar es Salaam. It portrayed bars and cafés, particularly cosmopolitan locations like the New Africa and Kilimanjaro hotels, as sites where enemies of the nation might elicit or overhear idle chatter that endangered national security. It tried to crack down on the foreign propaganda which was pumped into the city's public sphere by the Cold War powers. This suspicion of political gossip and subversion drew on a broader disdain for urban life which characterised the official

---

[19] Priya Lal, *African Socialism in Postcolonial Tanzania: Between the Village and the World* (New York: Cambridge University Press, 2015), 67–69.
[20] 'Stability and Change in Africa', in Julius K. Nyerere, *Freedom and Development: A Selection from Writings and Speeches, 1968–1973* (Dar es Salaam: Oxford University Press, 1973), 111.

language of socialist Tanzania. Government rhetoric and street discourse presented the capital's inhabitants as a parasitical class, which diverted human and financial resources away from TANU's revolution. In a similar vein, Dar es Salaam's public sphere echoed with criticisms of the liberation movement leaders for leading indulgent lifestyles in the city rather than fighting at the front alongside the rank-and-file.

However, Dar es Salaam's political life was not always viewed in such a negative light. As a revolutionary capital, the city produced more optimistic visions of a postcolonial future. The liberation movements contributed to a more dynamic, forward-looking political scene marked by the language of pan-Africanism and Third World solidarity. The popular euphoria which greeted TANU's landmark 'Arusha Declaration' of 1967 tapped into this feeling of postcolonial possibility, even as its proponents recognised the challenges which they faced in fulfilling their aims. Just as students elsewhere in the world struck out against imperialism and injustice, Dar es Salaam's youth condemned superpower interventions from Vietnam to Czechoslovakia. Its university established an international reputation as a centre for radical scholarship in Africa. Chapter 5 examines the elaboration of youth protest and mobilisation in an urban context, as the government attempted to channel the popular forces of the 'global sixties' towards its socialist political goals.

Like other African cities, Dar es Salaam's population grew rapidly in the twentieth century. In 1900, it was estimated at around 20,000, rising to 93,000 by 1957, and then trebling in size again to 273,000 by 1967.[21] The city has been the subject of a range of historical studies linked to this phenomenon of urbanisation. These histories recognise that the city's human landscape represented dangers for governments seeking to maintain control over this expanding population, as well as opportunities for citizens to bend the urban order towards their own agendas. Andrew Burton investigates colonial-era policing practices for managing these expanding numbers. James Brennan explores how city planning and the provision of social services were enwrapped in the formation of national and racial identities. Andrew Ivaska examines

---

[21] James R. Brennan and Andrew Burton, 'The Emerging Metropolis: A History of Dar es Salaam, circa 1862–2000', in James R. Brennan, Andrew Burton, and Yusuf Lawi (eds.), *Dar es Salaam: Histories from an Emerging African Metropolis* (Dar es Salaam: Mkuki na Nyota, 2007), 26, 53.

the postcolonial government's attempt to develop and define a 'national culture'. Recent work has pushed beyond the colonial and immediate postcolonial years to reflect on the urban histories during the period of acute economic crisis from the late 1970s onwards. Emily Callaci addresses the contribution of 'popular intellectuals' to Dar es Salaam's public sphere amid the breakdown of socialism. Chambi Chachage traces the trajectories of the city's African entrepreneurs from colonial origins to the neoliberal present. Emily Brownell shows how the capital's inhabitants responded creatively to environmental degradation and commodity shortages.[22] Breaking with the focus on urbanisation but still informed by its plural experiences in Dar es Salaam, this book transposes these fruitful approaches to the plane of high politics in the capital.

Anticolonial State-Making After Empire

Tanzania fashioned itself as a spearhead of Third World revolution. Whereas many of Africa's postcolonial governments were fearful of rattling the cages of stronger powers, Tanzania routinely adopted the most radical stances towards questions of anticolonial liberation on the international stage. Revolution beyond its borders went hand in hand with revolution within them, as TANU embarked on an 'African socialist' path to development. The idea of *ujamaa* ('familyhood') located the basis for socialist development in the supposed communal traditions of the African peasantry rather than Marxist theories of class antagonism. Following the blueprint set out in the Arusha Declaration, TANU emphasised rural transformation over heavy industrialisation. The most striking of the state's subsequent interventions was the mass

---

[22] Andrew Burton, *African Underclass: Urbanisation, Crime and Colonial Order in Dar es Salaam* (London: British Institute in Eastern Africa, 2005); James R. Brennan, *Taifa: Making Nation and Race in Urban Tanzania* (Athens: Ohio University Press, 2012); Andrew Ivaska, *Cultured States: Youth, Gender, and Modern Style in 1960s Dar es Salaam* (Durham, NC: Duke University Press, 2011); Emily Callaci, *Street Archives and City Life: Popular Intellectuals in Postcolonial Tanzania* (Durham, NC: Duke University Press, 2017); Chambi Chachage, 'A Capitalizing City: Dar es Salaam and the Emergence of an Entrepreneurial Elite (c.1862–2015)', PhD diss. (Harvard University, 2018); Emily Brownell, *Gone to Ground: A History of Environment and Infrastructure in Dar es Salaam* (Pittsburgh, PA: University of Pittsburgh Press, 2020). See also the essays in Brennan, Burton, and Lawi (eds.), *Dar es Salaam*.

relocation of millions of peasants from scattered hamlets into centralised *ujamaa* villages – a phenomenon which has become a magnet for social scientists and historians.[23] This book turns in the opposite direction: away from the countryside and grassroots experiences of socialism and towards the capital and governing elite.

Tanzania's socialist project was among the most ambitious of the Third World's responses to the challenges of decolonisation. Even as TANU enshrined the principle of African liberation at the forefront of its national credo, the country's leaders recognised that political self-determination could not be an end in itself. As the political theorist Adom Getachew has explained, anticolonial thinkers like Nyerere appreciated the need for the genuine decolonisation of the continent's economies.[24] Whereas Kwame Nkrumah had urged Africans to 'seek ye first the political kingdom', Nyerere argued that real independence required what he termed *kujitegemea* ('self-reliance'). This concept underpinned the developmental logic of *ujamaa*, which aimed to end Tanzania's dependence on aid and investment from abroad. It also informed Nyerere's foreign policy. He challenged prevailing ideas of the Cold War order by arguing that the main division in the world was between 'imperialists' and 'anti-imperialists' or a wealthy global North and poorer postcolonial South, rather than communist East and capitalist West.

This historical study of Tanzanian socialism and its entwinement with foreign policy challenges persistent trends in the literature on state formation in Africa. Much political science work subscribes to the premise that the modern state was simply a colonial imposition on Africa, that the anticolonial forces which challenged it took their inspiration from European nationalism, and that the failure of

---

[23] For recent examples, see Lal, *African Socialism*; Yusufu Qwaray Lawi, 'Tanzania's Operation *Vijiji* and Local Ecological Consciousness: The Case of Eastern Iraqwland, 1974–1976', *Journal of African History*, 48 (2007), 69–93; Leander Schneider, *Government of Development: Peasants and Politicians in Postcolonial Tanzania* (Bloomington: Indiana University Press, 2014); Husseina Dinani, 'Gendering Villagization: Women and Kinship Networks in Colonial and Socialist Lindi', *International Journal of African Historical Studies*, 50 (2017), 275–99.

[24] Adom Getachew, *Worldmaking after Empire: The Rise and Fall of Self-Determination* (Princeton, NJ: Princeton University Press, 2019). See also Christopher R. W. Dietrich, *Oil Revolution: Anticolonial Elites, Sovereign Rights, and the Economic Culture of Decolonization* (Cambridge: Cambridge University Press, 2017).

postcolonial governments to deliver on the hopes of independence was therefore unsurprising. Instead, this literature holds, ruling elites turned to the violent practices of their colonial predecessors to maintain control over their populations and exclude rival claims to power.[25] Another branch of work on the state takes its cue from the school of dependency theory. It presents African societies as being trapped in a world of neocolonial capitalist exploitation, abetted by the comprador ranks of postcolonial elites. Both these bodies of work suffer from tendencies to generalise and dehistoricise.[26] They present the scope for African governments to shape their own futures in a positive fashion as minimal.

These teleological interpretations of the genesis of the African state obscure histories of choice, possibility, and agency in the making of a world after empire. Historians have challenged assumptions that the path from colonial territory to postcolonial nation-state was inevitable. They have demonstrated how African politicians and intellectuals gave serious consideration to a plethora of regional federations, continental unions, and reconfigured relationships with the metropole.[27] Taking inspiration from this work, historians are now revisiting the early decades of independence. They have shown how, from rural communities to urban centres of power, Africans debated and pursued a wide range of approaches to state-making and development. The postcolonial era was replete with choices: for governments deciding on domestic and foreign policies; for politicians looking to translate the fruits of the nationalist struggle into new instruments of power; and for a whole

---

[25] Basil Davidson, *The Black Man's Burden: Africa and the Curse of the Nation-State* (Oxford: James Currey, 1992); Siba N'Zatioula Grovogui, *Sovereigns, Quasi Sovereigns and Africans: Race and Self-Determination in International Law* (Minneapolis: University of Minnesota Press, 1996); Mahmood Mamdani, *Citizen and Subject: Contemporary Africa and the Legacy of Late Colonialism* (Princeton, NJ: Princeton University Press, 1996); Crawford Young, *The Postcolonial State in Africa: Fifty Years of Independence, 1960–2010* (Madison: University of Wisconsin Press, 2012). For a critique, see Frederick Cooper, 'Possibility and Constraint: African Independence in Historical Perspective', *Journal of African History*, 49 (2008), 167–96.
[26] See Jean-François Bayart's critique in *The State in Africa: The Politics of the Belly* (London: Longman, 1993 [1989]), 7–12.
[27] Frederick Cooper, *Citizenship Between Empire and Nation: Remaking France and French Africa, 1945–1960* (Princeton, NJ: Princeton University Press, 2014); Gary Wilder, *Freedom Time: Negritude, Decolonization and the Future of the World* (Durham, NC: Duke University Press, 2015).

range of actors, such as businessmen, journalists, bureaucrats, for whom independence opened new vistas of possibilities. These choices involved brokering relationships inside and outside of the country, developing ideological visions of the future, and securing new-found nodes of power through patronage relationships.[28]

This book foregrounds the creative state-making endeavours of this postcolonial political elite. In the early years of independence, political scientists strove to pinpoint the origins and characteristics of this new ruling class.[29] This book does not seek to make such definitive interventions: it recognises that they were a diverse and constantly evolving cast. The term 'elite' then, used here, refers to a heterogeneous group of actors who were involved in various capacities in high-level debates about state-making in Tanzania. It encompasses cabinet ministers, senior bureaucrats, prominent members of parliament, party leaders, journalists, and intellectuals. In a mixture of private and public spaces, mainly located in Dar es Salaam, they participated in a national but globally informed conversation. To adopt this top-down perspective is not to deny that actors outside of these circles exercised significant agency in shaping the socialist experience in Tanzania. But the individuals found in the pages of this book – mostly, though not exclusively men – played a critical role in setting the parameters of debate about political economy and the country's engagement with the rest of the world. In doing so, this book also moves beyond the figure of Julius Nyerere. Tanzania's first president remains an influential, often decisive voice in the histories which follow. Yet his ideas were neither uncontested nor always triumphant.

This elite owed their positions to opportunities for self-advancement which arose during the late colonial era. Some had gained leadership experience as businessmen, through the cooperative movement, or in trade unions. Others had staffed the lower ranks of the colonial bureaucracy. They were wealthy by comparison with the average Tanzanian, but scarcely so in international terms. More significantly,

---

[28] Abou B. Bamba, *African Miracle, African Mirage: Transnational Politics and the Paradox of Modernization in Ivory* Coast (Athens: Ohio University Press, 2016); Jeffrey S. Ahlman, *Living with Nkrumahism: Nation, State, and Pan-Africanism in Ghana* (Athens: Ohio University Press, 2017); Kara Moskowitz, *Seeing Like a Citizen: Decolonization, Development, and the Making of Kenya, 1945–1980* (Athens: Ohio University Press, 2019).

[29] For a review, see Robert A. Miller, 'Elite Formation in Africa: Class, Culture, and Coherence', *Journal of Modern African Studies*, 12 (1974), 521–42.

they were relatively well-educated. Almost all had experience of secondary school in Tanzania at a small number of colonial institutions. Some had travelled abroad for higher education. During the liberation struggle and the post-independence years, they acquired further cosmopolitan experience through international conferences and on visits to Cold War capitals. As they travelled around the globe and became exposed to technocratic practices at home, this elite became socialised into a world which was inflected by a certain global cosmopolitanism and urbane sensibility. They were at ease in the genteel surroundings of diplomatic receptions in Dar es Salaam, on the conference circuit, and on aid-seeking missions. This was a world characterised by cordiality rather than confrontation. These experiences attuned them to the significance of Tanzania's foreign relations and image abroad, even as they differed as to how these might be conducted and represented.

Tanzanian politics in the time of *ujamaa* was marked with ideological pluralism and power struggles that were often masked by official rhetoric and its emphasis on national unity. Tanzania's elites drew on a pastiche of ideological influences, including from among the Cold War's protagonists and other Third World revolutionaries.[30] Yet African politicians neither swallowed whole the superpowers' world views nor talked in Cold War tongues simply to access external patronage.[31] In fact, the key split in this elite did not align with the 'left-right' spectrum which dominated the interpretative frameworks of contemporary onlookers and academic commentators. Instead, it came to run along rough divisions which pitted a small number of more economically versed ministers, senior bureaucrats, and technocratic

---

[30] On Tanzania, see Priya Lal, 'Tanzanian *Ujamaa* in a World of Peripheral Socialisms', in Chen Jian, Martin Klimke, Masha Kirasirova, Mary Nolan, Marilyn Young, and Joanna Waley-Cohen (eds.), *The Routledge Handbook of the Global Sixties: Between Protest and Nation-Building* (London: Routledge, 2018), 367–80. Recent work on this cosmopolitan ideological landscape includes Byrne, *Mecca of Revolution*; Elidor Mëhilli, *From Stalin to Mao: Albania and the Socialist World* (Ithaca, NY: Cornell University Press, 2017); Tuong Vu, *Vietnam's Communist Revolution: The Power and Limits of Ideology* (New York: Cambridge University Press, 2017).

[31] Elizabeth Schmidt, *Cold War and Decolonization in Guinea, 1946–1958* (Athens: Ohio University Press, 2007); Miles Larmer and Erik Kennes, 'Rethinking the Katangese Secession', *Journal of Imperial and Commonwealth History*, 42 (2014), 741–61; Justin Pearce, 'Global Ideologies, Local Politics: The Cold War as Seen from Central Africa', *Journal of Southern African Studies*, 43 (2017), 13–27.

expatriate advisers who advocated a more cautious way forwards, against a growing number of TANU leaders, who viewed development as a political task to be attained through popular mobilisation through party institutions. The latter group became an increasingly dominant force in Tanzanian politics during the *ujamaa* years.

Another source of division concerned the conduct, if not principles, of foreign policy. Under Nyerere's guidance, Tanzania became a prominent voice in continental and global international forums. However, it proved a difficult task to balance its commitment to the cause of Third World liberation with that of non-alignment, while also cultivating an aid-friendly public image and maintaining a sense of international respectability. Among the paradoxes of *ujamaa* was that the drive for 'self-reliance' required external support.[32] While Nyerere and other senior figures around him remained suspicious of imperialist machinations, they were convinced that Tanzania's socialist project required development aid. Even powers which were routinely pilloried in Tanzania for their neocolonial interventions in Africa remained desirable partners. The Tanzanian government did not want to endanger these relationships through needless provocation or a misrepresentation of its foreign policy. On occasions, this involved the intervention of Nyerere himself, in ordering party activists, journalists, and even government ministers to tone down their language. Their protests and polemics may have been motivated by the same anticolonial logic that formed the basis of official policy, but they were not deemed the respectable behaviour of a state which was demanding that its arguments be taken seriously on the international stage.

However attractive it might be to bask in the lights cast by Dar es Salaam's phosphorescent revolutionary moment, this book argues that Tanzania's commitment to the cause of anticolonial liberation was closely related to its shift towards a more authoritarian state during the *ujamaa* era. In its support for wars of liberation against the white minority regimes and attempts to overcome the Cold War order, Tanzania created powerful enemies for itself. The government responded by becoming more and more insular and fearful of subversion by imperialist powers and their local accomplices. By the mid-1970s, Dar es Salaam was a far more austere city than it had been in

---

[32] Lal, *African Socialism*, 59–60.

1961, the year of *uhuru* ('freedom' or 'independence'). The opportunity for political dissent was minimal. The local media was in the hands of a one-party state. *Ujamaa* went from a rich source of debate to official doxa. The internationalist rhetoric of Tanzania's political elite, which promised freedom to the oppressed peoples of the Third World, rubbed up against a disciplinarian approach to their own citizens. Cold War rivalries, liberation struggles, and Tanzanian politics therefore proved to be deeply contingent upon one another. To excavate these connections, we must turn to the scattered records of the 'postcolonial archive'.

The Postcolonial Archive and International History

In much of sub-Saharan Africa, underfunded state archives lie in a state of neglect or environmental degradation. To a large extent, this reflects both a lack of resources and the consequences of institutional instability. Where paper records have been preserved, access can be problematic.[33] Research on politically sensitive topics is especially restricted, as incumbent governments recognise the potential of archives to unsettle hegemonic narratives which legitimise their claims to authority in the present. In denying researchers access to its documentary record, Achille Mbembe asserts, the state falls back on 'its ability to control time, to abolish the archive and anaesthetise the past'.[34] Paraphrasing Mbembe, Omnia El Shakry concludes that the postcolonial state 'devours the past through either the material destruction of the archives or the presentation of a history purified of antagonisms and embodied in empty commemorative accounts'.[35] This epistemological violence is sharpened by the charged circumstances of contemporary politics, which encourages the mutilation or muzzling of the archival record.[36]

---

[33] Stephen Ellis, 'Writing Histories of Contemporary Africa', *Journal of African History*, 43 (2002), 1–26; Samuel Fury Childs Daly, 'Archival Research in Africa', *African Affairs*, 116 (2017), 311–20.
[34] Achille Mbembe, 'The Power of the Archive and Its Limits', in Carolyn Hamilton, Verne Harris, Michèle Pickover, Graeme Reid, Razia Saleh, and Jane Taylor (eds.), *Refiguring the Archive* (Dordrecht: Kluwer, 2002), 23.
[35] Omnia El Shakry, '"History Without Documents": The Vexed Archives of Decolonization in the Middle East', *American Historical Review*, 120 (2015), 920.
[36] Moses E. Ochonu, 'Elusive History: Fractured Archives, Politicized Orality, and Sensing the Postcolonial Past', *History in Africa*, 42 (2015), 290.

These verdicts may well be too pessimistic. Certainly, they overgeneralise a situation which varies from state to state.[37] Historians *have* worked in state archives in various African countries – like Ethiopia, Ghana, and Zambia – in order to write international histories of the postcolonial era, as well as move beyond the overquoted public speeches and writings of 'great men'.[38] But it remains the case in Tanzania that access to archival material on the inner workings at the top level of government is highly restricted. This book does draw on small amounts of material from the Tanzania National Archives in Dar es Salaam and the National Records Centre in Dodoma, including minutes of important TANU meetings. However, like many researchers in recent years, I was unable to access the archives of the *Chama cha Mapinduzi* (Party of the Revolution, CCM), which include TANU papers on the period covered by this book. The most insightful unpublished Tanzanian documents used in this study come from the private papers of Amir Jamal, a long-serving cabinet minister and Nyerere's economic guru. Perhaps tellingly, they are housed at Makerere University in Kampala, Uganda.

---

[37] Alexander Keese, 'Just Like in Colonial Times? Administrative Practice and Local Reflections on "Grassroots Neocolonialism" in Autonomous and Postcolonial Dahomey, 1958–65', *Journal of African History*, 60 (2019), 257–76.

[38] For Ethiopia, see Lovise Aalen, 'Ethiopian State Support to Insurgency in Southern Sudan from 1962 to 1983: Local, Regional and Global Connections', *Journal of Eastern African Studies*, 8 (2014), 626–41; Belete Belachew Yihun, 'Ethiopian Foreign Policy and the Ogaden War: The Shift from "Containment" to "Destabilization"', 1977–1991', *Journal of Eastern African Studies*, 8 (2014), 677–91; Belete Belachew Yihun, 'Ethiopia's Troubled Relations with the Sudan, 1956–1983', *International Journal of Ethiopian Studies*, 10 (2016), 67–88. For Ghana, see Ahlman, *Living with Nkrumahism*; Grilli, *Nkrumaism*; Frank Gerits, '"When the Bull Elephants Fight": Kwame Nkrumah, Non-Alignment, and Pan-Africanism as an Interventionist Ideology in the Global Cold War (1957–66)', *International History Review*, 37 (2015), 951–69; Naarborko Sackeyfio-Lenoch, 'The Ghana Trades Union Congress and the Politics of International Labor Alliances, 1957–1971', *International Review of Social History*, 62 (2017), 191–213; Nana Osei-Opare, 'Uneasy Comrades: Postcolonial Statecraft, Race, and Citizenship. Ghana-Soviet Relations, 1957–1966', *Journal of West African History*, 5 (2019), 85–111. For Zambia, see Andy DeRoche, *Kenneth Kaunda, the United States and Southern Africa* (London: Bloomsbury, 2016); Lynn Schler, 'Dilemmas of Postcolonial Diplomacy: Zambia, Kenneth Kaunda, and the Middle East Crisis', *Journal of African History*, 59 (2018), 97–119; Miles Larmer, 'Nation-Making at the Border: Zambian Diplomacy in the Democratic Republic of Congo', *Comparative Studies in Society and History*, 61 (2019), 145–75.

Given both the paucity of relevant collections in Tanzania and the international scope of this book, it turns to archives which are mainly located outside of Africa. As Jean Allman argues, Africa's postcolonial archive 'does not reside in one place or even two or three. It is a global, transnational archive.'[39] This book therefore draws on a wide range of source media in multiple languages, including newspapers, memoirs, oral interviews, and official publications. However, the substance of the evidence which drives the histories below comes from foreign diplomatic archives. These sources provide us with insights into the evolution of the foreign policies of various external powers, which were important participants in Dar es Salaam's politics in their own right. Used critically, they can also serve as sources on the city's African politicians and other actors, especially in terms of their transnational connections.[40] A multiarchival, multilingual approach not only permits an examination of Dar es Salaam's political life from various vantage points, but also provides paths into Tanzanian affairs which were hidden from the public gaze at the time.

The archival research involved in this book was the outcome of intellectual and practical choices. To some extent, these decisions were intended to account for the various geopolitical and ideological perspectives which different state archives reveal. Yet these choices were also constrained by the questions of accessibility and my own language proficiencies. In particular, the latter rendered impossible work in several Eastern Bloc archives, which are providing fresh insights into Africa's experience of the Cold War. I conducted longer periods of research, totalling a month or more, in archives in Britain, France, Germany, Portugal, and the United States. In addition, I made a series of shorter visits to Belgium, the Netherlands, and South Africa,

---

[39] Jean Allman, 'Phantoms of the Archive: Kwame Nkrumah, a Nazi Pilot Named Hanna, and the Contingencies of Post-Colonial History-Writing', *American Historical Review*, 118 (2013), 126. See also Luise White, 'Hodgepodge Historiography: Documents, Itineraries, and the Absence of Archives', *History in Africa*, 42 (2015), 309–18; Branwen Gruffydd Jones, 'Comradeship, Committed, and Conscious: The Anticolonial Archive Speaks to Our Times', in Shiera El-Malik and Isaac A. Kamola (eds.), *Politics of African Anticolonial Archive* (London: Rowman and Littlefield, 2017), 57–82.

[40] For an effort to understand the postcolonial politics of Togo through mainly Western diplomatic archives, see Kate Skinner, 'West Africa's First Coup: Neo-Colonial and Pan-African Projects in Togo's "Shadow Archives"', *African Studies Review*, 63 (2020), 375–98.

plus Poland, where I worked with the assistance of a translator. This research also draws on digitalised documents from the Australian and Indian national archives. The travel involved was made possible not only by generous funding, but also my own education and nationality, which equipped me with the skills for multilingual research and a passport which permitted flexible freedom of movement. Such privileges are not available to all. While acknowledging the benefits of multi-archival work, global and international historians must be wary of the danger that the transnational methodologies that characterise their work foreclose opportunities for many of their colleagues in the global South.

An immediate criticism of this approach might be that it risks writing a 'Eurocentric' history of Dar es Salaam's revolutionary politics. Certainly, the documents contained within these archives are characterised by the ideological, geopolitical, and racial world views held by their authors, who were mostly white men from outside of Africa. Reports written by American and British diplomats interpreted developments in Tanzania through the lens of the Cold War, seeking to understand manoeuvres in their relationship to the Soviet Bloc or China, often accompanied by implicit racial assumptions. The despatches of their West and East German counterparts reveal a remarkable, near obsessive and all-consuming fixation with the day-to-day activities of their rivals in Dar es Salaam. Whereas Tanzanian newspapers often referred to the liberation movements as 'freedom fighters', Portuguese and South African reports classify them as 'terrorists' and highlight their 'communist' connections. But as Luise White argues, with regard to Zimbabwean revolutionaries, the use of such labels assumes 'that individuals can be fixed in political positions'. Cosmopolitan Third World politicians were adept at speaking in different voices to different audiences. Therefore, White continues, 'the worlds in which one was a nationalist, pro- or anti-Chinese, or alternating between Moscow and Washington during the 1970s were complicated and contentious'.[41]

Rather than simply retelling a history that reproduces these ideological and geopolitical world views, this book understands them as part of the mental landscape of the global Cold War. By structuring

---

[41] Luise White, *The Assassination of Herbert Chitepo: Texts and Politics in Zimbabwe* (Bloomington: Indiana University Press, 2003), 32.

contemporary interpretations of African politics, they shaped the responses of foreign actors in Dar es Salaam. For example, as Chapter 3 demonstrates, the tendency of East German officials to interpret developments through the rigid framework of Marxism-Leninism accounts for some of their ill-judged decisions when brokering alliances with Tanzanian politicians. When Western diplomats and journalists depicted Dar es Salaam as being overrun by extremist revolutionaries acting as communist proxies, they moved the Tanzanian government to curate the public image of a non-aligned state more carefully still. In truth, no state's archives are free of such assumptions and representations. Even if this book had been able to draw extensively on Tanzanian documents, it would have faced a challenge in narrating a history that did not reproduce the official nomenclature of *ujamaa*.

The 'Cold War' diplomatic archive is replete with African voices, captured in memoranda of official meetings and reports of more informal encounters. Yet some are more visible than others: the diplomats tended to deal with government ministers, rather than TANU leaders, who often wielded greater influence. Certain sections draw heavily on certain relevant archives: American files when discussing the war in Vietnam; Portuguese documents when addressing Mozambican liberation movements; German files when exploring the 'German Cold War' in Dar es Salaam, and so on. But the footnotes are also studded with more surprising references, acknowledging that an anecdotal detail originated in a Polish telegram or a magazine clipping in a South African file. The archives of foreign ministries represent more than a paper trail of official communications: they contain newspaper clippings, transcripts of speeches, government circulars, documents from other diplomatic missions, mimeographed flyers, and other ephemera. Nonetheless, these archives are certainly *not* complete records of diplomatic activity in Dar es Salaam. In many instances, details have been redacted, individual documents have been excised, and whole files remain inaccessible to researchers. Those are just the officially acknowledged 'gaps': scandals regarding secret caches of colonial-era documents point to what else might be kept away from the public.[42] The intelligence archives of the major powers are essentially off limits to researchers.

[42] David M. Anderson, 'Mau Mau in the High Court and the "Lost" British Empire Archives: Colonial Conspiracy or Bureaucratic Bungle?', *Journal of*

This book supplements these archival sources with a range of other material. Local Tanzanian newspapers, in both English and Swahili, are valuable sources of information and commentary, while also a subject of inquiry in their own right, as Chapter 6 demonstrates.[43] The international press, some of which can now be keyword-searched online, offers perspectives on how Dar es Salaam and Tanzanian socialism were represented outside of the country.[44] Oral interviews with a number of Tanzanian politicians, bureaucrats, and journalists provided reflections on the *ujamaa* years even as they proved less helpful in providing the nuts and bolts of the granular histories which this book addresses. Finally, there is a growing body of autobiography in Tanzania (and also in Mozambique, as Chapter 4 shows).[45] As a corpus of evidence, these sources allow us to revisit revolutionary Dar es Salaam from a sweeping range of perspectives – sometimes corroborating, sometimes conflicting.

The histories set out in this book are full of twists and turns. At its heart is the idea of contingency in state-making in Africa after empire. However, taken together, these stories illuminate the rise and fall of Dar es Salaam as a 'Cold War city' and mecca of liberation in East Africa. From multiple angles, they follow the genesis of Tanzania's revolutionary state-making project, which involved not just the construction of a socialist society but the liberation of Africa. These include the perspectives of a range of Tanzanian politicians, liberation movement cadres, Cold War diplomats, radical journalists, and youth activists. This book contends that, against an international backdrop which highlighted the threat to the country's body politic from external subversion, Tanzania's socialist project became increasingly inward-looking. Space for dissent became highly circumscribed and political organisation beyond TANU almost impossible.

Imperial and Commonwealth History, 39 (2011), 699–716; Caroline Elkins, 'Looking Beyond Mau Mau: Archiving Violence in the Era of Decolonization', *American Historical Review*, 120 (2015), 852–68.
[43] On the African press as a historical source, see Ellis, 'Writing Histories', 15–19.
[44] See however Lara Putnam's assessment of the dangers of digitalised resources, including newspapers: 'The Transnational and the Text-Searchable: Digitized Sources and the Shadows They Cast', *American Historical Review*, 121 (2016), 377–402.
[45] On biography and African History, see Ochonu, 'Elusive History'.

The book begins by explaining how Dar es Salaam became a 'Cold War city' in Africa. This chronological and geographic exposition sets out the principles which informed the basis of Nyerere's engagement with the outside world – a set of foreign policy coordinates which remained remarkably consistent throughout the period covered by this book. It then shows how a violent revolution in the Zanzibar archipelago pushed Tanganyika into a hasty union with the islands, while an army mutiny in Dar es Salaam exposed the fragility of Nyerere's government. A series of foreign policy crises with major Western states followed. Meanwhile, Tanzania reached out to the socialist world and developed close connections with China. By the mid-1960s, Dar es Salaam had attracted the attention of the Cold War world. The remainder of Chapter 1 then demonstrates how a 'Cold War political culture' became inscribed into Dar es Salaam's political geography and public sphere.

The political debates about the future of the Tanzanian state in the mid-1960s, which culminated in the Arusha Declaration, form the theme of Chapter 2. It sets out the contours of conversations about development in the 1960s, as Tanzania's elites groped for a path forwards that would translate independence into meaningful socio-economic progress. After showing how Nyerere's decision to embark on a radical programme of socialist reform was motivated by local unrest and the fate of postcolonial regimes elsewhere in Africa, it then revisits the little-understood politics of the Arusha Declaration and its fallout. Offering an alternative dimension to readings of Arusha as a stimulant for national unity, the chapter demonstrates how Tanzania's revolution created fissures among the political elite. It represented a critical turning point in Tanzania's postcolonial history that narrowed space for dissent, while also sowing the seeds for future challenges to the TANU party-state.

Chapter 3 examines the 'inter-German Cold War' in Dar es Salaam. The chain of upheavals in East Africa in 1964–65 led to Dar es Salaam becoming the first African capital south of the Sahara in which the German Democratic Republic (GDR) maintained a diplomatic mission. This turned the city into a propaganda battlefield. East Berlin strove for full recognition from Tanzania, while Bonn tried to prevent such a development from coming to pass. In the face of this rivalry, Nyerere's government sought to pursue a non-aligned foreign policy and broker aid agreements to further its socialist project. Adopting a triangular approach, this chapter demonstrates how Tanzania's relationship with the two German states turned on developments in Central Europe, especially West Germany's *Ostpolitik*. It reveals the challenges of upholding non-alignment in a Cold War world which did not revolve around simple binaries and was complicated by politics 'on the ground' in Dar es Salaam.

In Chapter 4, the focus shifts from international diplomacy to liberation movement politics. The presence of the guerrilla leaders in Dar es Salaam was fundamental to its emergence as a 'Cold War city'. This chapter shows how their activities became embedded in the capital's political life through the case of the assassination of the president of FRELIMO (*Frente de Libertação de Moçambique*, Mozambique Liberation Front). Eduardo Mondlane was a skilful politician who used the city's international connections to publicise his movement's cause and canvas for foreign support. However, as FRELIMO sought to draw on Cold War patronage to wage war against the Portuguese, it was gripped by an internal crisis that split the movement's leadership along ethno-racial and ideological lines. Powerful gatekeepers within the Tanzanian political establishment aligned with Mondlane's enemies to challenge him in public and undermine his security in private. These schisms facilitated the assassination of Mondlane in 1969 and clouded the waters of subsequent inquiries into the crime's perpetrators.

Chapter 5 locates Dar es Salaam's urban politics in the context of the 'global sixties'. Tanzanian youths shared common ground with their contemporaries around the world in protesting against Cold War interventions in Vietnam and Czechoslovakia. In doing so, they drew inspiration from the landscape of radical ideas and texts of revolutionary Dar es Salaam. But in contrast to the dynamics of counter-hegemonic protest elsewhere, the Tanzanian government's foreign policy meant that it could channel radical critiques of superpower imperialism into its own nation-building project. The language of anti-imperialism could also be deployed against more immediate threats, as the case of Malawi's claims to Tanzanian territory demonstrate. While recognising the significance of transnational Afro-Asian and Third Worldist solidarities in these movements, the chapter integrates these dynamics into a national story. The state circumscribed the autonomy of youth activism, especially when it risked upsetting Nyerere's carefully calculated foreign policy.

Similar dynamics become apparent in Chapter 6, which analyses the evolution of the press in Dar es Salaam after *uhuru*. By the mid-1970s, Tanzania had just two national daily newspapers, one of which was owned by the party, the other by the state. But this was not the outcome of a teleological slide from an independent to a muzzled media, as liberal Cold War-era conceptions of the 'freedom of the press' would have it. This chapter shows how the press became a contested site of socialist politics in Dar es Salaam's internationalised media world. Stakeholders debated questions of who should own newspapers, who should work for them, and what they should write in them. Even when the government nationalised the country's only independent English-language newspaper, it placed it under the control of a radical, foreign editor and emphasised the need for it to serve as a critical voice. However, when this editorial independence transgressed Tanzania's foreign policy, the state moved to bring the press under closer control, justified by Third World trends towards 'development media'.

The final chapter explores the circumstances in which Tanzanian politics became radicalised further in the early 1970s, and with what consequences. It shows how a combination of internal unrest and an array of developments in Africa – read in Tanzania as 'neocolonial interventions' – pushed TANU into a gear-change in its socialist revolution, the 'Guidelines', or *Mwongozo*. These steps were taken with misgivings from Nyerere and proved fractious among several of his trusted colleagues. While the government continued to talk the language of continental revolution, this was accompanied by a toughening of the national institutions of the party-state. Power became concentrated in the hands of TANU. The motor for development was increasingly believed to be popular mobilisation through party organs rather than economic planning, which had previously tempered revolutionary interventionism. Meanwhile, the troublesome regime in semi-autonomous Zanzibar was brought to heel. National unity was achieved and enforced from above but came at a political (and likely economic) cost.

This book is not intended to be a comprehensive history of Dar es Salaam's experience of decolonisation and the Cold War, and still less a history of *ujamaa*-era Tanzania. Readers with some knowledge of Tanzania's postcolonial history will observe that there is little direct discussion of the country's relations with China, or its involvement in the Zimbabwean endgame, or the rise and fall of regional integration in East Africa. These and many other topics would all be worthy of dedicated books of their own. The history of FRELIMO presented in Chapter 4 comes with its own nuances, though an account of the exile experience of any one of the liberation movements would have been equally illuminating. Rather, the intention is for the selected threads, as expressions of dynamics rather than case studies, to serve as a keyhole into Dar es Salaam's central position in the international politics of the era.

1 | *The Making of a Cold War City in Eastern Africa*

In late 1964, a 29-year-old African American journalist named Ida Lewis visited Dar es Salaam. In an article published in *Life* magazine, she described a city alive with grand visions of Africa's postcolonial future. Meeting Tanzanian government ministers, she heard about plans for the liberation of southern Africa. Chinese support, she was told, would be critical in bringing down apartheid. 'It will be our pleasure to strip Verwoerd of all his white glory and hang him from the highest pole in Johannesburg', an unnamed minister told her. The Dar es Salaam which Lewis portrayed was also characterised by an overbearing sense of suspicion and secrecy. After a Kenyan newspaper published a recent photograph of Lewis posing next to a controversial revolutionary in Uganda, the Tanzanian authorities put her under surveillance and confiscated her passport. Lewis' experiences reached audiences far beyond *Life* subscribers in the United States: an annotated photocopy of her story was filed away for reference by the South African Defence Forces in Pretoria, in a folder labelled 'Tanzania – Terrorism'.[1]

Lewis' *Life* article was part of an emerging subgenre of writing on Dar es Salaam, in which Western correspondents depicted the city as a centre of revolutionary subversion in Africa. These claims were not entirely baseless. As this chapter explains, a combination of President Julius Nyerere's principled but provocative foreign policy and a series of upheavals in East Africa turned the city into an epicentre of radical politics in the region (Map 1.1). Reading these events through the rigid frameworks of the Cold War, Western observers interpreted the organisation of anticolonial struggle as a conduit for communist intrigue, whereby the Soviet Union and China manipulated pliable African politicians to serve their ideological ends. In a political context marked by fears of superpower-sponsored coups, the Tanzanian regime became

---

[1] Ida Lewis, 'Angry Mask of Black Africa', *Life*, 2 April 1965, enclosed in SADF, AMZ-IHDZ, GP15, Box 181, Tanzania – Terrorism.

near paranoid about subversive activities in the capital. The consequence was the emergence of a 'Cold War city', simultaneously a concrete site of revolutionary encounters and a mental construct that captured a sense of insecurity on the part of Africans as well as outsiders.

This chapter provides an explanation of the 'making' of a Cold War city, followed by an examination of its political geography. The first part establishes how Nyerere developed a postcolonial foreign policy which was intended to protect Tanzania's and Africa's sovereignty through a remarkably enduring matrix of principles. It then argues that the outbreak of revolution in Zanzibar and a mutiny at home turned Dar es Salaam not just into a mecca for liberation movements, but also a critical site of Cold War competition. Further episodes of tension with major Western powers demonstrated just how serious the Nyerere government was about its principled foreign policy, while revealing the extent to which it had become sensitive to its own insecurity. Finally, the chapter shows how the urban fabric of Dar es Salaam became saturated in the tropes of the Cold War. From diplomatic receptions to hotel bars, the Tanzanian capital became a notorious site of rumour, propaganda, and espionage.

The Pillars of Nyerere's Foreign Policy

Tanganyika's (and, from 1964, Tanzania's) foreign policy was defined by three key principles, as elaborated by Nyerere: African liberation, pan-Africanism, and non-alignment. They essentially represented different facets of the same world view, which revolved around the extension and preservation of African sovereignty, whether at the scale of the whole continent or through the unit of the nation-state. More broadly, Tanzania supported the sovereign claims of anticolonial movements from across the Third World. To this end, Nyerere remained committed to the idea of the United Nations as a forum for resolving international disputes. Yet by making Dar es Salaam a focal point for Third World liberation struggles and remaining open to no-strings-attached aid from almost any source, these foreign policy precepts pulled Tanzania more closely into the Cold War rivalries that Nyerere resisted.[2]

---

[2] For an extensive overview of Tanganyika's foreign policy, see Paul Bjerk, 'Postcolonial Realism: Tanganyika's Foreign Policy under Nyerere, 1960–1963', *International Journal of African Historical Studies*, 44 (2011), 216–47.

The first pillar was an unwavering commitment to the liberation of African peoples still living under white minority rule. In Addis Ababa in May 1963, where heads of state founded the Organisation of African Unity (OAU), Nyerere emphasised the continent's duty to free those still living under colonial oppression. African leaders, he argued, should view the endurance of colonialism elsewhere 'with the same gravity and same seriousness' as the continued occupation of their own territories. 'The real and humiliating truth is that Africa is not free', Nyerere said, 'and therefore it is Africa which should take the necessary collective measures to free Africa'.[3] Paul Rupia, an official at the Ministry of Foreign Affairs at the time, recalled that Tanganyika's foreign policy was 'dictated' from the outset by its involvement in the liberation struggle in southern Africa.[4] Initially, Nyerere encouraged peaceful negotiations with the white minority states. But as their intransigence became clear, he concluded that there was no alternative to armed struggle. As Nyerere reasoned, 'when the door of peaceful progress to freedom is slammed shut, and bolted, then the struggle must take other forms; we cannot surrender'.[5]

Dar es Salaam's credentials as a centre for trans-territorial anticolonial mobilisation were established even before Tanganyika's independence. The Pan-African Freedom Movement of Eastern and Central Africa (PAFMECA), founded in 1958 as a regional organisation for anticolonial leaders, set up its headquarters in the city.[6] As *uhuru* loomed, Tanganyika's geographic location turned Dar es Salaam into a muster point for dissidents from the repressive settler regimes of southern Africa. Its central position in these liberation networks was confirmed after the establishment of the OAU. The organisation's founder members decided that a body should be created to coordinate support for the exiles – 'a bank of blood', as Algeria's Ahmed Ben Bella put it.[7] Dar es Salaam was an obvious home for this Liberation Committee, which was chaired by Oscar Kambona, then foreign minister of Tanganyika and secretary-general of TANU. In Dar es Salaam,

---

[3] 'Addis Ababa Conference, 1963', in Julius K. Nyerere, *Freedom and Unity: A Selection from Writings and Speeches, 1952–65* (Dar es Salaam: Oxford University Press, 1966), 216.
[4] Interview with Paul Rupia, central Dar es Salaam, 3 August 2015.
[5] 'Policy on Foreign Affairs', in Nyerere, *Freedom and Development*, 115–16.
[6] Chris Vaughan, 'The Politics of Regionalism and Federation in East Africa, 1958–1964', *Historical Journal*, 62 (2019), 519–40.
[7] Quoted in Byrne, *Mecca of Revolution*, 197.

the liberation movements' offices clustered around the city centre, especially around Arab Street (later Nkrumah Street). They became central actors in the city's revolutionary and Cold War politics, as explored in Chapter 4.

Pan-Africanism represented the second pillar of Nyerere's foreign policy. Like many of his contemporaries, he believed that the continent's shared 'Africanness' could help to form a common front against neocolonial predation. 'Indissoluble African Unity is the stone bridge which would enable us all to walk in safety over this whirlpool of power politics', Nyerere wrote.[8] But Africa's leaders were hopelessly split into rival blocs. Some, like Ghana's Kwame Nkrumah, called for a rapid movement towards complete African unity. Others advocated a slower approach. Events in Congo, which demonstrated the vulnerability of the continent's states to external intervention, focused minds. The formation of the OAU represented a victory for Tanganyikan diplomacy: adopting a pragmatic role, Nyerere was instrumental in finding sufficient common ground among his fellow heads of state. Yet the intergovernmental structures of the OAU ultimately consolidated the primacy of the nation-state in Africa. By the 1970s, a disillusioned Nyerere had become fiercely critical of the OAU as a 'trade union' for despots, who used its charter's principle of non-interference in the internal affairs of member states as cover for committing atrocities against their own people.

Unlike more radical pan-Africanists, Nyerere believed in a gradualist path to continental unity. The formation of regional blocs had to precede any immediate leap to a 'United States of Africa'. During the independence struggle, TANU had mapped out a future East African Federation with Kenya and Uganda. However, the same problems that dogged the wider pan-African project also affected these attempts to forge regional unity. Divergent interests in Kenya and Uganda made their leaders sceptical of the idea. Critics portrayed the proposed federation as a neocolonial manoeuvre to smother national sovereignty. Ultimately, the rhetorical commitment to federate made by Nyerere, Jomo Kenyatta, and Milton Obote in June 1963 was never fulfilled.[9] Tanzania, Kenya, and Uganda did eventually come together in 1967 to

---

[8] 'A United States of Africa', in Nyerere, *Freedom and Unity*, 188.
[9] Vaughan, 'Politics of Regionalism'; Ismay Milford, 'Federation, Partnership, and the Chronologies of Space in 1950s East and Central Africa', *Historical Journal*, 63 (2020), 1325–48.

form the East African Community (EAC), an economic bloc which represented a diluted version of earlier visions. The EAC's ten-year existence was characterised by continual disputes, as its member states set out on contrasting economic and political trajectories. In a pattern repeated elsewhere in the continent, postcolonial elites jealously guarded the fragile sovereignty of their new nation-states.[10]

The final pillar of Tanganyika's foreign policy was non-alignment. In 1961, representatives of an array of mostly Third World states met in Belgrade, where they committed themselves to remaining outside of the rival Cold War blocs. Although their own understandings of 'non-alignment' differed, these countries believed that it offered the possibility of maintaining an independent foreign policy and thereby preserve their sovereignty.[11] For a state like Tanganyika, short of financial capital and technical expertise, this was no easy task. Days after *uhuru* in December 1961, Nyerere told the UN General Assembly that Tanganyika had no 'feelings of enmity toward any peoples in the world'. Non-alignment did not mean staying equidistant from the superpowers, but rather refraining from adopting foreign policy positions out of Cold War sympathies. 'Internationally, we believe that we have entered a world riven by ideological dissensions', said Nyerere. 'We are anxious to keep out of these disputes, and anxious to see that the nations of our continent are not used as pawns in conflicts which very often do not concern them at all.'[12] Over time, the accent of Nyerere's non-alignment shifted from the political to the economic. He saw the movement as representing a 'trade union' of the poor whose opponents were not the Cold War powers, but industrialised states

---

[10] Paul Bjerk, *Building a Peaceful Nation: Julius Nyerere and the Establishment of Sovereignty in Tanzania* (Rochester, NY: University of Rochester Press, 2015), 194–98.

[11] The literature on non-alignment has expanded rapidly in recent years. For a sample, see Nataša Mišković, Harald Fischer-Tiné, and Nada Boškovska (eds.), *The Non-Aligned Movement and the Cold War: Delhi-Bandung-Belgrade* (Oxford: Routledge, 2014); Lorenz M. Lüthi, 'Non-Alignment, 1946–1965: Its Establishment and Struggle Against Afro-Asianism', *Humanity*, 7 (2016), 201–23; Lorenz M. Lüthi, 'The Non-Aligned Movement and the Cold War, 1961–1973', *Journal of Cold War Studies*, 18 (2016), 98–147; Jürgen Dinkel, *The Non-Aligned Movement: Genesis, Organization and Politics (1927–1992)*, trans. Alex Skinner (Leiden: Brill, 2019).

[12] 'Independence Address to the United Nations', in Nyerere, *Freedom and Unity*, 154.

which kept nominally independent Third World countries in a relationship of dependency.

While non-alignment remained a constant feature of Nyerere's diplomacy, it was the most complex of these three tenets to elaborate and put into practice. The non-aligned world view was simultaneously an attempt to transcend the Cold War and an admission of its geopolitical and ideological pervasiveness. As a Tanzanian diplomat put it, 'non-alignment is a meaningless phrase except in relation to something else; a house can only be out of alignment if there is a street with which it is non-aligned!'[13] Non-alignment represented a creative response to the Cold War – but it was a response, nonetheless. It was also difficult to implement. Whereas Nyerere could leave other junior party and government spokespersons to attack 'imperialist' powers and acclaim the liberation struggle, the careful calibrations involved in maintaining a non-aligned stance were less suited to such rhetoric. Indeed, interventions on questions about the global struggle against colonialism frequently elicited complaints that Tanzania was anti-Western. Tanzania had to appear non-aligned to observers of all Cold War inclinations, while also entering into aid relationships, intervening in liberation movement disputes, and setting out a socialist development strategy. As this book demonstrates, Nyerere spent years fighting rearguard actions against Western accusations which alleged that Tanzania was too close to the communist powers.

The compass constituted by these three principles – liberation, pan-Africanism, and non-alignment – was intended to navigate a complex world in the time of decolonisation and superpower rivalry. Its needle deliberately pointed Tanzania's foreign policy in a direction that ran perpendicular to the simplified Cold War binaries through which many observers outside of Africa sought to interpret Nyerere's approach.[14] On paper, these principles were logical counterparts to one another: full, meaningful decolonisation of the continent would only come about through a united, liberated Africa, which protected its sovereignty by avoiding entanglements with the Cold War powers.

---

[13] George Kahama, 'The Policy of Non-Alignment as Practised by Tanzania', *Foreign Affairs Bulletin: An Official Record of Foreign Policy of the United Republic of Tanzania*, July 1966, 4–13.
[14] Emma Hunter, 'Julius Nyerere', in Steven Casey and Jonathon Wright (eds.), *Mental Maps in the Era of Détente and the End of the Cold War, 1968–91* (Basingstoke: Palgrave Macmillan, 2015), 87–88.

Translating this logic into practice was difficult. Although these principles were shared by most of Africa's first generation of leaders, there were different opinions about *how* African unity was to be reached, *how* liberation struggles should be conducted, and *what* non-alignment actually meant. A world in flux at the height of the Cold War and the process of decolonisation threw up new geopolitical dilemmas which confounded easy resolution, as Chapter 3 shows with reference to the 'German question'.

Africa's newly independent states were essentially novices in the world of 'official' foreign policy. Struggles for liberation had certainly demanded a degree of international diplomacy. But although colonial administrations left behind the framework for various government departments, African states had to create a postcolonial foreign affairs apparatus from scratch. Under-resourced foreign ministries hastily set up embassies in key diplomatic centres, especially in Europe and the capitals of the superpowers. In Dar es Salaam, the Ministry of Foreign Affairs operated out of a former colonial administrative building on the waterfront. When Paul Rupia joined the Ministry as a civil servant in 1963, he had just one colleague in the Division of African Affairs – a young Benjamin Mkapa, later the third president of Tanzania.[15] Even though the number of officials rose from 30 in 1961 to 364 in 1967, the Ministry remained underfinanced and faced, in its own assessment, a 'serious' problem in recruiting trained staff.[16] This shortage of diplomatic experience led Nyerere to consolidate control of foreign policy in the presidency. 'Mwalimu Nyerere was always the [de facto] minister for foreign affairs', a former Tanzanian diplomat recalled. A minister 'knew there were decisions he could not make without reference to the president'.[17]

Although Nyerere may have set the guidelines for Tanzania's foreign policy, he never had total control over it. Certainly, in terms of making high-level geopolitical decisions, his word was almost always final. However, the implementation of foreign policy involved a whole gamut of other actors, including government officials, junior ministers, and the OAU Liberation Committee secretariat. In public, Tanzanian intellectuals and journalists debated the foreign affairs issues of

---

[15] Interview with Paul Rupia, central Dar es Salaam, 3 August 2015.
[16] *Foreign Affairs Bulletin: An Official Record of Foreign Policy of the United Republic of Tanzania*, July 1966, 15–18.
[17] Interview with Anthony Nyakyi, Masaki, Dar es Salaam, 28 July 2015.

the day. While they did so largely within the scope of Nyerere's own policy, the tone and accent of this discussion posed public relations problems for the government. As Chapters 5 and 6 demonstrate, party youth activists and ideologues in government newspapers expressed opinions which shared Nyerere's overarching world view yet did so in a manner that risked diplomatic embarrassment or upsetting the public face of non-alignment. In early 1964, as the next section shows, a series of regional upheavals put these foreign policy principles to a severe test.

Revolution, Mutiny, and Union

Seventy-four kilometres north of Dar es Salaam lies the main port to the archipelago of Zanzibar.[18] Over the course of the nineteenth century, the Omani sultanate of Zanzibar become a regional superpower in Eastern Africa, through a booming clove trade and its involvement in the Indian Ocean slave trade. The imposition of European colonial rule severely diminished this status. From 1890, Zanzibar was ruled as a British Protectorate. After a fractious period of democratic elections, the islands attained independence in December 1963. Just a month later, in the early hours of 12 January 1964, the coalition government of the Zanzibar Nationalist Party (ZNP) and Zanzibar and Pemba People's Party (ZPPP) was overthrown in a violent coup d'état. Members of the youth wing of the Afro-Shirazi Party (ASP), acting in collaboration with a Ugandan migrant named John Okello, seized the police headquarters, post office, and radio station. As the ruling sultan fled into exile, the coup makers installed Abeid Karume, the leader of the ASP, as president of the revolutionary regime. Thousands of Zanzibaris, mostly of Arab descent, were killed in racial pogroms. Perhaps a third of Zanzibar's Arab population died or were forced into exile.[19]

Zanzibar had a population of just 300,000. Yet news of the revolution panicked Western onlookers beyond proportion. The United States feared that the coup had been backed by outside communist forces and offered openings for Marxist encroachment in Africa. Washington's ambassador to Tanganyika cautioned that Zanzibar

---

[18] The Zanzibar archipelago consists of the islands of Unguja and Pemba.
[19] The best account of events remains Anthony Clayton, *The Zanzibar Revolution and Its Aftermath* (London: Hurst, 1981).

could become 'a base for subversive and insurgency operations against [the] mainland from Kenya to the Cape'. The CIA's reports drew on sketchy knowledge of Zanzibaris who were known to have spent time in Cuba to paint a nightmarish picture of communist penetration. The press echoed these concerns. The *New York Times* warned that 'Zanzibar is on the verge of becoming the Cuba of Africa'. It suggested that the Cuban embassy in Dar es Salaam was orchestrating these communist grand designs.[20] Britain and the United States consequently delayed their recognition of the Karume regime. Washington even tried to pressure London into military intervention in the islands.[21]

American diplomats and journalists were particularly troubled by the inclusion in the revolutionary government of two 'extremists': Kassim Hanga and Abdulrahman Mohammed 'Babu'. Hanga was an ASP member, who had trained as a schoolteacher before heading abroad. In 1960 he travelled to Moscow, having obtained a scholarship to study at Lumumba University. Babu, who was intellectually and politically the sharper of the pair, had a similarly cosmopolitan background, although he gravitated towards China rather than the Soviet Union. From 1951 to 1957, Babu studied and worked in London, where he became immersed in overlapping political circles of British socialism and African nationalism. On his return home, Babu earned a reputation as a brilliant political organiser for the ZNP. He travelled widely on the anticolonial conference circuit around Africa and beyond. Following a visit to China, Babu became the Zanzibar correspondent for the New China News Agency. These connections created friction with the Arab patricians who led the ZNP, as well as with the British colonial administration. In May 1962, Babu was arrested on suspicion of arson and imprisoned. Shortly after his release in June 1963, he broke with the ZNP leadership to form the self-styled revolutionary Umma Party. A handful of Umma cadres received guerrilla training in Cuba. After the seizure of power, Hanga became Zanzibar's vice-president and Babu its foreign minister.[22]

[20] Quoted in Gleijeses, *Conflicting Missions*, 57–59.
[21] Ian Speller, 'An African Cuba? Britain and the Zanzibar Revolution, 1964', *Journal of Imperial and Commonwealth History*, 35 (2007), 283–302.
[22] On Hanga, see Ahmed Rajab, 'Maisha na nyakati za Abdulla Kassim Hanga', unpublished paper presented at the Zanzibar Institute for Research and Public Policy (2016). On Babu and Umma, see Haroub Othman (ed.), *Babu: I Saw the Future and It Works: Essays Celebrating the Life of Comrade Abdulrahman Mohamed Babu* (Dar es Salaam: E&D, 2001); G. Thomas Burgess, 'An

In Western eyes, the presence of Babu and Hanga at the prow of the revolution was evidence that the forces of global communism were at work in Zanzibar. This misunderstood the pair's role in the uprising and its underlying causes. Babu was not even present in Zanzibar during the coup itself, which was primarily the work of the ASP Youth League. Moreover, Western onlookers' fixation on the Cold War dimensions of events led them to overlook the deeper communal tensions which precipitated the violent revolution. As Jonathon Glassman has shown, the legacies of slavery and socio-economic disparities between the archipelago's ethno-racial groups shaped the fraught years of democratic politics which preceded independence. While the generally wealthier Arab minority tended to support the ZNP, the ASP drew most of its members from the poorer African and 'Shirazi' populations. These racial tensions were exacerbated by the rhetoric of Zanzibari intellectuals and politicians as they searched for votes. In the June 1963 elections, a ZNP-ZPPP coalition gained a majority of seats in the legislature, despite the ASP winning the popular vote. After independence in December, the ZNP-ZPPP government cracked down on opposition parties, restricted press freedoms, and dismissed African members of the bureaucracy and police force. Both the ASP and ZNP did employ transnational political languages to mobilise support and attack their rivals: the ASP, for example, presented itself as part of a pan-African movement, while red-baiting the ZNP by drawing attention to its connections with Nasser's Cairo and the socialist world. But this was largely a means of translating older, local cleavages into the political discourse of the day. The ASP revolutionaries fundamentally acted to overthrow what they felt was an unjust, undemocratic continuation of Arab domination.[23]

After the seizure of power, the new regime set about consolidating its control over the islands. Babu believed that he and his Umma followers transformed a 'lumpen uprising' into a 'popular, anti-imperialist

Imagined Generation: Umma Youth in Nationalist Zanzibar', in Gregory H. Maddox and James L. Giblin (eds.), *In Search of a Nation: Histories of Authority and Dissidence in Tanzania* (Oxford: James Currey, 2007), 216–49; Hashil Seif Hashil, *Mimi, Umma Party na Mapinduzi ya Zanzibar* (Paris: DL2A Buluu, 2018).

[23] Jonathon Glassman, *War of Words, War of Stones: Racial Thought and Violence in Colonial Zanzibar* (Bloomington: Indiana University Press, 2011); see also Michael F. Lofchie, *Zanzibar: Background to Revolution* (Princeton, NJ: Princeton University Press, 1965).

revolution'. This might overplay Umma's influence, but certainly Babu, Hanga, and other leading socialist thinkers in the ASP steered Zanzibar towards social revolution.[24] The government created a thirty-man Revolutionary Council as the supreme authority in Zanzibar. Umma was dissolved and Zanzibar became a one-party state. The regime began implementing a range of redistributive reforms, announcing the nationalisation of land and seizing housing from Arabs and Asians.[25] But it was the West's prevarication over recognising the revolutionary regime, based on suspicions that it was a communist proxy, which opened the space for the socialist powers to increase their presence in Zanzibar. China offered a $518,000 grant. The Soviet Union agreed to purchase $318,000 in stockpiled cloves. Babu became the first foreign minister of a non-communist Third World regime to recognise the GDR, which made an ambitious commitment to build apartment blocks to house 40,000 Zanzibaris. This financial support was complemented by an influx of communist aid workers.[26]

A violent uprising with a long, complex genealogy in Zanzibar's cosmopolitan but unequal society thereby became a major Cold War flashpoint in Africa. The revolution's origins lay in a history of slave labour and racial stratification, which became foundational narratives for political parties in the series of tense elections that preceded independence. Yet figures like Babu and Hanga were also part of a new generation of well-travelled, well-educated organisers who had close connections in socialist Cold War capitals. The American response to the coup focused overwhelmingly on this handful of revolutionaries, at the expense of the broader context. This was the outcome of poor intelligence, but also representative of a mentality in Washington which interpreted developments in Africa primarily through the prism of the Cold War. However, by delaying recognition of

---

[24] A. M. Babu, 'The 1964 Revolution: Lumpen or Vanguard?', in Abdul Sheriff and Ed Ferguson (eds.), *Zanzibar under Colonial Rule* (London: James Currey, 1991), 220–47. Cf. Issa G. Shivji, *Pan-Africanism or Pragmatism? Lessons of the Tanganyika-Zanzibar Union* (Dar es Salaam: Mkuki na Nyota, 2008), 63–65.
[25] Clayton, *Zanzibar Revolution*, 182–202.
[26] G. Thomas Burgess, 'A Socialist Diaspora: Ali Sultan Issa, the Soviet Union, and the Zanzibari Revolution', in Maxim Matusevich (ed.), *Africa in Russia, Russia in Africa: Three Centuries of Encounter* (Trenton, NJ: Africa World Press, 2007), 277.

Karume's government, the United States abetted the emergence of the very spectre of Third World communism of which it was so afraid.

—

One week after the outbreak of revolution in Zanzibar, Dar es Salaam was convulsed with its own bout of political turmoil. On the morning of 20 January, residents woke to the sight of soldiers on the city's streets. In an apparent echo of events in Zanzibar, the *askaris* of the Tanganyika Rifles had set up roadblocks around the city, and seized the radio station, post office, and police headquarters. They locked up senior officers in storerooms at the Colito Barracks. Troops surrounded State House and demanded an audience with Nyerere. To demonstrate their seriousness, they trained a mortar on the building. An army mutiny was under way, which quickly spread: first to Tabora in central Tanganyika, then in the following days to troops in Kenya and Uganda.[27]

Nyerere had already fled Dar es Salaam to a beach house several kilometres away. Unable to locate the president, the troops entered the National Assembly at the nearby Karimjee Hall. Amid the confusion, rioting broke out in the commercial district of Dar es Salaam, as Africans attacked Asian-owned shops: as many as thirty people may have died, with hundreds injured. Rumours swirled around the city, including the suggestion that Oscar Kambona, whom Nyerere had left to negotiate with the *askaris*, had himself been plotting a coup. Events across the Zanzibar Channel heightened tensions. But although they certainly alerted troops to the possibilities of armed insurrection, the mutiny had very different causes from the revolution. The mutineers were dissatisfied with their low pay, poor living conditions, and the government's decision to retain white European officers within the army rather than fully embrace a policy of Africanisation.

On 21 January, Nyerere slipped back into Dar es Salaam. In a radio broadcast, he said that there had been 'minor troubles' in the capital. Yet just as the government seemed to be regaining its authority, events took a critical turn. Tanganyikan intelligence reported the discovery at a trade unionist's house of a list of opposition figures who would

---

[27] On the mutiny, see Bjerk, *Building a Peaceful Nation*, 131–54; Timothy H. Parsons, *The 1964 Army Mutinies and the Making of Modern East Africa* (Westport, CT: Praeger, 2003).

purportedly form a new government following a seizure of power that would take place on 25 or 26 January. Fearing that mutiny was about to mutate into a trade union-backed coup, Nyerere requested British military assistance. The following morning, British commandos took control of the barracks, to minimal resistance. The mutiny was over. But the resort to military intervention from the former colonial power was a major embarrassment to Nyerere, who described 'a week of most grievous shame for our nation'.[28]

On the continental stage, Nyerere faced accusations of double standards. Since independence, he had talked of the need to escape the shackles of postcolonial dependency. But in its time of need, Tanganyika had fallen back on its imperial connections with Britain. To explain his actions, Nyerere hastily convened an emergency meeting of OAU foreign ministers in Dar es Salaam in mid-February. Nyerere partly justified the recourse to British intervention by drawing attention to Tanganyika's position as a 'border-state' and the home of the Liberation Committee. He argued that any situation in Tanganyika that interfered with the 'effectiveness' or 'psychological comfort' of the liberation movements was 'the concern of the whole of Africa'. On 20 March, a contingent of Nigerian troops arrived to replace the British forces.[29] In light of Nyerere's embarrassment, it seems fanciful, as one historian has done, to describe the British intervention as 'a spectacle of power by a sovereign head of state, exercising authority both within the nation and as a member of the international community'.[30] More accurately, the mutiny laid bare the fragility of the Tanganyikan government.

The events of early 1964 enhanced Dar es Salaam's reputation as a revolutionary node in Eastern Africa, at a time when the liberation movements had established themselves as central actors in the city's political life. However, just as Nyerere used their presence in Dar es Salaam to justify his decision to recall colonial troops, he was aware that the movements themselves were bound up in the challenges of urban control. Just before the outbreak of the Zanzibar Revolution, an Algerian ship had docked in the port, carrying a cargo of arms. Speculation was rife that they were destined for Mozambican

---

[28] Quoted in Parsons, *1964 Army Mutinies*, 132.
[29] 'O.A.U. Emergency Meeting of Foreign Ministers', in Nyerere, *Freedom and Unity*, 288–89.
[30] Bjerk, *Building a Peaceful Nation*, 131.

guerrillas, or even Zanzibari rebels. To silence the rumours, Kambona asserted that they were intended for the Tanganyika Rifles.[31] Although the liberation movements played no role in the mutiny, the government became increasingly anxious about their activities. In February, two members of the African National Congress (ANC) were arrested after they were overheard making remarks in a bar that the government had shown signs of weakness during the mutiny, especially in calling in the British troops.[32] In October, the government announced that the liberation movements would be limited to four official representatives in Dar es Salaam. Surplus officials, the British high commission reported, were to move to 'a more remote place than the capital, where they would be less able to stir up trouble' or be subverted by 'foreign diplomats'.[33] In response, the ANC relocated its headquarters from Dar es Salaam to the provincial town of Morogoro, though it maintained an office in the capital. This allowed the ANC to operate with a larger staff but came at the cost of reducing its contact-work among Dar es Salaam's international networks.[34]

The government responded to the mutiny by undertaking a major overhaul of key state institutions and strengthening TANU's control over them. First, the Tanganyika Rifles was replaced with a new Tanzania People's Defence Force (TPDF), which was closely tied to the ruling party. To minimise the potential for the army to develop into a rival power bloc, service was limited to three years. Mrisho Sarakikya, who had demonstrated his loyalty to the government during the Tabora mutiny, was appointed head of this new force.[35] Second, following the discovery of trade union involvement in the mutiny, the government dissolved the Tanganyika Federation of Labour and established the National Union of Tanganyika Workers (NUTA), a state-affiliated umbrella organisation.[36] Third, TANU introduced a system which grouped communities into ten-house 'cells', each led by a party activist. Already mooted in 1963, the cell block system was a means of popular mobilisation and conduit for communication between the

---

[31] Parsons, *1964 Army Mutinies*, 104.
[32] MacRae to Price-Jones, 7 February 1964, UKNA, DO 213/123.
[33] MacRae to de Burlet, 2 November 1964, UKNA, DO 213/123/15A.
[34] Arianna Lissoni, 'The South African Liberation Movements in Exile, c.1945–1970', PhD diss. (School of Oriental and African Studies, London, 2008), 167.
[35] Parsons, *1964 Army Mutinies*, 164–69.
[36] Cranford Pratt, *The Critical Phase in Tanzania, 1945–1968* (Cambridge: Cambridge University Press, 1976), 189–94.

party leadership and the people. But it also sought to extend surveillance over the general population, justified by reference to the international threat posed to the country. Cell leaders in Dar es Salaam were told they must be 'the eyes of the nation' and 'expose dangerous characters like thieves and other infiltrators who may poison our nation and put its safety at stake'.[37]

Against this backdrop of institutional change, the country became a de jure one-party state. These plans were already afoot before the events of early 1964: a year earlier, TANU's National Executive Committee determined to abolish the multiparty system. This decision did not emerge solely from an authoritarian attempt by TANU leaders to crush their remaining rivals, although there was certainly an element of this involved. Rather, as Emma Hunter has shown, the ending of multiparty politics represented the culmination of a vibrant conversation about the meaning, purpose, and value of democracy which had begun during the late colonial era. Nyerere weighed in on these debates himself, arguing that multipartyism was unhelpful and even inimical to the practices of democracy and the pursuit of development in a situation where TANU already commanded such mass support. After the mutiny, he established a presidential commission which canvassed views about a new system. This process received a sense of urgency from the upheavals of January. A system of 'one-party democracy' was formally introduced with the 1965 constitution. Subsequent years witnessed intense debates about the ideological substance which would flesh out this institutional apparatus, as we will see. But the political space for challenging TANU's authority became increasingly limited.[38]

———

On 23 April 1964, Tanganyikan radio suddenly announced that Nyerere and Karume had signed an act of union. This brought together

[37] Katherine Levine, 'The TANU Ten-House Cell System', in Lionel Cliffe and John Saul (eds.), *Socialism in Tanzania: An Interdisciplinary Reader. Vol. 1: Politics* (Nairobi: East African Publishing House, 1972), 329–37, quotation on 330.

[38] James R. Brennan, 'The Short History of Political Opposition and Multi-Party Democracy in Tanganyika, 1958–64', in Maddox and Giblin (eds.), *In Search of a Nation*, 250–76; Emma Hunter, *Political Thought and the Public Sphere in Tanzania: Freedom, Democracy and Citizenship in the Era of Decolonization* (New York: Cambridge University Press, 2015), 187–209.

the mainland with Zanzibar to form the state that became the United Republic of Tanzania. Under the new constitutional arrangements, Zanzibar ceded certain powers, including its foreign and defence policy, to a new union government based in Dar es Salaam, while retaining control over most of its internal affairs.[39] Nyerere explained that the union was motivated by pan-African sentiment alone. He described it as a stepping-stone to African unity. 'There is no other reason', he told parliament. 'It is insult to Africa to read cold war into every move towards African unity ... We do not propose the Union to support any of the 'isms of this world.'[40] Two days later, Nyerere announced the first union cabinet. Five portfolios were awarded to members of Zanzibar's Revolutionary Council. They included Hanga, who became minister of industries, mines, and power, and Babu, who was appointed minister of state in the Directorate of Development and Planning.[41]

No other episode in Tanzanian history has attracted such heated debate as the union.[42] Some portray it as a constitutional coup, orchestrated by mainlanders, that deprived Zanzibar of its independence.[43] Another viewpoint maintains that Nyerere was forced into the union by the imperialist machinations of the United States.[44] Accepting Nyerere's rhetoric at face value, others continue to see it as a lasting success of the pan-African moment.[45] Certainly, the pan-African spirit invoked by both mainland and island governments to justify the union over the following years was not pure gloss. In 1958, TANU and the ASP had announced their commitment to unite their states after both had gained independence. TANU had supported the ASP during

---

[39] The full legal framework is explained in Shivji, *Pan-Africanism*, 94–97.
[40] 'The Union of Tanganyika and Zanzibar', Nyerere, *Freedom and Unity*, 293.
[41] This account of the union is based mainly on Shivji, *Pan-Africanism*; Ethan R. Sanders, 'Conceiving the Tanganyika-Zanzibar Union in the Midst of the Cold War', *African Review*, 41 (2014), 35–70.
[42] Marie-Aude Fouéré, 'Recasting Julius Nyerere in Zanzibar: The Revolution, the Union, and the Enemy of the Nation', *Journal of Eastern African Studies*, 8 (2014), 478–92.
[43] Harith Ghassany, *Kwaheri Ukoloni, Kwaheri Uhuru!* (n.p.: self-published, 2010).
[44] Amrit Wilson, *US Foreign Policy and Revolution: The Creation of Tanzania* (London: Pluto, 1989); Amrit Wilson, *The Threat of Liberation: Imperialism and Revolution in Zanzibar* (London: Pluto, 2013).
[45] Godfrey Mwakikagile, *The Union of Tanganyika and Zanzibar: Product of the Cold War?* (Pretoria: New Africa Press, 2008).

Zanzibar's pre-*uhuru* elections and the ASP had joined other liberation movements in opening an office in Dar es Salaam. Yet Nyerere's soaring pan-Africanist rhetoric in parliament elided the geopolitical realities which brought the two leaders into their secretive deal.

Instead, the union was the product of Nyerere's pragmatic response to a situation which threatened to destabilise East Africa and submerge the region in Cold War conflict. Nyerere had long regarded Zanzibar, with its toxic racial politics, as a problem on the horizon. 'If I could tow the island out into the middle of the Indian Ocean, I'd do it', he had once said in private.[46] The growing communist presence in Zanzibar exacerbated these concerns. However, instead of trying to distance Tanganyika from this offshore crisis, Nyerere decided to pull Zanzibar closer to the mainland. After talks over an East African Federation with Kenya and Uganda fell through, Nyerere pushed forward with plans for a bilateral union with Zanzibar. Although American and British diplomats encouraged the Tanganyikan government to intervene, the driving forces behind the negotiations were Nyerere and Kambona. Karume was less committed to the idea of a union, but his power in Zanzibar had been slipping away to the socialists on the Revolutionary Council, led by Hanga and Babu. Anxious to maintain his grasp on power, Karume exchanged Zanzibar's autonomy for security.

The union bill sailed through the Tanganyikan parliament, but its passage in Zanzibar was mired in legal opacity. The articles were only discussed by the Revolutionary Council and never formally ratified. Some of its members were unwilling to forfeit the islands' autonomy.[47] When the act of union was signed on 22 April, Babu was in Indonesia, negotiating a triangular trade agreement that also involved the GDR. In his later writings and following personal fall outs with both Karume and Nyerere, Babu was deeply critical of the union. He believed that Nyerere had caved into American pressure to derail the Zanzibar Revolution.[48] Other accounts claim that Babu was initially supportive of the union, since it would give him a wider arena to realise his socialist goals.[49] Yet the coincidence of the signing of the union with the absence of Zanzibar's foreign minister suggests that negotiators felt that Babu

---

[46] William Edgett Smith, *Nyerere of Tanzania* (London: Victor Gollancz, 1973), 90.
[47] Shivji, *Pan-Africanism*, 88–90.
[48] Babu's foreword to Wilson, *US Foreign Policy*, 1–7; Babu, '1964 Revolution'.
[49] Shivji, *Pan-Africanism*, 82; Glassman, *War of Words*, 293.

was a likely obstacle.[50] The transfer of Babu and Hanga into the mainland government had the intended effect of taking the heat out of Zanzibari politics. Socialist aid workers and technicians continued to arrive in Zanzibar from Eastern Europe and especially China into the 1970s. But Western fears of Zanzibar becoming a 'Cuba in Africa' faded away as media attention died down. Instead, the kleptocratic state ruled by Karume and the Revolutionary Council became a source of embarrassment for Nyerere, as explained in Chapter 7.

Cold War Plots and Broken Relations

If Nyerere hoped the union with Zanzibar would insulate the new country against Cold War threats, events over the course of the next twelve months proved otherwise. A dispute with West Germany over the question of East German diplomatic representation in Dar es Salaam ended with Nyerere rejecting all capital aid from Bonn – events which are covered in detail in Chapter 3. This was an argument about the sticky details of diplomatic protocol, however. More dramatic were the disputes that jolted Tanzania's relationship with the United States and the break in diplomatic relations with Britain over Rhodesia's Unilateral Declaration of Independence (UDI).

On 9 November 1964, the Tanzanian ambassador to Congo-Leopoldville brought a clutch of photocopies to Dar es Salaam. These documents were supposedly obtained from the office of Moïse Tshombe, the Congolese prime minister. They indicated that the United States was plotting a coup against the Tanzanian government. Nyerere was on holiday at the time and so entrusted the issue to Oscar Kambona, his foreign minister. Rather than first summoning the American ambassador, as Nyerere might have done, Kambona chose to make the matter public. He had the incendiary text printed in the TANU newspaper, the *Nationalist* and then made the accusations against the United States official at a press conference. The American ambassador, William Leonhart, quickly concluded that the letters were clumsy forgeries. At a rally in Dar es Salaam on 15 November, Nyerere attempted to defuse the situation without conceding ground. He challenged the Americans to show that the letters were forged and asked for sympathy. What other reaction, Nyerere pointed out, could be expected from Tanzania? Washington had been

---

[50] Sanders, 'Conceiving the Tanganyika-Zanzibar Union', 44–45, 52.

hostile towards his country since the Zanzibar Revolution. After FRELIMO began its liberation struggle in Mozambique in September, there was now a serious military threat to Tanzania from Portugal. 'A man who has once been bitten by a snake starts if he sees even a palm leaf', Nyerere said, quoting a Swahili proverb.[51] In December, he announced that he had accepted an American statement that the letters were fakes. But he did not offer a full apology. The letters' origins remain shrouded in mystery. Claims that they were produced by the Czechoslovakian or Portuguese secret services rest on thin evidence.[52]

The situation was aggravated by events across Tanzania's western border. Tanzania had been providing concealed support for the 'Simba' rebel forces in eastern Congo, where followers of the assassinated Lumumba had established their capital in Stanleyville. Fearing the disintegration of the pro-Western regime in Leopoldville, Belgium and the United States colluded to recruit a force of mercenaries, mainly drawn from Rhodesia and South Africa. When these troops closed in on Stanleyville, the Simbas took hundreds of white hostages. On 24 November, Belgian paratroopers jumped from American aeroplanes to seize control of the city. This news was met with outrage in Dar es Salaam. The *Nationalist* described Stanleyville as 'a ruthless, crushing intervention supported by the full blast of malevolent propaganda and protestations of sickening hypocrisy to cover the exercise of naked power'.[53] University students demonstrated outside the American embassy.[54] Nyerere gave his permission for Cuba to use Tanzania as a base for aiding the remaining Congolese rebels. In April 1965, Che Guevara launched an armed expedition across Lake Tanganyika, which ultimately ended in failure. Guevara returned to Dar es Salaam, disillusioned with the prospects of revolutionary war in Africa. He spent the next few months secretly living in the Cuban embassy, writing his memoirs of the Congo expedition.[55]

[51] 'Tanzania and Plotomania', *Africa 1964*, 4 December 1964, 1–3.
[52] On the 'letter plot', see Pratt, *Critical Phase*, 144–47; Bjerk, *Building a Peaceful Nation*, 236–46; James R. Brennan, 'Intelligence and Security: Revolution, Espionage, and the Cold War in Tanzania', unpublished paper in author's possession, 33–34.
[53] 'Congo: Our Stand', editorial, *Nationalist*, 27 November 1964, 4.
[54] 'Dar Students Demonstrate', *Nationalist*, 27 November 1964, 1, 5.
[55] Gleijeses, *Conflicting Missions*, 77–157; Ernesto 'Che' Guevara, *The African Dream: The Diaries of the Revolutionary War in the Congo*, trans. Patrick Camillier (London: Harvill Jamie Monson, *Africa's Freedom Railway: How*

Just two months after the 'letter plot', the United States found itself at the centre of another scandal in Tanzania. On 15 January 1965, the Tanzanian authorities announced the expulsion of two American diplomats: Frank Carlucci, consul in Zanzibar, and Robert Gordon, deputy chief-of-mission in Dar es Salaam. The origins of the affair were innocuous. Discussing the appropriate American response to the first anniversary of the Zanzibar Revolution over the telephone, the pair felt that a simple statement of congratulations would be insufficient, and that 'bigger guns' were required – a reference to a potential visit to Zanzibar by the under-secretary of state for Africa, G. Mennen Williams. A Stasi-trained Zanzibari intelligence officer was listening in on the conversation. He interpreted the phrase 'bigger guns' literally and believed that he had uncovered an American plot against the Karume regime. Both Carlucci and his assistant in Zanzibar at the time have alleged that the tape was doctored by the East Germans. On this occasion, Nyerere seemed convinced that the threat was real. He made clear that this was a private matter involving two rogue officials and that neither the State Department nor ambassador Leonhart were implicated. Yet if his aim was to prevent the deterioration of relations with Washington, Nyerere failed. The Tanzanian ambassador was swiftly expelled from the United States.[56]

The passage of time renders the level of misunderstanding in these incidents almost farcical. But it cannot obscure the genuine sense of fear of outside intervention that preoccupied the Tanzanian elite following events in Zanzibar and Congo. Regardless of their exact origins and circumstances, the Congo letters and Zanzibar phone tap exhibited the nervousness – even paranoia – about external plotting against the new Tanzanian state. 'We should look at history and watch out', Nyerere told a rally. 'What happened in Congo could happen here.'[57] The letters from Leopoldville represented the tip of the iceberg of a culture of textual forgery and misinformation that became characteristic of Cold War

a Chinese Development Project Changed Lives and Livelihoods in Tanzania (Bloomington: Indiana University Press, 2009), 2001); Andrew Ivaska, 'Liberation in Transit: Eduardo Mondlane and Che Guevara in Dar es Salaam', in Jian et al. (eds.), *Routledge Handbook of the Global Sixties*, 27–38.

[56] American officials have given different accounts of the exact words used, some suggesting 'more ammunition' was the phrase. Brennan, 'Intelligence', 38–41. See also Bjerk, *Building a Peaceful Nation*, 246–49.

[57] 'The President's Speech at the 1964 Republic Day Rally', Information Service Press Release, 10 December 1964, NAN 2.05.253/254.

politics in Dar es Salaam. Equally, the 'phone tap' served as a warning about the insecurity of communications systems, as the city became a centre for espionage. Dar es Salaam's public sphere was replete with anti-American sentiment. While the United States rebuilt its relationship with Tanzania, it remained the subject of continuous talk about 'imperialist' plots and a common target of attacks from TANU's radicals, as subsequent chapters demonstrate.

Whereas neither the 'letter plot' or the 'phone tap' brought about a breach in Tanzania's relations with the United States, Rhodesia's UDI led Nyerere to take this ultimate diplomatic step. The crisis of Rhodesian decolonisation had been brewing for several years. Leaders of the two banned opposition parties, ZAPU and its breakaway faction ZANU, were already familiar faces in Dar es Salaam's exile scene. Tensions reached their height in 1965, when Ian Smith's Rhodesian Front became deadlocked in negotiations with Harold Wilson's Labour government in London. Nyerere expressed his strength of feeling in June, when he refused to sign the final communiqué at a Commonwealth conference after Wilson failed to provide assurance that Britain would not give independence to Rhodesia without majority rule.[58]

Like Stanleyville a year earlier, Rhodesia's UDI of 11 November 1965 provoked outrage in Dar es Salaam. Having been denied permission to hold a protest involving thousands of schoolchildren, university students pushed ahead with a demonstration outside the British high commission. The protest quickly turned violent: students tore down and burned the union flag, wrecked the high commissioner's car, and smashed windows. The police dispersed the crowd using tear gas. Around one hundred protesters were rounded up and driven to State House, where they were admonished by Nyerere for this ill-discipline. The students then returned to the high commission to apologise for their actions.[59] The Ministry of Information warned that the police would deal severely with any repeat of this 'unfortunate incident'.[60] As this episode showed, Nyerere's foreign policy struggles were inward- as well as outward-looking. This sort of violent protest embarrassed the Tanzanian leadership, which was

---

[58] Pratt, *Critical Phase*, 149.
[59] Leonhart to State Dept, 13 November 1964 (two dispatches), NARA, RG 59, SNF 1964–66, Box 2693, POL 23-8 TANZAN.
[60] 'Government Warns of Severe Action on Rioters', *Nationalist*, 15 November 1965, 1, 6.

sensitive to the risks it posed to its own moral authority. The government's response to the protest was a precursor to future interventions in both street demonstrations and the press, as later chapters show.

Meanwhile, a meeting of OAU foreign ministers in Addis Ababa on 3 December called on African states to sever diplomatic relations with Britain if it did not 'crush' the Rhodesian rebellion within two weeks. When the OAU ultimatum expired, Tanzania was one of nine African states to break relations with London. The decision came at significant cost, as Britain froze a £7.5 million development aid loan.[61] However, three-quarters of African states failed to follow through on the OAU's resolution, to Nyerere's dismay. 'Do African states meet in solemn conclave to make a noise? Or do they mean what they say?', he asked parliament.[62] Nyerere remained steadfast to the principle of 'no independence before majority African rule' in Rhodesia. Diplomatic relations between Britain and Tanzania were not restored until July 1968. To avoid the appearance of having caved into British pressure, Nyerere's volte face was accompanied by a refusal to turn back on a decision to cancel pensions to British expatriates who had worked for the colonial government. Britain responded by terminating all aid and technical assistance to Tanzania.[63] The new high commissioner in Dar es Salaam urged London that any concession to Smith's regime would be inimical to Britain's broader interests in Africa. He warned that a Rhodesian settlement 'unfavourable to African opinion' would create 'a situation which Communist Governments (particularly Peking) would relish as a success scored by them without effort on their part'.[64] The question of Zimbabwean liberation, bound up in the politics of the global Cold War, thereby became a mainstay of Britain's relations with Tanzania.

Tanzania and the Socialist World

While Tanzania became embroiled in disputes with Western powers, it attempted to strengthen its connections with communist China and the

---

[61] Arrigo Pallotti, 'Post-Colonial Nation-Building and Southern African Liberation: Tanzania and the Break of Diplomatic Relations with the United Kingdom, 1965–1968', *African Historical Review*, 41 (2009), 60–84.
[62] 'The Honour of Africa', in Julius K. Nyerere, *Freedom and Socialism: A Selection from Writings and Speeches, 1965–1967* (Dar es Salaam: Oxford University Press, 1968), 128.
[63] Pallotti, 'Post-Colonial Nation-Building'.
[64] Phillips, 15 January 1969, UKNA, FCO 31/432/21.

Soviet Union. The United Republic was keen to diversify its sources of aid, including by approaching the socialist superpowers. This meant, as Nyerere stressed time and time again, that Tanzania was following a genuinely non-aligned course. In the zero-sum calculations of Western diplomats, it represented something more dangerous altogether. From Nyerere's point of view, the transfer of the Zanzibari revolutionaries to his cabinet was therefore both an asset and a problem. On the positive side, their connections with Moscow and Beijing represented potential conduits for deepening relationships with the communist world. At the same time, the presence of Hanga and Babu at the centre of government increased the fearmongering in the West about Tanzania's geopolitical tilt. They provided grist to the mill for journalists whose sensationalised articles talked up communist subversion in Dar es Salaam.

The communist powers were disappointed at the turn of events since the Zanzibar Revolution. They believed that the union with the mainland had extinguished the flame of a promising revolutionary moment in the islands. The Chinese ambassador to Zanzibar sounded his concern that the Nyerere government 'wanted the revolution to stop' and was 'pulling it back'.[65] In November 1964, Soviet and East German intelligence officials described the union as 'a victory of the Western powers and Nyerere', who had 'played an extraordinarily negative role'. As we will see in Chapter 3, the East Germans were unhappy at losing their embassy in Zanzibar, as Dar es Salaam became the diplomatic capital of the new republic. Nonetheless, they sought to make the best of the new circumstances. The KGB and Stasi resolved that Zanzibar still had to be supported as a 'base for progress' and a 'fist within Tanzania'. They agreed that they should continue to look to Babu and Hanga in order to influence the situation in the country.[66]

Nyerere had similar thoughts. He sought to use the Zanzibari revolutionaries in the mainland government to build bridges with the socialist world. The president initially tried to draw on Hanga's influence to push for aid agreements from the Eastern Bloc. In August 1964,

---

[65] Quoted in Gregg A. Brazinsky, *Winning the Third World: Sino-American Rivalry During the Cold War* (Chapel Hill: University of North Carolina Press, 2017), 259.

[66] 'Stasi report of meetings with the KGB, 30 November-1 December 1964', 2 December 1964, BStU, MfS, SdM 576, 1–30, consulted via CWIHP digital archive, trans. Bernd Schaefer.

Hanga supported a delegation led by second vice-president Rashidi Kawawa on a tour of Czechoslovakia, Poland, and the Soviet Union. However, the Tanzanians received a cold reception in Moscow. The Soviet authorities declined to invest in any major development projects and told the Tanzanians to focus on expanding light industries that would yield immediate returns. The loan they proposed to fund these initiatives came with a high interest rate of 2.5 per cent, plus a requirement for Tanzania to purchase Soviet equipment and pay the costs of any technical expertise. Hanga was dismayed that Moscow 'should be saying things that would normally be expected of a capitalist country'.[67] The Soviet response to Tanzanian overtures reflected its disillusionment with sub-Saharan Africa in the early 1960s, as postcolonial leaders proved wary of Moscow's intrusive approach and narrow conceptions of revolutionary development, which offered little space for local forms of African socialism.[68]

This icy encounter with the Soviet Union contrasted sharply with Tanzania's experience of the other communist superpower, China. In the early 1960s, Beijing was on the offensive in the Third World. The acrimonious rift with Moscow meant that it sought to counter Soviet as much as Western influence. As Jeremy Friedman argues, China's own historical trajectory offered an advantage here. Whereas Moscow presented itself as the vanguard of anti-capitalist global struggles, China emphasised its anticolonial revolutionary credentials. The experience of China – a poor, non-white, Third World state which had suffered at the hands of imperialism – chimed with many leaders in postcolonial Africa. After Mao Tse-tung abandoned the disastrous industrialisation policies of the 'Great Leap Forward', China's renewed attention to rural development and strategy of mass mobilisation appealed to African governments.[69] Although disappointed by its setbacks in Zanzibar, China saw the union as an opportunity to spread its influence on the mainland, especially given Dar es Salaam's growing reputation as a centre for revolutionary activity in Africa.

Babu played a leading role in the strengthening of relations between Tanzania and China. In June 1964, he accompanied Kawawa to Beijing, where the Tanzanian delegation received a warm welcome.

---

[67] Pratt, *Critical Phase*, 159–61.
[68] Jeremy Friedman, *Shadow Cold War: The Sino-Soviet Competition for the Third World* (Chapel Hill: University of North Carolina Press, 2015), 82–83.
[69] Ibid.

They returned home with a £16 million aid package, including an interest-free £10 million loan. A trade agreement, negotiated by an economic delegation led by Babu, preceded Nyerere's own highly successful tour of China in February 1965.[70] In June, the Chinese premier Zhou Enlai made a return visit to Dar es Salaam, to a rapturous reception. The most consequential outcome of these exchanges was Beijing's verbal agreement to support the construction of a railway between the port of Dar es Salaam and the Zambian Copperbelt. Landlocked Zambia, which became independent in 1964, was dependent on railway arteries passing through Rhodesia, South Africa, and the Portuguese colonies for transporting copper to the coast for export. This problem was exacerbated by Rhodesia's UDI. Nyerere's initial meeting paved the way for the signing of a tripartite agreement between China, Tanzania, and Zambia in September 1967, under which Beijing pledged an interest-free £150 million loan to fund the 1,860-kilometre TAZARA railway. Work began in 1970 and was completed in 1974, with the assistance of 30–40,000 Chinese workers. Blending a major modernisation scheme with the spirit of anticolonialism, this epic infrastructure project was part of China's drive to become a superpower while remaining a member of the Third World, as Jamie Monson has shown.[71]

The deepening Sino-Tanzanian relationship sent alarm bells ringing in the West. Recognising both the appeal of Beijing's anticolonial credentials and Nyerere's desire to diversify the sources of foreign aid, the British high commissioner noted that the Chinese were 'batting on almost a perfect wicket' in Tanzania. The nightmarish images of communist penetration which had accompanied the Zanzibar Revolution were conjured up again. The British surmised that Chinese policy was to use Dar es Salaam in the east and Brazzaville in the west 'for subversion across the waist of Africa'.[72] The United States drew similar conclusions. In June 1966, the National Security Council classified Tanzania as a 'steady nuisance in Africa'. It judged that

---

[70] Alicia N. Altorfer-Ong, 'Old Comrades and New Brothers: A Historical Re-Examination of the Sino-Zanzibari and Sino-Tanzania Bilateral Relationships', PhD diss. (London School of Economics, 2014), 128.
[71] Jamie Monson, *Africa's Freedom Railway: How a Chinese Development Project Changed Lives and Livelihoods in Tanzania* (Bloomington: Indiana University Press, 2009).
[72] Fowler, 15 February 1965, UKNA, DO 213/100/11.

'under the mercurial and fiercely independent leadership of Nyerere, Tanzania is the bastion of radicalism in East Africa. Soviet and Chinese influence is considerable, especially in Zanzibar.'[73] These sentiments were also to be found in the media. Visiting Western correspondents built up a caricature of Dar es Salaam as a centre of subversion and communist penetration, often drawing a tired contrast with the meaning of its Arabic name, 'the haven of peace'.[74] Britain's *Daily Telegraph* dubbed Dar es Salaam 'the arsenal for the Communist arms build-up in East Africa'.[75] The *Wall Street Journal* called the city 'a focal point for African extremists of every type'.[76] The West German newspaper *Die Zeit* described Tanzania as a Chinese 'corridor of revolution'.[77]

Nyerere sought to maintain his non-aligned credentials in the face of this hyperbolic Western commentary. He tried to assuage his critics by emphasising the dilemmas facing Tanzania, a poor country faced by powerful white minority enemies, in a world dominated by superpower money and weapons. In January 1966, Nyerere gave an interview to American radio. He faced a barrage of hostile questions about armed liberation struggles and China's presence in Tanzania. 'I hope that before you go back to the United States you will try to move around either in Dar es Salaam or Tanzania to verify the idea that we are part of Peking or a springboard of Peking', he told his interviewers. 'But let me say that if we have to fight we are not going to fight with bows and arrows. We have to fight with modern arms. There is not an [arms] factory in Dar es Salaam.' Nyerere admitted that he was 'willing to get those arms from Washington, from London, from Paris'. However, he concluded, 'if I can't get them from there, I will get them from Moscow or from Peking'.[78] The Tanzanian press shared his frustration. 'The snakes have sung their usual song that Tanzania is heading towards communism', complained the popular Swahili tabloid *Ngurumo*.

---

[73] Haynes to Rostow, 8 June 1966, *FRUS*, 1964–1968, vol. 24, doc. 212.
[74] Ronald Payne, 'Russians and Chinese Use Tanzania as Arms Centre', *Sunday Telegraph*, 21 March 1965, 1–2; Lawrence Fellows, 'Nyerere Upholds Chou View of U.S.', *New York Times*, 9 June 1965, 7.
[75] Richard Beeston, 'Tanzania: Haven of Intrigue', *Daily Telegraph*, 23 November 1964, 14.
[76] Ray Vicker, 'Africa's Moderates', *Wall Street Journal*, 10 December 1965, 16.
[77] 'Chinas Stützpunkte in Afrika', *Die Zeit*, 5 March 1965, 8.
[78] CBS 'Face the Nation' interview with Julius Nyerere, 2 January 1966, Herskovits Library of African Studies Audio Collection, Northwestern University.

'Enough, we'll have no more of it! If those who are insulting the people and leaders of this country think that one day we will listen to them, they are wrong.'[79]

Inside the Cold War City

Nyerere's bold foreign policy, the regional concatenations, and especially the presence of the exiles turned Dar es Salaam into a major hive of revolutionary politics in Africa. The encounters which resulted were not simply confined to the spheres of formal diplomacy and official policymaking which are the typical focus of international histories. The city's public sphere became engrained with the insecurities of what Priya Lal has dubbed a 'global Cold War political culture' in Tanzania.[80] The belief that the nation's sovereignty was under constant threat from imperialist intervention, working with stooges inside the country, formed a rationale which justified the gradual militarisation of society and a vocabulary which cast dissenters as reactionary traitors, as subsequent chapters show. These same anxieties also influenced elite political behaviour in the capital. Dar es Salaam's spaces and places were believed to pose security risks through the spreading of rumour, the subversion of individuals, and the leaking of sensitive knowledge. Read from an alternative angle, of course, the city's transnational political networks also provided interested parties with channels for disseminating information and gathering intelligence.

By 1968, forty-seven foreign states had some form of diplomatic representation in Dar es Salaam. The political geography of this diplomatic scene mapped onto Cold War divisions. Western representations were clustered around the city centre. The American, Australian, French, and West German missions were all located in the National Bank of Commerce Building, near the Askari Monument, the city's central landmark. The Canadian high commission, which also housed the British Interests Section after Tanzania severed relations with London, was nearby on Independence Avenue, the main commercial thoroughfare. North of the centre, the communist embassies were scattered along Upanga Road, earning it the *nom de guerre* of 'Red

---

[79] 'Kusingiziwa', editorial, *Ngurumo*, 7 September 1965, 2.
[80] Lal, *African Socialism*, 69.

Boulevard'.⁸¹ They were joined by a smattering of representations from radical non-aligned states, like Algeria and Indonesia.

Diplomats mixed freely on the circuit of embassy and government receptions, where they brushed shoulders with Tanzanian officials and members of Dar es Salaam's liberation movements. These social opportunities helped to break down Cold War rivalries, yet they were far from devoid of tensions. The French ambassador expressed his concern that Western diplomats became 'submerged' at receptions by representatives of the 'revolutionary' countries.⁸² The Tanzanian government also worried about subversion of its employees at diplomatic gatherings. In December 1964, it informed officials that they required permission from their head of department before accepting invitations and must submit a report immediately after the event.⁸³ Diplomats from across the Cold War spectrum sought to gain the ear of the liberation movement leaders, whose faces were a common sight on this circuit. The ANC's Ben Turok recalled that, on these social occasions, 'there was some personal corruption' and that 'it was extremely difficult to maintain a sense of integrity in the face of this pressure'. The presence of the guerrilla leaders in these salubrious surroundings was also a regular issue of grievance for their Tanzanian hosts and the movement's rank-and-file, as Chapter 4 shows.⁸⁴

The diplomatic reception was the official manifestation of the vibrant social scene that characterised Dar es Salaam's clubs, restaurants, and bars. The New Africa, Kilimanjaro, and Twiga hotels were upmarket venues which attracted a cosmopolitan clientele, including liberation movement leaders, foreign correspondents, and Western diplomats.⁸⁵ A radical crowd propped up the bar at the Palm Beach Hotel, next to the Cuban embassy on Upanga Road. Babu and his followers met there, where they were often joined by communist diplomats who dropped by for a beer after finishing work nearby.⁸⁶ The liberation movement leaders took their lunch in restaurants near to

---

⁸¹ Schroeder to Auswärtiges Amt, 26 August 1965, PAAA, NA 13473.
⁸² De Bourdeille to MAE-DAL, 4 May 1965, CADN, 193PO/1/24 AIII1.
⁸³ Othman, 8 December 1964, enclosed in Miles to Aspin, 9 January 1965, UKNA, DO 213/103/21.
⁸⁴ Ben Turok, *Nothing but the Truth: Behind the ANC's Struggle Politics* (Johannesburg: Jonathan Ball, 2003), 205.
⁸⁵ See the description in Ryszard Kapuściński, *The Shadow of the Sun: My African Life*, trans. Klara Glowczewska (London:Allen Lane, 2001), 76.
⁸⁶ Interview with Mohamed Said, Magomeni Mapipa, Dar es Salaam, 8 July 2015.

their offices, including the New Zahir Restaurant on Mosque Street or the Canton Restaurant on Nkrumah Street. According to Portuguese intelligence and the Rhodesian press, the Canton and its adjacent Tanganyika Bookshop were run by a Chinese agent in Dar es Salaam, Ho Lin.[87] The Canton, the American embassy reported, was 'an excellent meeting place outside of the official Chinese mission'.[88] All of these spaces simultaneously provided places for socialising and opportunities for intelligence gathering.

Another key locus of politics in Dar es Salaam was the university, set in rolling green hills to the northwest of the city. University College (renamed the University of Dar es Salaam in 1970, when it became independent from the University of East Africa) was far removed from the noise of the city centre but became a site of confrontation between TANU's nation-building imperatives and students' own expectations of the future. By the late 1960s, the 'Hill' had emerged as a hotbed of radical politics in Africa of international renown. A permissive academic culture and the allure of Nyerere's philosophy attracted leftwing intellectuals from across the world.[89] As Chapter 5 explains, the organisation of students into a far-left revolutionary group which criticised *ujamaa* socialism ultimately led to a government crackdown. Even then, however, the university continued to sit at the centre of transnational networks that formed a radical Dar es Salaam counterculture, comprising Marxist politicians, communist diplomats, guerrilla leaders, anti-apartheid activists, and members of the African American diaspora.[90]

---

[87] SCCIM, 4 January 1967, enclosed in Deslandes to MNE, 28 January 1967, AHD, MNE, PAA 819.
[88] Gordon to State Dept, 22 December 1964, NARA, RG 59, SNF 1964–66, Box 2688, POL 2–3 TANZAN.
[89] See Ivaska, *Cultured States*, 124–65.
[90] Andrew Ivaska, 'Movement Youth in a Global Sixties Hub: The Everyday Lives of Transnational Activists in Postcolonial Dar es Salaam', in Richard Ivan Jobs and David M. Pomfret (eds.), *Transnational Histories of Youth in the Twentieth Century* (Basingstoke: Palgrave Macmillan, 2015), 188–210. On Tanzania's African American diaspora see Seth M. Markle, *A Motorcycle on Hell Run: Tanzania, Black Power, and the Uncertain Future of Pan-Africanism, 1964–1974* (East Lansing: Michigan State University Press, 2017); Monique A. Bedasse, *Jah Kingdom: Rastafarians, Tanzania, and Pan-Africanism in the Age of Decolonization* (Chapel Hill: North Carolina University Press, 2017).

Dar es Salaam's cosmopolitan political scene, containing so many competing ideological and geopolitical agendas, produced a vibrant and complex information ecology. Chapter 6 explores the complicated and multilayered relationship between the government, TANU, and the press in developing a revolutionary newspaper sector. But at times it felt like Tanzanian voices were struggling to be heard through the welter of propaganda issued by foreign powers in Dar es Salaam. This material was situated at various points on a spectrum between subtle, 'soft' propaganda to unapologetic attacks against other states or ideologies. A kaleidoscopic range of newspapers, magazines, and books were available for purchase. Swahili translations of Mao's *Little Red Book* and the *Communist Manifesto* were commonplace. The major embassies produced regular information bulletins, which were distributed to ministries and the press.

The more eye-catching publications came from the communist powers. In 1964, the Chinese embassy published a pilot issue of *Vigilance Africa*, which could be purchased for a pittance from the Tanganyika Bookshop. Proclaiming 'a relentless war on COLONIALISM, IMPERIALISM and NEO-COLONIALISM', it vowed that it would 'not spare a moment in exposing fearlessly colonialist intrigues, manoeuvres and any puppetish accomplices in monstrous schemes designed to negate the independence and freedom of the African peoples'.[91] In 1968, the Soviet Union began to produce a similar Swahili newspaper, *Urusi Leo* ('Russia Today'). Reflecting the acrimonious state of Sino-Soviet relations, it was directly arraigned against China rather than the West. 'We have much Chinese political literature here condemning Moscow', wrote its Tanzanian reporter. 'We want to give the public the true picture of what the Soviets stand for and what is the real picture of what Peking stands for in Africa.'[92] However, the socialist world did not have a monopoly on foreign propaganda material. In 1971, the British reported that their policy of supplying around two hundred newspapers and periodicals to senior Tanzanians was a 'highly worthwhile means of orientating the "ruling few" towards things British', to the 'envy' of less well-resourced diplomatic missions.[93] Cultural institutions like the British Council, West Germany's Goethe Institute, and the United States Information Service

[91] 'Policy', *Vigilance Africa*, 4 May 1964, inside cover.
[92] Belcher, 28 June 1968, NARA, RG 59, CFPF 1967–69, Box 393, PPB TANZAN.
[93] Phillips to Grey, 23 August 1971, UKNA, FCO 26/746/8.

maintained public libraries, stocked with literature friendly to the Western cause. Propaganda also took forms beyond the written word. Photographic exhibitions, dance troupes, and football teams all travelled to Dar es Salaam in an attempt to foster cultural relations. Film was an especially powerful medium of mass communication in the urban sphere.

This suffusion of propaganda also dismayed the Tanzanian government. In 1967, the *Nationalist* bemoaned the 'bundles of foreign literature' in government offices, including *BBC Listener*, *Korea Today*, the *Economist*, *Time Magazine*, *Moscow News*, and *Peking Review*. The editorial called on receptionists to stock up on Tanzanian publications to end this 'humiliation' (although its suggestion of copies of the country's Five-Year Plan was unlikely to have been particularly absorbing competition).[94] Government attempts to control the softer elements of foreign cultural propaganda were conjoined with *ujamaa*'s campaign against forms of moral decadence. TANU was particularly concerned about the corrupting influence of Hollywood film on its nation-building efforts. In non-aligned Tanzania, the Cold War content of these films also risked offending potential donor countries. Government censors banned a string of Western espionage movies.[95] The authorities' opposition to the development of television was rooted in similar concerns about moral corruption. A report submitted to cabinet in 1962 by the Tanganyika Broadcasting Corporation emphasised the 'morally degraded' character of American television. 'The early foreign traders in Africa bought our land and our birth-right with coloured beads, gin and firearms', the report concluded. 'Are we going to sell our minds in the same innocent way to their descendants, the cheap-jacks who dazzle us with their gaudy television goods?'[96]

But there were limits to the measures to which the Tanzanian government was prepared to resort to insulate the country against this foreign material. In August 1967, Nyerere stated that although he would not tolerate any attempts by outsiders to influence the country's policies, he would not 'draw an iron curtain around Tanzania to prevent foreign propaganda'.[97] Echoing this sentiment, a former

---

[94] 'Literature in Gov't Offices', editorial, *Nationalist*, 30 December 1967, 4.
[95] James R. Brennan, 'Democratizing Cinema and Censorship in Tanzania, 1920–1980', *International Journal of African Historical Studies*, 38 (2005), 505; see also Laura Fair, *Reel Pleasures: Cinema Audiences and Entrepreneurs in Twentieth-Century Urban Tanzania* (Athens: Ohio University Press, 2018).
[96] Mdoe, 'Television', 23 May 1962, Ivan Smith Papers, BL, MSS Eng. c. 6470, 174.
[97] 'No Iron Curtain Around Tanzania', *Nationalist*, 22 August 1967, 1, 8.

bureaucrat at the Ministry of Foreign Affairs recalled that Tanzania 'did not want to become like a police state' with 'the culture that was part and parcel of Eastern European countries'.[98] The Tanzanian government's policing of such activities was inconsistent, and often contingent on the political alignment of the officials directly responsible. Chinese, North Korean, and North Vietnamese representations appeared free to attack the United States and its allies with few restrictions. Gauging the actual impact of any propaganda is difficult. African audiences were certainly neither passive nor uncritical absorbers of this material. Nevertheless, the cumulative effect of this steady drip was the suffusion of Tanzanian political discourse with the language and tropes of the Cold War, as the genre of rumour shows.

On 15 November 1964, Nyerere addressed a rally at the Jangwani grounds in Dar es Salaam. He aimed to dampen the foment which Kambona had whipped up through his 'exposure' of the American 'letter plot'. In his speech, Nyerere drew attention to the problem of rumour in the capital.

Someone has told me that we should now call Dar es Salaam 'Rumorville'. Rumors are always rife in Dar es Salaam to the extent that not three days pass without rumors being spread, especially in the shopping areas. ... The difficulty is that there are rumor experts and professors here in Dar es Salaam. ... Someone has whispered to me that some of your leaders thoughtlessly talk in bars about government affairs. This is a very bad thing. ... There are already enough troubles in our country. We are surrounded by enough dangers, and we do not want to have more trouble from among ourselves.[99]

The 'Rumourville' tag stuck. Even by the standards of a Third World capital during the Cold War, the Tanzanian capital developed a reputation as a hotbed of rumour, which was routinely decried by local politicians and journalists. The idea of 'Rumourville' captured the sense in which rumour became associated with Dar es Salaam's urban fabric of bars, cafés, hotels, and marketplaces.[100]

Controversy about rumour was not a new phenomenon to East Africa, of course. Late colonial Dar es Salaam, for example, had

---

[98] Interview with Paul Rupia, central Dar es Salaam, 5 August 2015.
[99] FBIS Daily Report, 18 November 1964, I 16.
[100] See for example Philip Ochieng, 'Rumourville', *Sunday News*, 23 April 1972, 9.

witnessed riots in response to rumours of *mumiani*, people who supposedly killed Africans for medicinal purposes.[101] Less dramatically, after independence gossiping became associated with the stereotypical idle urbanite, who hung around on Dar es Salaam's streets rather than working to build the nation. Nyerere compared the gossipy behaviour of the capital's residents to the productive agricultural conversations which took place in provincial market towns. 'If you are in Tabora you talk about tobacco and its price, if you are in Mwanza you talk about cotton and what its price will be, if you are in Mtwara you talk about cashew nuts', he told a rally, 'but in Dar es Salaam they talk about people'.[102] Nyerere's example reflected a broader anti-urban sentiment which ran through the political language and practice of *ujamaa*. Although immediately after *uhuru* the government celebrated the modernising potential of urban life, it gradually abandoned these visions in favour of a development project oriented economically and rhetorically towards the countryside. Someone who gossiped away while drinking in the bars of the capital was the stereotype of what a Tanzanian nationalist should *not* be.[103]

In Dar es Salaam, the global Cold War imbued rumour with a more subversive quality. Gossiping was not just a waste of human time and energy, but also represented a serious threat to Tanzania's political stability by sowing misinformation. Regardless of their veracity, the study of rumours sheds light on prevalent attitudes and insecurities, as historians of Africa have shown. 'Rumors cannot be fed to a crowd as one force-feeds a goose', as Jonathon Glassman reminds us, here in the case of late colonial politics in Zanzibar. Rather, they 'will take hold only if they echo fears and convictions already in place'.[104] Luise White has shown how rumour can 'offer historians a way to see the world the way the storytellers did, as a world of vulnerability and unreasonable relationships'.[105] The talk of coups and plots in Dar es Salaam, as well as the Tanzanian state's public response to them, reflected a pervasive sense of insecurity, especially when connections were drawn between

---

[101] James R. Brennan, 'Destroying Mumiani: Cause, Context, and Violence in Late Colonial Dar es Salaam', *Journal of Eastern African Studies*, 2 (2008), 95–111.
[102] Quoted in Brennan, *Taifa*, 171.
[103] Ivaska, *Cultured States*; Callaci, *Street Archives*.
[104] Glassman, *War of Words*, 232.
[105] Luise White, *Speaking with Vampires: Rumor and History in Colonial Africa* (Berkeley: University of California Press, 2000), 5.

local figures and foreign powers. Reports and crackdowns on rumour tended to occur during times of political uncertainty, in Tanzania or elsewhere in Africa. Allegations that Tanzanian politicians, guerrilla leaders, bureaucrats, journalists, and other individuals in positions of authority were in the pay of the superpowers also represented a powerful means of smearing opponents. They demonstrated the degree to which Dar es Salaam's political culture was saturated in the tropes of the global Cold War.

Condemnations of oral rumourmongering and the circulation of libellous 'black literature' became a common refrain in the party newspapers and political speeches. They denounced rumour as a deliberate tactic to destabilise the state. Nyerere himself alleged that there were organisations committed to spreading gossip in Dar es Salaam. He described 'rumour committees', with their own 'chairmen' and 'secretaries'.[106] In private, Nyerere spoke about 'deliberate rumour factories'.[107] While these included Tanzanian citizens, they were also believed to be run by outsiders, pursuing imperialist or Cold War ends. In his pseudonymous column in the *Nationalist*, A. M. Babu instructed Tanzanians to treat rumour as 'an instrument of the imperialists', and trust only official news sources. 'We must never repeat [rumour] or if we do we shall be playing into our enemy's hands.'[108] Yet Babu himself was subject to accusations of the same practices which he decried. Babu recalled that he had asked a friend at a party about a rumour he had heard regarding a coup in Uganda. The following day, Babu was summoned to State House and asked why he was circulating such 'dangerous rumours'. He explained that 'this was something I had heard, and in order to know what to think, I merely wanted to find out whether others had heard it'.[109]

Where, though, were residents of Dar es Salaam to find out reliable information about political events? The workings of the upper echelons of the party and government were shrouded in secrecy. The government papered over divisions and power struggles in the name of national unity and development. As we will see in Chapter 6, it also extended its control over the production and dissemination of information. By the mid-1970s, Tanzania's domestic media was essentially in the hands of the party-state.

[106] 'The Union Is Firm and Strong – Nyerere', *Nationalist*, 27 April 1966, 1, 4.
[107] Smith, *Nyerere*, 154.
[108] [A. M. Babu], 'Pressman's Commentary', *Nationalist*, 22 April 1966, 4.
[109] 'African Symposium', *Index on Censorship*, February 1986, 16–17.

Though it was not devoid of criticism of the government, the press steered clear of political controversy. This secrecy and top-down control opened avenues for spreading rumour. 'When everything is done transparently and openly, the rumourmongers don't have much to benefit', recalled Salim Ahmed Salim, a diplomat who held top positions in the Tanzanian government, the OAU, and the UN. 'But when things are done in a clandestine manner, however genuine, it gives them ammunition to create stories, to fabricate stories.'[110]

The boundary between rumour and news was always unclear. The 'noise' created by the former complicated the production of the latter. 'Dar-es-Salaam remains one of the most difficult capitals in Africa in which to get firmly based information', admitted the London newsletter *Africa Confidential* in 1967. 'We have ourselves run the gauntlet of rumour-mongering charges, while attempting to reflect what was being said in Dar.'[111] Similarly, British diplomats bemoaned the problem of having to 'sift the minimal amount of hard fact out of the welter of rumour which abounds in this city'.[112] These grievances serve as important reminders for the historian. Diplomats and journalists wrote with an eye on the interests and expectations of their audiences, whether they were ministerial superiors or editors and readers. Rumour which conformed to Cold War logics and assumptive world views was probably more likely to find its way into their telegrams and copy. Foreign actors tended to overplay the international dimensions of Tanzanian developments or liberation movement politics at the expense of a local context which they all too often misunderstood. Nonetheless, their complaints also draw attention to Dar es Salaam's reputation as a particularly rumour-filled city, even compared to other postcolonial capitals at the height of the Cold War. In turn, this does not necessarily indicate that rumour was any more prevalent than elsewhere but reflects how the Tanzanian government perceived itself to be exposed to subversion, and therefore sought tighter control over Dar es Salaam's information economy.

Like rumour and propaganda, espionage was central to the making of the Cold War city. As superpower rivalry turned global, the CIA, KGB,

[110] Interview with Salim Ahmed Salim, Masaki, Dar es Salaam, 29 August 2015.
[111] 'Tanzania: Questions on Arusha', *Africa Confidential*, 4 August 1967, 6.
[112] Ewans to Dawbarn, 4 January 1967, UKNA, FCO 31/1285/6.

and the intelligence agencies of their allies extended their espionage networks into the Third World. Dar es Salaam's position on the frontline of Africa's liberation struggles and Cold War politics turned it into a centre of intelligence gathering on the continent. In 1965, the CIA briefed a new American ambassador that increasing the number of intelligence operatives in Tanzania was among 'their top priorities in Africa'.[113] Any attempt to appreciate the extent and influence of this intelligence activity runs into the perennial problem of access to documents. This book does draw on material produced by various intelligence agencies, including the CIA, the Stasi, and Portuguese organisations, but these collections shed little light on their day-to-day activities and nature of their networks in Dar es Salaam. The operations of Tanzania's own intelligence services are even more obscure.

We can draw firmer conclusions about the extent of the Tanzanian state's anxiety about the threat to Africa's liberation struggles from foreign intelligence agencies. Nyerere and his government feared that agents working for the Portuguese, Rhodesians, and South Africans had infiltrated the guerrilla movements and were working to destabilise Tanzania. In 1963, Nyerere broke up the Special Branch (the intelligence services Tanganyika had inherited from the colonial government) having realised that the post-independence arrangements left his country with intelligence links to not just the British MI5, but also to the Southern Rhodesian government. The decision was preceded by the expulsion from Tanganyika of a number of South Africans and Rhodesians, including several ZAPU members, who were accused of spying for Salisbury.[114] Suspicions about Europeans with links to the forces of white minority rule and neocolonialism in Africa remained paramount in the city. In 1968, a Belgian national working as a pastry chef in a Dar es Salaam hotel was given forty-eight hours to leave Tanzania after it emerged that he had previously been a mercenary commander in Congo.[115]

The government's fears about clandestine activity in Dar es Salaam led to the establishment of a massive counter-subversion apparatus. In 1965, the American embassy discovered from a technician working at

---

[113] Interview with John H. Burns, FAOHC.
[114] Brennan, 'Intelligence and Security', 14–15.
[115] AFP, 'Expulsion d'un Belge', 24 January 1968, AN, 19850665/75.

the central post office that there were more than two hundred tapped telephone lines in the city, including those belonging to diplomats and cabinet ministers.[116] The Tanzanian intelligence services were not solely concerned with eavesdropping on their known enemies. When Gamal Abdel Nasser visited Tanzania in 1966, a British telephone engineer discovered some 'stray wires' in the vicinity of the hotel where the Egyptian delegation was staying. After tying these up, he was later hauled in front of the security services and told that he had destroyed connections laid for the purpose of listening in on the visitors' telephone conversations.[117] Foreign diplomats became attuned to these operations: the Australian ambassador unplugged his telephone before beginning any sensitive discussion. His American counterpart held team meetings at his residence, rather than the embassy, which was 'a security nightmare'.[118]

These efforts to monitor foreign activity on Tanzanian soil went hand in hand with attempts to clamp down on sensitive information leaking out to the country's enemies. The burden assumed in housing the continent's liberation movements imbued the otherwise mundane work of typists and clerks in government departments or the Liberation Committee secretariat with serious responsibilities. Tanzanians were warned against careless talk in bars and cafés. Introducing an Official Secrets Act in parliament in 1963, the home minister, Job Lusinde, regretted that 'our people are not security conscious, they don't know that there are spies everywhere, you find people sat in bars talking about themselves about their work and their meetings and other meetings with ministers who have been in government'.[119] A culture of secrecy developed among the Tanzanian bureaucracy. When one Western researcher visited a civil servant's office in the mid-1960s, he found a typed note on the desk:

1. Beware of spies, love, bar gossip.
2. Beware, spies are everywhere.
3. Personal security comes first.[120]

---

[116] Millar to State Dept, 30 November 1965, NARA, RG 59, SNF 1964–66, Box 2693, POL 23-7 TANZAN.
[117] Dawson to Scott, 1 October 1966, UKNA, FO 371/190203.
[118] Burns, 14 January and 11 April 1966, NARA, RG 59, BAA, OEAA, Tanzania and Zanzibar, Box 1, Burns Correspondence.
[119] Lusinde, 12 September 1963, *Hansard* (Tanzania), 8th meeting, cols. 191–92.
[120] Raymond F. Hopkins, *Political Roles in a New State: Tanzania's First Decade* (New Haven, CT: Yale University Press, 1971), 114.

In this context, relationships between government employees and foreigners were viewed as potentially dangerous. Just as in Nkrumah's Ghana, women who served in secretarial roles were perceived as prone to gossip and susceptible to manipulation.[121] A Tanzanian civil servant told an Australian diplomat a story about a Soviet representative who brought sweets for a female receptionist in the Second Vice-President's Office, which was responsible for the liberation movements' security. The civil servant reminded the receptionist that she must not divulge any official information. Shortly afterwards, she was transferred to a different office.[122] Similar sentiments appeared in the press, mixing anxieties about security with social commentary on young people who pursued relationships with foreigners. For example, *Ngurumo* warned that young people who dated outsiders risked divulging secret information. 'The time has come for our youths to be told to bite their lips [*kuchungua midomo yao*]', it warned.[123]

Dar es Salaam thereby earned a reputation as a city paranoid about leaks of rumour-spreading, information leaks, and espionage. One American writer described scenes at 'cocktail parties and embassy receptions ... which make the average spy film seemed like a kindergarten vaudeville'.[124] A correspondent for *Time* magazine, who became Nyerere's biographer, noted that 'a sort of free-flowing paranoia sometimes seems to hang suspended in Dar es Salaam's heavy air'.[125] This tone reflected the broader genre of Western commentary on the city's radical politics and its links, exaggerated though they were, with the communist world. But even more sober observers, such as the perceptive French ambassador André Naudy, identified that the city's information politics were characterised by 'an atmosphere often devoid of trust ... Suspicion is the rule'.[126] Tanzanian elites preferred to tout Dar es Salaam's credentials as a spearhead in the anticolonial struggle, and justifiably so. But the constant admonitions about rumourmongering and calls for vigilance against subversion

---

[121] Ahlman, *Living with Nkrumahism*, 172–73.
[122] Hearder, 3 July [1968], NAA, A1838, 3107/40/184, 18.
[123] '"Fumba Mdomo"', editorial, *Ngurumo*, 25 May 1965, 2.
[124] Robert Carl Cohen, 'Black Foreign Legion', *Saga Magazine*, December 1968, enclosed in AHD, MNE, PAA 516.
[125] Smith, *Nyerere*, 153.
[126] Naudy, January 1971, CADN, 193PO/1/48 ADM7.

demonstrated an insecurity about the risks which the country had assumed in shouldering this revolutionary burden.

Conclusion

In 1965, Tanzanians went to the polls in the country's first exercise in 'one-party democracy'. Nyerere, as the sole candidate, was returned as president with 96 per cent of the vote. The parliamentary elections were much more hotly contested. Several high-profile figures, including government ministers, lost their seats. Derek Bryceson, the only European member of cabinet, fared better. He successfully defended his Dar es Salaam North constituency. However, his convincing win followed a controversial candidate selection process, which sheds light on the extent to which even the capital's domestic politics was immersed in the Cold War. Sam Kajunjumele was overlooked by TANU's National Executive Committee as one of the constituency's two candidates to face the electorate, despite coming second in a local party caucus. The NEC's decision was rumoured to have been a consequence of Kajunjumele's links to China. He was the editor of *Vigilance Africa* and had led a delegation of Tanzanian journalists to Beijing the previous May. Another rumour alleged that he had misappropriated funds from the Tanganyika Bookshop, a distributor of Chinese propaganda.[127] We will encounter Kajunjumele again in his capacity as a journalist in Chapter 6.

Kajunjumele's failed attempt to get his name on the ballot paper exemplified the degree to which Dar es Salaam's political life had become embedded in superpower rivalry and Third World revolution. TANU's commitment to the cause of African liberation turned the city into a cosmopolitan staging ground for the organisation of armed struggles against white minority rule. A chain of dramatic events in early 1964 – the revolution in Zanzibar, the army mutiny, and the act of union – propelled the region into global headlines. Western onlookers portrayed Nyerere's pursuit of a non-aligned foreign policy as a step towards communism. In an African political environment marked by a sense of insecurity, the Tanzanian government felt

---

[127] FBIS Daily Report, 19 May 1965, JJJ 11; Millar to State Dept, 12 October 1965, NARA, RG 59, SNF 1964–66, Box 2690, POL 14 TANZAN; Daudi Mwakawago, 'Dar es Salaam: Two Urban Campaigns', in Lionel Cliffe (ed.), *One-Party Democracy: The 1965 Tanzania General Elections* (Nairobi: East African Publishing House, 1967), 214–15.

Conclusion

especially vulnerable to outside subversion. These anxieties became imbricated into daily political life in Dar es Salaam. The state urged Tanzanians to stay vigilant against neo-imperialist subversion and avoid careless gossip, or even worse, rumourmongering.

Paul Bjerk brings his history of mainland Tanzania's early years of independence to a close at the end of 1964. By then, he writes, 'Nyerere had established overarching authority' in the country.[128] But Bjerk's focus on the words and actions of the president masks a much more unsettled picture. While TANU dominated the country's public life, its institutional strength alone could not deliver the economic development which many had hoped that *uhuru* promised. The reality was that the trappings of statehood meant little as long as Tanzania remained a poor, dependent Third World state. On the international front, Tanzania had fallen out with its three largest bilateral donor partners: Britain, the United States, and West Germany. The union was an emergency solution to a Cold War crisis, which developed into a painful headache for the mainland government. Superpower rivalry encroached further on political life, even as Nyerere attempted to distance his country from it. It was this connection between Tanzania's continued economic dependence and its fragile political sovereignty – in other words, the incomplete state of decolonisation – which paved the road to the Arusha Declaration, which forms the subject of the next chapter.

---

[128] Bjerk, *Building a Peaceful Nation*, 258.

2 | Revisiting the Politics of the Arusha Declaration

On 5 February 1967, a crowd estimated at more than 100,000 people gathered at the Mnazi Mmoja grounds in Dar es Salaam. For two-and-a-half hours, they listened to President Nyerere explain a new landmark party document, quickly dubbed the Arusha Declaration. '*Ndiyo! Ndiyo!*' shouted the crowd – 'yes! yes!' – as Nyerere extolled the virtues of TANU's policies of socialism and self-reliance.[1]

The full text of the Declaration was carried by the following day's press. 'The policy of TANU is to build a socialist state', it began. The tone was polemical:

> We have been oppressed a great deal, we have been exploited a great deal and we have been disregarded a great deal. It is our weakness that has led to our being oppressed, exploited and disregarded. Now we want a revolution – a revolution which brings to an end our weakness, so that we are never again exploited, oppressed, or humiliated.[2]

To escape the constraints of a global order which subordinated the Third World's developing economies to Europe and North America, the Arusha Declaration called upon Tanzanians to build a state which was 'self-reliant', rather than dependent on foreign aid or investment. The Declaration eschewed industrial growth in preference for agricultural development. This principle would later underpin a campaign of mass resettlement of the peasantry into centralised *ujamaa* villages. In the meantime, the immediate effect of the Declaration was electrifying: thousands of Tanzanians joined marches in support of its goals. It became a banner around which Tanzanian nationalism rallied.

However, this popular image of socialism and unity masks the heated politics that surrounding the drafting of the Arusha

---

[1] 'Nyerere Explains Tanzania's Socialism', 'Masses Hail Declaration', *Nationalist*, 6 February 1967, 8.
[2] 'The Arusha Declaration: Socialism and Self-Reliance', in Nyerere, *Freedom and Socialism*, 231.

Declaration and the deeper fissures which it brought about. The Arusha Declaration, as Lionel Cliffe recognised on its twentieth anniversary, sent 'shock waves' through the political elite, but this is 'scarcely acknowledged' in official statements or scholarship.[3] He bemoaned the tendency to consider the politics of Arusha only in abstract terms. 'Tanzania seems to have class forces, policies and programmes, but no debates and no in-fighting', he argued. As this chapter shows, the politics of the Arusha Declaration involved ideological differences, factional rivalries, and the pursuit of personal self-interest. These developments have been understood in earlier political science literature through institutional structures[4] or the forces of class struggle.[5] This chapter restores the agency of individual politicians to the contested politics of Arusha.

The years between the upheavals of 1964 and the beginning of 1967 featured intense debates about the direction of Tanzania's economic development. Sluggish growth and murmurs of popular unrest presented cause for concern, which received a sense of urgency from events elsewhere in Africa. The rise of the military coup demonstrated the fragility of postcolonial governments and impelled Nyerere to avoid the same fate by driving forwards a socialist plan of action. By the end of 1967, Nyerere seemed to have reasserted his authority over the Tanzanian state. But in the process, he had created several powerful opponents and stirred fears abroad about the aspirations of his regime. More generally, the Arusha Declaration became installed as the non-negotiable basis for political debate in Tanzania. If the introduction of the one-party state provided the apparatus for the authoritarian turn that later followed, then the enshrinement of the ideological principles of the Declaration in Tanzanian nationalist discourse made dissenting voices easier to dismiss and castigate, often as neo-imperial collaborators.

---

[3] Lionel Cliffe, 'Political Struggles Around the Adoption and Implementation of the Arusha Declaration', in Jeanette Hartmann (ed.), *Re-Thinking the Arusha Declaration* (Copenhagen: Centre for Development Research, 1991), 106–107.
[4] See for example Hopkins, *Political Roles*; William Tordoff, *Government and Politics in Tanzania* (Nairobi: East African Publishing House, 1967); Henry Bienen, *Tanzania: Party Transformation and Economic Development* (Princeton, NJ: Princeton University Press, 1970).
[5] See for example Issa G. Shivji, *Class Struggles in Tanzania* (London: Heinemann, 1976); John S. Saul, *The State and Revolution in East Africa* (London: Heinemann, 1979).

The Arusha Declaration was not only a response to a national set of problems, but among the most coherent of the Third World's ripostes to the global predicament of decolonisation. Political independence had not meant economic emancipation from relationships of dependency to wealthier states.[6] Indeed, as the Arusha Declaration argued, full political sovereignty was impossible while the underdeveloped economic sector of African states remained dominated by foreign capital and propped up by external aid. In theory, the achievement of the goal of self-reliance would mean Tanzania no longer had to enter into agreements with stronger powers that used aid to press their own agendas. It therefore was an effort to transcend the Cold War rivalries which had infused political life in Dar es Salaam, as the previous chapter showed. But the paradox, as recognised by a number of more pragmatically minded politicians, was that Tanzania continued to require external support in order to pursue these objectives. Nyerere and other senior ministers emphasised that the country remained open for foreign investment and donor aid, even as TANU cadres agitated for more radical change. Western onlookers proved more difficult to convince. Escaping the Cold War order was no easy task, as Tanzania's revolutionaries were to find out.

Politics in the Time of *Ujamaa*

We saw in the previous chapter that foreign commentators, especially Western diplomats and journalists, regarded Tanzania's willingness to engage with the socialist world as evidence that it was drifting down the path of communism. The government flatly denied these claims, and rightly so: its aid-seeking policies and socialist inclinations were bound up in its own brand of state-making. Like other Third World capitals, Dar es Salaam's public sphere contained lively debate about the future of the nation and its path to development.[7] While we cannot speak of clearly defined factions competing against each other for influence, we can detect the presence of loose groupings of politicians. Their different

---

[6] More generally, see Dietrich, *Oil Revolution*; Getachew, *Worldmaking*.
[7] Daniel Speich, 'The Kenyan Style of "African Socialism": Developmental Knowledge Claims and the Explanatory Limits of the Cold War', *Diplomatic History*, 33 (2009), 449–66; Alden Young, *Transforming Sudan: Decolonization, Economic Development, and State Formation* (Cambridge: Cambridge University Press, 2018).

understandings of the state of affairs were influenced by their own backgrounds. Even when they had links with external powers, these views did not map onto the Cold War spectrum through which many outsiders interpreted Tanzanian affairs. We should rather think about debates concerning development and economic policy in socialist Tanzania as being characterised by a scale of speed: the politics of fast change versus the politics of slow change.

Nyerere's ideological agenda was profoundly shaped by his formative experiences in East Africa and abroad. Born in 1922 in the village of Butiama on the shores of Lake Victoria, Nyerere was the son of a Zanaki chief. He attended Tabora Boys School, which was the territory's elite school for educating Africans to staff the colonial bureaucracy. After concluding his secondary education, Nyerere trained to be a teacher at Makerere College in Kampala, Uganda, which at the time was the only higher education institution in East Africa. Nyerere then gained a colonial scholarship to study at the University of Edinburgh, where he attained a master's degree in 1952. Beyond the moral, ideological, and political influences which this education had on him, Nyerere's trajectory left him with a network of personal connections among a rising Tanganyikan elite, many of whom had trod similar paths, at least as far as Tabora and Makerere. As one of the most educated, articulate, and well-connected politicians in the territory, Nyerere was drawn into nationalist circles. In 1954, he was instrumental in the transformation of the Tanganyika African Association into the more robust and explicitly anticolonial TANU.[8]

Nyerere's concept of African socialism crystallised around the idea of *ujamaa* ('familyhood'). His first full exposition of this concept came in a pamphlet issued in 1962. 'Socialism, like democracy, is an attitude of mind' rather than 'the rigid adherence to a standard political pattern', Nyerere argued. He criticised the acquisitive behaviour of capitalists and the parasitical earnings of landowners. But Nyerere consciously sought to establish a distance between *ujamaa* and 'European socialism'. He argued that there had been no class struggle in Africa and therefore set its societies outside of Marx's evolutionary model of history. *Ujamaa*, he concluded, was 'opposed to capitalism,

---

[8] Issa G. Shivji, Saida-Yahya Othman, and Ng'wanza Kamata, *Development as Rebellion – Julius Nyerere: A Biography* (Dar es Salaam: Mkuki na Nyota, 2020), vols. 1–2; Thomas Molony, *Nyerere: The Early Years* (Woodbridge: James Currey, 2014).

which seeks to build a happy society on the basis of exploitation of man by man; and it is equally opposed to doctrinaire socialism which seeks to build its happy society on a philosophy of inevitable conflict between man and man'. He reiterated this point again and again over the following years, mainly to ward off his Cold War critics. Instead, his socialism was located in the familyhood of 'traditional African society', prior to the ruptures of colonialism, in which everyone 'could depend on the wealth possessed by the community of which he was a member'.[9]

Nyerere's pamphlet was an eloquent meditation on socialist ethics, but an imprecise statement of intent. As Emma Hunter argues, *ujamaa* was a 'polysemic' idea which drew substance from vibrant debates in late colonial Tanganyika's public sphere.[10] In the hands of ordinary Tanzanians, it represented a fluid language for the articulation of social issues, such as the problem of inequality. Some politicians opposed the idea of 'African socialism' with calls for 'scientific socialism', although the addition of another nebulous term only muddled matters further. From the grassroots membership to the party leadership, among cabinet ministers and bureaucrats, socialism meant different things to different people at different times. Translating the abstract set of morals which were bound up in the concept of *ujamaa* into economic policy was therefore a contested and contentious process.

The formulation of Tanzania's development strategy after independence was overseen by a small coterie of economically minded cabinet ministers. All of them had received education abroad and had experience in running capital-intensive operations, as businessmen, cooperative managers, or agriculturalists. They were conversant in the language and practices of economic planning, which was then in vogue among postcolonial states. They travelled the international conference circuit, acting as spokesmen and ambassadors for the new nation. Crucially, they retained the confidence of Nyerere himself, even if their politics did not always align with the more vocal wings of TANU. That is not to argue that these men were neither African nationalists nor less committed to principles of *ujamaa*. But they were all, to a lesser or greater extent, concerned that the drive towards

---

[9] '*Ujamaa* – The Basis of African Socialism', in Nyerere, *Freedom and Unity*, 162–71.
[10] Hunter, *Political Thought*, 212.

socialism must be underpinned by sound economic thinking, as opposed to development via political mobilisation. This led them to adopt a more cautious approach towards development policy. They were supported in their jobs by a number of foreign technocrats. Together, they set out the parameters of Tanzania's planned economy.

Amir Jamal was perhaps the most astute of this group of men. Born into a prominent Asian family in Tanganyika, Jamal received a degree in commerce in Calcutta. Back in Tanganyika, he pursued a career in his family's business. Jamal then entered public life through the Asian Association in Dar es Salaam. Unusually for an Asian, he developed close links with TANU and Nyerere. After independence, Jamal held a number of key financial ministerial portfolios and became the president's economic guru, even as heated debate about the status of the Asian minority rumbled on in Tanzania.[11] Derek Bryceson, a European, was another enduring presence in Tanzania's post-independence cabinets. He had arrived in East Africa as a settler farmer but aligned himself with TANU as *uhuru* loomed on the horizon. Bryceson established himself as a reliable minister for agriculture.[12] Paul Bomani was the most business-friendly member of this group. He owed his rise to the success of the cooperative movement in his home region of Lake Victoria, which he used as a springboard for a prominent role inside TANU.[13] Nsilo Swai also built his reputation in the cooperative movement, following a university education at Makerere and in India. His experience representing TANU abroad led to his appointment as Tanganyika's first permanent representative to the UN.[14] Finally, Edwin Mtei was another well-travelled Tanzanian who had trod the well-worn path from Tabora Boys to Makerere and into the colonial civil service. He represented Tanzania at meetings of the International Monetary Fund, worked for the East African Common Services Organisation, and was then appointed the first governor of the Bank of Tanzania in 1966.[15] Jamal, Bryceson,

---

[11] Emma Hunter, 'Jamal, Amir Habib', in Emmanuel A. Akyeampong and Henry Louis Gates, Jr (eds.), *Dictionary of African Biography* [*DAB*], vol. 3 (Oxford: Oxford University Press), 190–91.
[12] 'Bryceson, Derek Noel Maclean', enclosed in Hobden to Holmes, 9 May 1969, UKNA, FCO 31/434/17.
[13] Paul Bjerk, 'Bomani, Paul', in *DAB*, vol. 1, 484–85.
[14] 'Asanterabi Zaphaniah Nsilo Swai', enclosed in Strong to State Dept, 13 July 1965, NARA, RG 59, SNF 1964–66, Box 2692, POL 15–1.
[15] Edwin Mtei, *From Goatherd to Governor: The Autobiography of Edwin Mtei* (Dar es Salaam: Mkuki na Nyota, 2009).

Bomani, Swai, and Mtei were senior figures in the Tanzanian state apparatus who prioritised sound economic and fiscal management above political revolution. Bomani and Jamal, in particular, were highly regarded by Nyerere for their economic acumen, especially when dealing with international trade and aid. When Bomani suffered a shock defeat in the 1965 elections, Nyerere restored him to parliament as a presidential nominee, on the basis that his skills were 'badly needed in the immediate future'. Bomani became minister for economic affairs and planning.[16]

The First Five-Year Plan, which covered the period from 1964 to 1969, was broadly representative of the political outlook of this group. Swai oversaw the formulation of the plan, although its content was largely the work of a French expatriate expert. Following the launching of the plan, Nyerere created a new Directorate of Development and Planning, headed by the triumvirate of Swai, Jamal, and A. M. Babu, the Zanzibari who was moved to the mainland cabinet after the union. In comparison with the radical economic policies pursued after the Arusha Declaration, the plan was a relatively conservative document. It gave a considerable role to foreign investment, both in terms of donor aid and private capital. The plan also sought to preserve the role of the private sector in internal trade, which remained dominated by Tanzania's Asian population.[17] This did not satisfy certain revolutionary voices inside government. The Moscow-trained Kassim Hanga, as minister for industries, attempted to introduce what one political scientist called a Stalinist 'storm economy', including large-scale farming and heavy industrialisation. His proposals received short shrift from Nyerere. In a cabinet reshuffle in November 1964, Hanga was moved to the position of minister for union affairs.[18]

There were no real analogues of either Babu or Hanga, the two Zanzibari Marxist revolutionaries, in mainland Tanzania, at least not in central government. Yet there were a number of senior TANU figures whose own trajectories had taken them into the socialist world. Oscar

---

[16] Nyerere, 'Opening of the New National Assembly', in *Freedom and Socialism*, 96.

[17] On the plan, see Bienen, *Tanzania*, 281–306.

[18] Ibid., 221–23. Al Noor Kassum, a civil servant in Hanga's ministry, recalls in his memoirs how Nyerere had placed him there 'to help look after Hanga'. *Africa's Winds of Change: Memoirs of an International Tanzanian* (London: IB Tauris, 2007), 45.

Kambona was widely considered as an ardent socialist by observers from across the Cold War's divisions, but he represents a much more slippery character for the historian. He met Nyerere at Tabora Boys, trained as a teacher, and then studied in London, with the assistance of TANU. There Kambona formed a number of friendships with other African nationalists, including Hanga. On returning to Tanganyika in 1959, he became a leading TANU organiser. After *uhuru*, Kambona held several powerful ministerial portfolios and in 1963 he was appointed as minister for foreign affairs. Kambona also chaired the OAU Liberation Committee, which was established in Dar es Salaam in 1963. One of the most popular politicians in the country, he emerged as a hero after negotiating with the mutinying troops in January 1964, even though rumours circulated about his own involvement in the uprising.[19]

In the process of leading a liberation struggle, TANU had established a sprawling apparatus of branches across the country. However, the party's ideological direction was provided by a smaller set of power-brokers at the centre. As TANU's chairman, Nyerere's voice carried particular weight across the party's various bodies, but it did not go unchallenged.[20] A National Conference, which met biennially from 1965 onwards, was the ultimate source of authority within the party, but in reality power was concentrated in a National Executive Committee of elected officeholders, which met around once every three months to discuss high-level matters. The NEC's meetings were pivotal moments in the development of *ujamaa* socialism and often politically fraught. A Central Committee met regularly at the party's headquarters in the Kariakoo area of Dar es Salaam to oversee the day-to-day running of TANU. In addition, the party's women's and youth wings provided avenues for ambitious Tanzanians to pursue their own political ambitions outside of the central party and government structures.

In contrast to government figures, many TANU MPs and senior cadres tended to favour direct political solutions to economic problems. They were by no means parochial figures, but their engagement with questions of socialism had a quite different slant: this was

---

[19] 'Oscar S. Kambona', enclosed in Strong to State Dept, 13 July 1965, NARA, RG 59, SNF 1964–66, Box 2692, POL 15–1.
[20] Bienen, *Tanzania*, 158–202.

socialism as *politics*, rather than socialism as *policy*. This was in part a consequence of their different formative trajectories. They lacked the more technocratic education of many of the government ministers or expatriate bureaucrats. Instead, their political rise was owed mostly to their involvement in TANU. But they were also vulnerable to the preferences of their constituents or other party members, on whose votes they depended. If the details of economic planning were beyond the comprehension of many TANU officials, then ordinary Tanzanians were even less well informed. They expected *uhuru* to bring tangible benefits to their own daily lives. The high numbers of incumbents defeated in the 1965 elections showed that MPs had to be responsive to these expectations. As the sociologist Ronald Aminzade writes, the TANU radicals were therefore 'less concerned with technical rationality and problem-solving expertise than with mobilizing ideological commitments and competing for political constituencies'.[21] Though there were rarely clean-cut lines of division, the party generally agitated for development through political *mobilisation*, while the bureaucracy and key ministers alike pressed for the prioritisation of political *economy*.[22]

Throughout the first half of the 1960s, the issue of Africanisation was the major source of debate in Tanzanian politics. Europeans had dominated the colonial bureaucracy even as small numbers of Africans were brought into lower-level positions as independence approached. The pace of this transformation quickened after *uhuru*. Africans occupied just 26 per cent of mid- and high-level civil service posts in 1961; by 1966, this proportion had risen to 72 per cent. By the time of the Arusha Declaration, the Africanisation of the bureaucracy was no longer a real political problem, even if there was still criticism of the government's reliance on expatriate experts at the top end of policy formulation and implementation.[23] However, the Africanisation of private trade was much more complicated and controversial. Party activists called for the expansion of the cooperative sector or even

[21] Ronald Aminzade, *Race, Nation, and Citizenship in Post-Colonial Africa: The Case of Tanzania* (New York: Cambridge University Press, 2013), 12.
[22] More generally on the bureaucracy, see Andreas Eckert, '"We Must Run While Others Walk": African Civil Servants, State Ideologies and Bureaucratic Practices in Tanzania from the 1950s to the 1970s', in Thomas Bierschenk and Jean-Pierre Olivier de Sardan (eds.), *States at Work: Dynamics of African Bureaucracies* (Boston: Brill, 2014), 205–19.
[23] Pratt, *Critical Phase*, 129–33, figures on 130.

nationalisation to displace private traders, where European and particularly Asian capital continued to predominate. This meant that questions of economic justice and the redistribution of private capital became bound up in debates about racial belonging in the postcolonial nation. In parliamentary debates, party meetings, and newspaper columns, TANU activists called for trade to be brought into the hands of the state.[24] These frictions were felt most acutely in Dar es Salaam, where Asians dominated commercial life in the city centre, which had been designated an Indian zone under colonial rule.[25]

The government's policy was much more cautious. The Five-Year Plan was premised on the continued investment of foreign and private capital in Tanzania. Even if in theory it supported the expansion of cooperatives, the government warned that there was not enough trained manpower to enact such swift change responsibly. Jamal, for example, drew parliament's attention to the 'stark economic facts staring us in the face' and advised that 'to have revolutions just for the sake of having them is to commit a deception on our people'.[26] Clarifying its policy on Africanisation in 1965, the government emphasised the need to 'gradually extend the collectively-owned sector of the economy and thus ensure both growth itself and the capability of our economy to serve the national interest at all times'. The government argued that Africanising the management of firms with 'untrained' staff 'would be as disastrous to the economy as the Africanisation of hospitals with witchdoctors would be to the health of the nation'.[27]

Even Babu cautioned against hasty intervention. The Western depiction of Babu as a communist extremist and a conduit for Chinese influence in East Africa was always a caricature. Yet his revolutionary credentials could not be doubted. While Nyerere tried to carve out a distinct ideological concept of 'African socialism', Babu adhered to the teachings of Marxism-Leninism. Nonetheless, he maintained a pragmatic streak that militated against counterproductive, politically motivated disruption to economic structures, which would drain resources away from more fundamental tasks. 'I want to remind you

---

[24] Chachage, 'Capitalizing City', 142–88.   [25] Brennan, *Taifa*, esp. 153–67.
[26] Quoted in Jeannette Hartmann, 'Development Policy-Making in Tanzania: A Critique of Sociological Interpretations', PhD diss. (University of Hull, 1983), 131–32.
[27] 'Africanising the Economy', *Nationalist*, 15 March 1965, 5. See also Chachage, 'Capitalizing City', 168–69.

that if we undertake to do something very rapidly we can fall', Babu told parliament in 1964, when arguing against displacing private trade with cooperatives without adequate trained manpower.[28] In private, he argued that the nationalisation of Tanzania's limited industrial sector would only involve obstructive bureaucratisation and paralyse the 'spontaneous creative energies of the people'.[29] As we will see, this became a recurring theme in Babu's economic thinking even as the *ujamaa* revolution entered a more radical phase.

Nyerere shared these concerns and was reluctant to meet the clamour for mass nationalisation. He believed that Tanzania lacked enough trained manpower to run major commercial assets. However, his position was made more difficult by examples set elsewhere in Africa. In September 1966, Gamal Abdel Nasser paid a fêted state visit to Tanzania, where he explained how the United Arab Republic had struck out at 'strongholds of feudalism and corrupt capitalism' to restore the 'the ownership of national wealth' to the workers.[30] Babu told Eastern Bloc diplomats that Nyerere had expressed his concern at Nasser's speech. 'Nasser has given me a great headache', Nyerere reportedly said at a cabinet meeting. 'Our people will also want [nationalisation], but how can I do that?'[31] Even as Nyerere incanted that 'we must run while others walk', his government cautioned against hasty change. In this view, Tanzania had to move swiftly, but not recklessly.

By late 1966, there was rising discontent at the lack of clear direction for socialist state-building in Tanzania. Michael Kamaliza, the secretary-general of NUTA, the country's sole trade union, called for the appointment of a commission to study the question of socialism.[32] He found support from the *Nationalist*, TANU's newspaper, which pointed out that 'every leader has at present his own interpretation of socialism'.[33] Babu, on the other hand, used his pseudonymous column in the same newspaper to savage NUTA for simply pointing fingers and shirking responsibility rather than proposing solutions itself.[34] A secret TANU

[28] Quoted in Hartmann, 'Development Policy-Making', 138–39.
[29] 'Tanzanie – opinions de Babu sur l'économie politique', 20 February 1966, ADB, 15.056.
[30] 'Africa Is Powerful – Nasser', *Nationalist*, 28 September 1966, 1–2, 4.
[31] Fischer, 15 October 1966, BA-B, SAPMO, DY 30/98143, 1–2.
[32] Pratt, *Critical Phase*, 191; 'Too Slow to Socialism', *Standard*, 3 January 1967, 1.
[33] 'Commission on Socialism', editorial, *Nationalist*, 28 December 1966, 4.
[34] [A. M. Babu], 'Nuta and Socialism – Part 2', *Nationalist*, 7 January 1967, 5.

paper on the 'Policy for the Transformation of the Party', produced by Kambona, argued that the problem was not that there were different interpretations of *ujamaa*, but that the party's leaders had not fully grasped *Mwalimu*'s teachings.[35] For all the expanding institutional apparatus of a party that increasingly exercised greater influence than cabinet, a heterogeneous elite therefore was yet to agree on a path forwards. 'There is no party at all', Babu told the East German consul-general. 'There are only large groups and small groups and individuals with different and often contradictory attitudes to the same problems.'[36]

In the period before the Arusha Declaration, Tanzania's future path to development and the policies it required were fiercely debated. Onlookers turned to the labels of 'left' and 'right' in order to understand this postcolonial elite. But this spectrum was a poor guide. Writing in 1970, the political scientist Immanuel Wallerstein acknowledged that the terms 'left' and 'right' were tricky categories to employ when talking about African politics. They bundled together positions on foreign affairs, economic policy, anticolonial liberation, and continental unification. In an attempt to extricate the terms from their Cold War associations, Wallerstein proposed returning to the nineteenth-century French idea of 'right' and 'left'. This pitted a more conservative 'party of order' against a 'party of movement'.[37] The latter term is particularly helpful here. Tanzanian politics in the time of *ujamaa* was a question not so much of alternative ideological visions of the future, but about the speed, means, and intensity of the journey to get there.[38] On the one hand, senior ministers, bureaucrats, and planners, all well-versed in international theories of political economy, urged caution.

---

[35] Oscar S. Kambona, 'Secretary-General's Report', TANU NEC Meeting, Arusha, 26–28 January 1967, TNA, 589, BMC 11/02 C, 28.
[36] Fischer, 28 October 1966, BA-B, SAPMO, DY 30/98143, 17–19.
[37] Immanuel Wallerstein, 'Left and Right in Africa', *Journal of Modern African Studies*, 9 (1971), 1–10.
[38] In their discussion of politics in Tanzania, William Tordoff and Ali A. Mazrui suggest that the terms '*siasa ya kali* [sic]' (the politics of radical change) and '*siasa ya pole*' (the politics of slow change) might be more appropriate. But there is little evidence of them being part of a recognised local political discourse in Tanzania. See 'The Left and the Super-Left in Tanzania', *Journal of Modern African Studies*, 10 (1972), 439. I am grateful to an anonymous reviewer for flagging this point.

On the other, TANU cadres and MPs looked to the party as an engine of transformation. They wanted socialism at speed.

Storm Clouds

The rumbles of thunder elsewhere in Africa seemed to amplify the sound of ticking clocks in Tanzania. As the lustre of liberation wore off Africa's postcolonial governments and the challenges of meeting the expectations of independence became starker, a wave of military coups toppled elected leaders. In January 1966 alone, the governments of Nigeria, Upper Volta, and the Central African Republic were swept away. International reputation provided no security: the previous June, Algeria's Ahmed Ben Bella had succumbed to a palace coup. Deteriorating economic conditions fuelled popular discontent with civilian regimes. Weak postcolonial democratic institutions proved flimsy opposition for disaffected militaries. There was suspicion that the coup makers received external support. In his pseudonymous *Nationalist* column, Babu pointed to parallels with Latin America, where the United States' reputation for engineering the end of left-leaning governments had already been established. 'Is there any doubt as to who is the master-mind in this African version of the Latin game?', asked Babu.[39] Political instability closer to home aggravated Tanzanian fears, as both Kenya and Uganda were wracked with cabinet crises. In Dar es Salaam, the mutiny loomed large in recent memory.

The Tanzanian government was concerned about the possibility of political unrest abroad emboldening would-be conspirators at home. On 10 February 1966, Nyerere addressed members of the TPDF and police at the Police Officers' Mess in Dar es Salaam, where he spoke about the coup in Nigeria. With dark humour, Nyerere said that if the army and police were thinking of doing the same in Tanzania, he hoped they would do so without bloodshed.[40] Then there were unverified reports that, on 23 February, Nyerere told a meeting of MPs that there was a plot to remove him and appealed for their vigilance. The

---

[39] [A. M. Babu], 'Are These Coups Spontaneous?', *Nationalist*, 7 January 1966, 4.
[40] Gilchrist to Dept for External Affairs, Canberra, 15 February 1966, UKNA, DO 213/103/65A. During the period covering the break in relations between Britain and Tanzania (1965–68), the British archives contain numerous Australian (as well as Canadian) documents.

text of his draft speech, passed by an expatriate journalist to the Americans, contained the allegation that there were 'some people who are cooking up plans to overthrow the government'. The same journalist said that Nyerere had several plotters under surveillance, including Oscar Kambona and Job Lusinde, the home affairs minister.[41]

The following day, news reached Dar es Salaam that Kwame Nkrumah had been overthrown in a military coup in Ghana. The effect in Tanzania was predictable. By this time, relations between Nkrumah and Nyerere had smouldered into animosity. Yet both men were high-profile, progressive African leaders committed to the unification and liberation of the continent, even if they disagreed as to how this was best achieved. The American ambassador described Dar es Salaam as being in 'a high state of edginess' with an 'audible buzz'.[42] There was suspicion of CIA involvement in the coup. Nyerere expressed disbelief. 'What is happening in Africa? What are all the coups about?', he asked a press conference. 'What is behind all this?' Pretoria and Salisbury were now 'jubilant'.[43] Nyerere was right: Tanzania's enemies did indeed lick their lips. Portuguese intelligence claimed that there existed 'an atmosphere which would greatly facilitate an action aimed at fomenting serious disturbances' in Tanzania, that would 'doubtlessly benefit the interests of Portugal in Africa'.[44]

On the international stage, the coup presented the Tanzanian government with a dilemma: should it recognise the military usurpers in Accra or not? On the one hand, Nyerere abhorred the fall of a progressive, elected African head of state. In March, he told the press that 'the gun or the revolver should not take the place of the ballot box'. On the other hand, given the emphasis in the OAU charter on non-interference in the internal affairs of member states, what choice did Tanzania have, other than to recognise the new regime? 'Do we organise subversion in Ghana? Do we promote or provoke civil war in Ghana?', Nyerere asked.[45] The answer, of course, was no: African unity had to take priority. As Jeffrey Byrne observes, 'alarming

---

[41] Burns to State Dept, 25 February 1966, NARA, RG 59, SNF 1964–66, Box 2692, POL 15–1.
[42] Burns to Meagher, 26 March 1966, NARA, RG 59, BAA, OEAA, Tanzania and Zanzibar 1963–75, Box 1, Burns Correspondence.
[43] 'Mwalimu Slams Coups', *Nationalist*, 1 March 1966, 1.
[44] SCCIM, 28 April 1966, AHD, MU, GM/RNP/RNP/82.
[45] 'Africa Going Through Difficult Times', *Nationalist*, 12 March 1966, 1.

as coups d'état were to postcolonial elites, they were becoming too common to ostracize those governments that came to power in that fashion; otherwise, Third Worldist conferences would become increasingly poorly attended events.'[46] Tanzania's decision to recognise the new Ghanaian regime, along with numerous lower-profile examples of coups in Africa, set an important precedent. As Chapter 7 explains, when Nyerere refused to recognise the military government of Idi Amin in Uganda, he broke with previous policy and in doing so destabilised East Africa's political landscape.

Nyerere's public deliberation on the question of recognising the military government in Ghana was a response not just to a dilemma of international politics, but complications thrown up by the apparent insubordination of Oscar Kambona. Shortly after the coup, Kambona led a Tanzanian delegation to an OAU conference in Addis Ababa. There was disagreement among the member states as to whether to seat a delegation from the new Ghanaian military regime.[47] When the new representatives were accepted, Kambona led a walkout. Nyerere was furious with Kambona, who apparently acted without the president's approval. Kambona had already been removed from his position of foreign minister after the 1965 elections and moved to the position of minister for regional administration. The CIA thought that his relationship with the president had broken down. 'We believe that Kambona has been on the skids for some time, but his unauthorized OAU walkout provided new grease', it filed.[48] Soon after his return from Addis Ababa, Kambona travelled to the Netherlands for medical treatment. His leave came with Nyerere's blessing, although rumours held that Kambona had essentially been sent into exile.[49]

Meanwhile, Dar es Salaam was gripped by a period of heightened attention to the phenomenon of rumourmongering. The gossip about Kambona was picked up abroad. His trip to the Netherlands featured in an article in the London-based newssheet *Africa*, which summarised the flurry of rumours circulating in Dar es Salaam. Alongside

---

[46] Byrne, *Mecca of Revolution*, 289.
[47] Nora McKeon, 'The African States and the OAU', *International Affairs*, 42 (1966), 405. This discord was aggravated by a resolution on Rhodesia that diluted the OAU's stance against maintaining relations with Britain.
[48] 'CIA Comments on the Situation in Tanzania', 11 April 1966, UKNA, DO 213/103.
[49] Gilchrist to Dept for External Affairs, Canberra, 24 March 1966, UKNA, DO 213/103.

Kambona's illness, it contained talk of coups, the dissolution of the union, Babu's attempted resignation, and food riots in Pemba.[50] The article was reprinted and then denounced in the *Nationalist*. An editorial described the 'filthy sheet' as evidence of 'the evil designs' of foreign plotters.[51] Babu himself used his column in the *Nationalist* to launch a furious attack on *Africa*, a publication which sowed discord by pitting 'hypothetical groups' against one another in a 'literary Punch and Judy'. He sketched out the spread of such rumours via Dar es Salaam's embassies. 'The public can now see the source of the recent spate of rumours and counter-rumours which made Dar es Salaam regain its reputation of a lively, gossipy town.'[52] Launching an explicit campaign against rumourmongering, Nyerere himself claimed that certain ambassadors were at fault for spreading malicious gossip.[53] *Uhuru*, TANU's Swahili newspaper, warned that if this was found to be true, it would ask Nyerere to shut down their embassies.[54]

These developments came against a backdrop of slow economic growth, widening inequality, and growing social tensions in Tanzania. By 1966, it was apparent that the prospects of growth in both Tanzania's agrarian and industrial sectors were poor. In rural areas, *uhuru* had brought little material progress to the peasantry, whose disposable income had scarcely altered since independence. This contrasted with significant gains for urban workers. The Five-Year Plan was not generating the desired growth: foreign capital investment failed to match expectations, manpower demands overstretched limited resources, and government ministries failed to coordinate their approaches. Nor, as Tanzania's disputes with Western donors had demonstrated, was dependence on external aid a solution. Meanwhile, the number of Tanzanians leaving school with a secondary education outstripped the capacities of the labour market to absorb their expectations of a middle-class career. Internal discontent mounted. There was growing criticism of a governing class – the *wabenzi*, 'those who own Mercedes-Benz' – that appeared to be benefiting from the fruits of the Africanisation of the bureaucracy.[55]

---

[50] 'Tanzania's Uncomfortable Union', *Africa 1966*, 8 April 1966, 2–3.
[51] 'Vicious Document', editorial, *Nationalist*, 23 April 1966, 4.
[52] [A. M. Babu], 'Pressman's Commentary', *Nationalist*, 22 April 1966, 4.
[53] 'Mwalimu Exposes Rumour-Mongers', *Nationalist*, 16 May 1966, 1.
[54] Editorial, *Uhuru*, 17 May 1966, 3.
[55] Pratt, *Critical Phase*, 215–22, 228–31; Andrew Coulson, *Tanzania: A Political Economy* (Oxford: Oxford University Press, 2013), 183–213.

A confrontation between Nyerere and the students at University College epitomised these tensions.[56] In November 1966, students staged a demonstration in which they declared their unwillingness to participate in a programme of compulsory national service for all university graduates. Pointing to the high salaries that civil servants and politicians earned, the students claimed they were being unfairly treated. Nyerere met the demonstrators outside State House. He reacted angrily. 'You are demanding a pound of flesh; everyone is demanding a pound of flesh except the poor peasant', he railed.[57] A total of 412 demonstrators – around two-thirds of the student body – were rusticated. The incident shook Nyerere. Not only had he faced a rare instance of significant, outspoken opposition, but the issues highlighted by the students' demands tallied with the president's own judgement. While the students' rejection of national service could be presented as unpatriotic, their critique of the current state of Tanzanian society exposed fundamental problems. Student complaints were mirrored by discontent among the workers, whose rising income since independence had only whetted their appetite for further gains. They were therefore unhappy with the government's decision to hold wage increases at 5 per cent per annum and called for the introduction of fixed prices.[58] In a prevailing climate of political uncertainty and economic disillusionment, Nyerere concluded that a major intervention was necessary.

Six Days in Arusha

In January 1967, Nyerere undertook a tour of provincial Tanzania. In a series of speeches, he reflected on the country's experience since independence and the economic challenges that it continued to face. Nyerere observed the dangers posed by the forces of neo-imperialism, as demonstrated by the fall of Ben Bella and Nkrumah. He described 1966 as a 'year of humiliation and shame' for Africa. To cut loose of its ties of dependency and insulate its sovereignty from imperialist predations, Tanzania required its own revolution. These speeches prepared the ground for the Arusha Declaration.[59] Over time, the document

---

[56] On the student protests, see Ivaska, *Cultured States*, 135–46.
[57] Quoted in Pratt, *Critical Phase*, 234.   [58] Ibid., 189–94.
[59] Shivji et al., *Development as Rebellion*, vol. 3, 112–19.

became directly associated with *Mwalimu*, as the president's personal initiative. 'Where other post-colonial leaders were overthrown in coups or pushed aside by rivals', writes Emma Hunter, 'Nyerere was able to create a new narrative which put himself at the centre of the struggle against illegitimate accumulation and corruption in politics, redefining politics as a moral struggle.'[60] However, as Issa Shivji has argued, the events which prefigured the grand proclamation in Dar es Salaam were a contentious process. Shivji's account provides much-needed insights on the contested nature of the behind-closed-doors party meetings in Arusha. It highlights that while the text of the Declaration was primarily the work of the president, it was not his work alone.[61]

There were actually two major TANU meetings in Arusha in late January 1967, not one. At the first, from 23 to 25 January, Nyerere explained his proposed course of action to TANU's regional commissioners. He established an eight-person committee, chaired by Edward Barongo, which drew up a set of recommendations. These were taken up by a meeting of the NEC, which lasted from 26 to 28 January. The NEC debated and ultimately accepted the proposals made by the Barongo Committee – though not without some fierce dissent. The party secretariat then drafted the text that became the Arusha Declaration, to which Nyerere added a lengthy passage on his key theme, self-reliance. The TANU meetings did not therefore simply rubber stamp Nyerere's proposals. Rather, they contained junctures at which other politicians raised their concerns and sought to influence policy. Critically, these were meetings of the party, rather than the cabinet, which had been sceptical of radicalising Tanzania's development. Previous proposals to appoint a commission on socialism were abandoned in favour of a swift process that hurried through the Arusha Declaration. Finally, the document was publicly unveiled by Nyerere on 5 February at Mnazi Mmoja in Dar es Salaam.

The central thrust of the speeches which Nyerere made at the Arusha meetings was the theme of *kujitegemea* ('self-reliance'). Tanzania might have won its formal independence, Nyerere argued, but it remained shackled to the world's wealthier states, which exploited the country's

---

[60] Emma Hunter, 'Julius Nyerere, the Arusha Declaration, and the Deep Roots of a Contemporary Political Metaphor', in Marie-Aude Fouéré (ed.), *Remembering Julius Nyerere in Tanzania: History, Memory, Legacy* (Dar es Salaam: Mkuki na Nyota, 2015), 85.

[61] Shivji et al., *Development as Rebellion*, vol. 3, 119–35.

underdevelopment. 'Did we really take power ourselves?', he asked the NEC.[62] Nyerere's solution to this problem – *kujitegemea* – was a flexible idea. As Priya Lal argues, self-reliance was simultaneously a method of action and aspirational outcome, operating at multiple scales, from the hard-working family to the nation-state. Economic growth required not foreign capital, but disciplined labour and the full mobilisation of Tanzania's natural resources, especially in the agricultural sector.[63] Nyerere's speeches in Arusha mixed popular local metaphors with references to the inequalities of the international economic order. He deployed the image of 'straw-sucking', drawing on the tradition of African elders sucking alcohol from a common pot and thereby living off the hard work of the masses.[64] But he extended the metaphor beyond Tanzanian society, to highlight the exploitation of the national economy by foreign powers.

To sell his socialist vision, Nyerere set Tanzania's predicament in a global context informed by contemporary political developments. Powers like Britain, West Germany, and the United States could not be relied upon to provide aid, Nyerere stated. He pointed to the fall in American support to Africa under the Johnson administration. The break in relations with Britain had cost Tanzania £7.5 million in development aid. Worse, the support these states did offer came with political strings attached, as the imbroglio with West Germany demonstrated. Nyerere drew attention to the situation in India, where the United States had attached conditions to food aid to Delhi with an eye to its Cold War objectives in Vietnam. He pointed out that while the Tanzanian government considered the likely international response of powerful Western countries to its decision-making, the same was not true vice-versa. 'In Britain they decide something in cabinet or within the party without asking whether Julius will like it or not.' In contrast, Nyerere praised the Third World countries which resisted such exploitation. He spoke highly of China's anti-imperialism and self-reliant development policies. Turning to the case of the Democratic Republic of Vietnam, Nyerere suggested that this small, revolutionary state offered guidance in the struggle against neocolonial exploitation.

---

[62] Minutes of the TANU NEC Meeting, Arusha, 26–28 January 1967, TNA, 589, BMC 11/02 D, 1.
[63] Priya Lal, 'Self-Reliance and the State: The Multiple Meanings of Development in Early Post-Colonial Tanzania', *Africa*, 82 (2012), 212–34.
[64] On this metaphor, see Brennan, *Taifa*, 163–67.

'They don't accept even one *mrija* [straw-sucker] there', he said.[65] Cuba, too, had demonstrated the ability of the weak to stand shoulder to shoulder with the powerful. 'When Castro coughs, Americans listen', he told the regional commissioners, to laughter. 'As for India, they don't care!'[66] These international references were central to Nyerere's pitch at the Arusha meetings, but were absent from the final document.

However, neocolonialists from beyond Africa's borders were not Tanzania's sole enemy. According to Nyerere, self-reliance required the ending of exploitation in Tanzania by local businessmen. The egalitarian principles of *ujamaa* therefore required party and government leaders to not be 'associated with the practices of capitalism and feudalism', as the 'Arusha Resolution' that was appended to the final document put it. Under what was eventually formalised as a 'leadership code', they could not hold shares or directorships in private companies, or own houses for renting out to others. This was Nyerere's response to the economic disparities which had been exposed by the student protests of the previous November. It was also a predictably bitter pill for the Tanzanian elite to swallow. After Nyerere unveiled his plans in his opening speech to the regional commissioners, his audience had been left, in the words of one eyewitness, 'stupefied'.[67]

In pushing through this leadership code, Nyerere was forced to concede ground on the question of nationalisation. As explained earlier, the president was wary of the risks of en masse nationalisation. Nyerere told the regional commissioners that there were two methods for putting the economy under the control of the peasants and workers. The first involved the government taking ownership of key economic assets. The second, as in the case of cooperatives, involved the people themselves directly taking control of means of production. Nyerere argued that the first model carried particular dangers, since it placed the government as an intermediary between the means of production and the workers; only if the government was genuinely democratic would workers really control the economy. The Nazis had nationalised

---

[65] Minutes of the TANU NEC Meeting, Arusha, 26–28 January 1967, TNA, 589, BMC 11/02 D, 1.
[66] F. Lwanyantika Masha, *The Story of the Arusha Declaration (1967)* (Mwanza: self-published, 2011), 29. Masha's account must be treated with caution. He was TANU's publicity secretary at the time, but also a close associate of Kambona. Masha was expelled from TANU in 1968, as Chapter 7 explains.
[67] Ibid., 44.

a lot, Nyerere remarked, but they had hardly put those assets in the hands of the German people. 'If there is no democracy, government ownership of the economy can be very unjust.'[68]

However, under the influence of more radical members of TANU, nationalisation became a core plank of the Arusha Declaration.[69] According to Fortunatus Masha, the party's publicity secretary, a faction led by Kambona successfully pressured the Barongo Committee to call for the nationalisation of major economic assets.[70] The previous week, Kambona had told party youth activists that the time had arrived for the government to take over 'all major industries presently owned by minority groups', adding an allusion to race to Nyerere's colour-blind discussions of exploitation.[71] More circumspect voices at the meeting in Arusha called for caution. Edwin Mtei, the governor of the Bank of Tanzania, urged the NEC members to proceed carefully but decisively. He was especially concerned by the outflow of capital which nationalisation would likely provoke, though recalled that the mood of the meeting prevailed against any detailed exposition of these economic consequences.[72] Under the influence of TANU leaders, the Arusha Declaration therefore took on a more radical appearance than Nyerere had initially planned. As he stressed, self-reliance, not nationalisation, was intended to be the main theme of the document.[73] Nonetheless, in the space of a few days – and without consulting his cabinet – Nyerere had his socialist manifesto.

The Revolution and Its Discontents

Although the Arusha Declaration established many principles, it had little to say about their implementation. It committed the government to bringing 'all the major means of production and exchange' under the control of the workers and peasants, but it set out no policy measures for achieving this goal. The first move came on the day after Nyerere's Mnazi Mmoja speech. On the morning of 6 February, Nyerere held a short cabinet meeting at which he presented the imminent nationalisation of the banking sector as a fait accompli.[74] That evening,

[68] Ibid., 20. [69] Hartmann, 'Development Policy-Making', 188–91.
[70] Masha, *Story*, 35–36.
[71] 'It's Time for Take-Over – Kambona', *Nationalist*, 20 January 1967, 1.
[72] Mtei, *Goatherd to Governor*, 107–108.
[73] Hartmann, 'Development Policy-Making', 188. [74] Ibid., 201.

Nyerere announced that all foreign banks operating in Tanzania had been nationalised, prompting jubilation across the city. Bars overflowed with people who drank to 'the success of Socialism and Self-Reliance'.[75] After nationalising the banks, the government turned its attention to other economic sectors. Every day, Nyerere revealed the details of nationalised businesses to huge crowds in Dar es Salaam. The government either totally nationalised or took controlling shares in eight grain-milling firms, six import-export houses, all insurance businesses, plus seven subsidiaries of multinational corporations. It assured that it would pay 'full and fair' compensation.[76]

The feverish reception of the Arusha Declaration contrasted with the sense of uncertainty among Dar es Salaam's business community, dominated by Tanzanian Asians and foreigners. A cautiously worded editorial in the *Standard*, their preferred newspaper, asked whether 'the same end' might have been achieved with 'less shock to the commercial and industrial sector and to foreign confidence?'[77] These concerns were shared by the 'political economists' in the government. The nationalisation of the banks caused particular alarm. Mtei as governor of the Bank of Tanzania, was reportedly distraught by developments and tendered his resignation, which Nyerere did not accept.[78] Amir Jamal, the finance minister, was less ideologically opposed to the nationalisation of the banks, but the news still caught him off guard. At a dinner hosted by the East German consul-general on the same day as the decision was announced, Jamal admitted to the Soviet ambassador that he had not been consulted about the takeover.[79] Both Mtei and Jamal were worried about the danger of serious capital flight. They quickly introduced currency controls to prevent Tanzanian shillings from being converted into their Kenyan or Ugandan equivalents.[80] In anticipation of a potential run on the banks, armed police were

---

[75] 'Take-Over of Banks Hits London Stock Prices', *Nationalist*, 8 February 1967, 1.
[76] Coulson, *Tanzania*, 217.
[77] 'Nationalisation', editorial, *Standard*, 8 February 1967, 4.
[78] Emmanuel Onah, Chinwe Okoyeuzu, and Chibuike Uche, 'The Nationalisation of British Banks in Post-Colonial Tanzania', *Business History* (forthcoming).
[79] The story was relayed to the Australian high commission via the Indonesian chargé d'affaires, who was party to the conversation between Jamal and Timoshenko. Bullock, 6 March 1967, NAA, A1838, 154/11/87, 252.
[80] 'Exchange Control Tightened', *Nationalist*, 8 February 1967, 1.

dispatched to guard their premises across the city.⁸¹ Other 'moderate' ministers shared this anguish. Paul Bomani told a foreign journalist that 'Julius is out of his mind' and that 'we will not live under a crazy Nyerere dynasty'.⁸² Derek Bryceson informed the Canadian high commissioner that he considered Arusha socialism to be idealistic and impractical, and that he had even contemplated resigning.⁸³ Meanwhile, Jamal resolved himself to the task of negotiating the nationalisation terms and compensation arrangements.

Then, as suddenly as the wave of nationalisations had begun, Nyerere brought them to an abrupt halt. In an article in the *Sunday News* on 12 February, he announced that there would be no further takeovers. While the idea of 'self-reliance' meant many things in Tanzania, economic autarky was not among them. The 'political economists' in central government recognised foreign aid and private investment would be vital in driving forwards Tanzania's socialist revolution. Nyerere clarified that self-reliance meant an end to neither aid nor investment, but that Tanzania would accept both as a 'catalyst' towards economic progress.⁸⁴ He argued that 'it would be as stupid for us to assume that capitalists have horns as it is for people in Western Europe to assume that we in Tanzania have become devils'.⁸⁵ Government representatives continued to court private capital. Babu gave the Joint Chambers of Commerce of Tanzania a 'categorical assurance' that the 'limited nationalisation programme' was over. He encouraged his audience to see the measures as 'sharp swords of deliverance', rather than 'clumsy boulders designed to stifle enterprise and initiative'.⁸⁶ Nyerere used an interview with the *New York Times* to call for investment in Tanzania on a 'partnership' basis.⁸⁷ Quite clearly, the government wanted to reassure the West that Tanzania remained open for business.

---

[81] McGill to Min. External Affairs, Ottawa, 7 February 1967, UKNA, FCO 31/52/29.

[82] Quoted in James R. Brennan, '*Julius Rex*: Nyerere Through the Eyes of His Critics', *Journal of Eastern African Studies*, 8 (2014), 468.

[83] McGill to Min. External Affairs, Ottawa, 1 March 1967, UKNA, FCO 31/156/8A.

[84] 'Public Ownership in Tanzania', in Nyerere, *Freedom and Socialism*, 254.

[85] 'Socialism Is Not Racialism', ibid., 259.

[86] Executive officer, Tanganyika Tea Growers' Association, 7 March 1967, UKNA, FCO 31/73/70.

[87] 'Nyerere Appeals to U.S. Investors', *New York Times*, 25 May 1967, 9.

Nonetheless, the Western response to the Arusha Declaration was predictably critical. Again, it was framed by Cold War precepts. From London, a *Daily Telegraph* editorial under the headline 'Building Marxania' predicted 'a sharp recession' in Tanzania.[88] Several observers incorrectly jumped to the conclusion that the Arusha Declaration was the product of external influence. 'Tanzania is to attempt a "great leap forward" on Sino-Zanzibari lines', stated the *Times*.[89] One Nairobi financier described the Arusha Declaration as a 'Nasser-inspired take-over by decree with Chinese encouragement'.[90] British diplomats echoed this unease, sharing similar pathological ideas about the 'spread' of communism in the African body politic. The high commissioner to Kenya feared that Nyerere would be 'drawn inexorably' towards the communist camp. A meeting of British diplomats in Nairobi judged that it was preferable for Arusha socialism to fail, 'to prevent the infection spreading to neighbouring countries'. It concluded that Britain should therefore 'avoid doing anything to cushion the Tanzanian Government from the full economic consequences of their actions'.[91] Nyerere bristled at the charge that he was under foreign influence. He used a set-piece speech in Cairo in April to put clear distance between *ujamaa* and Marxism-Leninism. Criticising the 'theology' of socialism, he stated that 'this idea that there is one "pure socialism", for which its recipe is already known, is an insult to human intelligence'.[92]

These crude Cold War assumptions misinterpreted both the content of debate in Arusha and realities in Dar es Salaam's corridors of power. The Arusha Declaration, as we have seen, was driven neither by the communist powers nor the more revolutionary members of the Tanzanian elite. For example, the *Sunday Times* in London noted that some observers considered the nationalisations 'a triumph for the Chinese-inspired Zanzibar Communist Commerce Minister Mohamed Babu'. This was well wide of the mark.[93] In fact, Babu was privately unconvinced about the new policy. As he propounded

---

[88] 'Building Marxania', editorial, *Daily Telegraph*, 9 February 1967, 14.
[89] 'Green Guards in Tanzania', editorial, *Times*, 13 February 1967, 13.
[90] Quoted in Ahmed Mohiddin, 'Ujamaa na Kujitegemea', *Mawazo* (December 1967), 24.
[91] Peck to Norris, 10 April 1967, UKNA, FCO 31/160/2.
[92] 'The Varied Paths to Socialism', in Nyerere, *Freedom and Socialism*, 301–302.
[93] 'Traders Start Cold War in Tanzania', *Sunday Times*, 19 February 1967, 6.

in his later writings, Babu was sceptical about the Arusha Declaration's emphasis on the intensification of agricultural production. Instead, he had favoured an industrialisation policy geared to transforming Tanzania's economic base.[94] In particular, he felt mass nationalisation was reckless and premature. Babu feared that the government was overextending its operations beyond the limited capacity of the state. He had already clashed with Nyerere on these grounds: shortly before the Arusha Declaration, Babu had rejected the president's request to develop plans for a price control mechanism in Tanzania, arguing that it would be expensive and bureaucratically cumbersome.[95]

On 22 February, Nyerere used a minor government reshuffle to switch Babu from the ministry of commerce and cooperatives to the less economically pivotal position of minister for health. Babu told the East Germans that this was a purely tactical move by Nyerere, designed to reassure Western investors by putting the portfolio into the hands of the moderate Paul Bomani.[96] On the face of it, this would not seem an unlikely scenario. However, snippets of intelligence suggest that this was more than a public relations matter. Both Oscar Kambona and his close ally, the civil servant Dennis Phombeah, informed Eastern Bloc officials that Babu had been moved due to his failure to draw up a list of foreign firms for nationalisation.[97] (Another casualty of this reshuffle was Nsilo Swai, the minister for industries, who also objected to mass nationalisation.) Undeterred, Babu used a speech in Nairobi to warn against overreliance on agricultural exports, which were vulnerable to fluctuations in the global marketplace. East Africa could not afford to become a region of 'banana republics', Babu argued, and therefore had to develop its heavy industry.[98] This was in direct contradiction to the message of the Arusha Declaration. This ideological friction between Nyerere and Babu would remain concealed at the heart of government

---

[94] A. M. Babu, 'The Tanzania That Might Have Been', in Salma Babu and Amrit Wilson (eds.), *The Future That Works: Select Writings of A. M. Babu* (Trenton, NJ: Africa World Press, 2002), 16–23.

[95] A. M. Babu, 'Entrepreneurs in Tanzania: A Minister's Story', in Stephen Ellis and Yves-A. Fauré (eds.), *Entreprises et entrepreneurs africains* (Paris: Editions Karthala, 1995), 348–49.

[96] Lessing to Kiesewetter, 27 February 1967, BA-B, SAPMO, DY 30/98143, 94–97.

[97] Brzezinski to Spasowski, 18 March 1967, MSZ, DV, 1967, 57/70 W-5; memcon (Schüssler, Phombeah), 7 March 1967, BA-B, SAPMO, DY 30/98136, 333–37.

[98] 'Heavy Industry the Only Way for East Africa – Babu', *Standard*, 20 May 1967, 3.

for the next half-decade. Among the Tanzanian cabinet, responses to the Arusha Declaration did not therefore follow any 'left-right' split. If anything, its most revolutionary member was critical of the new policies, even as he defended them in public.

If the reaction of the 'political economists' to the Arusha Declaration was concern about the country's stability, some party members believed that Tanzania's socialist revolution did not go far enough. These criticisms generally took two forms. First, they called for a more radical, interventionist approach to Africanisation. For example, Michael Kamaliza, the minister of labour and NUTA secretary-general, urged Nyerere to nationalise *all* industries and farms in Tanzania.[99] Second, radicals argued that the party must play a more active role in spearheading the implementation of socialism. At a TANU special conference held in late February, the MP Joseph Kasella-Bantu called for the development of an ideologically committed vanguard party.[100] The TANU Youth League (TYL), packed with party radicals, was particularly vocal in demanding an accelerated drive to socialism.[101] In one instance, this enthusiasm descended into reckless behaviour. In March, the MP and TYL secretary-general, Eli Anangisye, was accused of inciting an attack on the recently nationalised General Bank of the Netherlands, in which a portrait of the Dutch Queen Juliana was defaced. Nyerere apologised to the Dutch government for this 'act of hooliganism'. The incident was particularly embarrassing as the Dutch government had just given Tanzania £100,000 towards a fish processing plant. For a state wishing to reassure foreign donors, this was hardly a good look. Anangisye was quickly stripped of his TYL role but became an embittered backbencher in parliament.[102]

In response to demands for further radicalisation, Nyerere stressed the need for moderation over recklessness. He flatly rejected the idea of turning TANU into a vanguard party. Nyerere again employed the language of slow change. 'It would make us adventurists and opportunists not revolutionaries', he said. 'We cannot go "full speed" into socialism.'[103] Rebutting calls for the nationalisation of local capital at

---

[99] 'Takeover Will Go Fast', *Nationalist*, 10 February 1967, 1, 8.
[100] Hartmann, 'Development Policy-Making', 206–207.
[101] 'Youths Demand More Action', *Nationalist*, 8 February 1967, 1, 8.
[102] Schlegel, 5 April 1967, BA-B, SAPMO, DY 30/98143; 'President Apologises to Holland', *Standard*, 17 March 1967, 1.
[103] Quoted in Pratt, *Critical Phase*, 246.

the TANU special meeting, he made a comparison with the typical arrangement whereby Asians ran shops and Masai raised cattle. 'Now to move an Asian and ask him to raise cattle and a Masai to run a shop', he told laughing TANU delegates, would be for 'self-amusement' alone. He urged Tanzanians to keep one eye on the direction of the path to socialism, and the other on the 'mud, thorns, termite-mounds, and hills' along the way.[104] As we will see in Chapter 7, these arguments remained unresolved as TANU sought to navigate the implementation of the Arusha agenda into the 1970s.

For all the clamour for more radical action, the bulk of discontent with the Arusha Declaration arose from the leadership code, which threatened the personal wealth and property of the elite. An NEC meeting held in Iringa between 29 May and 1 June affirmed that TANU leaders must either abide by the code or step down.[105] Some felt that the terms had been imposed unjustly, without adequate discussion or warning. Again, this reflected the 'top-down' nature of the Arusha Declaration, which was imposed from above without discussion in parliament or lower party ranks. When Nyerere solicited questions from MPs about the Arusha Declaration, he was disappointed by their priorities. In the icy preface to a booklet carry a selection of his responses, Nyerere expressed his displeasure that almost all those received concerned the leadership qualifications, and none socialism or self-reliance.[106] However, open criticism remained muted. The 1965 elections had been highly competitive, with several high-profile incumbents losing their seats. For any MP to dissent in public to these popular measures would have been political suicide. One former MP recalled that the conditions were 'like someone holding a sharp knife to one's side in such a way that it could not be pulled away without getting hurt'.[107]

Although the vast majority of the elite therefore eventually relinquished their private assets, a few chose otherwise. One high-profile case was Bibi Titi Mohammed, the most prominent female member of

---

[104] Hartmann, 'Development Policy-Making', 217.
[105] Minutes of the TANU NEC Meeting, Iringa, 29 May–1 June 1967, TNA, 589, BMC 11/02 D, 27.
[106] United Republic of Tanzania, *Arusha Declaration: Answers to Questions* (Dar es Salaam: Government Printer, 1967).
[107] Aili Mari Tripp, *Changing the Rules: The Politics of Liberalization and the Urban Informal Economy in Tanzania* (Berkeley: University of California Press, 1997), 174.

the party, who resigned as the head of the Tanganyika Women's Union and from the TANU Central Committee. In 1967, she ascribed her decision to stand down from her party positions to back pains; later, in an interview with a researcher, she made no mention of any injury and explained her opposition to the hasty and undemocratic adoption of the Arusha Declaration. But at the time, popular gossip held that she simply did not want to give up her private properties.[108] In some cases, TANU leaders who had previously championed accelerated Africanisation now baulked at giving up their own assets. Ali Saidi Mtaki, a junior minister who was once referred to as the 'Karl Marx of Tanganyika', chose not to comply with the leadership code. He relinquished his government and party offices to take up a managerial position in a British tobacco multinational.[109]

More seriously for Nyerere, the leadership code jarred with an even bigger figure in Tanzanian politics: Oscar Kambona. In public, Kambona talked up the Tanzanian revolution – indeed, he tilted towards a more radical approach. Interviewed in *Jeune Afrique* after the Arusha Declaration, he stated that there was no such thing as 'African socialism', only an undefined 'scientific socialism'.[110] At the Iringa NEC meeting, he presented a report calling for the reorganisation of TANU into 'the revolutionary vanguard of the people', thus setting him at odds with Nyerere, who had already ruled out the idea.[111] Kambona later cited the Iringa meeting as being the moment when he believed that Nyerere intended to crush TANU's freedom through the apparatus of the state.[112] As we have seen, Kambona's relations with Nyerere were already strained. Yet Kambona's chief complaints about the Arusha Declaration appear to have arisen not from its insufficient radicalism, but the consequences it had for his personal assets and wealth. Job Lusinde, another cabinet minister, recalled receiving a telephone call from Kambona immediately after

---

[108] Wilson to Scott, 13 June 1967, UKNA, FCO 31/157/29; Susan Geiger, *TANU Women: Gender and the Making of Tanganyikan Nationalism* (Portsmouth, NH: Heinemann, 1997), here esp. 172–73.
[109] Chachage, 'Capitalizing City', 197–99, cf. 145–48; Tordoff and Mazrui, 'Left', 438.
[110] Ania Francos, '"Il n'y a pas de socialisme africain . . ."', *Jeune Afrique*, 23 April 1967, 28–29.
[111] 'Kambona Calls for Changes in Tanu', *Standard*, 2 June 1967, 1.
[112] Oscar Kambona, 'TANU Head Quit Because of State Power over Party', *Guardian*, 7 April 1971, 4.

the pivotal NEC meeting in Arusha. Kambona seemed panicked about the implications of the leadership code for his numerous private properties.[113] Rumours fluttered around diplomatic circles. According to the Polish embassy, for example, Kambona had three houses in Tanzania and large sums of money stashed away in European bank accounts.[114] Even as the country rallied to the Arusha Declaration, the socialist revolution seemed to be opening cleavages within the Tanzanian elite rather than soldering it together.

Reshuffle and Rupture

On 7 June, Nyerere announced a long-anticipated cabinet reshuffle and restructuring of central government. He rung the changes for various reasons. Tensions between the state and NUTA saw Michael Kamaliza replaced as minister of labour. Kassim Hanga was dropped as minister for union affairs, almost certainly due to pressure placed on Nyerere by Karume, with whom Hanga had experienced a troubled relationship since the union three years earlier.[115] Babu switched positions again, becoming minister for lands, settlement, and water development. Derek Bryceson (agriculture and cooperatives) and Amir Jamal (finance) kept their posts. Paul Bomani reverted to being minister for economic affairs and planning, resuming the role he had occupied prior to the minor February reshuffle. The retention of Bomani, Bryceson, and Jamal in portfolios with key economic responsibilities demonstrated Nyerere's prioritisation of competent administration over political revolution and desire to maintain the confidence of foreign donors and investors. In the end, the loyalty of these 'moderates' to Nyerere, plus the element of compromise built into the Arusha Declaration, ensured their continued support for the government. The reshuffle reassured Western onlookers. The French ambassador's snap judgement was that Nyerere had placed in key economic positions men 'who were not suspected of colluding

---

[113] 'Lusinde akumbuka Kambona alivyogoma kubadilishwa uwaziri', *Raia Mwema*, 31 May–1 June 2017, 12–13. See also Nyerere's own account of Kambona's private assets in his letter to Howell at the Tanzanian Interests Section of the Canadian high commission in London, 30 August 1967, Jamal Papers, AR/MISR/157/2.
[114] Brzezinski to Dept V, MSZ, 9 September 1967, MSZ, DV, 1967, 57/70 W-5.
[115] Stewart to CO, 8 June 1967, UKNA, FCO 31/157/20; Lessing to Stibi, 3 August 1967, BA-B, SAPMO, DY 30/98136, 351–67.

with extreme-left subversion' and 'capable of inspiring confidence after the quirks [foucades] of the Arusha Declaration'.[116]

However, the most significant development came after Nyerere's decision to appoint Kambona, previously minister for regional administration, to the newly created portfolio for local government and rural development. Kambona promptly resigned both from his new ministerial role and as secretary-general of TANU. At a press conference, in the company of Hanga, Kambona announced that he had resigned on health grounds.[117] The previous year, Kambona had indeed travelled to the Netherlands for treatment for high blood pressure. However, by mid-1967, he was cured: the real reasons lay in a series of disputes with the president and his supporters. On 11 June, Kambona, again flanked by Hanga, addressed his constituents in Morogoro, where he made veiled criticisms of Nyerere's authoritarian tendencies.[118] Dar es Salaam swirled with rumours about Kambona's connections with the Eastern Bloc. In May, Lady Marion Chesham, a Nyerere confidante, told an American official that the president had proof that Kambona was receiving money from the Soviet Union and would 'take strong action' against Kambona.[119] It is difficult to establish any solid factual ground here, but Kambona did turn to the East Germans for assistance, without success, as the next chapter reveals. When MPs passed a motion calling for Kambona to explain his decision to resign, he declined to attend parliament.[120]

By this time, Dar es Salaam was a febrile city. Despite the fact they all belonged to the same party, the session of parliament was characterised by the trading of insults between MPs. The budget passed by just 69 votes to 37. Paul Bomani implored members to show self-restraint in order to 'to prevent [the] imperialist press from exploiting disagreements between Parliament and Government, thereby sowing confusion among the public'.[121] That was just the open disagreement: the precise

---

[116] Naudy to MAE-DAL, 12 June 1967, CADN, 193PO/1/2 A5.
[117] 'Kambona Resigns', *Nationalist*, 10 June 1967, 1, 8.
[118] 'Kambona Tells Why He Resigned', *Standard*, 12 June 1967, 1.
[119] Butterfield to Burns, 24 May 1967, NARA, RG 59, BAA, OEAA, Tanzania and Zanzibar, 1963–75, Box 2, POL 15–1 TAN. Chesham was born in the United States before settling in Tanganyika. She had entered politics during the late colonial period and then became aligned with TANU. She took Tanganyikan citizenship after independence and served as an MP.
[120] 'MPs End Long Session of Parliament', *Standard*, 21 July 1967, 3.
[121] Quoted in Hartmann, 'Development Policy-Making', 21.

details of the behind-the-scenes disputes remain hazy. It seems that on 15 July, Nyerere called a meeting of MPs at State House. He warned them that neither opposition to the Arusha Declaration nor the spreading of rumours would be tolerated. Anangisye, the disgraced former TYL leader, then went immediately to the Lugalo barracks, where he tried to incite troops into agitating against the government.[122] He was arrested, along with Hamisi Salumu, who was formerly Hanga's bodyguard.[123] On 23 July, three more men – all known Kambona associates – were arrested on charges of subversion.[124]

Recognising that his room for manoeuvre was narrowing, Kambona fled Tanzania. He drove first to Kenya, probably with the knowledge of Tanzanian intelligence. In Nairobi, his friend Oginga Odinga tried to persuade Kambona to return home and even spoke to Nyerere on the telephone. But Kambona refused to turn back and flew on to London.[125] The Tanzanian government remained silent about the issue until 1 August. Finally, it stated that Kambona had fled to Kenya 'with a lot of money' and without paying his income tax.[126] In London, Kambona gave an interview in which he alleged that there was a plot to remove Nyerere, involving the upper ranks of the Tanzanian security services and army.[127] Nyerere responded by calling Kambona a liar. 'Anybody who believes in this talk of conspiracy can well believe that his parents are donkeys', he told a rally in Dar es Salaam. 'If you accept these lies you can well accept anything.'[128] When a Dutch associate of Kambona, Ernst van Eeghen, tried to mediate between the 'sick' Kambona and Nyerere, the president rejected any attempt at reconciliation. He described Kambona as 'a renegade and traitor to my country ... He can't wriggle out of the mess he has created for himself.'[129] The rupture was irreversible. By September, Kambona had

---

[122] Burns to State Dept, 18 July 1967, NARA, RG 59, CFPF 1967–69, Box 2513, POL 2 TANZAN.
[123] The Stasi thought that the charge against Salumu was fabricated and simply intended as a warning to Hanga. MfS, 18 September 1967, BStU, MfS, HV A, no. 227, 105–12.
[124] 'Three More Detained', *Nationalist*, 26 July 1967, 1.
[125] Shivji et al., *Development as Rebellion*, vol. 3, 144.
[126] 'Kambona Left "In Secret"', *Standard*, 2 August 1967, 1.
[127] 'Kambona Talks in London', *Standard*, 11 August 1967, 1.
[128] 'There Is No Conspiracy', *Nationalist*, 14 August 1967, 1, 8.
[129] Nyerere to van Eeghen, 4 September 1967, Jamal Papers, AR/MISR/157/2. Van Eeghen had business interests in Tanzania and had served as the country's honorary consul in the Netherlands.

been joined in London by two close allies, Hanga and Phombeah.[130] The verbal spat between Kambona and Nyerere carried on intermittently over the following years. As Chapter 7 explains, Kambona was later accused of masterminding an amateurish conspiracy to overthrow Nyerere's government in a plot orchestrated from London. He became a convenient bogeyman through which the TANU party-state whipped up support for its message of national vigilance.

If there was any remaining doubt about Kambona's pariah status in Tanzania, it was dispelled by Hanga's ill-fated return to the country. Since joining his friend in exile, Hanga had travelled backwards and forwards between London and Conakry, where his wife lived. In conversations with acquaintances in London, Hanga seemed oblivious to the consequences of his association with Kambona and the dangers awaiting him should he return to Tanzania.[131] But Hanga would not be deterred. On 21 December, he flew back to Dar es Salaam. He claimed that he had been sent by the Guinean president, Sékou Touré, to patch up the split between Kambona and Nyerere. Just ten days after his return, Hanga was placed in preventative detention, alongside Kambona's brothers, Otini and Mattiya. This prompted further heated exchanges. From London, Kambona branded Nyerere a 'dictator'. At a rally in Dar es Salaam to mark the anniversary of the Zanzibar Revolution, Nyerere responded with a blistering attack on Kambona, dubbing him a 'traitor', a 'thief', and a 'prostitute'. Nyerere humiliated Hanga by parading him before the crowd and calling him an 'idiot' who had accomplished nothing as a minister. Nyerere said that Hanga was detained after claiming that he had been asked by the Zanzibari TPDF to lead a coup.[132] In an unconvincing and defensive interview given from prison, Hanga protested his innocence.[133] Hanga remained in preventative detention until December 1968. The following year, he

---

[130] Hanga was dismissed from his position as vice president of Zanzibar on 18 August. No explanation was given: 'Hanga Loses Appointment', *Standard*, 19 August 1967, 1. Phombeah's services as a civil servant were 'terminated' on 29 August. 'Phombeah's Service Terminated', *Standard*, 31 August 1967, 1.
[131] Rajab, 'Maisha na nyakati'.
[132] 'Kambona Breaks Silence', *Standard*, 4 January 1968, 1; 'Kambona a Thief, Lackey', *Nationalist*, 13 January 1968, 1, 8; 'Give Us Hanga – TPDF Zanzibar', *Nationalist*, 13 January 1968, 8; 'Hanga Brought Before Rally', *Standard*, 13 January 1968, 1, 3.
[133] 'Hanga Tells His Story', *Standard*, 5 February 1968, 2–3.

met a grim fate at the hands of the Zanzibari authorities, as Chapter 7 explains.

More generally, the idea that the Arusha revolution was being undermined by 'mercenaries' in the pay of nefarious foreign governments became a staple of government rhetoric. In a speech on 7 July 1967 at the Jangwani grounds, Nyerere declared that 'the biggest danger facing Africa today is that leaders can be bought. There are known and unknown Tshombes, some are very big and other [sic] are small.'[134] He later privately admitted that he already had Kambona in mind.[135] The president's language caught on. The *Nationalist* piggy-backed on a speech made by Nasser, in which he warned of the neocolonial threat. '*Wananchi* [citizens] must beware', the editorial stated. 'The imperialists may try to use local "politicians" to lure you with money.'[136] The concept of an 'enemy within', who sold out to neocolonial subversives, became commonplace in Tanzanian discourse. It connected the long-standing local idiom of the 'exploiter' with a Cold War political culture of insecurity and subversion. The trope became a powerful charge that could be levied at all sorts of dissident figures in years to come.

Conclusion

The Arusha Declaration represented a decisive answer to the tensions of decolonisation which drew a line in the sand of Tanzanian politics. The language of *ujamaa*, now backed up with tangible policies, fleshed out the structural bones of the one-party state. As Lionel Cliffe reflected, through 'the development of an "official" ideology with some concrete content ... it is now possible to sort out the sheep from the goats far more rigorously than was the case when leaders at various levels could make up their own orthodoxy so long as they related it to a handful of slogans'.[137] The confused debate about the direction of socialism was replaced by a clear development strategy. Yet clarity also allowed the establishment of sharper lines of division between rival groups. Figures who challenged the precepts of the Arusha Declaration could be marked out as enemies of the Tanzanian

[134] 'No Dignity for Africa Yet – Nyerere', *Nationalist*, 8 July 1967, 1, 8.
[135] Nyerere to Howell, 30 August 1967, Jamal Papers, AR/MISR/157/2.
[136] 'Nasser's Message', editorial, *Nationalist*, 25 July 1967, 4.
[137] Lionel Cliffe, review of Bienen, *Tanzania*, in *African Review*, 1 (1971), 129.

Conclusion

revolution, working in cahoots with the country's imperialist enemies. In codifying the ethics of *ujamaa* into a socialist manifesto, the Arusha Declaration formed a blueprint for bringing about genuine decolonisation while also providing the ideological foundations for TANU's turn towards authoritarian rule.

The genesis of the Arusha Declaration was not a straightforward process. Amid the insecurities brought about by the encroachment of the global Cold War into postcolonial African politics, as well as rising socio-economic tensions within the country, Nyerere compromised between the two rough power groupings inside the Tanzanian state. His morally charged 'leadership code', which assuaged popular complaints about the elite's self-enrichment, was sweetened by concessions to mass nationalisation. More moderate government ministers, who favoured the politics of slow change, were far from content at the hasty imposition of the nationalisation measures. But they were at least reassured by the pragmatism which Nyerere showed in not conceding too much ground to those TANU members who called for more radical change – for the meantime, at least. In the longer term, the events of 1967 marked a general shift of power from the 'political economists' inside government to an increasingly assertive and vocal group of party leaders, shrinking the latitude for debate.

The Arusha Declaration was a manifesto for national development, but one forged in a context that stretched beyond Tanzania's borders. As governing elites watched their fellow liberation heroes elsewhere fall to military coups, with disconcerting rumours of foreign complicity, they recognised the need to regain a sense of momentum as the lustre of *uhuru* wore off. The irruption of Cold War crises over the course of 1964–65 convinced Nyerere that genuine political sovereignty required economic decolonisation rather than flag independence. Although Nyerere drew on the examples of China, Vietnam, and Cuba in justifying the case for a policy of self-reliance, it was not the direct influence of communist states or their allies in the Tanzanian elite which galvanised the shift towards a socialist development agenda. As the ripples which the Arusha Declaration sent through the Western diplomatic and business community demonstrate, it also had global implications and posed new questions of Tanzania's foreign policy. Some onlookers perceived Arusha as an opening for expanding their influence in the country, including the states of divided Germany. The next chapter shows how Tanzania navigated the whirlpool of the 'German Cold War'.

3 | Dilemmas of Non-Alignment: Tanzania and the German Cold War

In January 1969, a pamphlet entitled 'China and the Devil Slaves' dropped into the in-trays of politicians, diplomats, and journalists in Dar es Salaam. According to its title page, it was written by Walter Markow, an East German Africanist, with the assistance of Stephen Mhando. Mhando was Tanzania's recently appointed minister of state for foreign affairs. The publisher was named as the 'German-African Society in the German Democratic Republic'. The pamphlet began:

> Why do the Chinese, when they talk among themselves, always refer to the Africans as the 'devil slaves?' Because for many centuries they have regarded the Africans as inferior beings. Beings suitable only for slavery, or to be sterilised, or to be wiped off the face of the earth.

The tract offered a batch of 'historical' examples to back up these wild accusations.[1] Characteristic of much of the 'black literature' in circulation in Dar es Salaam, the pamphlet raised multiple questions. Was it a genuine East German production? Or a false-flag forgery by their West German counterparts? Why the attack on China? And why did it claim the co-authorship of a senior figure in the supposedly non-aligned – or, to many observers, China-inclined – Tanzanian government?

This chapter explores how Dar es Salaam became a battlefield in a Cold War subplot: the global struggle waged between the two German states. In so doing, it pushes beyond Eurocentric conceptions of the Cold War, while also not purely adopting a 'subaltern' view of international affairs which emphasises the agency of Third World states like Tanzania. Rather, it analyses the engagement of both German states with Tanzania through a triangular framework. On the higher plane of diplomacy, the chapter demonstrates how a Cold

---

[1] 'China and the Devil Slaves', enclosed in Burns to State Dept, 20 March 1969, NARA, RG 59, CFPF 1967–69, Box 1511, CSM TANZAN.

War struggle became defined in Tanzania as much by North-South divisions over issues of self-determination and economic decolonisation than the East-West rivalry in which its origins lay. At a lower level, this chapter also shows how the German Cold War was waged within the political and communication networks of Dar es Salaam, as the two rival states sought to besmirch each other in the city's public sphere while cultivating relations with local powerbrokers.

From a Tanzanian perspective, the 'German Cold War' presents an opportunity for understanding the nuanced realities involved in putting into practice a 'non-aligned' foreign policy. The diversification in approaches to the global Cold War has included a renewed interest in states which pursued alternative foreign policies outside of the ideological and geopolitical divisions of the superpower-dominated world order. Among the most prominent of these was the contested and evolving concept of 'non-alignment'. In 1961, representatives of an array of mostly Third World states met in Belgrade, where they formed a loose association of states committed to remaining outside of the rival Cold War blocs. They avowed that 'peoples and Governments shall refrain from any use of ideologies for the purpose of waging cold war, exercising pressure, or imposing their will'. But non-alignment meant remaining neither equidistant from both superpower blocs or aloof from world affairs. Rather, it was a positive, constructive policy that aimed to empower Third World states in navigating a divided international order.[2]

As explained in Chapter 1, non-alignment was a key pillar of Nyerere's conception of Tanzania's foreign relations, which logically arose out of his commitments to self-determination and liberation. According to Nyerere's rationale, Tanzania could only preserve its newly won independence by refusing to enter into alliances with foreign powers or accept aid with political conditions attached. Adopting a non-aligned position would also allow Tanzania to trade widely and accept development aid from any nation, rather than restrict itself to arrangements with a particular Cold War bloc. But the complex and contradictory situations thrown up by the international order meant that espousing a non-aligned position on paper was far easier than translating it into actual policy. Following recent literature, this chapter seeks to cut through the hazy conference rhetoric of solidarity to

---

[2] Quoted in Westad, *Global Cold War*, 107.

understand non-alignment as it existed in practice.³ As Nyerere himself urged, '[a]ny real discussion of the "non-alignment" of Tanzania's foreign policy should therefore be based on an examination of what we do, more than what is said publicly'.⁴ We should also resist the temptation to see Third World states like Tanzania as 'playing off' the superpowers (or, in this case, the two German powers) against one another. To do so overlooks the constraints imposed on 'non-aligned' actors by global power imbalances, as well as setting the parameters of Third World foreign policymaking within the strictures of the Cold War.

The division of Germany after the Second World War was confirmed by the de jure creation of the Federal Republic and the GDR in 1949. The two states soon began a global struggle over the question of the international status of the GDR. Under the so-called Hallstein Doctrine, West Germany threatened to sever relations with any state that opened relations with the East. For both German states, the matter became a zero-sum game that structured their foreign policies: the GDR pressing for international recognition, the Federal Republic seeking to avoid exactly that.⁵ Frozen out in the West, the GDR saw the wave of decolonisation that swept over Africa as a fresh opportunity. The GDR's broader anti-imperial ideological world view, informed by the teachings of Marxism-Leninism, also propelled it into supporting independence struggles and socialist development in the Third World. The GDR's goal of establishing itself as a sovereign state therefore overlapped with anticolonial campaigns for self-determination.⁶ Its political and material support for African liberation movements

---

³ Lüthi, 'Non-Alignment'; Lüthi, 'Non-Aligned Movement'; Robert Vitalis, 'The Midnight Ride of Kwame Nkrumah and Other Fables of Bandung (Ban-Doong)', *Humanity*, 4 (2013), 261–88; Jeffrey James Byrne, 'Beyond Continents, Colours, and the Cold War: Yugoslavia, Algeria, and the Struggle for Non-Alignment', *International History Review*, 37 (2015), 912–32.
⁴ 'Principles and Development', in Nyerere, *Freedom and Socialism*, 195.
⁵ William Glenn Gray, *Germany's Cold War: The Global Campaign to Isolate East Germany, 1949–1969* (Chapel Hill: University of North Carolina Press, 2003); Werner Kilian, *Die Hallstein-Doktrin: Der Diplomatische Krieg zwischen der BRD und der DDR, 1955–1973* (Berlin: Duncker und Humblot, 2001); Young-Sun Hong, *Cold War Germany, the Third World, and the Global Humanitarian Regime* (New York: Cambridge University Press, 2015).
⁶ See George Bodie, 'Global GDR? Sovereignty, Legitimacy and Decolonization in the German Democratic Republic, 1960–1989', PhD diss. (University College London, 2019).

increased over the course of the 1960s, including to FRELIMO and the ANC. In stark contrast, West Germany maintained relations with Portugal and South Africa, clinging to the line that it separated out trade from politics. This was a major asset for East German propaganda in the Third World. The GDR portrayed itself as an anticolonial, anti-racist state committed to international cooperation in its own search for recognition, while painting the Federal Republic as a supporter of white minority rule that betrayed continuities with its imperialist and fascist past.[7]

In the early 1960s, the GDR went on a diplomatic offensive in Africa. Its early endeavours in the radical states of West Africa came tantalisingly close to success. In 1960, the Federal Republic required frantic efforts to prevent Guinea from recognising the GDR. The following year, an East German delegation to West Africa obtained promises from Ghana, Guinea, and Mali that their states would press the GDR's case at the upcoming Non-Aligned Conference in Yugoslavia. 'Everyone knows that there are two Germanies', argued Kwame Nkrumah in Belgrade. 'The nations of the world should therefore recognize the existence of these two States to ensure them to co-exist peacefully.' But amid the crisis over the construction of the Berlin Wall, the non-aligned states found no common position. The conference's final communique refrained from taking a firm stance on the 'German question' and simply called for a 'peaceful solution'.[8] Moreover, none of the GDR's supporters in Africa was willing to risk the consequences of recognition, with the explicit threat of severed relations with Bonn, the attendant loss of much-needed aid, and the

---

[7] For a clear articulation of this logic, see Sebastian Gehrig, 'Reaching Out to the Third World: East Germany's Anti-Apartheid and Socialist Human Rights Campaign', *German History*, 36 (2018), 574–97. On West German relations with Portugal and South Africa, see Rui Lopes, *West Germany and the Portuguese Dictatorship, 1968–1974: Between Cold War and Colonialism* (Basingstoke: Palgrave Macmillan, 2014); Tilman Dedering, '*Ostpolitik* and the Relations between West Germany and South Africa', in Carole Fink and Bernd Schaefer (eds.), *Ostpolitik, 1969–1974: European and Global Responses* (New York: Cambridge University Press, 2009), 206–31; Susanna Schrafstetter, 'A Nazi Diplomat Turned Apologist for Apartheid: Gustav Sonnenhol, *Vergangenheitsbewältigung* and West German Foreign Policy Towards South Africa', *German History*, 28 (2010), 44–66.

[8] Gray, *Germany's Cold War*, 107–115, 125–29. See also Lüthi, 'Non-Aligned Movement', 102–11; Amit Das Gupta, 'The Non-Aligned and the German Question', in Mišković et al. (eds.), *Non-Aligned Movement*, 143–60.

general opprobrium that it would bring from the West. Although several African states permitted the opening of GDR trade missions in their capitals, none chose to recognise it.

This chapter draws heavily on state archives located in today's reunified Germany. The collections of the now obsolete GDR include the records of its Ministry for Foreign Affairs (*Ministerium für Auswärtige Angelegenheiten*, MfAA) and the organs of the Socialist Unity Party of Germany, as well as documents from the intelligence services or 'Stasi'. West German records come mainly from the Foreign Office (*Auswärtiges Amt*), plus the archives of the Federal Ministry for Economic Cooperation and Development. As with all the 'Cold War' state archives used in this book, these documents reveal a particularly ideologically and geopolitically slanted view on Tanzanian affairs. However, they also exhibit an extraordinary preoccupation with the activities of the 'other' Germany in Dar es Salaam. Lengthy reports written by West and East German diplomats demonstrate ultrasensitive attitudes towards even the most minor movements of their rivals. They show that the German Cold War was an all-consuming struggle for its participants, which frequently obscured the real significance of local events. The GDR was afflicted by the Marxist-Leninist frameworks of analysis through which it interpreted and reported developments in Tanzania. The strict Marxist categories which it employed not only failed to capture the realities of socialist politics in Tanzania, but also misguided the GDR's responses to them. This became especially clear after the Arusha Declaration. But to find the origins of the 'German Cold War' in Dar es Salaam, we need to rewind back to 1964 and shift our focus to Zanzibar.

'One of the thorniest diplomatic problems in the modern world'

On 28 January 1964, two weeks after the Zanzibar Revolution, A. M. Babu became the first foreign minister of a non-communist state to recognise the GDR.[9] The move took the West Germans by surprise. Bonn had initially claimed that it would recognise the revolutionary government on the condition that no East German diplomatic mission was established in Zanzibar. Under the influence of the

---

[9] Quotation from 'Understanding Friends', editorial, *Nationalist*, 25 June 1964, 4.

hardline ambassador to Tanganyika, Herbert Schroeder, the West German cabinet announced that it would not countenance relations with a Zanzibari government that maintained them with the GDR. Meanwhile, large numbers of East German diplomats, aid workers, and intelligence officers began arriving in Zanzibar. In the context of the meagre returns on the GDR's search for recognition in the Third World, this was a major breakthrough for East Berlin.[10]

This triangular 'diplomacy of recognition' – *Anerkennungsdiplomatie* – was complicated further by the Tanganyika-Zanzibar union. Among the powers that Zanzibar relinquished to the mainland government was control over its foreign policy. Bonn, like its Western allies, therefore welcomed the union as an opportunity to reverse the GDR's recent success in Zanzibar. After all, Nyerere had previously shown no inclination to rock the diplomatic boat in extending recognition to East Germany. He anticipated no difficulties in relegating the GDR embassy in Zanzibar to the status of a trade mission in Dar es Salaam, similar to situations in other African states at the time. Zanzibari politicians had other intentions. The two prominent Marxists who had been appointed to the union government, Babu and Kassim Hanga, wanted to retain full relations with the GDR.[11] So did the president of Zanzibar, Abeid Karume, who told the East German ambassador that '[i]f Tanganyika was not prepared to recognise the GDR, then we would prefer to break the union'.[12] Conversely, 'moderates' within the union cabinet, like Paul Bomani and Austin Shaba, who had both been involved in negotiations for West German assistance, baulked at the prospect of upsetting a major donor.[13]

Nyerere was therefore left in a truly German *Zugzwang*, to borrow a term from chess: he was forced to take a decision in which any of the moves available would weaken his country's position vis-à-vis the status quo. To recognise the GDR would lead to a dispute with Bonn, which had been Tanganyika's third largest bilateral donor since

---

[10] On *Anerkennungsdiplomatie*, see Kilian, *Die Hallstein-Doktrin*, 171–214; Gray, *Germany's Cold War*, 155–57, 160–61, 178–79; Timothy Niblock, 'Aid and Foreign Policy in Tanzania, 1961–68', PhD diss. (University of Sussex, 1971), 215–63; Ulf Engel, '"I will not recognise East Germany just because Bonn is stupid". Anerkennungsdiplomatie in Tansania, 1964 bis 1965', in Ulrich van der Heyden and Franziska Benger (eds.), *Kalter Krieg in Ostafrika: Die Beziehungen der DDR zu Sansibar und Tansania* (Berlin: Lit Verlag, 2009), 9–30.
[11] Memcon (Phombeah), 29 July 1964, BA-B, SAPMO, DY 30/98130, 38–47.
[12] Kilian, *Die Hallstein-Doktrin*, 195.   [13] Pratt, *Critical Phase*, 140.

independence, as well as cast his non-aligned government as an associate of the Eastern Bloc. To refuse to do so would risk the future of the union with Zanzibar. Nyerere attempted to charter a middle course in offering the GDR a consulate in Zanzibar, which would have jurisdiction for the whole of Tanzania. But even this was rejected by Bonn. Meanwhile, Karume refused to close the GDR's embassy on the islands. He signed a 'Friendship Agreement' with the East German ambassador. This angered Nyerere. On 26 June, the TANU newspaper, the *Nationalist* claimed that it had 'evidence that the East Germans are attempting to destroy our Union in the interests of their own desires... Through intrigue and sharp practice they are trying to secure, through the Union, a diplomatic status in Africa which has up to now been denied them.'[14] The article came with Nyerere's blessing. The next day, Oscar Kambona, the union foreign minister, announced that all embassies in Zanzibar were to be downgraded to consulates by the end of June. But even after the deadline passed, the East Germans continued to operate a de facto embassy in Zanzibar. Nyerere sought time for the situation to cool. Bonn agreed, and the dispute was placed on ice until the new year.

The impasse was ultimately resolved on 19 February 1965, when the Tanzanian government announced that the GDR would be permitted to open a low-level consulate-general in Dar es Salaam, provided it downgraded its Zanzibar embassy to a consulate. Tanzania explicitly stated that this did *not* constitute diplomatic recognition. Five days later, Bonn responded by cancelling military assistance for Tanzania, where West Germany had been providing training for the air force. Nyerere's response was even stronger. Angered by what he regarded as Bonn's attempts to manipulate his foreign policy through economic pressure, Nyerere announced that Tanzania would forgo all forms of aid from West Germany, worth around $32.5 million. On 16 March, the West German cabinet cancelled all outstanding capital assistance to Tanzania.[15] As Nyerere later reflected, 'we had to choose whether to become a puppet state of Germany in return for any charity she cared to give us'.[16] Or, as he put it in a letter to other African heads of

---

[14] 'Were We Wrong?', editorial, *Nationalist*, 26 June 1964, 4. Zanzibar responded by banning the *Nationalist*.
[15] This covered only federal aid and so exempted assistance from the churches, state governments, and volunteer organisations.
[16] 'Principles and Development', in Nyerere, *Freedom and Socialism*, 190.

state, the decision was 'a rather absurd way of demonstrating that our foreign and diplomatic position has nothing to do with aid'.[17] In private conversation with the UN secretary-general's personal representative, Nyerere said that the experience would make the government 'doubtful' about accepting aid 'from a country that is prone to playing the cold war game'.[18] The episode, together with the diplomatic run-ins with Britain and the United States explained in Chapter 1, shaped Nyerere's evolving world view. The West German threat demonstrated the need for greater economic independence. It helped pave the way to the Arusha Declaration and the notion of self-reliance.

The outcome of *Anerkennungsdiplomatie* left all three participant states in varying degrees of dissatisfaction. The GDR now had half a diplomatic loaf in East Africa, where little more than a year earlier it had none, but not quite the prized embassy it had held briefly in Zanzibar. It had also been accused of meddling in the internal affairs of a sovereign state. The Federal Republic had averted the establishment of a full East German embassy in Tanzania, but the episode had exposed chinks in the armour of the Hallstein Doctrine. It also projected the image throughout the Third World of Bonn as an uncompromising power, preoccupied with playing Cold War games rather than supporting poor post-colonies. Nyerere's bold diplomacy earned Tanzania the moral high ground, but at considerable financial cost. He immediately tried to mend fences in Bonn, although he found the West German government resolutely opposed to renewing capital aid. To many Western eyes, Tanzania confirmed its reputation as a bastion of communist subversion in Africa. Perhaps the biggest winner was Bonn's and East Berlin's mutual Chinese rival, which seized on Nyerere's gesture for propaganda capital. 'Naturally a proud people prefer lean liberty to fat slavery', remarked the *Peking Review*.[19]

The diplomatic struggle between the two German states did not end with the establishment of the GDR's consulate general. Instead, the unsatisfactory resolution to the crisis localised the German Cold War in Dar es Salaam, as the one African city in which both states had some form of diplomatic representation. The GDR was by far the more active. Frozen out at the diplomatic level, it launched an *Öffentlichkeitsarbeit*

[17] Quoted in Pratt, *Critical Phase*, 141.
[18] Ivan Smith to Thant, 13 April 1965, Ivan Smith Papers, BL, MSS Eng. c. 6466, 171.
[19] 'Lean Liberty and Fat Slavery', *Peking Review*, 19 March 1965, 21.

('publicity work') campaign, led by its consul-general, Gottfried Lessing.[20] This targeted ministers and officials who were known or likely sympathisers to Eastern European socialism. These included Babu and Hanga, whose Marxist proclivities were well established. Kambona had visited the GDR in 1962 as part of what the East Germans described as a scheme to establish 'good working relations' between 'progressive forces in East Africa' and 'Communist parties in socialist countries'.[21] He became another regular GDR contact-point among the TANU leadership. The GDR also found sympathy among the radical staff at the party newspapers, some of whom socialised at the Palm Beach Hotel, a short walk from the consulate-general. The *Nationalist* occasionally attacked the West German press over its negative coverage of Tanzanian affairs.[22] In November 1965, it reproduced an article from *Christ und Welt* which portrayed Dar es Salaam as a centre of extremism and regional destabilisation. This was accompanied by an editorial which alleged that 'this campaign seeks to discredit German friends of Tanzania [i.e., the GDR] by suggesting that they are unpatriotic, uninterested in German unity, and pro-Communist'.[23]

Despite the small size of the consulate-general, the GDR ran an intense programme of print propaganda.[24] A recurrent theme was the connection, often exaggerated, between West Germany and Tanzania's principal adversaries, Portugal and South Africa. GDR bulletins,

---

[20] Lessing's fascinating career deserves a biographical sidenote. Born in St Petersburg in 1914 of partial Jewish descent, he fled from Nazi Germany to Britain in 1938 and then moved to Rhodesia during the war. There, he worked as a lawyer, co-founded the Southern Rhodesian Communist Party, and was briefly married to the author Doris Lessing. In 1950, he relocated to the GDR and served in various government positions, including as trade representative to Indonesia. From 1962, Lessing worked as the head of MfAA's Africa Section before taking up his position as consul-general in Tanzania in 1965. He was killed in violence during the Uganda-Tanzania war in 1979, while serving as the GDR's ambassador to Kampala. See 'Lessing, Gottfried', in Helmut Müller-Enbergs, Jan Wielgohs, and Dieter Hoffmann (eds.), *Wer war wer in der DDR? Ein biographisches Lexikon* (Berlin: Ch. Links Verlag, 2000), 520.

[21] Foreign Policy and International Relations Division, SED, 16 April 1962, BA-B, SAPMO, DY 30/98129, 7–9.

[22] 'What Enemies Say', *Nationalist*, 18 October 1965, 4.

[23] 'How German Press Spreads Evil against Tanzania' and 'An Evil Intention', editorial, *Nationalist*, 8 November 1965, 4.

[24] George Roberts, 'Press, Propaganda and the German Democratic Republic's Search for Recognition in Tanzania, 1964–72', in Philip Muehlenbeck and Natalia Telepneva (eds.), *Warsaw Pact Intervention in the Third World: Aid and Influence in the Cold War* (London: IB Tauris, 2018), 152–53.

brochures, and newspaper inserts claimed these relationships as evidence that West Germany had not escaped from its own colonial and fascist past. In an appeal to local sensibilities, this propaganda also highlighted the violence perpetrated by German colonialism in Tanganyika.[25] Bonn lamented the greater resources which the GDR pumped into this publicity work. After visiting Tanzania, a federal minister expressed his concern at the 'well-produced' handouts distributed by the East Germans and Bonn's incapability of mounting a comparable operation.[26] But the dark arts of propaganda could also backfire. In December 1965, the West German embassy complained to the Tanzanian government about the circulation of the so-called *Braunbuch*, which listed prominent West German politicians and officials who had associations with the Nazi regime. After Nyerere banned the book, Lessing was hauled before the Tanzanian authorities and severely reprimanded. Shortly afterwards, the Ministry of Foreign Affairs issued a circular prohibiting attacks on third-party states in Tanzania. 'We will have to be more cautious and reserved from now on', wrote an East German diplomat, tellingly.[27]

For all this publicity work, the GDR made little progress in Tanzania during the two years after the opening of the consulate-general. Its aid remained concentrated in Zanzibar, but it understood that full recognition could only come about through negotiation with the more circumspect union government. Talks in late 1965 over long-term aid, technical assistance, and trade agreements gave little encouragement.[28] In March 1966, the GDR tabled an aid package worth £600,000 to Tanzania, one-third in 'humanitarian relief' for homeless people, the rest in an interest-free loan. Despite divisions in cabinet, Tanzania rejected the offer, holding out hope of future aid from Bonn.[29] At the turn of 1967, a Stasi report observed that the Federal Republic's hard-line policy had been ultimately successful. No other African states had since established official ties of any sort with the GDR. Meanwhile, Bonn had been 'gradually and quietly improving its

---

[25] Hong, *Cold War Germany*, 290–94.
[26] Leber to Brandt, 21 March 1967, PAAA, NA 6408.
[27] Roberts, 'Press', 153–54.
[28] Helmut Matthes, 'Zur Entwicklung außenpolitischer Grundlagen der Beziehungen zwischen der Deutschen Demokratischen Republik und der Vereinigten Republik Tansania bis Mitte der siebziger Jahre', in van der Heyden and Benger (eds.), *Kalter Krieg*, 73.
[29] Kilian, *Die Hallstein-Doktrin*, 219.

relations with Tanzania'.³⁰ More generally, the Eastern Bloc looked at China's growing importance in Tanzania with concern. For the GDR, the situation on the eve of the Arusha Declaration was gloomy.

The Arusha Declaration and the Eastern Bloc

The events of 1967 provided the GDR with new hope, while also exposing the shortcomings of its political and ideological approach in Tanzania. As we saw in the previous chapter, Western observers in Dar es Salaam received the Arusha Declaration with alarm. In contrast, the Soviet Union and its allies responded with quiet optimism. The document's idea of African socialism may not have been congruent with Marxist doctrine, but they welcomed its revolutionary intent all the same. On the basis of flawed ideological assumptions, the GDR sensed an opportunity and intensified its publicity work in Dar es Salaam. However, this led them into the bitter post-Arusha disputes among the Tanzanian elite. Guided by rigid Marxist-Leninist assumptions, GDR diplomats attempted to strengthen their influence among what they believed to be the Tanzanian 'left'. The result was that East Germany's reputation in the eyes of Nyerere was sullied further still.

The Eastern European socialists greeted the Arusha Declaration as an opportunity for increasing their limited foothold in Tanzania.³¹ The East Africa specialist at the Soviet Ministry of Foreign Affairs told Lessing that after the Arusha Declaration, the Warsaw Pact states had to 'strengthen their cooperation with Tanzania, in order to encourage progressive development and to counter the influence of China'.³² The Stasi believed that encounters with the leaders of Guinea, Mali, and the United Arab Republic had all been influential in shaping Nyerere's turn to socialist revolution. It presented the Arusha Declaration as the continued effect of events in Zanzibar three years earlier. 'The fact is that without the existence of the Zanzibar Revolution, the present developments on the mainland would have been unthinkable.'³³ This 'diffusionist' understanding of developments in the region ironically shared much ground with the hyperbole about communist encroachment that characterised the Western responses to Arusha. It was hopelessly wide of the

[30] 'Uschi', 13 January 1967, BStU, MfS, HV A, no. 221, 438–39.
[31] 'Tanzania: Soviet Views on the Arusha Programme', *Mizan*, 9 (1967), 197–201.
[32] Lessing, 24 February 1967, PAAA, MfAA, M3, 136, 1–8.
[33] 'Oskar', 25 February 1968, BStU, MfS, HV A, no. 222, 318–23.

mark: the Arusha Declaration had a totally different ideologically trajectory from the Marxism and racialism of the Zanzibar Revolution. Nonetheless, the GDR responded to these rays of hope by increasing its publicity work in Dar es Salaam. The ADN, the East German news agency, introduced a new Swahili-language bulletin. It also provided Tanzanian bureaucrats with copies of articles from the West German press which were critical of the Arusha Declaration.[34]

More importantly, the GDR consulate-general intensified efforts to forge links with 'progressive politicians' in Tanzania. It singled out Babu, Hanga, and Kambona.[35] Throughout the first half of 1967, East German diplomats held a series of meetings with these individuals, as they attempted to establish the shifting power dynamics in the post-Arusha landscape.[36] Even after Kambona's resignation from government in June, GDR officials continued to consult him on fast-moving developments. Kambona explained that Tanzania was heading to the 'right'. He cited the retention of 'reactionaries' in key positions in the government as evidence. Such descriptions tallied with the GDR's own ideological outlook.[37] This 'contact work' with the likes of Kambona proved to be a major misjudgement. As the previous chapter established, the Arusha Declaration opened up a number of rifts among the Tanzanian political elite, which did not split along the 'left-right' political spectrum through which the GDR interpreted events. The ideological readings of East German diplomats led them to cooperate with politicians whose influence waned after Arusha: at best, they were marginalised; at worse, they became pariahs.

For Kambona, the GDR also offered a potential means of extricating himself from his dispute with Nyerere. Shortly after the reshuffle, Kambona sought to engineer an invitation to East Germany. He did so via his close ally, Dennis Phombeah, a civil servant and the GDR's key contact in Tanzania, as well as sometime Czechoslovakian intelligence informer.[38] At an international trade meeting in Geneva, Phombeah

---

[34] Fischer to Press Division, MfAA, 6 April 1967, BA-B, SAPMO, DY 30/98143, 121.
[35] Lessing to Kiesewetter, 14 February 1967, BA-B, SAPMO, DY 30/98143, 58–59.
[36] Lessing to Kiesewetter, 27 February 1967, BA-B, SAPMO, DY 30/98143, 94–97.
[37] Fischer to Kiesewetter, Kern, Schüssler, 4 July 1967, BA-B, SAPMO, DY 30/98143, 160–62.
[38] James R. Brennan, 'The Secret Lives of Dennis Phombeah: Decolonization, the Cold War, and African Political Intelligence, 1953–1974', *International History Review*, 43 (2021), 153–69.

approached a representative of the East German delegation. He said that Kambona had resigned from his government and party positions after major disagreements with Nyerere, particularly over Hanga's departure from government. Phombeah asked whether the GDR might be able to provide Kambona with an excuse to travel to East Germany, perhaps for further medical treatment or a 'study visit'.[39] East Berlin told the consulate-general in Dar es Salaam that this would not be possible.[40] The GDR seemed to have already realised that it had backed the wrong horses in Tanzania.

Too late, the East Germans began to question their post-Arusha strategy of consolidating their ties with a 'progressive' faction of the Tanzanian political elite. 'This contact work could at the present time be used by right-wing forces and the West Germans against the position of the GDR', noted a MfAA report, which also questioned Kambona's motives and trustworthiness. East Berlin therefore instructed the consulate-general to break off all contact with the 'Kambona group'.[41] Yet even after Kambona's flight into exile, the GDR did not cut all ties with his associates. For example, on 27 July, an East German diplomat met Oscar's brother, Otini, for dinner at the Palm Beach Hotel.[42] The acrimonious war of words between Nyerere and the exiled Kambona left the GDR in no doubt that continued contact of this type was dangerous. By October, the GDR seemed to have learned its lessons, when it blocked an attempt by Hanga and Kambona to fly to East Berlin. The pair had been in Conakry and obtained tickets from Air Guinée to return to London via the GDR. However, the East Germans intervened to amend their tickets. When Kambona and Hanga changed aeroplanes in Algiers, they found they had been rerouted to London via Paris instead. But by this point the damage to the GDR's reputation had already been done.[43] Kambona and Phombeah were in exile; within days of his ill-fated return to Tanzania in December, Hanga was in prison.

Nyerere's opinion of the GDR had never been high. East Germany's attempts to cut deals directly with the Zanzibari authorities at the height of the crisis over recognition in 1964 had already drawn the

[39] Rose to Scholz, 16 June 1967, PAAA, MfAA, M1, C1469/72, 13–15.
[40] Fritsch to Rose, 5 July 1967, PAAA, MfAA, M1, C1469/72, 12.
[41] Africa Division, 10 July 1967, PAAA, MfAA, M1, C763/74, 16–24.
[42] Uhlig, 1 August 1967, BA-B, SAPMO, DY 30/98143, 178–81.
[43] Hückel, 25 October 1967, PAAA, MfAA, M1, C1469/72, 1–2.

president's wrath. He was wary about reports of the GDR's subversive activities elsewhere in Africa. In 1966, after the coup in Accra, it was revealed that Ghanaian intelligence officers were being trained at a special school by the Stasi. Nyerere responded by reducing the number of employees at the consulate-general in Dar es Salaam from ten to six.[44] The GDR's shadowy relations with Kambona and Hanga during the unrest of 1967 confirmed these doubts. So, too, did further suspicions that the GDR was spreading rumours to smear West Germany's supporters in Tanzania. In December, a leaflet signed by the 'Revolutionary Committee of the TANU Youth League' alleged that '[i]mperialists and bootlickers have formed a perfidious conspiracy to divert our nation from its socialist way'. It accused Austin Shaba, the minister of housing, of working for the CIA.[45] Shaba was among the most pro-West German members of cabinet. An official at the Ministry of Foreign Affairs told the American ambassador that Nyerere thought that the GDR was behind the flyer, which was denounced in the Tanzanian press.[46] At the time, these doubts only reached the GDR through murmurs in Dar es Salaam. It was not until 1970, when confronted with the GDR's foreign minister's desperate appeals for diplomatic recognition, that Nyerere brought up the issue. He accused the East Germans of 'meddling' in Tanzanian affairs in 1967, by talking to 'disloyal MPs and other officials' in order to encourage them to do 'stupid things'.[47]

The GDR's mistakes in Tanzania were more than just a series of blunders. They were the product of the inflexible Marxist-Leninist framework through which the East Germans interpreted politics in the country. As explained in the previous chapter, Tanzanian politics in the time of *ujamaa* did not fit neatly into the left-right Cold War grids favoured by foreign observers. The language of scientific socialism induced East German officials to force Tanzanian politicians into pigeonholes which did not reflect their ideological leanings and flattened out all manner of personal disagreements. This problem affected Western diplomats' understandings of Tanzanian affairs too, but their

---

[44] Gray, *Germany's Cold War*, 189.
[45] Enclosed in Burns to State Dept, 7 December 1967, NARA, RG 59, CFPF 1967–69, Box 151, CSM TANZAN.
[46] Memcon (Nyakyi, Pickering), 27 December 1967, NARA RG 59, CFPF 1967–69, POL TANZAN-US.
[47] Memcon (Nyerere, Winzer), 10 April 1970, PAAA, MfAA, M1, C779/75, 12–23. Nyerere referred to 'some of your officials', hinting that he meant junior diplomats, rather than the senior consul general, Lessing.

approach was more tolerant than their Eastern counterparts. Tanzanians were adept at touching the correct ideological buttons here: both Phombeah and Kambona told GDR diplomats that the 'right' had gained ground after the Arusha Declaration.[48] Reflecting back on events, an East German news agency correspondent identified that Lessing's reliance on 'Kambona and other "left" forces proved quite detrimental'.[49]

If at first glance the Arusha Declaration represented grounds for optimism for the GDR, by the end of 1967 its outlook in Tanzania was more negative. An East German report coldly concluded that Tanzania's 'conception of socialism does not comply with modern science' and so 'will not lead to the construction of socialist society'.[50] Yet, pessimistic though this forecast was, the GDR still regarded Tanzania as a 'key point' in its foreign policy towards sub-Saharan Africa.[51] After all, its primary task was not to help build a Marxist-Leninist state, but to gain diplomatic recognition. Prospects looked better for the West, including the Federal Republic. Nyerere emphasised that Tanzania still remained receptive to offers of aid, provided they came without strings attached. He stressed that 'self-reliance and socialism' did not mean severing aid relationships with any potential partner, including in the West. 'Tanzania has not said it does not want international assistance', clarified Nyerere, pointing to the example of the railway to Zambia. 'Overseas capital will also be welcome for any project where it can make our own efforts more effective – where it acts as a catalyst for Tanzanian activity.'[52] Ultimately, West Germany rather than East Germany emerged the stronger in this new stage in Tanzania's postcolonial history.

Ostpolitik in Afrika

While Tanzania experienced the internal transformations of the Arusha Declaration, West German foreign policy was also going through

---

[48] Rose to Scholz, 16 June 1967, PAAA, MfAA, M1, C1469/72, 13–15; Fischer to Kiesewetter, Kern, Schüssler, 4 July 1967, BA-B, SAPMO, DY 30/98143, 160–62.
[49] Peter Spacek, 'Die Anfänge in Sansibar und in Dar es Salaam', in van der Heyden and Benger (eds.), *Kalter Krieg*, 177.
[50] Africa Division, 5 January 1968, BA-B, SAPMO, DY 30/98137, 1–27.
[51] Africa Division, 11 April 1968, PAAA, MfAA, M1, C751/74, 10–36.
[52] 'The Purpose Is Man', in Nyerere, *Freedom and Socialism*, 322.

something of a revolution. In December 1966, the Christian Democratic Union (CDU) and the German Social Democratic Party (SPD) formed a 'grand coalition' government in Bonn, led by the CDU's Kurt Georg Kiesinger. Willy Brandt, the chairman of the SPD, was appointed foreign minister. His entry into government prefigured a major rethinking in West Germany's relations with Eastern Europe, which had overspill effects on its policy towards the Third World.

As mayor of Berlin since 1957, Brandt had long sought a way out of the Cold War impasse that divided his city and country. He sensed a grassroots desire for a fresh approach to foreign policy – a 'New Eastern Policy', or *Neue Ostpolitik*. Rather than isolate the communist regimes, Brandt wanted to reach out to Eastern Europe, building connections through trade negotiations and cultural exchanges across the Cold War divide. In a Europe stalemated by nuclear stand-off, Brandt believed that opening dialogue with communist societies would spread Western consumerism and liberal values to the East. In the short-to-medium term, this would lead to improved relations with the Warsaw Pact states and a *modus vivendi* with the GDR. In the long term, it might even pave the way for German reunification. The policy was encapsulated in the words of Egon Bahr, Brandt's close associate: 'change through rapprochement'.[53]

The historiography on Brandt's *Ostpolitik* overwhelmingly focuses on its European elaboration at the centre of the Cold War. Yet, as Sara Lorenzini acknowledges, *Ostpolitik* had much broader implications for West German foreign policy.[54] Bonn's decisions to establish relations with Romania in January 1967 and Yugoslavia in January 1968 were key steps in Brandt's initiative. But they contradicted the core principle of the Hallstein Doctrine, which hitherto had governed West Germany's foreign relations (even if, as the Tanzanian example demonstrated, it was scarcely watertight). This global dimension to *Ostpolitik* was problematic for West Germany: in the light of the agreements with Bucharest and Belgrade, other states might be tempted to recognise the GDR, with less fear of repercussions from Bonn. West German policymakers believed that this would weaken their

---

[53] The literature on *Ostpolitik* is vast. Among recent English-language work, see Gottfried Niedhart, 'Ostpolitik: Transformation Through Communication and the Quest for Peaceful Change', *Journal of Cold War Studies*, 18 (2016), 14–59.
[54] Sara Lorenzini, 'Globalising Ostpolitik', *Cold War History*, 9 (2009), 223–42; see also Fink and Schaefer (eds.), *Ostpolitik*.

bargaining position in Europe, since the GDR would be less prepared to make concessions to Bonn if international recognition was already forthcoming across the Third World.[55]

Neue Ostpolitik was paralleled by a shift in West Germany's *Afrikapolitik*. This was laid out by Brandt at a conference of West German ambassadors to sub-Saharan Africa held in early 1968 in Abidjan, Ivory Coast. There, as Lorenzini notes, 'the clash between the old thinking of the diplomatic establishment and the more open attitude of the new political leadership became manifest'. Brandt told the meeting that the priority of West Germany's relations in Africa was to drum up support for its stance on the German question. This, as such, was nothing new. But now it was to be linked to development assistance and West Germany's revamped image of an outward-looking social democratic welfare state. Brandt did not mention the Hallstein Doctrine. In contrast, a senior official at the Auswärtiges Amt restated West Germany's commitment to the Hallstein Doctrine and claimed that Bonn's policy towards Tanzania had been a success.[56] His line was characteristic of the Auswärtiges Amt's conservative approach to foreign policymaking in the late 1960s, which maintained an over-riding concern for European Cold War geopolitics and a scepticism towards Africa.[57]

In these circumstances, the appointment of a new West German ambassador to Dar es Salaam in October 1967 gave Bonn's approach to Tanzania a shot in the arm. Norbert Hebich was much more relaxed than his predecessor, who had overseen the crisis of 1965. Hebich told the Soviet ambassador that he accepted the existence of two German states and believed that the Hallstein Doctrine was unsustainable.[58] In December, he set out the case for bringing Tanzania in from the cold to the Auswärtiges Amt. Hebich expressed concern at East Germany's expanding presence in the country at the same time as more West German technical experts were being withdrawn. He noted that given the questions he was receiving about the Hallstein Doctrine, the Tanzanians had noticed the 'new orientation of our *Ostpolitik*'. Just as Yugoslavia was considered a special case in the communist world, he

---

[55] Gray, *Germany's Cold War*, 199–201.
[56] Lorenzini, 'Globalising Ostpolitik', 228–29.
[57] Schrafstetter, 'Nazi Diplomat'; Lopes, *West Germany*.
[58] Lessing to Kiesewetter, 14 October 1967, BA-B, SAPMO, DY 30/98143, 275–76.

argued, so Tanzania should be treated as such in Africa. He recommended a 'broad-minded policy towards Tanzania', to provide 'greater freedom of manoeuvre to defend our interests than the present insistence on barely tenable standpoints'.[59] Similar views could be found in the West German press. The *Frankfurter Allgemeine Zeitung* argued that there was little to be gained by 'crying over spilt milk'. It suggested that the change in ambassador was an opportunity for improving relations with Tanzania.[60]

However, the Auswärtiges Amt remained implacable in its stance towards Tanzania. In March 1968, it prepared a lengthy report on relations with Tanzania in response to a request made by Kai-Uwe von Hassel, the federal minister for expellees. Von Hassel had a personal interest in the matter: he had been born in Tanganyika in 1913 and then returned there to work as a businessman between the wars.[61] During the crisis of early 1965, von Hassel had spoken out in cabinet against imposing sanctions on Tanzania.[62] However, the Auswärtiges Amt proved unsympathetic. New capital aid for Tanzania would come at the expense of states which had greater respect for West German interests, it argued. Tanzanian policy was increasingly anti-Western and the country was becoming a 'military bastion for Red China'. It did nothing to stop the GDR's campaign against West Germany. Moreover, providing new capital aid to Tanzania would encourage other African countries to institutionalise contact with the GDR. There was therefore to be no immediate rapprochement with Tanzania.[63] Cold War concerns about Tanzania's orientation towards the socialist world and memories of 1965 prevented the Auswärtiges Amt from recommending the more conciliatory approach advised by Hebich. This changed as Brandt's *Ostpolitik* gathered momentum.

On the Tanzanian side, *Ostpolitik* appeared to represent a fresh opportunity to revive its relationship with West Germany. Ever since the crisis of 1965 Nyerere had sought to mitigate his damaged relationship with Bonn, albeit without much success. As argued earlier, he had

---

[59] Hebich to Auswärtiges Amt, 8 December 1967, PAAA, NA 6408.
[60] Herbert Kaufmann, 'Worüber zwischen Bonn und Tansania gesprochen werden könnte', *Frankfurter Allgemeine Zeitung*, 8 December 1967, 2.
[61] Britta Schilling, *Postcolonial Germany: Memories of Empire in a Decolonized Nation* (Oxford: Oxford University Press, 2014), 113–14.
[62] Engel, '"I will not recognise"', 24.
[63] Wever, 8 March 1968, PAAA, NA 6408.

also emphasised after the Arusha Declaration that Tanzania still welcomed no-strings-attached foreign aid. This becomes clear from encounters between senior Tanzanian politicians and Yugoslav officials. The Yugoslav ambassador reported to East German colleagues that he had pressed the GDR's case to the Tanzanian government. The second vice-president, Rashidi Kawawa, responded by stating that recognition was a pragmatic rather than an ideological question, as Tanzania wished to investigate economic cooperation with West Germany.[64] The external pressures placed upon Tanzania also contributed to this pragmatic position. On a visit to Belgrade in April 1968, Amir Jamal, the minister for finance, stressed to his Yugoslav hosts that a 'certain amount of frank talking was necessary'. Referring to Rhodesia and Portugal, Jamal drew attention to 'the geopolitical circumstances of our country' and 'the hostilities surrounding us', in asking for a degree of flexibility in straying from stringent non-alignment in economic matters.[65] Senior figures within the government felt that having taken on the burden of supporting Africa's liberation movements, Tanzania required some leeway in developing a non-aligned foreign policy. This included accepting aid from states that continued to work with the white minority regimes, like West Germany. Indeed, just prior to his visit to Belgrade, Jamal had discussed the implications of Bonn's renewed relations with Yugoslavia and Romania with Hebich, the West German ambassador. Jamal also raised the possibility of a visit to Bonn. In the new conditions created by *Ostpolitik*, the relationship between Tanzania and West Germany was beginning to thaw.[66]

'No recognition by the backdoor': The GDR's Travails in Tanzania

As Tanzania put out feelers to West Germany, the GDR continued to struggle for a diplomatic breakthrough. A belief that the recalibration involved in *Ostpolitik* might open up the possibility of Tanzanian recognition proved ill-founded. Instead, it experienced a series of

---

[64] Lessing, 17 October 1967, PAAA, MfAA, M1, C1467/72, 56–63.
[65] 'Resume of the Minister of Finance's Visit to Yugoslavia and Attendance in the Consultative Group Meetings in Paris', n.d. [April 1968], NRC, PMO, Box 312, T3/42, 4A.
[66] Hebich, 5 March 1968, PAAA, NA, 6408.

public relations disasters in the aftermath of further propaganda scandals and then the fallout from events in Czechoslovakia. This came against the backdrop of China's perceived rising influence in Dar es Salaam. The Tanzanian response to this nadir in its relations with the GDR is instructive: it sought to reassure the Eastern Bloc that it remained true to its non-aligned credentials, but this rapprochement fell short of the recognition of the GDR. Despite the GDR's support for African liberation movements, Nyerere calculated he had nothing to gain from its recognition, especially as *Ostpolitik* provided opportunities to re-engage with Bonn.

The Soviet Union and the GDR initially reacted to Brandt's *Ostpolitik* with concern. In the short-term, East Berlin believed that Bonn wanted to bypass and thereby isolate the GDR from its allies. Taking a longer-term perspective, the East German leadership also worried about the integrity of the communist bloc should Brandt succeed in opening up perforations in the Berlin Wall. After Romania opened relations with West Germany in January 1967, Eastern Bloc leaders gathered in Warsaw, where they adopted a common position in order to prevent any repetition. Moscow sent a memorandum to selected non-aligned leaders, including Nyerere, warning them of the 'neocolonial' nature of the Hallstein Doctrine, which was 'an expression of great power policy', in the same mould of Second Reich imperialism and Third Reich fascism. It called on the memorandum's recipients to recognise the GDR, without success.[67]

Navigating the implications of *Ostpolitik* became part of the GDR's routine diplomacy and publicity work in Dar es Salaam. Lessing reported that there seemed to have been a 'rethinking process' and 'change in tactics' in Bonn's policy in Tanzania.[68] The GDR noted an intensification in West German propaganda activity, including the launch of a Swahili-language news bulletin.[69] On the one hand, this posed a danger to the GDR. The consulate-general highlighted West Germany's practice of 'bridge-building', by which Hebich cultivated ties with Bulgarian, Czechoslovakian, Hungarian, and Polish diplomats in an attempt to isolate the GDR. On the other hand, the thaw in Bonn's relations with Eastern Europe provided the GDR with

---

[67] Gray, *Germany's Cold War*, 200–201.
[68] Lessing to Kiesewetter, 12 February 1968, BA-B, SAPMO, DY 30/98136, 428–34.
[69] Zielke to Fischer, 5 June 1968, BA-B, SAPMO, DY 30/98136, 441–44.

precedents which lent themselves to the argument that the Hallstein Doctrine no longer applied. A senior Tanzanian bureaucrat told Lessing in September 1967 that the West German government 'only formally maintains the Hallstein Doctrine and no longer believes in it'.[70] The GDR sought to capitalise on this perceived openness in Tanzanian attitudes. In early 1968, it used the example of Yugoslavia in both printed material and meetings with Tanzanian officials to make the case for recognition.[71] However, Nyerere seemed more interested in taking advantage of re-engaging with Bonn than using the relaxation of the 'German question' to strengthen relations with East Berlin.

Just as these openings offered the GDR a glimmer of hope, its standing in Tanzania suffered further blows. In mid-1968, the appearance of several anonymous pamphlets in Dar es Salaam stirred up minor controversy. The first, entitled 'Outlook from the Pamirs', contained a vicious assault on China. It claimed that Beijing planned to build an 'Asiatic Reich' and described Mao as a 'Socialist Genghis Khan'. Two Swahili tracts followed: one criticised government policy, the other was a scurrilous personal attack on Nyerere. Owing to its reputation, suspicion for this 'black literature' immediately fell on the GDR. An editorial in the *Nationalist* warned the Eastern Bloc against interfering in Tanzanian affairs. 'We did not fight against the Western colonialists to become the playthings of any Eastern country', it stated. Diplomats of all Cold War stripes felt it was written by Nyerere himself and addressed to East Germany.[72] This reflected the president's general dissatisfaction with East German propaganda, both overt and covert. When Hebich, the West German ambassador, complained about the content of the GDR's news bulletins, Nyerere did not hide his displeasure. He thought that East German propaganda was counterproductive: it was 'slapping itself in the face' and 'showing its inferiority complex'.[73]

Nyerere's disdain for the GDR went beyond just its propaganda activities. He was a firm supporter of German reunification, acknowledging that the country had been split in two by Cold War politics. As

---

[70] GDR consulate-general, Dar es Salaam, 14 November 1967, BA-B, SAPMO, DY 30/98136, 409–23.
[71] Lessing to Kiesewetter, 11 March 1968, BA-B, SAPMO, DY 30/98143, 431–35; Lessing, 3 April 1968, BA-B, SAPMO, DY 30/98143, 439–42.
[72] Roberts, 'Press', 159.
[73] Hebich to Auswärtiges Amt, 6 July 1968, PAAA, NA 6408.

early as December 1964, in the midst of the *Anerkennungsdiplomatie* saga, Nyerere compared the union between the previously divided peoples of Tanganyika and Zanzibar with the German situation. He told a rally in Dar es Salaam that 'when people cross the [Berlin] Wall to rejoin their brethren on the other side of the wall, they rejoice'.[74] Tanzania's ambassador to Bonn recalled similar sentiments. 'We were the United Republic of Tanzania', he said. 'So as a country which seeks to unite its people, we had every sympathy for [*Ostpolitik*]. That's why we welcomed the efforts of Willy Brandt.'[75] But this went hand in hand with a more negative view of the GDR. Nyerere believed that East Germany was fundamentally an illegitimate state. In July 1968, Nyerere told Hebich, that the East German government did not represent the people of the 'Zone' and was merely a Soviet puppet. In August, he drew a comparison between the GDR and the situation in South Korea or South Vietnam. Whereas the latter two countries were dependent on American support yet could at least claim to govern their own territory, he told Kai-Uwe von Hassel, the GDR was simply under Soviet occupation.[76]

The GDR's reputation in Tanzania was therefore already at a low when, on the morning of 21 August, news reached Dar es Salaam that a Soviet-led invasion of Czechoslovakia had brought a swift end to the reformist socialism of the 'Prague Spring'. Among African states, Tanzania was especially vocal in its condemnation.[77] Editorials screamed outrage and a demonstration led by university students ended with stones being thrown at the Soviet embassy. The Warsaw Pact states were accused of betraying the causes of international socialism and anti-imperialism. For the GDR, which flaunted its commitment to self-determination via its support for Third World liberation movements, this was a bitter blow. From an East German angle, the invasion also undermined its claims to be an advocate for self-determination. As Nyerere later pointed out to the West Germans, events in Czechoslovakia showed the narrow limits of freedom for the nominally sovereign states of the Eastern Bloc.[78]

---

[74] 'President's Speech at the 1964 Republic Day Rally', 10 December 1964, enclosed in NAN, 2.05.253/254.
[75] Interview with Anthony Nyakyi, Masaki, Dar es Salaam, 28 July 2015.
[76] Von Hassel to Kiesinger, 9 September 1968, BA-K, B136/3001.
[77] The Tanzanian reaction to the invasion is considered in detail in Chapter 5.
[78] Extracts from report on Eppler's visit to Tanzania and Kenya, April 1970, enclosed in BA-K, B213/7673.

However, this defiant Tanzanian response to the invasion of Czechoslovakia also posed a public relations problem for Nyerere. These frictions with the Eastern Bloc came at a time when Tanzania's non-aligned credentials were being questioned due to its close relationship with China. The conclusion of the TAZARA railway agreement was only the most eye-catching of a plethora of Sino-Tanzanian initiatives. In February 1969, the Tanzanian government decided that, on the expiration of arrangements with Canada, it would accept military aid from Beijing alone.[79] Nyerere therefore tried to dampen talk of Chinese influence in Tanzania. He told a reporter that 'we are a stubborn people. The Chinese will learn that if they want to control us they will get into trouble.'[80] Nyerere recognised the added layer of complexity that the Sino-Soviet split had added to the Cold War. Speaking at a meeting of non-aligned states in Dar es Salaam in 1970, he noted that the rise of China had complicated the Cold War: 'the so-called "Iron Curtain" has become less solid', he noted, with an implicit reference to *Ostpolitik*. Nyerere continued: 'whether a "Bamboo Curtain" exists or does not exist, the People's Republic of China does exist. The "Power Game" has become three-sided, and those wishing to stand outside it have further complications to deal with.'[81] Continuing to work with the Soviet Bloc was therefore an essential aspect of maintaining a triangular balancing act between the superpowers, especially as Eastern European states continued to finance, arm, and train African liberation movements.

The appointment of Stephen Mhando as minister of state for foreign affairs in a November 1968 cabinet reshuffle was part of this strategy to rebuild Tanzania's relations with the Eastern Bloc. Born in 1918, Mhando was one of the first Tanganyikans to have travelled what became the well-worn path from Makerere College into nationalist politics. He was among the most sympathetic members of TANU's inner circles to Eastern Europe, especially the GDR. Between 1961 and 1963, Mhando had taught Swahili in Leipzig, where he had married an East German. On his return to Tanzania, he had served in editorial positions for the TANU press. This gave him good

---

[79] CIA, 'Nyerere's Plans for Tanzania', 16 January 1970, RNL, NSCF, Box 745, Folder 3.
[80] 'Tanzania Stubborn – Nyerere', *Standard*, 7 May 1969, 1.
[81] 'Developing Tasks of Non-Alignment', in Nyerere, *Freedom and Development*, 161.

connections with Horst Schlegel, the local ADN correspondent.[82] Subsequently, Mhando was appointed the managing director of the Tanganyika Sisal Marketing Association, where he proposed a restructuring of trade arrangements which, according to the British high commissioner, would have facilitated sales to the socialist world.[83] He was also the president of the GDR's All-African Initiative Committee, a network of African elites committed to developing 'friendship' with the GDR.[84] Mhando privately told the East Germans immediately after the invasion of Czechoslovakia that the Tanzanian government's response had been inappropriate.[85]

In short, Mhando was the perfect intermediary for Nyerere as he attempted to demonstrate to the Soviet bloc that he was committed to the principle of non-alignment and sought only friendly relations with Eastern Europe. According to one former Tanzanian diplomat, Mhando used his background to maximise aid connections with the Eastern Bloc.[86] In January 1969, Mhando told Schlegel that Nyerere had given the all-clear to the conclusion of government-level agreements between the GDR and Tanzania.[87] The GDR recognised that these steps should not be seen as representing any sea change in the Tanzanian position. After all, Nyerere still retained full oversight over foreign relations (as with all foreign affairs ministerial appointments after Kambona relinquished the portfolio, Mhando was a 'minister of state', rather than full cabinet member). An East German delegation sent to attend the anniversary of the Zanzibar Revolution therefore perceived the olive branches offered by Nyerere and Mhando as being rooted in 'tactical-pragmatic considerations' rather than ideological inclination.[88] Nonetheless, this was clear progress from the nadir to which relations had slipped in mid-1968. It was in these circumstances that 'China and the Devil Slaves' appeared. Schlegel interpreted the 'forgery' as 'the first reaction among imperialist circles' against Mhando's appointment. The pamphlet's origins remained a mystery.[89]

---

[82] Schlegel, 15 December 1968, BA-B, SAPMO, DY 30/98131, 185–88.
[83] Phillips to Le Tocq, 20 November 1968, UKNA, FCO 31/434/4.
[84] Wessel, 13 January 1969, PAAA, MfAA, M1, C756/74, 9–14.
[85] Wessel, 26 August 1968, PAAA, MfAA, M1, C749/74, 65–66.
[86] Interview with Paul Rupia, central Dar es Salaam, 3 August 2015.
[87] Schlegel, 25 January 1969, BA-B, SAPMO, DY 30/98143, 601.
[88] Flegel, 22 January 1969, BA-B, SAPMO, DY 30/98129, 213–26.
[89] Roberts, 'Press', 161–62.

While Tanzania mended fences with the Eastern Bloc, the GDR won a flurry of diplomatic victories in the Third World. Between April and July 1969, Iraq, Cambodia, Sudan, and Egypt all recognised the GDR.[90] In Dar es Salaam, Eric Butzke, the new consul-general, told journalists that this string of recognitions reflected the fact that Third World governments now recognised 'the undisputable reality' that there were two German sovereign states.[91] However, Nyerere was resolute in his resistance to elevating the GDR's diplomatic status. In June, Mhando suggested to Nyerere that the GDR should be invited to send a ministerial-level delegation to the upcoming Saba Saba trade fair in July. Mhando argued that following the decisions taken elsewhere to recognise the GDR, the gesture would be a symbolic means of demonstrating the GDR's improved status. Mhando passed Nyerere's terse response to the East Germans. 'We do not recognise the GDR', wrote Nyerere. 'Certainly, the day will come when we recognise it', he admitted. But that decision 'will be taken in Tanzania and not in Cambodia or Sudan. And there will be no recognition by the backdoor.'[92]

The weakness of the GDR's position vis-à-vis Tanzania was exposed by the experience of Otto Winzer, the foreign minister, on a visit to the country in April 1970. He arrived in Dar es Salaam from Somalia, where he had secured recognition from Siad Barre's pro-Soviet regime. To the public eye, Winzer's brief stay in Tanzania seemed a glowing success. He signed bilateral agreements on trade and technical cooperation. Facilitated by Mhando, they represented the first intergovernmental agreements between Tanzania and the GDR.[93] But behind closed doors, the GDR's hopes of recognition were dashed. Nyerere offered various excuses and explanations for the non-recognition of East Germany. 'One must accept that the question of the development of relations between Tanzania ... and the GDR is not a cricket match, but rather an extraordinarily serious matter, which cannot simply be resolved by a simple cabinet decision.' In any case, if the German question was to be answered, the solution had to come from the

---

[90] Gray, *Germany's Cold War*, 205–12.
[91] 'G.D.R. Envoy Explains Recognition', *Standard*, 17 June 1969, 5.
[92] Information Division, MfAA, 30 June 1969, BA-B, SAPMO, DY 30/98131, 454.
[93] 'Trade Agreement Signed with GDR', *Nationalist*, 10 April 1970, 1; 'Tanzania Signs Pact with the GDR', *Nationalist*, 11 April 1970, 8.

major Cold War players. 'There could be two hundred recognitions from Malawi and Tanzania without the German problem being resolved', Nyerere told Winzer. Finally, Nyerere referred back to 1967, when East German diplomats in Dar es Salaam had 'meddled' in Tanzanian affairs. 'It is very easy to overthrow an African government', he warned. 'We are sensitive to any subversive activity.' Winzer left the meeting disappointed.[94]

Despite making advances elsewhere in the Third World, the GDR remained frustrated in Tanzania. The GDR continued to highlight Bonn's compromised relationship with Portugal and South Africa by disseminating its own propaganda and feeding stories to the local press.[95] It also increased its own commitment to African liberation movements, including FRELIMO, as the next chapter shows. Yet while these gestures won over the more radical elements of TANU, they made no tangible impressions with Nyerere and other more technocratically minded ministers. East Germany's relationship with Zanzibar deteriorated as the GDR's development projects fell flat and the government tired of its over-assertive behaviour.[96] On the mainland, the GDR lost its most committed supporter in November 1970, when Mhando was dismissed as minister of state for foreign affairs. The French ambassador noted that Mhando was prone to heavy drinking and occasionally engaged in 'scandalous' behaviour. But he also suspected that there were political reasons too: having initially been appointed to stabilise Tanzania's relationship with Eastern Europe, Mhando had overstepped his remit, and now appeared a threat to Nyerere's intention to build aid relationships across all superpower blocs.[97] Regardless of the truth of the French ambassador's explanation, the case of Mhando shows that keeping up the appearances of non-alignment was a delicate balancing act.

---

[94] Memcon (Nyerere, Winzer), 10 April 1970, PAAA, MfAA, M1, C779/75, 12–23.
[95] Roberts, 'Press', 162–66.
[96] Hong, *Cold War Germany*, 298–316; Eric Burton, 'Diverging Visions in Revolutionary Spaces: East German Advisers and Revolution from Above in Zanzibar, 1964–1970', in Anna Calori, Anne-Kristin Hartmetz, Bence Kocsev, James Mark, and Jan Zofka (eds.), *Between East and South: Spaces of Interaction in the Globalizing Economy of the Cold War* (Oldenbourg: De Gruyter, 2019), 85–115.
[97] Naudy to MAE-DAL, 10 November 1970, CADN, 193PO/1/11 K1.

Socialism and Détente: West Germany's Rapprochement with Tanzania

As the GDR's star fell in Tanzania, so the Federal Republic's rose. This was not simply a see-saw consequence of Nyerere's distaste for East Germany. Instead, the rapprochement between Bonn and Dar es Salaam was facilitated by Brandt's *Ostpolitik* and the extension of West German social democracy into its approach to the Third World. In the late 1960s, Brandt's and Nyerere's world views came into remarkable – though never total – alignment. Both leaders were non-doctrinaire socialists. Both believed there was a serious and widening gulf in the socio-economic trajectories of the global 'North' and the postcolonial 'South'. And both were committed to the broader goal of détente. Although Tanzania kept up its fierce criticism of West Germany's relationships with Portugal and South Africa in public, Nyerere prioritised deepening aid relations with Bonn in his pursuit of economic independence.

This change in West Germany's stance towards Tanzania was part of a continuing evolution of its broader foreign policy over 1969, as Brandt's SPD built a Third World development dimension into its *Ostpolitik*. Reflecting a wider interest shown by European social democrats and radical '68ers in the Third World, Brandt argued that a relaxation of tensions in Europe would free up resources for aid policies abroad. He suggested that détente 'might naturally bring to bear Europe's technological and research capabilities on development tasks much more strongly than hitherto'.[98] His hand was strengthened by the SPD's strong performance in September's federal elections, after which Brandt became chancellor. A distinction here needs to be made between the public image of change in West German development policy and the fundamental continuity which characterised its practice. As Heide-Irene Schmidt has shown, West German development aid had never been driven by the narrow goals of its Cold War struggle against the GDR. From the late 1950s onwards, West Germany had developed an overseas aid policy which combined a moral duty to the Third World with the development of Western economic interests, which would also guard against the spread of communism. The Brandt government's shift in approach was therefore more one of presentation

---

[98] Willy Brandt, 'Problems of the Second Development Decade', *Intereconomics*, 4 (1969), 244.

than substance. The proportion of West Germany's gross domestic product that was committed to aid actually fell under Brandt. But its public image was transformed.[99]

A key figure in the association of *Ostpolitik* with development policy was Erhard Eppler. In 1968, Eppler was appointed Bonn's minister for economic cooperation, a move engineered by Brandt in order to secure more support for his *Ostpolitik* from within the cabinet.[100] Even more so than Brandt, Eppler believed that West Germany could carve out a mutually beneficial niche as a development partner to the decolonised world. 'We do not forget for a moment that we are neither a supermarket nor a superpower', he said shortly after taking up his post. 'But this cannot mean that we avoid the task which others, especially in the Third World, ascribe to us. Now more than ever before, we cannot lose sight of the East-West conflict, but now more than ever before our foreign policy cannot be reduced to its function in this conflict.'[101] This ideological shift was accompanied by increasing West German confidence in the superior quality and quantity of its aid to that offered by the GDR. As Eppler said, West Germany did not have 'the slightest reason to be afraid of the GDR in the Third World', since what it could offer 'far exceeds the performance of the GDR'.[102]

Brandt's personal relationship with Nyerere assisted in the revival of a strong partnership between West Germany and Tanzania. Brandt was familiar with the country: as mayor of Berlin, he had visited Dar es Salaam in 1963 and spoke of the parallels between anticolonial struggles in Africa and Bonn's fight for reunification. The mayor of Dar es Salaam responded by repeating President Kennedy's phrase, 'Ich bin ein Berliner'.[103] In an interview with the *Nationalist* in December 1965, Brandt revealed that he had received a friendly letter from Nyerere. Referring to the Tanzanian president as 'a great and able statesman',

---

[99] Heide-Irene Schmidt, 'Pushed to the Front: The Foreign Assistance Policy of the Federal Republic of Germany, 1958–1971', *Contemporary European History*, 12 (2003), 473–507. Schmidt does however accept that there were instances when Bonn attempted to use aid for leverage over the 'German question', with Tanzania being the most prominent.

[100] Erhard Eppler, *Links Leben: Erinnerungen eines Weltkonservativen* (Berlin: Prophyläen, 2015), 130.

[101] SPD press release, 20 December 1968, AdsD, SP, 2897. See also Erhard Eppler, *Not Much Time for the Third World* (London: Oswald Wolff, 1972).

[102] SPD press release, 30 April 1971, AdsD, SP, 2897.

[103] Schilling, *Postcolonial Germany*, 118.

Brandt said he hoped that a normalisation of relations would take place. Brandt added that developing countries had 'considerable moral weight in the world' which could bring about a peaceful resolution to the German question.[104] The two leaders had thus developed a promising relationship even before Brandt entered government in Bonn.

In seeking to rebuild its relationship with Tanzania, the West German government also took confidence from the GDR's public relations travails. In September 1968, von Hassel wrote to Chancellor Kurt Georg Kiesinger about his conversation with Nyerere in July. Referring to both the 'Hands Off' editorial and the Tanzanian response to the invasion of Czechoslovakia, von Hassel argued that Tanzania's attitude towards the communist world was consistent with its approach to the West: it would fiercely protect its independence, regardless of Cold War alignment. As Tanzania 'would not be getting into communist waters in the foreseeable future', von Hassel recommended that Bonn should resume the suspended capital aid programme.[105] From Dar es Salaam, Hebich pointed out that Nyerere had held good to his position on the non-recognition of the GDR.[106] Having previously opposed the resumption of aid to Tanzania, the Auswärtiges Amt now swung behind this proposed shift in approach and instructed Hebich to explain West Germany's U-turn to Nyerere.[107]

Given notice of Bonn's revised position in January 1969, the Tanzanian government began to court aid in public as well as in private. 'You live in a rich country', Nyerere half-joked with a group of West German journalists in April, 'and therefore it would be good if you could give us a little more of your money!'[108] Nyerere entrusted the role of brokering this renewed relationship to his finance minister, Amir Jamal. After a visit to Bonn in October, Jamal told the West German Ministry for Economic Affairs that he now had 'a clear conviction' that the Federal Republic was 'committed to play the fullest part in assisting Tanzania in her self-development endeavours'.[109] Yet

---

[104] 'Brandt Hopes for Normalisation of Dar-Bonn Relations', *Nationalist*, 21 December 1965, 3.
[105] Von Hassel to Kiesinger, 9 September 1968, BA-K, B136/3001.
[106] Hebich to Auswärtiges Amt, 24 October 1968, PAAA, NA 6408.
[107] Auswärtiges Amt, 24 October 1968, BA-K, B213/7672; Berger to various, 2 January 1969, BA-K, B213/7672.
[108] Timmerman to Auswärtiges Amt, 29 April 1969, BA-K, B102/86803.
[109] Jamal to Schiettinger, 27 October 1969, BA-K, B102/86803.

Socialism and Détente

Nyerere's support for the change in course in West German foreign policy was not simply an aid-seeking tactic. He shared Brandt's view that détente in Europe could permit a reorientation of global politics away from East-West tensions and towards the widening gulf between North and South. In November 1969, Nyerere wrote to Brandt to congratulate him on becoming chancellor. In his message, Nyerere talked up the connection between *Ostpolitik*, détente, and Third World development.

> Many of us elsewhere in the world welcome your intention to work for the building of new and more harmonious relationships with Eastern European countries. . . . For the truth is that even small states like mine are affected by world conflict centering in Europe. Indeed, the friendship between Tanzania and the Federal Republic has in the past been adversely affected by decisions relating to a divided Germany . . . I am glad that in recent years our friendship has been growing stronger again, but there is room for much further improvement and I look forward to co-operation with your Government in affecting this.[110]

After Brandt became chancellor, *Ostpolitik* entered a new, more assertive phase. In March 1970, he met the chairman of the GDR council of ministers, Willi Stoph, in East Germany. The talks produced no concrete results – indeed, they were decidedly icy. But they carried symbolic capital around the world, as photographs of the two men meeting at Erfurt Hauptbahnhof were carried in the international press, including in Tanzania. Anthony Nyakyi, Tanzania's ambassador to Bonn, recalled the 'electrified' atmosphere of the visit. The crowd in Erfurt were chanting 'Willy! Willy! Willy!', he remembered. 'You didn't know which "Willy" they were talking about, Stoph or Brandt.'[111]

By chance, Erhard Eppler arrived in Dar es Salaam four days after the Erfurt talks. His reception was by no means cordial. Brandt's government had attracted criticism in Africa for providing credit for West German firms controversially involved in the Cahora Bassa hydroelectric scheme in Portuguese-occupied Mozambique. The previous month a Tanzanian representative had opened a meeting of the OAU Liberation Committee by condemning West German involvement in

---

[110] Nyerere to Brandt, 10 November 1969, BA-K, B136/6290.
[111] Interview with Anthony Nyakyi, Masaki, Dar es Salaam, 28 July 2015. There was little doubt that the crowd were chanting for Brandt, however.

the dam's construction as a 'slap in the face of Africa'.[112] In Tanzania, Eppler was handed a bitterly worded open letter to Brandt from FRELIMO and faced fierce questioning from local journalists.[113] When Eppler trotted out his government's usual line that its trade policy towards South Africa should be seen as separate from its political stance on apartheid, the recently nationalised *Standard* declared that Tanzania could not 'differentiate between principles and pfennigs'.[114]

However, in private talks with Eppler, this is precisely what Tanzanian leaders did. Leaving the public vitriol to TANU's radicals, Nyerere isolated the anticolonial and aid-seeking stands of Tanzania's foreign policy to strengthen relations with West Germany. While Eppler faced a barrage of criticism from the Tanzanian press, behind closed doors his hosts refrained from mentioning the Cahora Bassa dam project. This allowed a positive discussion about West German capital aid to Tanzania. Eppler made clear Bonn's commitment to assisting Tanzania with the implementation of its Second Five-Year Plan. The two states established a framework for regular bilateral consultations. Jamal told Eppler that he was impressed by West Germany's understanding of Tanzania's development policy, which was unmatched by any other industrialised country.[115] Eppler's trip was presented as a success in West Germany: *Die Zeit*'s correspondent wrote that it 'set something right for the Federal Republic' after the breakdown of relations in 1965.[116]

Relations between Bonn and Dar es Salaam flourished in the early 1970s. In 1971, a West German briefing paper described Tanzania as a 'focus country [*Schwerpunktland*] for German development aid'.[117] That year, West Germany gave grants worth $4.1 million and pledged a further $3.7 million in development loans, figures which set it among Tanzania's most important bilateral aid partners once more.[118] In his memoirs, Eppler wrote glowingly of his favourable impression of Arusha

[112] 'Step up Liberation Struggle, O.A.U. Told', *Standard*, 19 February 1970, 1.
[113] Extracts from report on Eppler's visit to Tanzania and Kenya, April 1970, enclosed in BA-K, B213/7673.
[114] Editorial, *Standard*, 24 March 1970, 1. The article sat alongside the famous photograph of Brandt and Stoph meeting at Erfurt Hauptbahnhof.
[115] Extracts from report on Eppler's visit to Tanzania and Kenya, April 1970, enclosed in BA-K, B213/7673.
[116] Peter Grubbe, 'Reicher Onkel aus Germany', *Die Zeit*, 10 April 1970, 9.
[117] Hanemann to Schiller, 13 October 1971, BA-K, B102/95608.
[118] Coulson, *Tanzania*, 350–51.

socialism, Nyerere's vision for Tanzania, and Jamal's ability to explain the state of the global economy from the perspective of the South.[119] The Cold War and the GDR played little role in Eppler's calculations. 'I never mentioned [to Nyerere] what the GDR did in Tanzania', he remembered. 'Our cooperation was built on mutual trust and sympathy.'[120] These sentiments were reflected in public statements made by Tanzanian officials. When a West German dignitary visited Tanzania in 1972, the minister for health, Lawi Sijaona, praised 'a friendship between a people determined to stand up and grow in the world and a people who in recognition and appreciation are putting out a helping hand'.[121] In the seven years since the *Anerkennungsdiplomatie* crisis, the Tanzanian-West German relationship had come full circle.

This improvement in relations only came about because of the flexibility in Bonn's global foreign policy initiated by Brandt. In transforming West Germany's image from cold warrior to broker of détente, he repositioned his government as a development-friendly partner to the Third World. This challenged the East-West model of international affairs with a North-South vision that chimed with Nyerere's own world view. In Brandt, Nyerere saw another leader committed to transcending the Cold War order, and so swung behind *Ostpolitik*. Nyerere conveyed to Hebich his admiration for Brandt as 'one of the few statesmen, who on the basis of a vision, wanted to overcome daily political problems to bring about fundamental change in Europe'. Nyerere also said that he had asked Yugoslavia's Tito to back *Ostpolitik*.[122] Despite their very different backgrounds, Brandt and Nyerere shared common cause. During the 1970s, the pair emerged as two of the most prominent and articulate voices in the campaign for the restructuring of the global economy. Later, after they relinquished power, both men also headed major international commissions into the widening gap between the global North and South.

Conclusion

On 18 December 1972, Tanzania finally recognised the GDR. The decision owed nothing to the GDR's policy in East Africa and

---

[119] Eppler, *Links Leben*, 148; Erhard Eppler, *Komplettes Stückwerk: Erfahrungen aus fünfzig Jahren Politik* (Frankfurt: Insel Verlag, 1996), 259–60.
[120] Email correspondence with Erhard Eppler, 31 December 2016.
[121] 'Sijaona Praises West German Friendship', *Standard*, 9 February 1972, 1.
[122] Hebich, 1 April 1971, PAAA, NA 13469.

everything to developments in Central Europe, propelled by the effects of *Ostpolitik*. Under the 'Basic Treaty', the two German states recognised each other's sovereignty. A deluge of Third World states almost immediately opened full diplomatic relations with the GDR.[123] Mhando wrote to consul-general Butzke to convey the 'great pleasure and excitement' with which he had received the news, adding in parentheses that 'this could have happened a few years ago'.[124]

In his authoritative history of 'Germany's Cold War', William Glenn Gray correctly concludes that East Germany did not '"win"' the fight for recognition. But his assessment that West Germany 'threw in the towel' underestimates the strength of Bonn's position in the Third World after Brandt came to office as chancellor.[125] In part, this reflects the fact that Gray brings his analysis to a close with the SPD's election victory in 1969. He therefore stops before Brant and Eppler set about reorienting West German development aid policy at the same time as *Ostpolitik* gathered pace. By the early 1970s, West German aid was simply superior to anything the GDR could offer in response, notwithstanding the latter's growing commitment to the liberation struggle in southern Africa. The constructive turn in Bonn's foreign policy marked by *Neue Ostpolitik* brought about a more flexible approach to the Third World, which opened up space for the outward extension of West German social democratic welfare politics. Ultimately, the levelling of the diplomatic playing field created by the Basic Treaty and the formal break with the Hallstein Doctrine strengthened rather than weakened Bonn's presence in Africa.

Beyond its contribution to the liberation struggles in southern Africa, the story of East Germany's experience in Dar es Salaam is essentially one of failure. The breakthrough moment of 1964, when it briefly opened an embassy in Zanzibar, proved a false dawn. The GDR's propaganda operations tested Nyerere's patience, while its association with a number of controversial figures due to its mistaken ideological reading of the local political scene also damaged its reputation. As long as recognising East Germany remained among the most controversial diplomatic steps which a Third World leader could take, Nyerere saw no reason to deepen Tanzania's relationship with East Berlin. Instead,

---

[123] Kilian, *Die Hallstein-Doktrin*, 226.
[124] Mhando to Butzke, 21 December 1972, PAAA, MfAA, M1, C61606, 23.
[125] Gray, *Germany's Cold War*, 5.

he tried to placate the GDR, the Soviet Union, and its allies. Following the invasion of Czechoslovakia, Nyerere recognised the commitment they had made to Africa's liberation movements, as well as the danger that he appeared too close to China. That is not to say that non-alignment was simply a façade. Rather, it required a public calibration that did not necessarily map onto its underlying political dynamics.

From a Tanzanian perspective, navigating the 'German Cold War' was a question of juggling different priorities and conceptions of national sovereignty. In 1965, Nyerere rejected West German aid in a moral gesture intended to demonstrate his nascent state's political sovereignty. The GDR, in its own drive for international recognition as a sovereign state, pointed to its own demonstrated support for self-determination in Africa, which it contrasted with West Germany's connections to colonial rule. Yet Nyerere himself believed that the GDR was an illegitimate state under the de facto occupation of the Soviet Union, a superpower that maintained its own empire in Eastern Europe. Moreover, at the core of Tanzania's socialist project was the belief that economic sovereign independence could only be achieved through the development of a self-reliant economy, which required the input of foreign aid. The emergence of a West German government with a substantial aid budget and an ideological outlook that overlapped with Nyerere's own world view therefore paved the way for a revival of close relations between Bonn and Dar es Salaam.

This history also shows the potential contradictions involved in pursuing non-alignment, supporting the liberation of Africa, and trying to build a self-reliant economy. In theory, all three principles followed in logical fashion, being intended to secure political sovereignty and genuine economic decolonisation in Africa. But putting them into practice was much more difficult and threw up apparent paradoxes. Tanzania had far better economic and diplomatic relations with West Germany, despite Bonn maintaining connections with Portugal and South Africa. Meanwhile, the GDR shared Tanzania's commitment to anticolonial struggles in the Third World yet remained out in the cold. These complex circumstances thrown up by the entwinement of anticolonial and Cold War agendas precluded any attempt by Third World states simply to play East and West off against one another in search of aid and arms, as non-alignment is sometimes crudely depicted. For Nyerere, non-alignment was a profoundly ideological project, which permitted Tanzania to transcend Cold War divisions in pursuit of constructive relations with governments that shared a world view with his own. These included China, as an anti-imperialist Third World power, but also states committed to addressing economic injustices at home and in the world, like the social democratic regimes of Scandinavia and Brandt's West Germany.

Finally, an analysis of Tanzania's conduct of foreign policy towards the 'German question' reveals the extent to which Nyerere kept control over his country's external relations. He was far from the only Tanzanian involved in the matter: as we have seen, the 'German Cold War' touched the working lives of politicians, journalists, and government officials. But as much as the GDR tried to work around Nyerere through its 'publicity work' in Dar es Salaam, they found these activities ultimately had little bearing on the fundamental issue of recognition that was at stake. Indeed, the East Germans' substitute for diplomatic negotiations – clumsy propaganda operations and clandestine meetings with controversial politicians – marked them out to Nyerere as Cold War actors who did not respect Tanzania's sovereignty. In these matters, the president's judgement was decisive. However, when we shift our gaze away from Tanzania's 'official' foreign policy and towards the more ambiguous area of liberation movement politics in Dar es Salaam, a more complex, contested picture emerges, as the next chapter shows.

4 | *The Assassination of Eduardo Mondlane: Mozambican Revolutionaries in Dar es Salaam*

At around ten o'clock on the morning of 3 February 1969, Dr Eduardo Mondlane pulled up outside 201 Nkrumah Street. The address housed the offices of FRELIMO, the guerrilla movement fighting for Mozambique's independence from Portugal beyond Tanzania's southern frontier. Mondlane was FRELIMO's president. He collected his mail and drove to the beachfront villa of an American friend in the leafy suburb of Oyster Bay. Mondlane preferred to work there, away from the city's noise and heat. He sat down with coffee and sifted through his post. Unwrapping a parcel bearing stamps from Moscow, Mondlane saw that it contained a rare French translation of the Russian Marxist, Georgi Plekhanov. He flipped through the pages. It was the last thing he did: when the Tanzanian police arrived on the scene minutes later, they found a room blown apart by a bomb.[1]

Who was responsible for the assassination of Mondlane? This chapter offers no clear answer, though it considers a plethora of possible culprits and alleged conspiracies. Instead, it uses the assassination as an aperture onto Dar es Salaam's liberation politics and the contested spheres of power they involved. The previous chapter demonstrated how Nyerere, as the leader of a sovereign state, maintained tight control of Tanzania's 'official' foreign affairs, despite the efforts of international actors to build their influence in the country via Dar es Salaam's political networks. The circumstances encountered by the city's African liberation movements were more complicated. The political status of their senior cadres was far from clear-cut. They were at once diplomatic missions, governments-in-waiting, guerrilla commanders, and political refugees. In Dar es Salaam, the liberation movements and the factions they contained drew on the support of

---

[1] Burns to State Dept, 13 February 1969, NARA, RG 59, CFPF 1967–69, Box 2354, POL 30 MOZ; David Martin, 'Interpol Solves a Guerrilla Whodunit', *Observer*, 6 February 1972, 4.

Tanzanian elites, OAU officials, and foreign diplomats. Just as these sources of external support sustained liberation struggles, so too they could pull movements in opposite directions. This dynamic also confounded attempts by outsiders to influence the movements. Even Nyerere found his own authority drowned in this whirlpool of entangled relationships, which brought global geopolitics into the same space as personal and ethnic rivalries.

This chapter builds on emerging work which reconsiders the history of Africa's liberation movements in transnational terms. Early literature tended to adopt a national (often national*ist*) framework in addressing these struggles, both mirroring and bolstering the 'official' histories set out by the movements once they assumed power after independence. But as Luise White and Miles Larmer write, '[t]he notion of a single one-way journey from tyranny to national liberation has arguably restricted the development of a more open-ended, fragmented and inclusive set of conflict histories in southern Africa'.[2] In contrast, new histories stress connections between liberation movements, as well as with foreign powers. They also highlight the tensions within them, often by moving the analytical lens from the political to the social in examining the experience of exile. They critically reassess the ways that liberation struggles were shaped by the dynamics of ethnicity, race, ideology, and class. The result is a messier history, rife with shifting factional and personal alliances.[3]

A common theme in the new historiography on transnational liberation movements is their mobility. In moving beyond a national framework, it shows how organising and fighting wars of liberation literally involved crossing borders. Refugees fled into exile. Leaders flew around the globe on diplomatic missions, to address the UN or the OAU. They

---

[2] Luise White and Miles Larmer, 'Introduction: Mobile Soldiers and the Un-National Liberation of Southern Africa', *Journal of Southern African Studies*, 40 (2014), 1271–74.

[3] See the overviews in Jocelyn Alexander, JoAnn McGregor, and Blessing-Miles Tendi, 'The Transnational Histories of Southern African Liberation Movements: An Introduction', *Journal of Southern African Studies*, 43 (2017), 1–12; Jocelyn Alexander, Paolo Israel, Miles Larmer, and Ricardo Soares de Oliveira, 'Liberation Beyond the Nation: An Introduction', *Journal of Southern African Studies*, 46 (2020), 821–28. Especially important here is Williams, *National Liberation*. On the problem of exile, see Nathan Riley Carpenter and Benjamin N. Lawrance (eds.), *Africans in Exile: Mobility, Law, and Identity* (Bloomington: Indiana University Press, 2018).

drummed up support in Cold War capitals. Soldiers travelled abroad for training and then were infiltrated across African borders to wage war. Rather than pursue these movements, this chapter takes the opposite position. By focusing on Dar es Salaam as a key node in the struggle for the liberation of southern Africa, it examines how the city served as a site of encounter between these transnational dynamics. Instead of foregrounding the liberation movements' international connections with the superpowers and their allies, it emphasises the significance of local Tanzanian actors in this political nexus.

This chapter begins by exploring the political world of the liberation movements in revolutionary Dar es Salaam. In particular it addresses how the movements became enmeshed in the city's public sphere, through their relationships with the media, their dependence on the support of the Tanzanian government, and their dealings with the OAU's Liberation Committee. These relationships were characterised by friction as much as cooperation. It then shows how Mondlane used FRELIMO's Dar es Salaam headquarters to build an organisation that commanded international legitimacy and support across Cold War divisions. However, FRELIMO was fractured by multiple splits, which gradually undermined Mondlane's authority. He had enemies as well as allies within the Tanzanian state, who worked with disaffected FRELIMO members against its president. Finally, it looks back at the assassination itself, the multiple conspiracy theories which surround it, and their significance in Mozambique's memory politics today.

Mecca of Revolution or Mecca of Mice?

As we saw in Chapter 1, supporting the liberation of Africa was the guiding star of Tanzania's foreign policy. The result was that Dar es Salaam became a 'mecca of liberation', especially for movements from southern Africa. These principally involved organisations representing Namibia, South Africa, Zimbabwe, and the Portuguese territories of Angola and Mozambique. They were joined by an array of lesser-known, smaller groups, including movements seeking the independence of the Indian Ocean archipelagos of Comoros and Seychelles. Outside of the 'official' realm of liberation movement politics, Dar es Salaam also hosted exiles from neighbouring Malawi and Uganda. Other itinerant Third World revolutionaries joined this vibrant scene, representing liberation causes as diverse as Vietnam, Palestine, and the

Canary Islands. From their offices, the major movements' leaders organised guerrilla wars, liaised with their Tanzanian hosts, and worked the circuit of embassy meetings and diplomatic receptions to canvass support. In the process, they became embedded not just in the capital's international affairs, but also in Tanzanian political life. These relationships were far from straightforward. Although the Tanzanian state trumpeted its support for the anticolonial cause, the status, activities, and behaviour of the liberation movement leaders were a hot topic in the city's public sphere.

Dar es Salaam had emerged as a mustering point for exiled anticolonialists even before Tanganyika formally gained independence. By the time the OAU was formed in 1963, it was the obvious location for the headquarters of its Liberation Committee.[4] The Committee was first based on Ingles Street (today's Azikiwe Street), before moving shortly after to premises on the nearby Garden Avenue. Oscar Kambona, then Tanganyika's minister for foreign affairs, acted as its chairman. The Liberation Committee's secretariat, which was also mostly staffed by Tanzanians, liaised with the institutions of the host government: the Second Vice-President's Office dealt with refugee affairs; the Tanganyika Broadcasting Corporation arranged broadcasts on Radio Tanzania; the TPDF oversaw training camps and the distribution of arms. All three of the Liberation Committee's executive secretaries during its lifetime were Tanzanians. Hashim Mbita, who held office between 1972 and 1994, recalled that he worked closely with Tanzanian ministers, the armed forces, the intelligence services, and Nyerere himself.[5] This meant that Tanzanians, both in the Liberation Committee and elsewhere in the government, occupied vital gatekeeper roles within the day-to-day politics of the movements.

---

[4] For institutional histories, see Emmanuel M. Dube, 'Relations Between Liberation Movements and the OAU', in N. M. Shamuyarira (ed.), *Essays on the Liberation of Southern Africa* (Dar es Salaam: Tanzania Publishing House, 1971), 25–68; Michael Wolfers, *Politics in the Organization of African Unity* (London: Methuen, 1976), 163–94; Zdenek Červenka, *The Unfinished Quest for Unity: Africa and the OAU* (London: Julian Friedmann, 1977), 45–63; C. O. C. Amate, *Inside the OAU: Pan-Africanism in Practice* (London: Macmillan, 1986), 211–316. For a case study, see Chris Saunders, 'SWAPO, Namibia's Liberation Struggle and the Organisation of African Unity's Liberation Committee', *South African Historical Journal*, 70 (2018), 152–67.

[5] Elias C. J. Tarimo and Neville Z. Reuben, 'Tanzania's Solidarity with South Africa's Liberation', in SADET, *The Road to Democracy in South Africa, vol. 5: African Solidarity, Part 1* (Pretoria: UNISA Press, 2013), 215.

The Liberation Committee played two key roles in shaping the 'late' decolonisations in Africa. First, it disbursed funds to the movements, allowing them to maintain offices, pay travel expenses, run training camps, and purchase arms and other war materiel. Second, the Committee had the power to recognise individual movements, which conveyed upon them a sense of international legitimacy as representatives of their respective territories. This was not always a straightforward process. In some cases, like the PAIGC for Guinea-Bissau, FRELIMO for Mozambique, and SWAPO for Namibia, a clearly dominant movement established strong relations with the Liberation Committee. In others, there were multiple, credible contenders to be the 'official' movement. In Angola, South Africa, and Zimbabwe, the struggle was characterised by profound divisions between the movements. The Liberation Committee tried to hedge its bets, in some instances recognising rival movements while seeking to reconcile them, with little success.

All of these processes were dogged by controversy. The Committee was accused of being excessively secretive and corrupt. Patronage and personal relationships between the governing elites of independent African states and claimants to the leadership of the competing liberation movements meant that any choices made by the Committee were politically loaded. Given the location of the Liberation Committee's offices and its close relationship with the Tanzanian state, much of this criticism was aimed at Nyerere's government. Nkrumah's Ghana engaged in a particularly acrimonious confrontation with Tanzania over the alleged mismanagement of the Liberation Committee and misappropriation of its funds. These concerns contributed to the reluctance of many of the OAU's members to pay their dues to the Liberation Committee, which only hamstrung its activities further. In February 1966, the Liberation Committee bemoaned that the majority of members had failed to meet their financial commitments. 'It cannot be possibly seen how the committee can carry out its work, achieve its objectives, and meet the ever-increasing demands of the various liberation movements without the spontaneous payment of these contributions', it stated. 'This reluctance will be sadly reflected on the seriousness of Africa to liberate its occupied territories – a humiliating ignominy that no African state can bear to face.'[6]

---

[6] OAU Liberation Committee, Report to the 6th Ordinary Meeting of the OAU Council of Ministers, February 1966, African Union Common Repository.

The entanglement of liberation politics with local affairs in Dar es Salaam went much further than these instrumental relationships. Far from being temporary guests in the city, several of the 'exiled' movements had much deeper roots in Tanzania, a factor which complicated relationships with the local government. As will be explained, the presence of a Makonde ethnic community which lived on both sides of the Mozambique-Tanzania border became a destabilising factor within FRELIMO. On an individual level, a number of well-educated liberation movement members were employed by the Tanzanian state. For example, ZANU's Herbert Chitepo was Tanzania's first director of public prosecutions;[7] the ANC's Ben Turok worked as a planner for the Ministry of Home Affairs;[8] and Frene Ginwala, another ANC member, edited the nationalised *Standard* newspaper.[9] There was no discrete sphere of liberation movement politics, as often implied by the earlier nationalist literature on the anticolonial struggles. Rather, liberation politics were engrained in local Tanzanian affairs and their transnational connections.

The liberation movement leaders were central figures in Dar es Salaam's international media networks. The foreign press pack gravitated towards their activities. The Polish journalist Ryszard Kapuściński, for example, wrote evocatively of tracking down Africa's 'fugitives, refugees, and emigrants' at the terrace bar of the New Africa Hotel. 'We, the correspondents, come by here frequently to pick up something', he noted. 'We already know all the leaders, we know who is worth sidling up to.'[10] The guerrilla leaders, especially those well-versed in the art of publicity, exploited these opportunities to gain global exposure for their cause through interviews and press conferences. They also contributed to Dar es Salaam's subculture of print propaganda, via publications which ranged from glossy magazines like the ANC's *Sechaba* to crude mimeographed bulletins, which were all poorer movements could afford. Liberation movement press releases were a staple of the local media, which carried exaggerated figures of enemy casualties. The movements also utilised Radio Tanzania Dar es Salaam's external service to broadcast their

---

[7] White, *Assassination of Herbert Chitepo*, 3. [8] Turok, *Nothing but the Truth*.
[9] See Chapter 6. [10] Kapuściński, *Shadow of the Sun*, 76.

propaganda across Africa, maintaining connections over the airwaves with the people whom they sought to liberate.

However, wars of liberation could not be fought by words alone. Since African states were unable to fulfil the movements' requirements for financial assistance, material aid, military training, and especially arms, they turned to the wider world. In turn, China, the Soviet Union, and other Eastern Bloc states perceived an opportunity to increase their influence in Africa. Supporting armed struggle against racist regimes bolstered the socialist states' competing claims to be global leaders of anticolonial revolution. Officials in Beijing and Moscow also hoped that influence among the movements during wars of liberation might translate into influence over future independent governments. But, contrary to the fears of especially Western diplomats, their targets demonstrated significant autonomy in brokering international relationships. Savvy guerrilla leaders knew that they could use inter-socialist competition as leverage for gaining the support of either Moscow or Beijing. However, geopolitical choices also had the potential to divide movements, as the case of FRELIMO reveals.[11]

The lives of members of Dar es Salaam's liberation movements were marked by stark contrasts. Many lived in refugee camps in the suburbs, including students who awaited scholarship opportunities to study abroad. Their compatriots in the guerrilla camps in provincial Tanzania endured austere barracks lifestyles and harsh training programmes. Even in the capital, the buildings from which the leadership organised their struggles were hardly polished embassies. One ANC cadre remembered his surprise at the state of his movement's offices, which occupied the 'ground floor of a shabby building, jammed between a row of struggling businesses'.[12] However, a small group of leaders maintained relatively opulent lifestyles in the city, leaving revolutionary visitors unimpressed. Che Guevara was disappointed to see that many of the liberation movement leaders 'lived comfortably in hotels and had made a veritable profession out of their situation, sometimes lucrative and nearly always

---

[11] Westad, *Global Cold War*, 207–18; Lena Dallywater, Chris Saunders, and Helder Adegar Fonseca (eds.), *Southern African Liberation Movements and the Global Cold War 'East': Transnational Activism, 1960–1990* (Oldenbourg: De Gruyter, 2019). Chinese support for Africa's liberation movements remains an under-researched topic.

[12] Ronnie Kasrils, *Armed and Dangerous: From Undercover Struggle to Freedom* (Johannesburg: Jonathan Ball, 1998), 79.

agreeable'.[13] Stokely Carmichael attacked the liberation movements on similar grounds, drawing a stinging rebuke from the ANC.[14] While the guerrilla leaders rejected such accusations, there was some substance to the idea that some preferred the high life to running liberation wars. Andreas Shipanga, a member of SWAPO's executive committee, recalled initially being impressed with Dar es Salaam's 'fine hotels', like the New Africa, but bemoaned their subsequent deterioration. After the Arusha Declaration, he wrote, 'when the waiter, the barman and the cleaner became the "ruling class", all discipline went by the board'.[15]

The quotidian life of Nkrumah Street and its environs, where the movements worked in close proximity, fostered a sense of collaborative struggle against shared colonial enemies. The leaders ate, drank, and chatted together on a daily basis. Cosmopolitan urban spaces provided opportunities for cementing pan-African solidarities, as some cadres forged affective relationships with local musicians through their involvement in Dar es Salaam's vibrant musical scene.[16] But their leaders' apparent preference for talking in bars over waging war against the colonialists drew criticism from their Tanzanian hosts. Nyerere described the Zimbabwean exiles as 'a few chaps here noise-making in Dar-es-Salaam and living in hotels, they are not the real ZAPU and ZANU. The real freedom fighters are in Rhodesia.'[17] Similar sentiments were freely expressed by the public, drawing on the anti-urban and anti-elite rhetoric of *ujamaa*, which castigated laziness and profligacy. The *Standard* remarked that the liberation movement leaders 'haunt the capital's hotels scrounging drinks, tour embassies asking for money and free flights to anywhere and continually squabble about leadership. The one thing they do not do is their job ... Unless someone acts soon, Dar es Salaam could become known as the Mecca of mice.'[18] One letter to the TANU

---

[13] Guevara, *African Dream*, 5. See also Ivaska, 'Liberation in Transit', 35.
[14] Toivo Asheeke, 'Black Power and Armed Decolonization in Southern Africa: Stokely Carmichael, the African National Congress of South Africa, and the African Liberation Movements, November 1967–December 1973', *Journal of African American History*, 104 (2019), 426–28.
[15] Andreas Shipanga with Sue Armstrong, *In Search of Freedom* (Gibraltar: Ashanti, 1989), 73.
[16] Maria Suriano, 'Transnational Music Collaborations, Affective Networks and Everyday Practices of Convivial Solidarity in Ujamaa Dar es Salaam', *Journal of Southern African Studies*, 46 (2020), 985–1008.
[17] Miles to CRO, 29 October 1965, UKNA, DO 183/700/94.
[18] 'Mice or Men', editorial, *Standard*, 28 July 1967, 4.

newspaper, the *Nationalist*, alleged that the freedom fighters could 'only make their revolution at the roof-tops of Dar es Salaam ... The struggle they can offer in revolution is the sweat they give while dancing to the bombshell music of duke boxes.'[19]

Tanzanian unease at the behaviour of the liberation movements was accentuated by the influx of arms from their foreign sponsors, which entered the continent via the port in Dar es Salaam. In 1966, Oscar Kambona told a meeting of the Liberation Committee that arms for the movements should be sent to other countries, since there were too many weapons in Tanzania. He complained that the first the Tanzanian authorities knew about arms orders was when they arrived at the port. Kambona reportedly suggested that the Liberation Committee should be moved out of the city and instead rotated among its members.[20] More generally, the government feared the danger posed by the presence of trained guerrilla troops in camps across the country as potential armed support for a challenger to Nyerere. The case of the treason trial of 1969, covered in Chapter 7, exposed the potential links between dissident Tanzanian politicians like Kambona, liberation movement leaders, and their armed rank-and-file. Acting as gatekeepers to the liberation struggle gave the Tanzanian state significant control over the movements' activities yet handing out weapons to refugee guerrillas came with inherent risks.

The Tanzanian authorities and the movements themselves were justifiably concerned at the potential for the subversion of the liberation cause by agents of the white minority states. Spotty evidence suggests that Portuguese, Rhodesian, and South African informers were planted into and recruited within Dar es Salaam's political networks and the inland camps. Phyllis Johnson and David Martin, the latter a long-time journalist at the *Standard* with privileged access to Nyerere, alleged that Tanzania had broken up a large Portuguese spy ring in the capital in the late 1960s. The men under question said that they had been recruited by a man who carried a Belgian passport and claimed to be a shoe salesman.[21] In 1968, the Kenyan press reported that a leaked list of twenty-two people being held in preventive detention contained six Goans believed to have being

---

[19] "Revolutionary", letter to the editor, *Nationalist*, 17 November 1967, 4.
[20] 'Tanzania: Liberation Movements and Refugees', n.d. [1966], UKNA, DO 213/123/92.
[21] Phyllis Johnson and David Martin, *Apartheid Terrorism: The Destabilization Report* (London: Commonwealth Secretariat, 1989), 153.

spying for Lisbon.²² A Portuguese informer in Tanzania later reported 'a number of Goans' had been arrested, but all except one had now been released. Those with Tanzanian citizenship were allowed to remain in the country; those without it were deported to India.²³ Here, concerns about Portuguese subversion blended with anti-Asian sentiment to root out 'exploiters' to the nation who might conspire with Tanzania's imperialist enemies abroad.

For all these reasons, the Tanzanian state's wholehearted public commitment to the cause of African liberation was not universally shared in private. Walter Bgoya, a former bureaucrat at the Ministry of Foreign Affairs, remembered that 'some high officials and politicians' believed that the country was 'unduly exposing itself to dangers' and 'expending financial and other resources it could ill afford' in supporting the liberation struggle. They did not say so in public, since 'who would dare question Mwalimu Nyerere?' Instead, they 'slowed things down' and 'occasionally resorted to calling [liberation movement leaders] CIA agents as a way to discredit them'.²⁴ This discontent was also in evidence among the general public. Dar es Salaam's workers grumbled when asked to make material sacrifices to the anticolonial struggle. In 1972, NUTA resolved that each worker should contribute a small portion of his or her income to the liberation fund. In any case, this was less than 1 per cent of the worker's salary.²⁵ But several wrote to the government-owned newspapers to complain about this imposition. One argued that 'over-taxed workers' would be 'digging our own graves'.²⁶ Another stated that he would not contribute a 'single penny' while 'the freedom fighters continue to marry Europeans, sit behind very expensive mahogany desks, and drive the most expensive cars'.²⁷

---

22 *Reporter*, 9 February 1968, 11–12.
23 Unsigned letter, 29 April 1968, enclosed in director, PIDE, to director general of political affairs, MNE, 7 November 1968, AHD, MNE, PAA 569.
24 Walter Bgoya, 'From Tanzania to Kansas and Back Again', in William Minter, Gail Hovey, and Charles Cobb Jr (eds.), *No Easy Victories: African Liberation and American Activists over a Half Century, 1950–2000* (Trenton, NJ: Africa World Press, 2007), 104; cf. evidence of popular discontent at the financial burden of supporting the liberation movements in Ghana: Ahlman, *Living with Nkrumahism*, 130–32.
25 'NUTA yaanzisha mchango wa ukombozi', *Uhuru*, 18 December 1972, 1.
26 Masudi S. Kidy, letter to the editor, *Daily News*, 9 February 1973, 9.
27 Ngila Mwase, 'The Liberation Fund Question', *Daily News*, 6 April 1973, 7. These letters appeared at the height of the strike action which followed TANU's *Mwongozo*, explained in Chapter 7.

That such mutterings made the letters page of the state-owned newspaper on an issue as sacrosanct as African liberation suggests wider grassroots unease at the costly burden it placed upon ordinary citizens, especially while the guerrilla leaders were perceived as having a lavish lifestyle in Dar es Salaam.

Nonetheless, by the mid-1960s, it was clear that in championing the cause of anticolonial self-determination, the Tanzanian government had turned its capital into a centre of revolutionary activity that rivalled Algiers or Cairo. Hosting the Liberation Committee gave the Tanzanian state a certain gatekeeping control of the movements' activities, often to the dismay of other African governments. However, this also brought dangers for Tanzania's own sovereignty, including the threat of military reprisals from the white minority states and the build-up of guerrilla forces inside Tanzania. More generally, Dar es Salaam became a vital centre for espionage and journalists seeking sensationalised stories. The liberation movement leaders were adept at working these networks. Yet these myriad connections, which blurred the lines between liberation activities and local politics, could also be appropriated in the internal struggles which afflicted the movements, as the case of FRELIMO demonstrates.

FRELIMO in the Cold War World

Eduardo Mondlane was born in Mozambique in 1920. He studied at university first in Johannesburg, from where he was expelled after a year, and then in Lisbon, before moving to the United States. There, he obtained degrees from Oberlin College in Ohio and Northwestern University in Illinois. He married a white American, Janet.[28] While working for the UN Trusteeship Council in New York, Mondlane came into contact with Julius Nyerere, then spearheading Tanganyika's fight for independence. On an official visit to Mozambique with the UN in early 1961, Mondlane was struck by a sense of frustrated anticolonial ambitions. He considered a future role in an independence struggle and was in communication with likeminded exiles. In the United States, he had already cultivated relationships with powerbrokers at the State Department. While a student

---

[28] On Janet Mondlane, see Nadja Manghezi, *O meu coração está nas mãos de um negro: uma história da vida de Janet Mondlane*, trans. Machado da Graça (Maputo: Imprensa Universitária, 2nd ed., 2001).

Mondlane developed a lasting friendship with Wayne Fredericks, who became assistant secretary of state for Africa under the Kennedy administration.

Meanwhile, Dar es Salaam was emerging as the focal point for Mozambican anticolonial mobilisation. The multiple origins of FRELIMO's liberation struggle are too complex to recount here.[29] The movement itself emerged from a fluid political situation involving several factions, each based on networks within the Mozambican diaspora in Africa. The Tanganyikan government, for its part, sought to forestall the influence of Nkrumah's Ghana over one particular group of Mozambican exiles. In June 1962, Mondlane travelled to Dar es Salaam in an attempt to provide coherence and leadership as these various factions sought to create a common front. In a series of political manoeuvres, Mondlane was overwhelmingly elected president of the new movement, FRELIMO. After resigning from his position at Syracuse University, Mondlane moved permanently to Dar es Salaam with his family in March 1963. Janet Mondlane directed the Mozambique Institute, a school for refugees located in the suburb of Kurasini.[30] Like Nyerere, Eduardo Mondlane initially pressed for a peaceful transition to independence. However, in the face of Portuguese intransigence, Mondlane decided that there was little alternative to armed struggle. FRELIMO launched its liberation war in September 1964.[31]

With his transcontinental education and connections, Mondlane was adept at promoting FRELIMO's cause around the globe. 'The most notable and refreshing African liberation figure I reported on was Eduardo Mondlane', remembered a journalist working in Dar es Salaam. 'He had his own press network and when he wanted particular

---

[29] After years of being obscured by narratives dominated by FRELIMO, its forerunner movements are now receiving due critical attention: Michel Cahen, 'The Mueda Case and Maconde Political Ethnicity: Some Notes on a Work in Progress', *Africana Studia*, 2 (1999), 29–46; Liazzat J. K. Bonate, 'Muslims of Northern Mozambique and the Liberation Movements', *Social Dynamics*, 35 (2009), 280–94; Joel das Neves Tembe, '*Uhuru na Kazi*: Recapturing MANU Nationalism Through the Archive', *Kronos*, 39 (2013), 257–79; John A. Marcum, *Conceiving Mozambique* (Cham: Palgrave Macmillan, 2018).

[30] Joanna T. Tague, *Displaced Mozambicans in Postcolonial Tanzania: Refugee Power, Mobility, Education, and Rural Development* (London: Routledge 2018).

[31] João M. Cabrita, *Mozambique: The Torturous Road to Democracy* (Basingstoke: Palgrave, 2000).

coverage he would use journalists from outside, to ensure better, more broad acceptance and coverage.'[32] Mondlane's engaging character, articulate delivery, and debonair style drew foreign admirers. An American doctor, who was well acquainted with the Mondlanes, recalled the scene at an Israeli independence day celebration held at the Kilimanjaro Hotel in 1967, in which Eduardo was 'surrounded by admirers hanging onto his every word . . . his booming voice and precise rhetoric carried throughout much of the noisy gathering'.[33] Following Mondlane's lead, FRELIMO's propaganda sought to present itself as a future-looking organisation through a visual iconography that focused on its state-like operations in Dar es Salaam. Over time, this gave way to a focus on the war and the liberated zones of northern Mozambique. Nonetheless, the initial impression of a modern, urban front was important in claiming legitimacy in the international sphere.[34]

This public relations strategy paid off. FRELIMO was the only Dar es Salaam-based liberation movement to receive aid from all three superpowers. Initially, FRELIMO's connections to the communist world were strongest with China. Soon after Mondlane first visited Beijing in 1963, Chinese small arms began arriving in Tanzania, accompanied by military instructors who trained the guerrillas in the south of the country.[35] Uria Simango, the movement's vice-president, was the closest member of FRELIMO's inner circle to Beijing. His Maoist sympathies were well known, and he was a familiar face at the Canton Restaurant, a short walk from FRELIMO's Nkrumah Street offices.[36] However, as the 1960s wore on, FRELIMO developed stronger ties with the Soviet Bloc. This reflected a growing irritation among African states and guerrilla movements at China's inflexible

---

[32] J. B. Thomson, *Words of Passage: A Journalist Looks Back* (n.p.: Xlibris, 2012), no pagination.
[33] Charles R. Swift, *Dar Days: The Early Years in Tanzania* (Lanham, MD: University of America Press, 2002), 49.
[34] Alba Martín Luque, 'International Shaping of a Nationalist Imagery? Robert van Lierop, Eduardo Mondlane and *A luta continua*', *Afriche e Orienti*, 19 (2017), 115–38.
[35] On China and FRELIMO, see Altorfer-Ong, 'Old Comrades', 149–50; Stephen R. Jackson, 'China's Third World Policy: The Case of Angola and Mozambique', *China Quarterly*, 142 (1997), 388–422.
[36] PIDE Mozambique, 21 June 1968, TT, PIDE, SC, SR 337/61, NT 3051, 1° pt., 488–89.

approach to bilateral relations (a trend to which the Tanzanian government was an exception). The Soviet Union harboured initial doubts about Mondlane's ideological position and his connections with the United States. It was more impressed with FRELIMO's secretary for foreign affairs, Marcelino dos Santos. Like Mondlane, dos Santos had been socialised into cosmopolitan political worlds while studying outside of Africa, in his case among radical intellectual circles in Paris. Dos Santos mixed political activism with poetry, leading to an introduction to the Soviet Union through an invitation to the Afro-Asian People's Writers Conference, held in Tashkent in 1958.[37]

After the Soviet Union rebuffed Mondlane's request to visit Moscow in 1963, a letter from dos Santos to the Soviet Afro-Asian People's Solidarity Organisation produced a breakthrough. Mondlane travelled to Moscow in 1964 and 1966, returning on both occasions with promises of aid and military training. FRELIMO delegations also received aid from Czechoslovakia and East Germany. Over the course of the 1960s, the feeling rose in the Eastern Bloc that Mondlane was coming over to their side. After Mondlane visited East Berlin in 1966, the GDR concluded that he had moved to the 'left', under the steady influence of colleagues such as dos Santos and Samora Machel, an Algerian-trained revolutionary who became FRELIMO's director of military affairs. Mondlane encouraged this change in perception by drawing on the split within the communist world. He complained to the East Germans about the treatment of a FRELIMO delegation in Beijing and China's 'divisive' intentions in the Third World.[38] Meanwhile, China began to support a rival organisation to FRELIMO, the Zambia-based Mozambique Revolutionary Committee (*Comité Revolucionário de Moçambique*, COREMO), though this alternative movement never proved a serious challenger.[39]

It might be surprising, given these links to China and the Eastern Bloc, that Mondlane remained well-regarded in the West. FRELIMO's relationship with Britain and the United States was certainly

---

[37] Natalia Telepneva, 'Mediators of Liberation: Eastern-Bloc Officials, Mozambican Diplomacy and the Origins of Soviet Support for FRELIMO, 1958–1965', *Journal of Southern African Studies*, 43 (2017), 67–81. See also Natalia Telepneva, 'Our Sacred Duty: The Soviet Union, the Liberation Movements in the Portuguese Colonies, and the Cold War, 1961–1975', PhD diss. (London School of Economics, 2015).
[38] Africa Division, MfAA, 12 December 1966, PAAA, MfAA, M1, A18984/1.
[39] Jackson, 'China's Third World Policy', 399–400.

complicated by Cold War geopolitics. António Salazar's regime used Portugal's membership of the North Atlantic Treaty Organization (NATO) as leverage to suppress criticism of its colonial policy.[40] Nonetheless, Washington provided covert support for FRELIMO. Senior figures in Washington recognised that Mondlane represented the best chance for a negotiated settlement in Mozambique and a counterweight to more radical elements within FRELIMO. In 1963, the CIA channelled $60,000 to FRELIMO via the African-American Institute in New York. The sum of $99,700 followed from the Ford Foundation to the Mozambique Institute. Even after FRELIMO launched its war of liberation, the United States retained a degree of cooperation with Mondlane. Despite FRELIMO's openness to receiving support from Beijing and Moscow, some Western observers trusted Mondlane's claims that he obtained arms from the communist powers simply because he could not from the West. The former ambassador to Tanzania, William Leonhart, told the National Security Council that Mondlane was a 'force for moderation' and that by supporting FRELIMO, 'we would reindorse [sic] Mondlane's pride and affection for the USA, buy some investment in stability for the movement and keep a better watch on the direction of the struggle'.[41]

By the mid-late 1960s, FRELIMO was the best-organised liberation movement operating out of Dar es Salaam. FRELIMO's leaders, especially Mondlane and dos Santos, had used their cosmopolitan connections to build relationships with numerous foreign donors, including the superpowers. Reputations earned via the daily rhythms of liberation movement diplomacy in Dar es Salaam were translated into material support during globetrotting visits to Cold War capitals.[42] Yet as Mondlane shook hands with foreign sponsors, the geopolitical and ideological choices which these aid agreements implied contributed to widening tensions inside his movement. Just as damaging, this same cosmopolitanism, which set the leadership apart from less privileged and educated Mozambican exiles, led to animosities inside FRELIMO.

---

[40] Witney W. Schneidman, *Engaging Africa: Washington and the Fall of Portugal's Colonial Empire* (Lanham, MD: University of America Press, 2004).
[41] 'Minutes of the Meeting of the 303 Committee, 27 October 1967', *FRUS*, 1964–68, vol. 24, doc. 449.
[42] Daniel Kaiser, '"Makers of Bonds and Ties": Transnational Socialisation and National Liberation in Mozambique', *Journal of Southern African Studies*, 43 (2017), 29–48.

Towards the Crisis of 1968

Like many African liberation movements, FRELIMO was an unhappy family. Its early years were plagued by splits, as the leaders of the parties which were subsumed into the unified movement under Mondlane resented their reduced status. This is obscured by FRELIMO's official history, which projected the image of a united movement, into which Mozambique's various ethnic groups coalesced into a singular, nationalist cause. The writing of this history began with the publicity activities of FRELIMO's leadership in its nascent years. Leaders like Mondlane and dos Santos, whose formative years had been spent in urban Lourenço Marques and had travelled far beyond Mozambique's borders, were inculcated into a world in which the modular European nation-state presented a model for postcolonial government. The self-presentation of a liberation movement as *national* in scope was essential in gaining recognition from intergovernmental bodies like the OAU and UN, which then conferred onto the movement a legitimacy through which to attract bilateral support from foreign powers.[43]

These visions of national liberation were not uniformly shared across FRELIMO's membership. In particular they jarred with the interests of the Makonde ethnic group, which straddled the Mozambique-Tanzania border. Under European colonial rule in East Africa, waves of Makonde had migrated north into Tanganyikan territory in flight from Portuguese taxes and labour demands. As Tanganyikan independence approached, some Makonde workers feared potential discrimination by a TANU government, and so explored the possibilities of returning to northern Mozambique. The violent colonial repression of demands for greater autonomy they encountered there pushed the Makonde into resistance to Portuguese rule, and later incentivised them to join FRELIMO. This meant that they did not all buy into the movement's national project. Rather, they saw FRELIMO as a vehicle for pursuing more parochial ends.[44]

---

[43] Michel Cahen, 'Nationalism and Ethnicities: Lessons from Mozambique', in Einar Braathen, Morten Bøås, and Gjermund Sæther (eds.), *Ethnicity Kills? The Politics of War, Peace and Ethnicity in SubSaharan Africa* (Basingstoke: Macmillan, 2000), 163–87.

[44] Cahen, 'Mueda Case'; Michel Cahen, 'Lutte d'émancipation anticoloniale ou movement de libération nationale?', *Revue Historique*, 637 (2006), 113–38.

Lazaro Kavandame emerged as the most powerful Makonde figure in FRELIMO. In the late 1950s, he had led a cooperative of cotton producers in Cabo Delgado province, which challenged exploitive colonial practices and was temporarily banned by the Portuguese. After FRELIMO took up armed struggle in 1964, Kavandame became an essential ally in the warzone of northern Mozambique. He was appointed as the movement's political secretary in Cabo Delgado. FRELIMO's early military successes expanded the territory in which Kavandame's cooperatives were able to function. However, according to the FRELIMO leadership, Kavandame abused his position to extort produce from the peasantry and, with the connivance of the local Tanzanian authorities, take a cut from cross-border trade. He subscribed to a narrower, more racially defined vision of anticolonial liberation, in contrast to the colour-blind approach embraced by the Dar es Salaam-based leadership.[45] Kavandame also commanded support outside of Cabo Delgado among the Makonde diaspora in Eastern Africa, for example from the FRELIMO branch in Zanzibar.[46]

The 'People's War' and model of social revolution in the 'liberated zones' adopted by the FRELIMO leadership clashed with the interests of Kavandame and his Makonde supporters. Mondlane advocated the creation of new structures of government to administer the freed territory, incorporate the peasantry into the revolutionary struggle, and thereby develop the political consciousness for a liberated Mozambican nation. This involved the extension of party control over regions where Kavandame had carved out an economic niche. Kavandame was not a 'traditionalist', but a new-era capitalist whose business practices broke with typical Makonde peasant economics. He lacked the cosmopolitan experience of Mondlane or dos Santos and was an anticolonialist rather than a Mozambican nationalist: the liberation of Makonde territory from Portuguese rule was his ultimate goal. The 'modernisation' versus 'traditionalist' dichotomy, propagated by FRELIMO after Mondlane's death and accepted by sympathetic historians, is therefore misleading. Instead, the conflict between Kavandame and the

---

[45] On Kavandame, see Cahen, 'Mueda Case', 45–46n27.
[46] See for example the request from FRELIMO's regional branch to the ASP secretary-general for Kavandame to visit Zanzibar: Mpinyeke Tatalo to Kombo, 1 November 1967, ZNA, AK26/98, 27.

leadership was over competing ideas of a liberated Mozambique, fuelled and complicated by other dynamics.[47]

Prominent among these other ingredients in FRELIMO's divisions were Mondlane's connections with the United States. These were subject to continual rumour in Dar es Salaam, a city rife with anti-American animosity. Such suspicions were increased by the sensational case of Leo Milas. To cut a long, twisting, and mysterious story short, Mondlane first encountered Milas' name in 1962. Milas was living in the United States, though he claimed Mozambican descent. At a time when FRELIMO was desperately short of trained staff, Mondlane was impressed with Milas' academic background and so invited him to Tanzania, where he served as FRELIMO's first publicity secretary. In Dar es Salaam, Milas proved a controversial figure and was soon embroiled in FRELIMO's fractious politics. He was eventually expelled from the movement in August 1964, after Mondlane discovered that he was actually an American named Leo Clinton Aldridge.[48] There was also a racially inflected aspect to this criticism of the FRELIMO leadership. Some of its members were white, like Mondlane's wife, Janet. Dos Santos also fell under suspicion, since he was a *mestiço* who had a white South African girlfriend, Pamela Beira, an ANC member who worked for the Swedish aid agency.[49]

Many of Mondlane's critics, both within FRELIMO and among the Tanzanian population, looked unfavourably on what they regarded as his distinctly un-revolutionary lifestyle. Whereas FRELIMO's rank-and-file occupied crowded student dormitories or camp barracks in rural Tanzania, Mondlane lived in comfort in Dar es Salaam's upmarket suburb of Oyster Bay.[50] While others faced Portuguese bullets or harsh training routines, Mondlane moved in a world of international jet travel and cocktail parties. This drew criticism from within his movement. 'Mondlane's dogs eat better than we do', grumbled one member.[51] In

---

[47] Georgi Derluguian, 'The Social Origins of Good and Bad Governance: Re-Interpreting the 1968 Schism in FRELIMO', in Éric Morier-Genoud (ed.), *Sure Road? Nations and Nationalisms in Angola, Guinea-Bissau and Mozambique* (Leiden: Brill, 2012), 79–101.
[48] This extraordinary story is told in Marcum, *Conceiving Mozambique*, 43–51.
[49] Nadja Manghezi, *The Maputo Connection: The ANC in the World of FRELIMO* (Auckland Park: Jacana, 2009), 15–25.
[50] Ivaska, 'Liberation in Transit', 30–31.
[51] Pickering to State Dept, 30 March 1968, NARA, RG 59, CFPF 1967–69, Box 2513, POL 2 TANZAN.

1968, a group of discontented Mozambican students in the United States attacked Mondlane's decision to stay in 'luxury hotels' on 'senseless journeys' to Europe and the United States – 'places where true revolutionaries like F. Castro would not set foot'.[52] We might see this friction as a form of 'class' politics, reflective of a gulf between the lived material and social experiences that split an elite like Mondlane from both the rank-and-file and more powerful figures who lacked his cosmopolitan background.

The expectations of Mozambican students in Dar es Salaam provided another source of tension within FRELIMO. They did not envisage the Tanzanian capital as the final point in their exile journeys, but rather a stepping-stone for gaining a university scholarship to study outside of Africa following the completion of their secondary education at the Mozambique Institute. For these young students, Dar es Salaam was less a 'mecca of revolution' than, as Joanna Tague puts it, a 'city of waiting'. Mondlane and the FRELIMO leadership feared that the students were more interested in their own educational self-advancement than waging the liberation war. There was probably some truth to this, again revealing the divergences between the leadership's top-down concept of a national liberation struggle and the diverse aspirations of FRELIMO's members. These tensions became aggravated in 1967, when the leadership resolved that failing students would be placed in the army and those who had already studied at university would have to serve time in the military before being permitted to study for a master's degree. The students reacted with dismay.[53]

Many of these frictions became misleadingly subsumed into a simplified division between 'northern' and 'southern' members of FRELIMO. Certainly, the political leadership in Dar es Salaam was dominated by southerners. Refugees and soldiers, who made up the vast majority of FRELIMO members in Tanzania, were naturally mostly from the northern provinces nearest the frontier, including the Makonde. In particular, the reorganisation of the armed forces in 1966 appeared to many dissatisfied northerners as evidence that FRELIMO's leadership were pursuing an anti-northern agenda. Samora Machel became the head of the army, replacing Filipe Magaia, who had been

---

[52] National Union of Mozambican Students, 'The Mozambican Revolution Betrayed', May 1968, reproduced in *African Historical Studies*, 3 (1970), 175.
[53] Tague, *Displaced Mozambicans*, 79–119.

killed in mysterious circumstances. Some FRELIMO members believed that he had been killed on the orders of the leadership.[54] Foreign powers with a stake in FRELIMO reputedly sought to latch onto these tensions. In mid-1967, the Portuguese secret police, the PIDE, reported that Chinese agents in Dar es Salaam were cultivating an opposition faction to Mondlane among Mozambican workers of Makonde background at the Friendship Textile Factory, a Chinese-funded scheme in the suburb of Ubungo.[55] The same shorthand of the north-south division has also come to serve as an axis for explaining splits inside the movement in recent histories which are critical of FRELIMO.[56]

Questions of ethnicity, race, ideology, regionalism, and a loosely-defined idea of 'class' all undoubtedly fed into tensions within FRELIMO. Yet these issues should not be understood as discrete categories. Simplified dichotomies, as Christian Williams remarks, 'overdetermine meaning and obscure exiles' daily lives'.[57] Used by liberation movement protagonists, diplomats, and journalists at the time, they have been sustained in FRELIMO's own 'official' history. There was not, Michel Cahen advises, a 'simple crisis' within FRELIMO, but rather 'tensions at the crossroads of numerous, varied factors, without the possibility of democratic control'.[58] Mondlane himself was alert to the problems posed by these entanglements. In the *Struggle for Mozambique*, he warned that '[t]he complexities of motive behind divisive conduct makes it the more difficult to guard against: individual neuroses, personal ambitions, real ideological differences are muddled up with the tactics of the enemy secret service'.[59] In early 1968, these tensions spilled over into violence.

---

[54] Cabrita, *Mozambique*, 44–49; Marcum, *Conceiving Mozambique*, 104–105.
[55] Secretary-general for national defence, 16 August 1967, TT, PIDE, SC, SR, 337/61, NT 3051, 1° pt., 776–77.
[56] Barnabé Lucas Ncomo, *Uria Simango: um homem, uma causa* (Maputo: Edições Novafrica, 2004); Lawe Laweki, *Mateus Pinho Gwenjere: A Revolutionary Priest* (Wandsbeck: Reach, 2019).
[57] Williams, *National Liberation*, 13.
[58] Michel Cahen, 'La "fin de l'histoire... unique": Trajectoires des anticolonialismes au Mozambique', *Portuguese Studies Review*, 16 (2008), 210.
[59] Eduardo Mondlane, *The Struggle for Mozambique* (Baltimore, MD: Penguin, 1969), 132.

In March 1968, Mondlane was on a publicity and lobbying tour of Britain when he received an urgent cable from Dar es Salaam that brought him rushing back to Tanzania. His hasty return was prompted by trouble at the Mozambique Institute. At the centre of the crisis was Mateus Gwenjere, a Roman Catholic priest, who had fled to Tanzania from Mozambique in August 1967. Mondlane was immediately impressed by Gwenjere, who was fast-tracked into FRELIMO's leadership. Accompanied by Simango, Gwenjere represented the movement at the UN General Assembly. In New York, Simango informed Gwenjere about rising discord inside FRELIMO with the Mondlane-dos Santos-Machel faction. This stemmed from the heavy-handed suppression of dissent within the army and the presence of white faces among the Dar es Salaam leadership, whom Simango claimed included Portuguese agents.[60]

On his return to Dar es Salaam, Gwenjere began to criticise FRELIMO's education policy. He fomented opposition to Mondlane by tapping into discontent at the Mozambique Institute regarding the lack of scholarship opportunities to study abroad and the leadership's insistence that students served at the front. The students called for the dismissal of the Institute's white teachers – with Gwenjere's encouragement, according to the leadership. The ensuing stand-off resulted in the temporary closure of the Institute and reached a climax when a FRELIMO party, including Machel, raided the student dormitories on 6 March. This precipitated Mondlane's return from London.[61] George Magombe, the Liberation Committee executive secretary, and Rashidi Kawawa, Tanzania's second vice-president, set up a commission of inquiry into the affair. Its report concluded that student unrest was the 'direct consequence of the interference in the affairs of the Institute by Father Mateus Gwenjere'.[62]

---

[60] Cabrita, *Mozambique*, 53; Marcum, *Conceiving Mozambique*, 101–104. For a more nuanced view of Gwenjere, see Éric Morier-Genoud, *Catholicism and the Making of Politics in Central Mozambique, 1940–1986* (Rochester, NY: University of Rochester Press, 2019), 103–108; for a biography explicitly written in his defence, see Laweki, *Mateus Pinho Gwenjere*.

[61] Michael G. Panzer, 'The Pedagogy of Revolution: Youth, Generational Conflict, and Education in the Development of Mozambican Nationalism and the State, 1962–1970', *Journal of Southern African Studies*, 35 (2009), 803–20.

[62] Quoted in Walter C. Opello Jr, 'Pluralism and Elite Conflict in an Independence Movement: FRELIMO in the 1960s', *Journal of Southern African Studies*, 2 (1975), 74.

Within weeks, FRELIMO was convulsed by more violence. On 6 May, a group of Makonde forcibly closed the movement's offices on Nkrumah Street. After FRELIMO's leadership succeeded in getting the offices reopened two days later, the Makonde returned, armed with clubs and machetes. The administrative workers inside attempted to flee to the ANC offices nearby. One member of the Central Committee was fatally wounded. The Tanzanian police arrested eighteen men. At the time, Mondlane was in Mozambique with representatives of the Liberation Committee.[63] The local press reacted with dismay. 'The place for using weapons is not the city of Dar es Salaam', stated *Uhuru*, TANU's Swahili newspaper. 'The place to use pangas [machetes] and sticks is in the wars in South Africa, Mozambique, Rhodesia, Angola, and elsewhere.'[64]

At a press conference on his return to Dar es Salaam, Mondlane tried to re-establish control. He stated that while two of the assailants were former members who had long deserted FRELIMO, the rest were unknown to the leadership.[65] The Makonde-dominated FRELIMO 'Council of Elders' rejected these claims. In a letter printed in the Tanzanian trade union newspaper, *Mfanya Kazi*, they criticised Mondlane's 'contemptuous designs' over the movement. They also accused Simango of conspiring against Mondlane, but then of shying away from cooperation with the Elders when they sought his help in forcing fresh presidential elections.[66] According to Mondlane, Gwenjere was also at the heart of this latest disturbance. In a letter to George Houser, the head of the American Committee on Africa, an anticolonial pressure group, Mondlane stated that Gwenjere had lobbied the Tanzanian civil service and the Liberation Committee to shut the FRELIMO offices and order elections. When this proved unsuccessful, so Mondlane claimed, Gwenjere encouraged members of his church, who were mostly Makonde, to first close the offices and then attack the reopened premises. After the fracas, the Tanzanian government arrested a number of Mozambican refugees in Dar es Salaam,

---

[63] For an eyewitness account, see Lopes Tembe Ndelana, *From UDENAMO to FRELIMO and Mozambican Diplomacy* (Terra Alta, WV: Headline Books, 2016), 96–97.
[64] Editorial, *Uhuru*, 11 May 1968, 2.
[65] Mondlane, press statement, 26 May 1968, OCA, HSC, Subgroup II, Series 4, Box 1.
[66] 'Chanzo na chokochoko katika FRELIMO ni hila na uongozi mbaya wa viongozi wake', *Mfanya Kazi*, 8 June 1968, 7.

among them Gwenjere, with the intention of removing them from the capital.⁶⁷

Meanwhile, Kavandame's supporters in Cabo Delgado continued to challenge the central leadership in Dar es Salaam. In the aftermath of the unrest at the Mozambique Institute, FRELIMO branch leaders wrote to the Central Committee (quite possibly with Kavandame's blessing) to express their dismay at the turn of events. They claimed that Gwenjere had been sent to Tanzania by the Portuguese to stir up trouble and accused him of being a *'lipyoto'* – a Swahili term for a large bird that pollutes water supplies. However, having sided with Mondlane in his opposition to Gwenjere, the Cabo Delgado leaders then turned their fire on their nominal superiors in Dar es Salaam. They dismissed reports that Kavandame was a PIDE agent and defended his economic activities in Cabo Delgado as the operations of a FRELIMO cooperative, rather than private business. It was not Kavandame who was doing the work of the Portuguese by dividing the movement, they alleged, but the leadership in Dar es Salaam. Although the Cabo Delgado leaders continued to speak in the name of FRELIMO, they called for a Congress and fresh elections to the Central Committee.⁶⁸ Mondlane's rivals were not united, as the denunciation of the 'traitor' Gwenjere from Cabo Delgado shows. Yet this only complicated Mondlane's position further still. He came under attack from multiple angles, with each critic tapping into different sources of discontent.

By mid-1968, Mondlane's position appeared particularly fragile. Word reached Lisbon that morale among the Mozambican exiles was low. One Portuguese informer in Tanzania predicted that 'at any moment now, there will be an attempt on the life of Dr. Mondlane to assassinate him'.⁶⁹ In these circumstances, Mondlane bowed to demands that FRELIMO hold a Special Congress in July. Kavandame wanted it to take place in southern Tanzania, where his support base was strongest. Instead, Mondlane decided to hold the meeting on liberated Mozambican soil. Fearing an anti-Makonde plot, Kavandame and his

---

⁶⁷ Mondlane to Houser, 5 June 1968, OCA, HSC, Subgroup II, Series 2, Box 2. Laweki disputes this interpretation: *Mateus Pinho Gwenjere*, 222.
⁶⁸ FRELIMO Regional Branch, Cabo Delgado, 9 March 1968, enclosed in FRELIMO Regional Branch, Zanzibar, to Office of Regional Commissioner, Zanzibar Urban, 11 May 1968, ZNA AK26/98, 16–18.
⁶⁹ Unsigned letter, 27 May 1968, enclosed in director, PIDE, to director-general of political affairs, MNE, 7 November 1968, AHD, MNE, PAA 569.

supporters boycotted the Congress, at which Mondlane and dos Santos strengthened their positions. The former was re-elected president, narrowly beating Simango in a secret ballot. The Congress passed a programme that transformed FRELIMO into a centralised 'vanguard party'.[70] 'FRELIMO is really more socialist, revolutionary, and progressive than before', Mondlane told an interviewer, 'and now tends more and more in the direction of the Marxist-Leninist variety'.[71] Yet beneath this bravado, there remained fundamental tensions between Mondlane and Simango. Furthermore, the problem posed to the leadership by Kavandame was unresolved. At this point, Nyerere intervened directly. In August, he brought Mondlane and Kavandame together in Mtwara, southeastern Tanzania, at a meeting attended by several FRELIMO leaders, plus officials representing TANU and the OAU Liberation Committee. But Kavandame refused to compromise. Instead, he pushed ahead with his attempt to set up a rival Makonde separatist movement.[72]

Mondlane's Enemies in Tanzania

FRELIMO's divisive politics were not purely a Mozambican affair. They also involved Tanzanians pursuing their own agendas in destabilising Mondlane's position. The longer the liberation movements were based in Dar es Salaam, the more they became 'domesticated' and entangled with local politics. Multiple institutions in the capital had oversight for the movements' activities: the OAU Liberation Committee, various government ministries, and the Second Vice-President's Office, plus the police, the TPDF, and the president himself. This placed multiple office-holders, often with contrasting aims, in crucial gatekeeping roles vis-à-vis the crisis inside FRELIMO. Critical commentary in the local press also played a role in aggravating the splits. Yet these were not just institutional divisions. Just like the tussles inside FRELIMO, individual Tanzanians were motivated by interwoven issues of ethno-racial identity, political views, and personal relationships.

In FRELIMO's early years, Mondlane was able to fall back on his good relations with the Tanzanian leadership for support. In

[70] Cabrita, *Mozambique*, 56–57.
[71] 'The Evolution of FRELIMO', in Aquino de Bragança and Immanuel Wallerstein (eds.), *The African Liberation Reader, vol. 2: The National Liberation Movements* (London: Zed, 1982), 121.
[72] Cabrita, *Mozambique*, 56.

particular, Nyerere and Kambona were powerful allies. The Tanzanian government's sovereign power to expel dissidents from the country had then enabled Mondlane to secure his own authority within FRELIMO.[73] However, after Kambona fled into exile in 1967, those Tanzanians tasked with overseeing the guerrillas' security were less inclined towards Mondlane. Rashidi Kawawa's Second Vice-President's Office was responsible for refugee affairs, which included the liberation movements' security. Kawawa himself expressed some scepticism about Mondlane's political credentials. He told a visiting Soviet delegation in 1967 that he did not believe Mondlane would be the leader of a future independent Mozambican state.[74] But if Kawawa's stance towards Mondlane was tepid, then the attitude of other figures at the Second Vice-President's Office was positively hostile.

Chief among these officials was Lawi Sijaona, a minister of state with responsibility for refugee matters. Sijaona built his career through his leadership of the TANU Youth League during the struggle for independence. After *uhuru*, he served in a number of cabinet roles, including as minister for home affairs from 1965 to 1967. His personal politics set him at odds with Mondlane on multiple grounds. Sijaona had a reputation, like many TYL cadres, for his hostility towards the presence of Asians and Europeans in Tanzania.[75] Mondlane's connections with the United States, his white wife, and upmarket lifestyle represented everything that Sijaona stood against. In addition, Sijaona and the TYL were closely associated with the Maoist streak inside TANU. This gave Sijaona common ideological ground with Uria Simango, who was reportedly unhappy with FRELIMO's gravitation away from Beijing and towards Moscow. Born in Mtwara, Sijaona was also a Makonde and so shared an ethnic background with Lazaro Kavandame and his supporters. A shared animosity towards Mondlane also seems to have pushed Sijaona towards collaboration with Mateus Gwenjere.[76] The Dutch embassy went as far as to describe

---

[73] Cabrita, *Mozambique*, 12, 17; Manghezi, *O meu coração*, 225; interview with Kingunge Ngombale-Mwiru, Victoria, Dar es Salaam, 26 August 2015.
[74] Lessing, 24 February 1967, PAAA, MfAA, M3, 136, 1–8.
[75] Burns to State Dept, 28 March 1969, NARA, RG 59, CFPF 1967–69, Box 2513, POL 2 TANZAN.
[76] Laweki, *Mateus Pinho Gwenjere*, 220–21; Helder Martins, *Porqué Sakrani? Memórias dum medico duma guerrilha esquecida* (Maputo: Editorial Terceiro Milénio, 2001), 350.

the priest as Sijaona's 'protégé'.[77] Finally, according to the American embassy, Sijaona disliked the manner in which Mondlane frequently bypassed him in preference for dealing directly with Kawawa.[78] In short, for ethnic, ideological, and personal reasons, Sijaona resented Mondlane.

Sijaona and senior bureaucrats in Kawawa's office actively undermined Mondlane, apparently against the inclinations of the second vice-president himself. After the trouble at the Mozambique Institute, Mondlane ordered the school's closure and for the students to be sent to rural camps. In Kawawa's absence, Sijaona countermanded Mondlane's order – until Kawawa returned and overruled his deputy.[79] In April, despite opposition from Sijaona, Mondlane won Kawawa's agreement for a round-up of FRELIMO deserters and dissidents in Dar es Salaam. These measures were never implemented.[80] After the attack on FRELIMO's headquarters, Kawawa rejected accusations published by *Mfanya Kazi* that his office could have prevented the violence by providing adequate police protection. He explained in parliament that the Tanzanian government would not interfere in FRELIMO's internal affairs, so long as they conformed with the laws of the country: Tanzania could not tolerate violence on its territory. On 29 May, the Tanzanian government expelled three white Portuguese teachers from the Mozambique Institute and gave them three days to leave the country. A FRELIMO official told the East Germans that the decision was again taken in the absence of Kawawa, suggesting the hand of Sijaona. On this occasion, when Kawawa returned, he did not overturn the order, but merely extended the deadline for the teachers' departure.[81]

Mondlane himself identified Sijaona as a problematic and influential figure within the Tanzanian state apparatus. He briefed diplomatic contacts on both sides of the Iron Curtain that Sijaona was scheming against him, alleging that there was possible collaboration with the Chinese involved. To Mondlane's relief, Sijaona was then removed

---

[77] Brink to Ministry of Foreign Affairs, 7 February 1969, NAN, 2.05.253/313.
[78] Burns to State Dept, 10 May 1969, NARA, RG 59, CFPF 1967–69, Box 2513, POL 2 TANZAN.
[79] Burns to State Dept, 28 March 1969, NARA, RG 59, CFPF 1967–69, Box 2513, POL 2 TANZAN.
[80] Burns to State Dept, 9 and 10 May 1968, NARA, RG 59, CFPF 1967–69, Box 2515, POL 13 TANZAN.
[81] Müller, 5 June 1968, BA-B, SAPMO, DZ 8/163.

from the Second Vice-President's Office. In October, Nyerere used a cabinet reshuffle to move Sijaona into the position of minister for health. Mondlane claimed to the British that this was the result of his own petitioning of Sijaona's superiors.[82] A FRELIMO militant also recalled that Sijaona's replacement was part of an effort by Nyerere to consolidate Mondlane's authority within the movement.[83] These concerns may well have played a part in Nyerere's reasoning, although the embarrassment caused by Sijaona's involvement in a raucous demonstration at the Soviet embassy following the invasion of Czechoslovakia also contributed to his relocation to a less politically sensitive role.[84]

This opposition to Mondlane from influential Tanzanian politicians went hand in hand with criticism in the party press. The *Nationalist* was strongly associated with TANU's radical wing, including members of the Youth League. Its journalists were ardent supporters of China. Like Sijaona, they too were hostile towards Mondlane's leadership style and geopolitical orientation. The day after the fight at 201 Nkrumah Street, a *Nationalist* editorial criticised the lack of democracy within FRELIMO and other liberation movements. It remarked that 'conferences are never called to allow for members to exercise their right to choose their leaders or to endorse their trust in existing ones'.[85] At a rally to mark African Liberation Day on 26 May, the president of Zanzibar, Abeid Karume, accused the guerrilla leaders of being more preoccupied with issuing news bulletins than liberating their territory.[86] The *Nationalist* hammered home the point. It accused certain unnamed leaders of living 'luxuriously in air conditioned bungalows in independent African countries at a time when their own people are suffering from untold colonial cruelties'.[87] Complaints about the behaviour of the liberation movement leaders were, as we have seen, not uncommon in the Tanzanian press at this time.

[82] Wilson to Scott, 21 October 1968, UKNA, FCO 45/174/7; José Manuel Duarte de Jesus, *Eduardo Mondlane: Um homem a abater* (Coimbra: Almedina, 2010), 325.
[83] Josefina Daniel Nkulunguila, 'Frente de Cabo Delgado', in Joel das Neves Tembe (ed.), *História da luta de libertação nacional* (Maputo: Ministerio dos Combatentes – Direcçao Nacional de Historia, 2014), 321.
[84] See Chapter 5.
[85] 'Fracas at FRELIMO Offices', *Nationalist*, 10 May 1968, 1.
[86] 'Victory Is Certain – Karume', *Nationalist*, 27 May 1968, 1.
[87] 'Freedom Fighters', editorial, *Nationalist*, 28 May 1968, 4.

Mondlane had already responded to such criticisms after the violence at the Mozambique Institute in March. 'In Dar es Salaam I don't even think you see even one per cent of the people who belong to the movements', he said. 'I think it is wrong to judge by the behaviour of two or three people who may do some outrageous things.'[88] But the press seemed to have made up its mind. Even if this criticism was not as visceral a threat as the armed thugs who ransacked the FRELIMO offices, it nonetheless helped to establish a discursive environment which facilitated challenges to Mondlane's authority.

The extent of this press opposition to Mondlane was revealed again in November, when the *Nationalist* reported on a visit he had made to Nairobi. It claimed that at a private dinner, Mondlane had briefed a group of Americans who were in Kenya to attend an 'American-African Dialogue' meeting, sponsored by the Ford Foundation. Some of them had connections in the State Department, including Wayne Fredericks, Mondlane's friend, though he had left his position two years previously.[89] The *Nationalist* repeated rumours that the CIA had penetrated FRELIMO.[90] Mondlane claimed that he had been in Kenya to meet President Jomo Kenyatta and had met the Americans by chance. He also questioned why the *Nationalist* had referenced his wife's race and nationality in the report.[91] The *Nationalist*'s selective use of information was another demonstration of its hostility: while condemning Mondlane's presence at the dinner, it neglected to mention that several prominent OAU and TANU officials, including President Nyerere's brother, had also attended.[92] Nyerere himself seemed unconcerned. He told George Houser that the *Nationalist* articles were 'ridiculous', adding that 'we don't censor everything that goes into the paper'.[93] But other members of the government were less convinced. The minister of state for foreign affairs, Stephen Mhando, told the East Germans that the Nairobi meeting confirmed Mondlane's proximity to the United States.[94]

---

[88] 'The War Against the Portuguese', *Weekly News*, 15 March 1968, 15.
[89] Schneidman, *Engaging Africa*, 102–103.
[90] 'Mondlane in Nairobi Dialogue', *Nationalist*, 23 November 1968, 1.
[91] Statement by Mondlane, 23 November 1968, Fundação Mário Soares, Arquivo Mário Pinto de Andrade, pt. 04322.005.011.
[92] Pickering to State Dept, 29 November 1968, NARA, RG 59, CFPF 1967–69, Box 2513, POL 2 TANZAN.
[93] Houser to Osborne, 31 December 1968, OCA, HSC, Subgroup II, Series 6, Box 2, Microfiche 3.
[94] Schlegel, 5 December 1968, BA-B, SAPMO, DY 30/98137, 262–63.

Trouble continued to mount inside FRELIMO in the aftermath of the fractious congress in July. In December, Paulo Kankhomba, a FRELIMO representative sent to implement the reforms agreed upon at the congress, was murdered by Makonde militants in Cabo Delgado. Meanwhile, Gwenjere set about planning fresh elections for a new FRELIMO president.[95] In response, Mondlane moved against his rivals. According to Gwenjere, on 27 December, Tanzanian officials raided his home; the following day, he was arrested and deported from Dar es Salaam to the northwestern town of Tabora.[96] Then, on 3 January 1969, the FRELIMO Central Committee suspended Kavandame from his duties as provincial secretary in Cabo Delgado. But Mondlane's actions brought only temporary respite. Portuguese intelligence in Mozambique reported that Dar es Salaam was 'swarming with people from all around, completely out of control and causing the FRELIMO leadership serious concerns'.[97] On 1 February, Mondlane met officials from the Second Vice-President's Office. He expressed concern about the continued threat posed to him by Kavandame and his Tanzanian supporters, including Sijaona.[98]

Two days later, Eduardo Mondlane was dead.

Who Killed Eduardo Mondlane?

Mondlane was not, of course, the only liberation movement leader to be murdered in the struggle for independence in southern Africa. In *The Assassination of Herbert Chitepo*, historian Luise White traces debate about the car bombing which killed the ZANU leader in Lusaka in 1975. Rather than attempt to identify the perpetrator, White deftly demonstrates how the various stories told about Chitepo's assassination represent attempts to shape the history of the liberation struggle as a source of authority in postcolonial Zimbabwe. The assassination of Mondlane in Dar es Salaam six years earlier has been subject to similar dynamics – though with the caveat that whereas multiple figures have 'confessed' to the murder of Chitepo, the debate about Mondlane's killers is marked by accusation and denial. Nonetheless, in both cases, the existence of plural, incompatible accounts of the

[95] Marcum, *Conceiving Mozambique*, 131–32.
[96] Laweki, *Mateus Pinho Gwenjere*, 235–36.
[97] SCCIM, 16 January 1969, TT, SCCIM/A/20-7/30, 135–36.
[98] Cabrita, *Mozambique*, 58.

assassination were only made possible by the circumstances of exile. Lusaka and Dar es Salaam were rumour-filled 'Cold War cities' characterised by a political cosmopolitanism that brought together issues of ethnicity, ideology, and personal rivalries. These conditions permitted the advancement of so many competing and intersecting agendas as to make disentangling the causes of the assassinations a near impossible task.[99]

In Dar es Salaam, Tanzania's Criminal Investigation Department (CID) took up the murder case. It soon identified the Soviet stamp on the parcel as a forgery. The remnants of the device – plus two identical bombs encased in further Plekhanov volumes, addressed to dos Santos and Simango in the following weeks and intercepted by the police – were sent to London for analysis. Through Interpol, Scotland Yard found that the batteries in the detonators had been manufactured in Osaka, Japan, and sold by a firm in Lourenço Marques. The Tanzanian police believed that the bomb had been constructed in Mozambique and then inserted into Mondlane's mailbag by a FRELIMO member in Dar es Salaam.[100] But after concluding its investigation in May 1969, the CID kept silent for three years. In February 1972, Radio Tanzania announced that the police knew who had killed Mondlane but refused to name him. These details were revealed in the *Observer* by David Martin, who used insider information from the Tanzanian police to establish the technical specifics involved in the bombing.[101]

Moving beyond this 'official story', we enter the territory of rumour and rumination. Chatter in Dar es Salaam's political circles considered the potential culpability of a whole gamut of suspects.[102] Both the Soviet Union and China might have had vested interests in eliminating Mondlane, who was perceived to be the moderate tip of a movement that appeared to be taking a more radical direction and who had

---

[99] White, *Assassination of Herbert Chitepo*.
[100] Burns to State Dept, 13 and 15 February 1969, NARA, RG 59, CFPF 1967–69, Box 2354, POL 30 MOZ.
[101] David Martin, 'Interpol Solves a Guerrilla Whodunit', *Observer*, 6 February 1972, 4. See also James R. Brennan, 'David Martin: Tracking the 1969 Killing of Mozambique's Independence Fighter, Eduardo Mondlane', in Anya Schiffrin and George Lugalambi (eds.), *African Muckraking: 75 Years of Investigative Journalism from Africa* (Auckland Park: Jacana, 2017), 11–19.
[102] For examples of these rumours, fanned by the international press, see Anthony Astrachan, 'Guerrillas' Leader Buried in Tanzania: Chinese Suspected', *Washington Post*, 7 February 1969, A24.

known connections with the United States.¹⁰³ As we have seen, there were already suspicions that the Chinese had sought to foment discontent among Makonde workers in Dar es Salaam. But would they risk an assassination attempt on a guerrilla leader who maintained the support of Nyerere, one of Beijing's closest allies in Africa? No hard evidence has emerged that links either communist superpower to the assassination. Talk of their involvement is nonetheless indicative of the degree to which FRELIMO had become embroiled in the Cold War world, as well as the predilection for speculating about the hidden hand of the superpowers among journalists and diplomats in Dar es Salaam.

Cutting through this Cold War 'noise', most accounts of the assassination suspect that the PIDE was behind the plot. Yet removing Mondlane was not unequivocally in Lisbon's interests. A Portuguese Overseas Ministry report concluded that although the turmoil arising from Mondlane's death represented a short-term benefit, the long-term consequences of a more revolutionary FRELIMO were far more disadvantageous.¹⁰⁴ One Portuguese intelligence source in Lourenço Marques expressed his fear to the Americans that an extremist turn within FRELIMO might lead to the beginning of an urban terror campaign in Mozambique, a strategy Mondlane had ruled out.¹⁰⁵ The South African consul in Mozambique reported that while the assassination had not been met with 'undue surprise' there, it was also 'not necessarily good news', given the likelihood of Simango taking over as president.¹⁰⁶ As we will see, FRELIMO did take a more explicitly Marxist-Leninist ideological direction after Mondlane's death, even if neither a turn to terror nor Simango's triumph ultimately came to pass.

The PIDE's own archives offer no real supporting evidence. An internal report did not hide the PIDE's disdain for Mondlane as Washington's 'pretty boy', whose 'sandcastle' had been undermined by 'sly' Chinese diplomacy. It concluded that the responsibility for his death lay with Beijing.¹⁰⁷ But even if we accept this denial as genuine,

---

103 Jesus, *Eduardo Mondlane*, 367–68.
104 Catalão, 4 February 1969, AHD, MU, GM/GNP/RNP/160, 10° pt.
105 Gossett to State Dept, 4 February 1969, NARA, RG 59, CFPF 1967–69, Box 2354, POL 30 MOZ.
106 Gleeson to Bureau of State Security, 4 February 1969, SADF, HSI-AMI, GP3, Box 953.
107 Jesus, *Eduardo Mondlane*, 345.

the absence of 'official' PIDE participation does not preclude the involvement of Portuguese agents. Multiple sources have claimed that the shadowy Aginter Press network attempted to disrupt the activities of FRELIMO in exile. Ostensibly a publishing house, Aginter was connected to Operation GLADIO, NATO's stay-behind network of sleeper cells in Western Europe. GLADIO was originally intended to coordinate resistance in the aftermath of a Soviet invasion, but later became associated with anti-communist terrorism with dubious links to conservative European governments.[108] Aginter may have been involved in stirring up trouble among FRELIMO during 1968 through the cover of a journalist who held interviews with prominent leaders, including Mondlane, dos Santos, and Gwenjere.[109] Aginter was also connected to Jorge Jardim, a Mozambique-based businessman who had a strong relationship with Salazar. Although Jardim denied any responsibility, the editor of the newspaper which he owned, *Notícias da Beira*, noted that on the day of Mondlane's assassination Jardim waited at the newspaper's office in expectation of 'important news'.[110] Several sources have claimed that the bomb which killed Mondlane was assembled by Casimiro Monteiro, a Goa-born explosives expert and Aginter operative. Monteiro was first named as a participant in the assassination plot by David Martin in 1975. This has been corroborated by two PIDE agents and a Rhodesian intelligence officer, as well as Monteiro's own son, though there remains some scepticism about the trustworthiness of their stories.[111]

Even if the matter of Portuguese culpability is accepted, the question of Mozambican collaboration remains a fraught political issue. From the beginning of the liberation struggle, FRELIMO's leadership has maintained a tightly policed 'official history'.[112] This equates

[108] Frederic Laurent and Nina Sutton, *L'Orchestre noir* (Paris: Éditions Stock, 1978); Daniele Ganser, *NATO's Secret Armies: Operation GLADIO and Terrorism in Western Europe* (London: Frank Cass, 2005); José Manuel Duarte de Jesus, *A guerra secreta de Salazar em África. Aginter Press: Um rede internacional de contra-subversão e espionagem em Lisboa* (Algragide: Dom Quixote, 2012).
[109] Laurent and Sutton, *L'Orchestre noir*, 151–54.
[110] Dalila Cabrita Mateus, *PIDE/DGS na guerra colonial, 1961–1974* (Lisbon: Terramar, 2004), 172.
[111] Mateus, *PIDE/DGS*, 172–73; Jesus, *Eduardo Mondlane*, 347; Cahen, 'La "fin de l'histoire..."', 213n85; Joaquim Furtado (dir.), *A Guerra* (RTP, 2012), episode 13 – 'Morte de Eduardo Mondlane'.
[112] For a recent example, see das Neves Tembe (ed.), *História da luta*.

FRELIMO with the Mozambican nation itself and casts any dissidents within the movement, like Simango and Gwenjere, in traitorous terms. More recent histories have challenged this official narrative, particularly through the genre of autobiography and biography.[113] The outcome has been a heated debate in memoirs, newspaper columns, and on the Mozambican blogosphere. The assassination of Mondlane forms a critical, dramatic juncture around which many of these competing histories pivot. In the absence of hard evidence about the actual bomb plot, explanations for the tensions of 1968 serve as means for casting aspersions as to who might have carried it out, even if there is no direct link between the two.[114]

FRELIMO's supporters usually identify three prominent Mozambicans as complicit in the assassination: Kavandame, Simango, and Gwenjere. When they began their investigation in 1969, the CID's prime suspect was Kavandame. Its chief for the Coast Region, Gerald Manikam, told the American embassy that, while conducting investigations a week after the assassination, he had encountered Kavandame in Mtwara, where he was being sheltered by the local TANU chairman. In response to Manikam's questions, Kavandame gave inconsistent and incomplete answers. In March, Kavandame defected to the Portuguese, giving FRELIMO scope to cast him as a bourgeois 'traitor' to the national liberation struggle.[115] The CID's other main suspect was Silvério Nungu, an official at FRELIMO's headquarters with access to Mondlane's mail. Shortly after the assassination, Nungu was moved to a new role inside liberated Mozambique. According to FRELIMO, he was caught while also attempting to defect and died of a hunger strike in prison. Simango claimed he was executed.[116]

---

[113] Rita Chaves, 'Autobiografias em Moçambique: A escrita como monument (2001–2013)', *Revista de História*, 178 (2019), 1–22.
[114] For discussion of these 'memory wars', see Alice Dinerman, *Revolution, Counter-Revolution and Revisionism in Post-Colonial Africa: The Case of FRELIMO, 1975–1994* (London: Routledge, 2006); Amélia Neves de Souto, 'Memory and Identity in the History of Frelimo: Some Research Themes', *Kronos*, 39 (2013), 280–96; Victor Igreja, 'Politics of Memory, Decentralisation and Recentralisation in Mozambique', *Journal of Southern African Studies*, 39 (2013), 313–35.
[115] Cabrita, *Mozambique*, 60; Burns to State Dept, 27 March 1969, NARA, RG 59, CFPF 1967–69, Box 2354, POL 30 MOZ.
[116] David Martin, 'Interpol Solves a Guerrilla Whodunit', *Observer*, 6 February 1972, 4.

Suspicion of Simango largely stems from his actions after the death of Mondlane. Under FRELIMO's constitution, the vice-president should have taken over the leadership. However, doubts about Simango's loyalty led the Central Committee to establish a 'Council of the Presidency' in April 1969, in which he shared power with dos Santos and Machel. The latter two developed into a stronger faction. In November, Simango published a pamphlet entitled 'Gloomy Situation in FRELIMO', which accused dos Santos and Machel of murder, tribalism, and nepotism, calling them 'vipers' and 'tools of imperialism'. He blamed the split not on ideological division, but rather on the predominance of southerners in FRELIMO.[117] Simango was expelled from FRELIMO and subsequently joined COREMO, the Chinese-backed movement operating out of Zambia. After Mozambique gained independence in 1975, Simango was forced to read a 'confession' of his guilt before a kangaroo court. He was sent to a 're-education camp' and eventually murdered in 1978.[118]

Gwenjere, the third major dissenter, appears to have met a similar end at the hands of FRELIMO. Gwenjere fled Tabora for Kenya in 1972. From Nairobi, he attempted to organise a party of FRELIMO dissidents, including Simango. He moved back to Mozambique after the revolution in Portugal, but then returned to Kenya when it became clear that FRELIMO would assume power. He was kidnapped in Nairobi in 1975 and never seen again.[119] In FRELIMO circles, Gwenjere is suspected of being a PIDE agent, who was sent to Tanzania to infiltrate the movement. For example, Helder Martins, a teacher at the Mozambique Institute, places Gwenjere at the centre of the bomb plot, which he alleges was only made possible by co-conspirators inside FRELIMO.[120] In his memoirs, Mondlane's former secretary, Sérgio Vieira, recounts a conspiracy in which the parcel bomb was transferred to Dar es Salaam via Portuguese agents in Malawi and Mozambicans in Tanzania, including Nungu and

---

[117] Uria Simango, 'Gloomy Situation in FRELIMO', 30 November 1969, in de Bragança and Wallerstein (eds.), *African Liberation Reader*, 125–27.
[118] Cabrita, *Mozambique*, 81–84.
[119] Laweki, *Mateus Pinho Gwenjere*, 247–52.
[120] Martins, *Porquê Sakrani?*, 357. Martins later claimed that he himself had unknowingly passed the package to Simango, as requested by a Belgian missionary friend of Gwenjere. Jesus, *Eduardo Mondlane*, 366.

Gwenjere. Vieira also claims that Kavandame and Simango knew of the assassination plot in advance.[121]

Since Mozambique's post-independence civil war came to an end and democratic space for dissent reopened inside the country, there has been a backlash against this 'official' history. Biographers of Simango and Gwenjere have sought to exonerate their subjects.[122] In particular, they blame the FRELIMO leadership's pursuit of factional agendas for the creation of a rift between 'northerners' and 'southerners', with the latter working closely with 'Mozambicans of non-native origin'. These divisions then translated into ideological differences. Gwenjere's biographer observes that the well-educated 'non-natives', together with the likes of Mondlane, 'displayed radical thinking' and were 'entrusted with the task of delineating the movement's line of thought, thus influencing its alignment during the Cold War [sic] geopolitics'.[123] These histories suffer from oversimplified categorisations, selective use of evidence, and chronological inconsistencies (Simango, a 'northerner', had his own international connections in the socialist world, for example). Nonetheless, they serve as important reminders of alternative interpretations to the dominant FRELIMO narrative of the Mozambican liberation struggle.[124]

Finally, there remains the question of Tanzanian complicity. These Mozambican 'memory wars' focus on the Mozambican protagonists, often isolating them from the entanglements of exile politics. Martins, who was among the white teachers at the Mozambique Institute who were ordered to leave Tanzania in 1968, believes that Sijaona was 'undoubtedly' involved.[125] The integrity of the police investigation has also been called into question by various sources. According to information given to the American embassy by Manikam, the police were assisted in their investigation by the Chinese. Manikam said that Sijaona was under surveillance by the security services, who were amassing evidence against him in connection with his embroilment in FRELIMO affairs.[126] Janet Mondlane has recalled that a police officer

---

[121] Sérgio Vieira, *Participei, por isso testemunho* (Maputo: Editorial Ndijira, 2010), 257–59.
[122] Laweki, *Mateus Pinho Gwenjere*; Ncomo, *Uria Simango*.
[123] Laweki, *Mateus Pinho Gwenjere*, 226.
[124] See also the critique of Ncomo in Cahen 'La "fin de l'histoire..."'.
[125] Martins, *Porquê Sakrani?*, 357.
[126] Memcon (Manikam, Pickering), 24 March 1969, NARA, RG 59, CFPF 1967–69, Box 2354, POL 30 MOZ.

working on the case with her was suddenly transferred to Moshi, as he 'was digging up things that the Tanzanian government did not want to reveal'. She has never seen the Tanzanian report into her husband's assassination.[127]

The potential implication of senior members of Tanzania's state and security apparatus may explain why the CID's findings have never been released. During both the liberation struggle against the Portuguese and Mozambique's post-independence civil war, FRELIMO depended on a close relationship with the Tanzanian government. Any evidence of Tanzanian involvement in the death of Mondlane would therefore have been a source of embarrassment for both sides. At the very least, as this chapter has shown, members of the Tanzanian government played a role in undermining Mondlane's position, even as others continued to support him. CCM today continues to draw political capital for itself as a 'liberation movement in power', as well as in promoting relationships with its now-independent southern neighbours. Tanzanians, too, are rightly proud of the role they played in the liberation of southern Africa. But a more critical reading of this period reveals a far more complex story.

Conclusion

1969 represented a low point in the struggle to liberate Africa. Both the guerrilla movements and the governments of independent Africa were split over the way forward. FRELIMO was fractured in the aftermath of Mondlane's assassination. The ANC and SWAPO held major conferences on Tanzanian soil to address factionalism inside their movements. The OAU Liberation Committee recommended to African states that, faced with the resolute position of the minority states, there was a need for a more comprehensive approach to the anticolonial cause. 'It might not only be imperative for Member-States to contribute materially towards the struggle, but also to take the concrete measures necessary for rehabilitating the African man and expelling the colonialists from our Continent.'[128] Yet some African governments seemed to be moving in the opposite direction. A few independent

---

[127] Furtado (dir.), *A Guerra*, episode 13.
[128] OAU Liberation Committee, Report to the 12th Session of the Council of Ministers, 17 February 1969, African Union Common Repository.

states, such as the Ivory Coast, responded positively to South African diplomatic overtures.[129] Although this détente with apartheid drew fierce criticism from states like Tanzania and Zambia, they too showed signs of softening their stance. In April, fourteen countries from East and Central Africa released the 'Lusaka Manifesto', which appeared to re-open the door for negotiated settlements with the minority states.[130] The ANC leadership was dismayed: this turn away from armed struggle seemed to undermine its own operations, as well as its position that the apartheid regime was essentially illegitimate, thus precluding any African negotiations with it.[131]

These tensions extended to the politics of the OAU's Liberation Committee. Both the guerrilla movements and member states challenged Tanzania's control of the organisation. At a meeting in Dakar in July, Stephen Mhando conceded that Tanzania would permit its headquarters to be moved from Dar es Salaam. In fact, he would not even oppose the abolition of the Liberation Committee altogether. But he reiterated that the liberation struggle itself had to continue. 'The proper place for these disillusioned gentlemen to talk tough is in Salisbury and not in Dar-es-Salaam', Mhando argued. 'They must not sit down in comfort in the capitals of free Africa ... and then have the impudence and the insolence to insult the governments which make possible the struggle in which some of these leaders are unwilling to play a full and physical part.'[132] When the Liberation Committee next met in Moshi in January 1970, George Magombe, its Tanzanian executive secretary, was glum. His report bemoaned 'the continued state of seemingly endless spiral of internecine disputes and ethnic disunity in the rank and file of some of the movements. Much energy and time is dissipated on resolving bickerings and clashes of personality'.[133] This

---

[129] Jamie Miller, *An African Volk: The Apartheid State and Its Struggle for Survival* (Oxford: Oxford University Press, 2016).
[130] N. M. Shamuyarira, 'The Lusaka Manifesto on Southern Africa', *African Review*, 1 (1971), 67–78.
[131] Sifiso Mxolisi Ndlovu, 'The ANC's Diplomacy and International Relations', in SADET, *The Road to Democracy in South Africa, vol. 2 (1970–1980)* (Cape Town: UNISA Press, 2006), 616–17.
[132] Quoted in Mohammed Omar Maundi, 'The Role of the Organisation of African Unity in the Liberation Struggle of Southern Africa', in Temu and das Neves Tembe (eds.), *Southern African Liberation Struggles*, vol. 9, 398–99.
[133] Report to 16th Session of OAU Liberation Committee, 19 January 1970, TNA, 589, BM/24.

nadir prompted Nyerere to restate Tanzania's commitment to armed struggle in the face of white intransigence in southern Africa. In Toronto in October 1969, he stated that 'if the door to freedom is locked and bolted ... the choice is very straightforward. Either you accept the lack of freedom or you break the door down.'[134]

The choice to take up arms against colonialism might have been straightforward, but its implications were not. Liberation movement affairs were characterised by conflicting and converging personal, ideological, geopolitical, regional, and ethnic agendas. This complicated the efforts of foreign powers to influence the struggles, as well as the Tanzanian government's attempts to maintain some control over their activities. By hosting the liberation movements in Dar es Salaam, Tanzanian state actors took on powerful gatekeeping roles. But the assassination of Mondlane served as a bleak reminder that Africa's revolutionaries had dangerous opponents. It was further grist to the mill to those within the Tanzanian state who cited the anti-imperialist threat as necessitating greater vigilance against the county's enemies abroad and their lackeys within, as we will see in later chapters. For all of this, Dar es Salaam rightfully earned its reputation as a revolutionary capital in Africa. The influence of the liberation movements extended far beyond their Nkrumah Street offices. Their daily activities, press coverage, and speeches at rallies or at the university instilled the city's politics with a militant anti-imperialism. As protesters took to the streets in Paris and Prague in the late 1960s, Tanzania's youth were therefore already at the forefront of a revolutionary moment which spanned Africa and the Third World. Their experience of the 'global 1968' forms the subject of the next chapter.

[134] 'Stability and Change in Africa', in Nyerere, *Freedom and Development*, 115–16.

5 | *Tanzania's '68: Cold War Interventions, Youth Protest, and Global Anti-Imperialism*

'Many astrologers have predicated a near-doom for the world in 1968', wrote 'Pressman' in his first *Nationalist* column of the new year. He then listed a series of ongoing crises: the economic exploitation of the developing world, war in Indochina, liberation struggles in Africa, and conflict in the Middle East. 'When the astrologers make their dismal forecasts what they are really saying is that a clash between the people and imperialism (and its lackeys) is drawing nearer and nearer. One does not need to be an astrologer to make this prediction', concluded 'Pressman' – *nom de plume* of A. M. Babu.[1]

The events of the year which followed might even have surprised Babu himself. Around the world, students and youths took to the streets. While their demands were diverse, their anger shared a common target: an unjust global order, dominated by the superpowers and upheld by ruling elites. The Third World played a central role in shaping these movements. In Europe and North America, protesters condemned the neocolonial interventions of their own governments and the widening economic gulf between the West and the postcolonial world. They pointed to the grim fate of Africa's revolutionaries, especially the martyred Patrice Lumumba, as evidence of the forces of imperialism at work. Lumumba and those who followed him, like Ahmed Ben Bella and Kwame Nkrumah, became, as Jean Allman puts it, 'canaries in the coal mine of postwar global politics'.[2] The Third World was not just an inspiration behind the events of the 'global 1968', but also a site of protest and dissent itself. Youth activists in

---

[1] [A. M. Babu], 'Significance of 1968', *Nationalist*, 5 January 1968, 1.
[2] Jean Allman, 'The Fate of All of Us: African Counterrevolutions and the Ends of 1968', *American Historical Review*, 123 (2018), 731. See for example Sean Mills, *The Empire Within: Postcolonial Thought and Political Activism in Sixties Montreal* (Montreal: McGill-Queen's University Press, 2010); Quinn Slobodian, *Foreign Front: Third World Politics in Sixties West Germany* (Durham, NC: Duke University Press, 2012); Jon Piccini, *Transnational Protest, Australia and the 1960s: Global Radicals* (London: Palgrave Macmillan, 2016).

the postcolonial world voiced their own criticisms of the status quo and articulated visions of alternative futures.[3]

This chapter situates Dar es Salaam amid this transcontinental landscape of protest and youth politics. As Victoria Langland argues in her study of Brazil, historians 'have tended toward noting the international context without integrating it into the local narrative of 1968'. She calls for greater attention to 'how contemporaneous beliefs, fears, and suspicions about such connections affected the course of local events'.[4] Dar es Salaam's central position in global revolutionary networks encouraged Tanzanians to speak out against imperialist interventions in distant states. However, unlike the bulk of protests elsewhere in the world, the demonstrations in the capital in 1968 and the broadsides which appeared in the city's press pledged support to their own government, rather than opposition to it. This chapter uses three protests as apertures through which to unpack these dynamics in Dar es Salaam. Two of these – against the United States' war in Vietnam and the Soviet-led invasion of Czechoslovakia – were central to the global wave of activism. The other – in response to Malawi's claims on Tanzanian territory – was a distinctly local affair but bound up in the politics of African liberation struggles.

Rather than take a strictly bottom-up approach to these protests, this chapter shows how they were entangled with the Tanzanian government's practices of state-building and foreign policy. Tanzanian students and youth activists cited examples of 'imperialism' intervention as justification for increased 'vigilance' and unity through TANU. The strength and nature of street protests and newspaper polemics were shaped not only by the government's anti-imperialist world view, but by the nuances of Tanzania's international relations with the superpowers and within Africa. In this way, the transnational motifs and languages which characterised the revolutions of '1968' were tethered to the nation-building and foreign policy aims of the Tanzanian party-state. However, this relationship between youth and state also meant that there were strict limits to the form and content of protest. On occasions, they upset the public image of Tanzanian foreign policy, as

---

[3] Samantha Christiansen and Zachary A. Scarlett (eds.), *The Third World in the Global 1960s* (New York: Berghahn, 2013).

[4] Victoria Langland, *Speaking of Flowers: Student Movements and the Making and Remembering of 1968 in Military Brazil* (Durham, NC: Duke University Press, 2013), 8–9.

we have already seen in the raucous scenes at the British high commission following Rhodesia's UDI in 1965, for example. At other times, they indirectly challenged the authority of TANU's leadership, which in some cases drew interventions from President Nyerere himself.

The Global Sixties Come to Dar es Salaam

In Africa, student and youth protest was bound up in the structural challenges of decolonisation. Student numbers across the continent expanded rapidly after independence, as states recognised the need to fill the ranks of bureaucracies and develop technical expertise. In turn, students acquired rising expectations of the individual economic prospects which they anticipated higher education would open up to them. This mutually beneficial relationship between students and state broke down in the mid-1960s, as progressive African governments fell prey to coups or abandoned investment in universities in the face of economic difficulties. Students and youths challenged this shift by repossessing and reasserting the revolutionary agenda of the anticolonial struggle. In some instances, the state responded with crackdowns, backed up by violence.[5] In Tanzania, as Chapter 2 explained, Nyerere responded to demonstrations against the imposition of national service with a mass rustication of the majority of the student body.

However, focusing on students can mask the role played by youth activists who were mobilised through other institutions, especially the militant wings of ruling parties.[6] From the beginning of the anticolonial campaign, Tanganyika's nationalist leadership recognised the potential of youth politics as a means for mobilising a growing, energetic, and marginalised group. The TANU Youth League was established in 1956. It provided a mechanism for enlisting young Tanzanians in the liberation struggle, but also for exerting top-down control over them, by bringing them under the party umbrella. After independence, the TYL assumed key security functions within the state apparatus. In

---

[5] Françoise Blum, Pierre Guidi, and Ophélie Rillon (eds.), *Étudiants africains en mouvements: Contribution à une histoire des années 1968* (Paris: Publications de la Sorbonne, 2016).

[6] For examples from West Africa, see Ahlman, *Living with Nkrumahism*, 84–114; Jay Straker, *Youth, Nationalism, and the Guinean Revolution* (Bloomington: Indiana University Press, 2009); on Zanzibar, see G. Thomas Burgess, 'The Young Pioneers and the Rituals of Citizenship in Revolutionary Africa', *Africa Today*, 51 (2005), 3–29.

1963, the government wound up the colonial Special Branch security forces. The more informal structures which replaced it were manned by TYL cadres. When the Tanganyika Rifles were disbanded after the mutiny of 1964, recruits to the new TPDF were scrutinised by the TYL.[7]

The student protests of November 1966 brought about a top-down recalibration of the relationship between the state and the student body. The students were not simply rusticated but vilified as unpatriotic in the press. Counterdemonstrations organised by the TYL and other party organisations took place in Dar es Salaam. At the same time as they chastised the students, TANU's spokesmen praised the revolutionary potential of the country's youth. A branch of the TYL was set up at the university in an attempt to tie the students into this party-sponsored youth movement, rather than allow them to pursue more individualist goals that ran counter to the government's development plans.[8] The Arusha Declaration continued this practice of foregrounding the youth as key actors in Tanzania's national revolution. As Nyerere told the TANU leaders who gathered in Arusha, '[o]ur country is a country of youth; we are all young and our blood is still hot'.[9] Thousands of young Tanzanians marched from across the country to Dar es Salaam to support *ujamaa*. On the first anniversary of the Declaration in 1968, TYL cadres returned to the capital for an inaugural 'National Youth Festival'. The TYL's activities also stretched beyond the nation. As a consequence of Dar es Salaam's pivotal position in the struggle against colonialism, the TYL was part of a continental network of youth activist organisations. It was appointed with the particular task of liaising between the Pan-African Youth Movement and the Dar es Salaam-based liberation movements.[10]

In driving forwards the agenda of *ujamaa* socialism, the TYL drew on strands of anti-imperialist ideology, rhetoric, and praxis emanating

---

[7] James R. Brennan, 'Youth, the TANU Youth League, and Managed Vigilantism in Dar es Salaam, 1925–73', *Africa*, 76 (2006), 221–46. See also Lal, *African Socialism*, 81–102.

[8] Ivaska, *Cultured States*, 145–47.

[9] Minutes of the TANU NEC Meeting, Arusha, 26–28 January 1967, TNA, 589, BMC 11/02 D, 1.

[10] 'Ripoti ya Mjumbe wa TANU Youth League katika Mkutano wa Kamati Maalum ya Kutayarisha Mkutano wa Pili wa Pan African Youth Movement, 25–29 Mai 1967, Algiers', TNA, 589, BMC 11/012.

The Global Sixties Come to Dar es Salaam 177

from elsewhere in the Third World.¹¹ In particular, it took inspiration from the language and tactics of Maoist China. Even as Nyerere insisted that Tanzania was not in Beijing's pocket, the TYL modelled itself on Chinese practices. Its uniformed members were known informally as the 'Green Guards', replacing the red of the Cultural Revolution's youth activists with the TANU colours. They were to perform a similar function in mobilising the population and defending the country against imperialism and its collaborators. But the deployment of Maoist symbols or slogans should not be taken for wholesale embrace of Chinese socialism and the Cultural Revolution. Rather, it was the boiled-down, anti-imperialist rhetoric of Maoism that was attractive to the Tanzanian youth.¹² They discussed the teachings of Mao alongside those of other revolutionary icons, like Che Guevara, Ho Chi Minh, and the African liberation movement leaders.

Curious students and party activists had no difficulties in accessing such revolutionary ideas. The city's public sphere was saturated with radical literature. Tanzanians encountered a barrage of anti-imperialist headlines that screamed from the *Peking Review*, a Chinese propaganda magazine. Even more popular was Mao's *Little Red Book*. As Alexander Cook notes, Mao's sayings were a 'flexible and dynamic script for revolution' which 'travelled easily from its contingent and specific origins to a great many different kinds of places'.¹³ In Tanzania, they were harnessed towards the building of *ujamaa* socialism. Perhaps just as powerful an influence on Dar es Salaam's youth was the *cri-de-cœur* for Third World revolution of Frantz Fanon's *The Wretched of the Earth*.¹⁴ The language of the liberation movements, whether in their in-house publications or speeches made by their

---

[11] For similar dynamics elsewhere, see Claire Nicholas, 'Des corps connectés: les Ghana Young Pioneers, tête de proue de la mondialisation de Nkrumahisme (1960–1966)', *Politique africaine*, 147 (2017), 87–107.

[12] Priya Lal, 'Maoism in Tanzania: Material Connections and Shared Imaginaries', in Alexander C. Cook (ed.), *Mao's Little Red Book: A Global History* (Cambridge: Cambridge University Press, 2014), 96–116.

[13] Alexander C. Cook, 'Introduction: The Spiritual Atom Bomb and Its Global Fallout', in Cook (ed.), *Mao's Little Red Book*, 19.

[14] Alamin Mazrui, 'Fanon in the East Africa Experience: Between English and Swahili Translations', in Kathryn Batchelor and Sue-Ann Harding (eds.), *Translating Frantz Fanon Across Continents and Languages* (New York: Routledge, 2017), 76–98.

leaders, drew heavily on such revolutionary ideas and stoked these radical fires further still.

The events of 1968 were an urban phenomenon. As elsewhere in the global sixties, Dar es Salaam provided concrete spaces for the distribution of this radical literature and a public sphere in which it was discussed.[15] Bookshops and embassy libraries formed access points to Marxist texts, which were then explored in student discussion groups and the pages of local newspapers. The National Library, which opened in the city centre in December 1967, sold Swahili translations of the ubiquitous *Little Red Book*.[16] Next to the Canton Restaurant on Nkrumah Street, the Chinese-run Tanganyika Bookshop offered literature on topics like 'The Great Proletarian Cultural Revolution in China', 'American Crimes in Vietnam', and communism in Laos.[17] A rival retailer, the African Bookshop, opposite the TYL headquarters in Kariakoo, advertised 'books from the world's biggest reading nation', distributed by the Soviet literature export house, Mezhdunarodnaya Kniga.[18] University students recalled visiting the Chinese, Cuban, and Soviet embassies to collect such print material or consult it in reading rooms.[19] There was no shortage of radical literature in the Cold War city – much to the chagrin of Western observers.

The contrast with Tanzania's northern neighbour here is instructive. As the Kenyan government moved towards the West, it became concerned about Chinese activities in the country, especially through Beijing's supposed connections with President Jomo Kenyatta's rival, Oginga Odinga. Sino-Kenyan relations became fraught.[20] In response, the Kenyan government cracked down on Chinese propaganda activities. It banned the *Little Red Book*, together with all publications by Beijing's Foreign Language Press and North Korean periodicals. It also tried to prevent material from entering the country via Tanzania. In 1968, several Kenyans were imprisoned for bringing Maoist literature across the border. According to a journalist for the *Guardian*, the Tanganyika Bookshop in Dar es Salaam had been 'identified as a well

---

[15] Mills, *Empire Within*; Piccini, *Transnational Protest*.   [16] Lal, 'Maoism', 97.
[17] Stuart to Ministry for External Affairs, 25 March 1968, NAA, A1737, 3107/40/184, 256.
[18] Advertisement, *Nationalist*, 2 July 1968, 6.
[19] Interview with Juma Mwapachu, Oyster Bay, Dar es Salaam, 12 June 2015; interview with Salim Msoma, Oyster Bay, Dar es Salaam, 2 July 2015.
[20] Jodie Yuzhou Sun, '"Now the Cry Was Communism": The Cold War and Kenya's Relations with China, 1964–70', *Cold War History*, 20 (2020), 39–58.

of political poison'.²¹ In Dar es Salaam, these same publications circulated freely, and thereby provided ideological inspiration for a Tanzanian youth increasingly engaged with the politics of Third World liberation, especially the long-running war in Vietnam.

Vietnam

As elsewhere in the West, the Eastern Bloc, and the Third World, the conflict in Vietnam performed a central role in spurring anti-imperialist protest and organisation in Tanzania.²² In Africa, shocking images of the war may not have reached television screens as they did in Europe and North America, but they found expression in newspaper columns and Cold War propaganda. The conflict contained a mixture of ingredients that made it a protest cause *par excellence* in Tanzania: a superpower interfering in the decolonisation of a small, poor state; a revolutionary guerrilla movement, led by the iconic Ho Chi Minh; and a sense of Afro-Asian and Third World solidarity. The Tet Offensive of early 1968 was celebrated as a deep, albeit only fleetingly successful, strike at the heart of American imperialism. These sentiments were shared by not only youth protesters, but also party and government leaders.

For the United States' enemies in Dar es Salaam, Vietnam was fertile soil. In particular, China reaped the propaganda value from this manifestation of violent American imperialism and the virtue of the Vietcong guerrillas. In November 1967, a touring Chinese dance troupe performed a politically inspired ballet, which depicted the 'heroic Vietcong' triumphing over 'American aggressors'.²³ The following month, John F. Burns, the American ambassador, complained to the Tanzanian Ministry of Foreign Affairs that North Vietnamese representatives were allowed to show anti-American 'atrocity films' at the university, while Tanzanian censors had prevented the United States from screening a film explaining the historical context of the

---

²¹ John Fairhall, 'Mr Moi Opens Attack on KPU', *Guardian*, 14 July 1969, 3; see also Lal, 'Maoism', 109.
²² See for example Slobodian, *Foreign Front*; James Mark, Péter Apor, Radina Vučetić, and Piotr Osęka, '"We Are with You Vietnam": Transnational Solidarities in Socialist Hungary, Poland and Yugoslavia', *Journal of Contemporary History*, 50 (2015), 439–64.
²³ Burns to State Dept, 20 November 1967, NARA, RG 59, CFPF 1967–69, Box 1511, CSM TANZAN.

conflict.[24] These incidents accompanied a steady drip of printed Chinese and North Vietnamese propaganda about the war. Officials responsible for policing this material often turned a blind eye to the activities of Beijing and its friends. When Burns raised the issue with Nyerere, the president acknowledged the problem and said that the perpetrators would continue to be admonished, though he accepted that this had hitherto had little impact.[25]

Nyerere himself was a stern critic of the United States' war in Vietnam. As we saw in Chapter 2, during his speeches to TANU leaders in Arusha in January 1967, he used the Democratic Republic of Vietnam as an example of a small state that stood up to imperialist aggression and exploitation. In October that year, Nyerere delivered a major speech on foreign policy to the TANU National Conference in the northern city of Mwanza. After setting out the basis of Tanzania's non-alignment, the president turned to specific issues, including the conflict in Indochina. Nyerere described Vietnam as 'probably the most vicious and all-enveloping war which has been known to mankind'. He called for an 'immediate and unconditional' end to the American bombing of North Vietnam and for a peace settlement on the basis of the Geneva Accords of 1954.[26] Nyerere's Mwanza speech represented an intensification of his criticism of the Vietnam war, which had emerged as a motif in his statements on foreign affairs over preceding years. In June 1965, Nyerere had refused Tanzania's participation in a Commonwealth peace mission to Vietnam on the grounds that the plan was simply an instrument of British foreign policy and thereby condoned American aggression.[27]

Behind closed doors, Nyerere's relations with the United States suggested a more constructive approach. In January 1968, Nyerere reached out to the United States in his own peacemaking efforts. In a letter to President Lyndon B. Johnson, he conveyed the danger to the world of escalating conflict in Indochina and expressed his belief that North Vietnam genuinely desired peace. Nyerere called on the United States to live up to the responsibility which superpower status

---

[24] Burns to State Dept, 8 December 1967, NARA, RG 59, CFPF 1967–69, Box 1511, CSM TANZAN.
[25] Burns to State Dept, 5 January 1968, NARA, RG 59, CFPF 1967–69, Box 2517, POL TANZAN-US.
[26] 'Policy on Foreign Affairs', in Nyerere, *Freedom and Socialism*, 369–71.
[27] Niblock, 'Aid', 342–46.

conferred upon it. 'No one really doubts that America could bomb North Vietnam out of existence and exterminate all of its people', he wrote. 'The real question now is whether the United States is powerful enough to be able to talk with the small nation which has defied it.'[28] Burns thought the letter contained an implicit offer from Nyerere to act as an intermediary in negotiations. With the Sino-Tanzanian relationship deepening, Nyerere's 'credentials in communist Asia' seemed an asset worth pursuing.[29] Moreover, Burns thought that Nyerere's initiative presented an opportunity for improving the United States' position in Tanzania. The letter, he thought, had 'set the stage for an exchange which could have a lasting impact on our understandings with him and our future relations'. He pressed Washington to send a special emissary to Tanzania to deliver Johnson's response.[30] However, Washington deemed a written reply from Johnson sufficient.[31] This simply recapitulated the United States' position: it was willing to end the bombing campaign and pursue peace talks if it received sufficient guarantees that North Vietnam would abide by a truce.[32] The short-lived diplomatic opening had no lasting consequence. Nonetheless, it demonstrated Nyerere's commitment to constructive diplomacy and contrasted sharply with the uncompromising language of party journalists and activists.

Vietnam was rarely out of the local headlines in Tanzania in 1968. TANU's newspaper, the *Nationalist*, carried a series of anti-American editorials. One particularly vitriolic feature condemned 'the most criminal war of aggression in history waged by the United States imperialists against the Vietnamese people'.[33] Newspapers carried front-page photographs of visiting Vietnamese delegations meeting Tanzanian officials. In March 1968, TANU participated in a 'Solidarity with Vietnam Week', which was 'being observed throughout the progressive

[28] Nyerere to Johnson, 2 January 1968, LBJL, NSF, SHSC, Box 52, Tanzania, 19m.
[29] Burns to State Dept, 3 January 1968, NARA, RG 59, CFPF 1967–69, Box 2517, POL TANZAN-US.
[30] Burns to State Dept, 4 January 1968, NARA, RG 59, CFPF 1967–69, Box 2517, POL TANZAN-US.
[31] Rusk to US emb., Dar es Salaam, 5 January 1968, NARA, RG 59, CFPF 1967–69, Box 2517, POL US-TANZAN.
[32] Johnson to Nyerere, 15 January 1968, LBJL, NSF, SHSC, Box 52, Tanzania, 19b.
[33] Nsa Kaisi, 'Heroic Vietnam', *Nationalist*, 19 March 1968, 4.

world'. It sent a message to Ho Chi Minh, which stated that '[t]he people of Tanzania are immensely encouraged by the staunchness and bravery of the Vietnamese people in standing as the greatest pillar of liberation in modern times'.[34] The TANU Youth League was at the forefront of these expressions of solidarity. In April, it donated a consignment of tinned beef to the 'youth and people of Vietnam' in their 'just struggle against imperialism aggression'. The cans were delivered to North Vietnam by Benjamin Mkapa, the *Nationalist* editor.[35] Kingunge Ngombale-Mwiru, a TYL leader, recalled how he had close relations with the North Vietnamese diplomats in Dar es Salaam. 'I learned quite a lot about the Vietnamese and the way they were facing the giants of the world – the Americans', he said. 'We were opposed to American aggression in solidarity with the Vietnamese people.'[36]

On 20 July, the TYL held a march in Dar es Salaam to mark the fourteenth anniversary of the Geneva Accords, which demarcated the division between the north and southern parts of Vietnam.[37] This was the first public protest in the capital since the student demonstration of 1966. It was organised by the University College branch of the TYL and led by its chairman, Juma Mwapachu. Between 100 and 150 Tanzanians participated, joined by members of the American community in the city, including Peace Corps volunteers. They ran through the streets of central Dar es Salaam, waving branches of foliage and placards with slogans like: 'In every grave will rise a raging ricefield', 'Long live Uncle Ho and the heroic people of Vietnam', and '*Marekani washenzi*' ('Americans are savages'). Burns refused to meet a student delegation in the presence of what he condescendingly described as 'a Roman circus' of reporters, photographers, and sound crew. Instead, he invited them in for tea. The protesters rejected this, asking, 'How can

---

[34] 'Tanu Greets Viet Week', *Nationalist*, 19 March 1968, 1, 8.
[35] 'T.Y.L. Gift to Vietnam Militants', *Nationalist*, 20 April 1968, 1; Benjamin William Mkapa, *My Life, My Purpose: A Tanzanian President Remembers* (Dar es Salaam: Mkuki na Nyota, 2019), 64.
[36] Interview with Kingunge Ngombale-Mwiru, Victoria, Dar es Salaam, 26 August 2015.
[37] This account of the protest is based on 'Militant Youth Protest Against US', *Nationalist*, 22 July 1968, 8; Burns to State Dept, 20 July 1968, NARA, RG 59, CFPF 1967–69, Box 2513, POL 2 TANZAN; Burns to State Dept, 20 July 1968, NARA, RG 59, CFPF 1967–69, Box 2516, POL 23 TANZAN; Naudy to MAE-DAL, 23 July 1968, CADN, 193PO/1/31 AII32; Markle, *Motorcycle*, 85.

you offer us tea when your hands are dripping with the blood of the people of Vietnam?'[38] The demonstrators settled on a note of protest, which called for the unconditional withdrawal of 'Yankee and their satellite troops from South Vietnam', condemned the use of napalm, and 'utterly abhorred the bestiality and callousness like castration, disembowelment, cutting of [sic] women's breasts committed in the name of American democracy and western civilisation'. Singing songs in praise of Ho and Nyerere, the protesters departed for the North Vietnamese mission. The demonstration may have been small scale, but its language and repertoire set a precedent for subsequent protests. Marches against the United States and in support of the North Vietnamese became regular features of Dar es Salaam's public life.

Czechoslovakia

A month later, the protesters were back on the streets of Dar es Salaam, and in greater numbers. This time they directed their anger at Moscow. On the night of 20–21 August, the forces of the Warsaw Pact invaded Czechoslovakia, bringing a swift end to Alexander Dubček's period of socialist reform. While the intervention reasserted Soviet control over Eastern Europe, it was a public relations disaster for Moscow and manna for its enemies, especially China. The Soviet Union, which touted itself as the vanguard of the struggle against imperialism across the world, appeared to have scant respect for independent governments in its own neighbourhood. As Jeremi Suri notes, '[w]hile Mao Zedong's followers waved a "little red book" pledging power to the masses, the Kremlin could only offer the so-called "Brezhnev Doctrine" – a commitment to use force in defence of the status quo'.[39]

As news of the invasion filtered through to capitals around the world, governments and political parties scrambled to formulate a response. Geopolitical and ideological inclinations shaped their reactions to the Soviet Union's actions. Some socialists resorted to particularly contorted rhetorical gymnastics in justifying Moscow's decisions. But Tanzania's response to the invasion was immediate and unambiguous.

---

[38] Robert Carl Cohen, *Black Crusader: A Biography of Robert Franklin Williams* (Secaucus, NJ: Lyle Stuart, 1st ed., 1972), 344.
[39] Jeremi Suri, 'The Promises and Failure of "Developed Socialism": The Soviet "Thaw" and the Crucible of the Prague Spring, 1964–1972', *Contemporary European History*, 15 (2006), 156.

On the evening of 21 August, a government statement condemned 'a betrayal of all the principles of self-determination and national sovereignty'. It accused Warsaw Pact states of showing total disregard for the UN charter and reiterated that 'Tanzania opposes colonialism of all kinds, whether old or new, in Africa, in Europe, or elsewhere.'[40] Having made his position clear, Nyerere then turned towards a public manifestation of the strength of Tanzanian feeling. He privately instructed student leaders to organise a demonstration.[41]

On 23 August, around 2,000 people marched to the Soviet embassy on Bagamoyo Road in Dar es Salaam. The crowd comprised student groups and members of the TANU Youth League. They chanted and waved placards emblazoned with slogans like 'To hell with the Warsaw Pact' and 'Russians are Hitler's hench men'. The demonstration then took an unexpected turn. Led by two government ministers who also held leadership positions in the TYL, Lawi Sijaona and Chediel Mgonja, protesters jumped over the fence of the embassy compound. They pelted the building with torn-up scraps of Soviet propaganda, which they had brought along in wheelbarrows. There were reports of thrown stones and smashed windows. In a moment of alarm, the protesters pounded on the roof of a diplomatic car carrying the Soviet flag, which had chosen an unfortunate moment to pass through the embassy gates. Tanzanian police officers looked on, unmoved. The students thrust a note through a grill to diplomats inside the embassy which described the invasion as 'a naked contravention of the sacred principles of international socialism'. After twenty minutes, the crowd crossed the Selander Bridge to the nearby Czechoslovakian embassy, where the chargé d'affaires gratefully accepted a letter of solidarity. Behind them, the shrubbery outside the Soviet embassy lay strewn with the shredded propaganda.[42]

---

[40] 'Tanzania Deplores Occupation', *Nationalist*, 22 August 1968, 1.
[41] Interview with Juma Mwapachu, Oyster Bay, Dar es Salaam, 12 June 2015.
[42] This account of the protest is based on 'Massive Protest March', *Nationalist*, 24 August 1968, 1, 8; 'Angry Students, TANU Youths in Demonstration', *Daily Nation*, 24 August 1968, 24; Pickering to State Dept, 23 August 1968, NARA, RG 59, Czechoslovakian Crisis Microfilm, Reel 2; Naudy to MAE, 24 August 1968, CADN, 193PO/1/27 AII27; Lessing to Kiesewetter, Kern, and Schüssler, 24 August 1968, BA-B, SAPMO, DY 30/98137, 190–91; Lessing to Kiesewetter, 27 August 1968, BA-B, SAPMO, DY 30/98137, 183–85; 'Czechoslovakia: Its Impact on Independent Africa', CIA, October 1968, cia.gov/library/readingroom/docs/CIA-RDP78-03061A000400030018-7.pdf;

The particularly assertive Tanzanian response to the invasion of Czechoslovakia must be understood in the context of its rapidly deteriorating relations with Moscow. This was in part the inevitable consequence of Dar es Salaam's strengthening friendship with Beijing. In June 1968, Nyerere paid a second visit to China, where he restated his admiration for Mao. Nyerere asserted that he had 'no reason to believe that friendship between Tanzania and China will not continue indefinitely, and grow stronger as time passes'.[43] At a banquet held in Nyerere's honour, Chinese premier Zhou Enlai outraged Soviet diplomats by remarking that Moscow and Washington had invented 'nuclear colonialism'. Representatives of the Soviet Union, other Warsaw Pact states, and Mongolia walked out of the dinner in protest.[44] The 'Hands Off' editorial in the *Nationalist*, which appeared just a week before the invasion of Czechoslovakia, served as further evidence of Nyerere's impatience with the behaviour of the Eastern Bloc in Tanzania.[45]

These Soviet-Tanzanian tensions were sharpened by their contrasting stances towards the ongoing war in Nigeria. Against the backdrop of coups and ethnic violence, the eastern region of Biafra had declared its independence from Nigeria in May 1967. The Federal Military Government in Lagos responded by imposing a blockade and then launching an armed intervention to end the secession. In April 1968, Tanzania broke rank with other African states when it announced the recognition of Biafra, citing the region's right to self-determination in the face of oppression from the federal government. This was a surprising move by Nyerere, given the OAU charter's pledge to maintain the borders inherited from colonial rule.[46] Moscow's decision to provide military support to Lagos therefore met with a bitter reaction in the TANU press. In March 1968, a *Nationalist* leader on 'Anglo-Soviet Collusion' in Nigeria, described the 'line of thinking of the Russians' as 'tantamount to the reasoning of the Americans with regard to Vietnam'.[47] This simmering animosity informed the strong

Reuters, 'Tanzania: Hundreds of Students March on Soviet Embassy in Czech Protest Demonstration', film report, 24 August 1968, BPRHC.
[43] 'Equality in Sovereign Relationships', in Nyerere, *Freedom and Development*, 41.
[44] 'Walkout at Banquet for Mwalimu', *Standard*, 20 June 1968, 1. The incident went unmentioned in the *Nationalist*.
[45] See Chapter 3.   [46] Lal, 'Tanzanian *Ujamaa*', 376–77.
[47] 'Anglo-Soviet Collusion', editorial, *Nationalist*, 16 March 1968, 4.

Tanzanian reaction to events in Czechoslovakia. Both press and protesters drew parallels between the Soviet Union's behaviour in Czechoslovakia and Nigeria. 'Hands off Biafra, down with Russian aggression', declared one placard at the embassy demonstration. Babu reminded the readers of his *Nationalist* column that 'as we shudder at the invasion of Czechoslovakia let us not forget the indirect invasion of the Biafran people'.[48]

In keeping with his desire to cut a statesmanlike figure who commanded international respectability, Nyerere's own response to the invasion was more measured. He was embarrassed by the scenes at the Soviet embassy, especially as he himself had ordered the demonstration. In a meeting with the Soviet chargé d'affaires, Nyerere calmly listened to Moscow's explanation for the intervention, which stated that the invasion had taken place at the request of the Czechoslovakian leadership. Nyerere then rejected this version of events and cited the overriding authority of the UN charter and the principle of national sovereignty, pointing to Tanzania's stance towards Vietnam.[49] The following morning, the *Nationalist* ran a leader entitled 'Pity the Ambassador'. It was written, though not signed, by Nyerere himself. Without naming states or individuals, it sympathised with the 'poor Ambassador', who was duty-bound to convey the views of his own government, no matter how preposterous. 'If his Government tells him it has decided that in future the sun will rise in the West and set in the East he must solemnly go to the Head of his host Government and report the decision', the editorial mused.[50] Nyerere here sought to take the heat off the local Soviet representatives, who were still reeling from the protest at the embassy three days beforehand, while also mocking Moscow's party line. In another attempt to defuse the situation, an anti-Soviet demonstration planned by NUTA, the party-affiliated trade union, was called off.[51] As Chapter 3 showed, relations between the Soviet Union and Tanzania quickly recovered, due to Nyerere's concern not to appear too close to Beijing or alienate a potential aid donor,

---

[48] [A. M. Babu], 'The World's So-Called Policemen', *Nationalist*, 23 August 1968, 4.
[49] Arkadi Glukhov, 'The Fateful August of 1968: Hot Summer in Dar es Salaam', in Russian Academy of Sciences Institute of African Studies, *Julius Nyerere: Humanist, Politician, Thinker*, trans. B. G. Petruk (Dar es Salaam: Mkuki na Nyota, 2005), 42–49.
[50] 'Pity the Ambassador', editorial, *Nationalist*, 26 August 1968, 4.
[51] Naudy to MAE-DAL, 1 October 1968, CADN, 193PO/1/27 AI127.

Malawi

Another month, another protest in Dar es Salaam. The numbers involved also grew once more. On 26 September, a crowd estimated at between 5,000 and 10,000 people marched through the capital. On this occasion, their grievances came not from some distant superpower intervention in Indochina or Central Europe, but a threat much closer to home: claims by Hastings Banda, president of Malawi, to a swathe of territory in southwestern Tanzania. The protesters again brandished placards: 'Banda – Africa will never forgive you', 'Malawians overthrow Banda regime', 'Down with Banda'. They chanted 'traitor, traitor' and dragged an effigy of Banda, which was then violently decapitated at the feet of Rashidi Kawawa, the Tanzanian second vice-president. TYL members carried a coffin that proclaimed 'Banda, we are burying you today'. Also present at the march was a small group of Malawian dissidents who had taken up residence in exile in Dar es Salaam.[52]

The dispute that triggered these protests ostensibly concerned the contested location of the border between Malawi and Tanzania, which had its origins in colonial-era ambiguities. But it was turned into such a heated issue by a number of interwoven political bones of contention between the two states that bridged international and domestic affairs. Principal among these was the presence of the Malawian exiles in the Tanzanian capital. In September 1964, long-running rivalries among Malawi's political elite, which had simmered away during the liberation struggle, burst out into the open once the collective cause of winning independence ceased to provide cohesion. A number of Banda's opponents inside cabinet fled into exile. Yatuta Chisiza and Kanyama Chiume were granted refuge in Dar es Salaam, where they became integrated into the local political scene. Chiume, who had grown up in Tanganyika, joined the staff of the *Nationalist*. In 1966,

---

[52] 'Put Gunboats on L. Nyasa – NUTA', *Nationalist*, 27 September 1968, 1, 8; 'Dar Challenge to Banda', *Daily Nation*, 27 September 1968, 1, 40; Burns to State Dept, 27 September 1968, NARA, RG 59, CFPF 1967–69, Box 2513, POL 2 TANZAN; Reuters, 'Anti-Banda Demonstration in Dar-es-Salaam', film report, 27 September 1968, BPRHC.

the exiles were joined by another ex-minister, Henry Chipembere, who had led a failed attempt to overthrow Banda the previous year and then fled to the United States. From Dar es Salaam, Chipembere canvassed support for his Panafrican Democratic Party (PDP), which campaigned against Banda, while also teaching at Kivukoni College, the TANU training school. Both Chiume and Chipembere were close childhood friends of Oscar Kambona, who was of Malawian descent. Kambona provided them with a contact point at the centre of power and, most likely, their jobs in party institutions.[53]

The Malawians became members of Dar es Salaam's exile scene, although they occupied an anomalous position within it. Unlike the likes of FRELIMO and the ANC, they were campaigning for the overthrow of an independent African government, rather than the liberation of a territory still under the colonial yoke. The Tanzanian government therefore treated their arrival with circumspection. In 1964, it announced it had granted asylum to the Malawians, but underlined that it would not tolerate them 'abusing our hospitality and undertaking any political or other campaign against the Malawi Government'. Despite this, the TANU press threw its support behind the dissidents. The *Nationalist* described Banda as a 'tin pot Cromwell'.[54] The exiles' supporters received military training in Tanzania and elsewhere in the socialist world. Banda repeatedly warned of the dangers of an attack from Tanzanian soil. Such fears were not without basis. In September 1967, Chisiza and his supporters launched an invasion of Malawi. But the mission, which ended in Chisiza's death, was a total catastrophe and illustrated the weakness of the ex-ministers' position. Exile life, as the previous chapter showed, was marked by division as much as solidarity. Chipembere and Chiume had cautioned Chisiza against his invasion, while the PDP was riven with factionalism and distrust.[55]

These tensions came against the backdrop of a fundamental cleavage between Malawi's and Tanzania's foreign policies. In contrast to Tanzania's hard-line opposition to Africa's white minority regimes,

---

[53] Colin Baker, *Revolt of the Ministers: The Malawi Cabinet Crisis, 1964–1965* (London: IB Tauris, 2001); Kanyama Chiume, *Autobiography of Kanyama Chiume* (London: Panaf, 1982); Kanyama Chiume, *Banda's Malawi: An African Tragedy* (Lusaka: Multimedia Publications, 1992).
[54] Quoted in Philip Short, *Banda* (London: Routledge, 1974), 231.
[55] Chiume, *Autobiography*, 237–42.

Malawi took a much more conciliatory approach. In pursuit of a modus vivendi with his powerful neighbours, Banda embraced negotiation rather than armed conflict. He recognised that a close relationship with Portugal would give landlocked Malawi access to the port of Beira in Mozambique. Banda reciprocated by restricting FRELIMO's operations on Malawian territory. This was, of course, anathema to Tanzania. In 1965, the OAU attempted to patch up these differences by recommending that Malawi be given a seat on its Liberation Committee. Nyerere reacted angrily. In return, Banda refused to commit funds to the Liberation Committee's work as long as its headquarters was located in the capital of a state which allegedly supported the Malawian dissidents. By the end of 1967, Malawi had signed trade and labour agreements with Portugal and Banda had announced his intention to establish diplomatic relations with South Africa.[56] The Malawi-Tanzania argument was also coloured by the two states' contrasting stances towards communist China. During the cabinet crisis of 1964, Banda had accused Chiume and other ministers, at a meeting with the Chinese ambassador in Dar es Salaam, of accepting a 'bribe' in agreeing to receive £18 million in aid in exchange for Malawi's recognition of China. Banda attacked China in public, claiming that Mao was seeking to resurrect the Mongol Empire. He also opened diplomatic relations with Taiwan.[57] Banda's allegations that communist countries were propping up the ex-ministers were not entirely baseless, since Chisiza had received military training in China prior to his ill-fated invasion in 1967.[58]

The interconnected matters of the anti-Banda dissidents, the geopolitics of anticolonial liberation, and Cold War tensions thus turned a cartographic technicality into a major international confrontation between Malawi and Tanzania. The lack of space here precludes a full exposition of the details of the border debate, which were the outcome of the confusion caused by multiple colonial regimes operating under different legal norms. Between independence and the Malawian cabinet crisis of 1964, the government in Dar es Salaam accepted the existing frontier, which ran along the Tanganyikan shoreline of Lake Nyasa[59]

---

[56] Banda's foreign policy awaits archive-grounded historical analysis, but see Short, *Banda*; Carolyn McMaster, *Malawi: Foreign Policy and Development* (London: Julian Friedman, 1974).
[57] Short, *Banda*, 236–37.   [58] Baker, *Revolt*, 274.
[59] The lake is known as Lake Malawi in Malawi and Lake Nyasa in Tanzania.

and therefore set its waters within Malawian jurisdiction. But the tensions which arose over Malawi's stance towards the white minority regimes and the perceived threat of a Portuguese invasion propelled Tanzania to revisit the matter, possibly with the encouragement of the Malawian exiles. In January 1967, pointing to inconsistencies in earlier maps, the Tanzanian government now claimed that the median line between the lake's two shores would be a just border. The actual legal foundations for the Tanzanian case, notes James Mayall, were 'weak' and the decision to publicise the call for the relocation of the border 'hardly prudent' given the geopolitical context. Banda responded by arguing that colonial boundary-drawing had already separated Malawians living in contemporary Mozambique, Tanzania, and Zambia from the territory of the postcolonial state of Malawi.[60]

The crisis came to a head in September 1968, when Banda offered his own, more radical reinterpretation of the border's location. At a rally in northern Malawi, Banda talked about restoring the country's 'natural frontiers', including swathes of southwestern Tanzania. Amid the broader tensions between the two states, these comments received an immediate rebuke from Nyerere. He warned that Banda 'must not be ignored simply because he is insane. The powers behind him are not insane.' Banda hit back by calling Nyerere 'a coward and a communist inspired jellyfish', as well as a 'betrayer' of the cause of African unity.[61] The liberation movements rallied to the defence of Tanzania, as the ANC, FRELIMO, ZANU, and ZAPU all condemned Banda.[62] Chipembere accused Banda of having 'grandiose designs of territorial self-aggrandisement'.[63] TANU then organised its own response. Unlike the Vietnam and Czechoslovakia protests, which had been led by students and members of the party's youth wing, the anti-Banda demonstrations were called by the trade union. NUTA's Executive Council decided to organise countrywide protests and alleged that Banda was being 'used by colonialists, imperialists and fascists to disrupt peace in Tanzania'.[64] The relatively large size of the Dar es Salaam march may

---

[60] James Mayall, 'The Malawi-Tanzania Boundary Dispute', *Journal of Modern African Studies*, 11 (1973), quotation on 624.
[61] Ibid., 619. [62] 'Reaction to Claim', *Nationalist*, 14 September 1968, 1.
[63] 'Banda's Land Claims Come Under Attack', *Daily Nation*, 20 September 1968, 11.
[64] 'Nuta to Organize Anti-Banda Demonstration', *Nationalist*, 21 September 1968, 8.

well have been indicative of both the broader base of the organisation and the nature of the threat against which the workers mobilised: a supposed 'puppet' of the white minority regimes across Tanzania's southern frontier felt like a more visceral danger to the body politic than superpower interventions on distant continents. Yet the anti-Banda protesters shared the same language of anti-imperialism with the students and youth activists who had demonstrated outside embassies in previous months.

However, the rationale of the Tanzanian response to the threat from Malawi was more complicated than its stance on Czechoslovakia and Vietnam. In these other examples, Tanzania's criticism had been based on the fundamental principle of national sovereignty against imperialist encroachment. But in demanding the end to Banda's regime, Tanzania's response went beyond simply the defence of its own territory. In doing so, it shared the aims of Chipembere and Chiume, who themselves participated in the demonstration. 'Malawians overthrow Banda', read one placard. Such calls were difficult to reconcile with the enshrined principle of non-interference into member states' internal affairs which underpinned the OAU's continental order. This tension was evident in an ambivalent and contradictory editorial in the *Nationalist*. 'It is not for us in Tanzania to solve the Banda problem. That is clearly the task of the Malawi [sic] people', it recognised. Yet the newspaper also called on Tanzanians 'to join hands with our Malawi brothers in any revolutionary task that they may undertake to deal with reactionary sell-out forces that want to take them back to the forgotten dark ages of slavery'.[65] This was, in effect, the organ of a ruling party in an African state explicitly calling for the overthrow of the government of its neighbour. By claiming that Malawi was in the hands of white racist puppeteers, TANU was implying that the Banda regime had relinquished its own sovereign claims.

The September demonstrations were the high-water mark in tensions between Malawi and Tanzania. Banda never followed through on his threats and the uproar in Tanzania died down, even as the Malawian president was still castigated as an imperialist stooge. Nonetheless, the incident serves as an example of the vulnerability which Tanzania felt from its powerful enemies to the south, lubricated by Nyerere's personal animosity towards Banda. At the height of the crisis, Nyerere had

---

[65] 'Dare Not Dr. Banda', editorial, *Nationalist*, 18 September 1968, 4.

stated that Banda's words 'do not scare us and do not deserve my reply', but the numbers that rallied to the Tanzanian cause on the streets of the capital revealed more widespread anxieties.[66] The American embassy thought that the Tanzanian government was genuinely concerned about Banda, with unconfirmed reports of cancelled military leave and the dispatch of troops to the border.[67] Meanwhile, the threat posed to Banda's regime from the dissidents in Dar es Salaam quietly fizzled out. Chisiza was already dead, while Chipembere and Chiume had lost their major sponsor in Tanzanian political circles following Kambona's own flight into exile. Chipembere was reportedly disillusioned with exile life and feared assassination in Dar es Salaam. Shortly after the death of his friend Eduardo Mondlane in 1969, he returned to California to pursue a doctorate and take up a university teaching position.[68] The problem of the boundary debate has been more enduring. Although the issue fell dormant after the conflagration of 1968, the discovery of fossil fuel reserves under the lake's waters has recently increased the stakes for both sides.[69] In the short term, the lasting material impact was much more symbolic: in October, the Dar es Salaam City Council voted to rename Banda Close in Oyster Bay as Chisiza Close, in memory of the 'Malawian freedom fighter Yatuta Chisiza'.[70]

Nationalising Transnational Protest

In recent years, it has become commonplace to characterise the revolutions of the 1960s as a transnational phenomenon. Indeed, texts and ideas produced elsewhere in the world circulated through Dar es Salaam's public sphere and shaped local responses to events abroad. Concepts of Afro-Asian solidarity, Maoism, and Third Worldism animated protests outside embassies and provided ideological fuel for newspaper columns. Yet whereas youth protesters across the world

---

[66] 'Expansionist Banda Warned', *Nationalist*, 14 September 1968, 1.
[67] Burns to State Dept, 4 October 1968, NARA, RG 59, CFPF 1967–69, Box 2513, POL 2 TANZAN.
[68] Baker, *Revolt*, 274; David Martin, 'Bitter Chipembere Leaves Africa', *Guardian*, 20 December 1969, 3.
[69] Tiyanjana Maluwa, 'Some Aspects of the Boundary Dispute Between Malawi and Tanzania over Lake Malawi', *Michigan Journal of International Law*, 37 (2016), 351–420.
[70] 'Banda's Name Struck Off', *Nationalist*, 23 October 1968, 1.

levelled their criticisms at the nation-state, their Tanzanian contemporaries rallied to it. Their primary vehicles for these mobilisations were TANU and its organs. The Tanzanian state was thus able to marshal protest in support of its foreign and domestic policies. It essentially nationalised the transnational dynamics of the 'global 1968'.

Despite the obvious differences between the geopolitical circumstances of the situations explored here – the war in Vietnam, the invasion of Czechoslovakia, and the dispute with Malawi – their language drew on a common world view structured by anti-imperialism. Tanzanian interlocutors sought to connect each incident with a wider pattern of imperialist violations of national sovereignty. 'We believe that imperialism is a global phenomenon', said Lawi Sijaona when opening an exhibition of photographs on the Vietnam conflict in June 1968. 'Vietnam is only one theatre where this struggle is going on.'[71] In the *Nationalist*, Babu stated that '[t]he horror of intervention in Czechoslovakia should remind us of the continuing horror and the larger scale of destruction of property, extermination of human life, and abuse of the dignity of a people, which describes the American oppression and occupation of Vietnam'.[72] The placards brandished by the demonstrators also made reference to powerful actors deemed to be at the root of the imperialist threat. 'U.$. Imperialism Hold Your Dogs', read one at the Malawi march – despite the United States having little directly to do with the dispute. Addressing the protest, second vice-president Kawawa drew parallels between the Malawian situation and the case of Biafra, alleging that in both cases imperialists were arming puppet regimes to set Africans against one another.[73] Almost totally lacking from this discourse was the language of East-West rivalry, despite the Cold War context of the Vietnam and Czechoslovakia examples.

Whereas in Western Europe and North America the protests of 1968 were arraigned against the state, in Dar es Salaam they were marshalled by the organs of the ruling party. The government's decision to permit demonstrations to take place (and even encourage them) represented a shift in approach. Since the ugly scenes at the British high commission following UDI in 1965 and the student protests against national service the following year, there had been no youth protests in the capital. When assessing the Vietnam demonstration in July, the French

[71] 'Sijaona Slates US on Vietnam', *Nationalist*, 5 June 1968, 8.
[72] [A. M. Babu], 'The World's So-Called Policemen', *Nationalist*, 23 August 1968, 4.
[73] 'Put Gunboats on L. Nyasa – NUTA', *Nationalist*, 27 September 1968, 1, 8.

ambassador noted that the most significant aspect of the protest, given its small size, was that it had been allowed to take place at all.[74] More explicit evidence of this dynamic comes from the Czechoslovakia march. Juma Mwapachu, chairman of the university branch of the TYL, remembered receiving a telephone call from Nyerere. Nyerere told Mwapachu that the students were to lead a demonstration against the Soviet Union. '*Mwalimu* was very clever', Mwapachu recalled. 'Instead of using state authority to say, "we don't agree with you", he allowed the youth movement to perform that particular task'. In Nyerere's concern not to aggravate Tanzania's already strained relations with Moscow, the country would speak through its youth rather than via official diplomatic channels. 'It was not spontaneous on our part', said Mwapachu. 'It was very much state driven.'[75] The state recruited the youth, via the party's apparatus, to express Tanzania's discontent with distant imperialist interventions.

This was the critical difference between Dar es Salaam's protesters and radicals in 1968, and most of their contemporaries elsewhere in the world. As in Western Europe and North America, superpower interventions were the target of Tanzanian protests. But whereas students elsewhere turned their anger against their own governments, in Dar es Salaam, the state, students, and youth shared similar world views.[76] The Arusha Declaration and the principle of 'self-reliance' were predicated on a similar critique of an unjust global economic order to that advanced by student protesters in the global North. For this reason, Nyerere himself was heartened by news of unrest in Europe. In his annual New Year's address to foreign diplomats in January 1969, he lauded the world's youth for their struggle against injustice and inequality.[77] The following year, Nyerere told Erhard Eppler, the West German minister

---

[74] Naudy to MAE-DAL, 23 July 1968, CADN, 193PO/1/31 AII32. The French report noted the irony that just two hours before the demonstration, Burns had signed an agreement under which the United States would give a $13 million loan to cover the construction of a road connecting Tanzania and Zambia – the American counterpunch to the Chinese-funded railway.

[75] Interview with Juma Mwapachu, Oyster Bay, Dar es Salaam, 12 June 2015.

[76] Compare with the situations in Congo-Brazzaville and Senegal, where youth activists criticised their governments for remaining dependent on French neocolonial support: Matthew Swagler, 'Youth Radicalism in Senegal and Congo-Brazzaville, 1958–1974', PhD diss. (Columbia University, 2017).

[77] Pickering to State Dept, 2 January 1969, NARA, RG 59, CFPF 1967–69, Box 2512, POL.

for economic development, that he believed that the 'spirit of the youth in the industrialised world' gave hope to the poorer countries of the global South.[78] This revolutionary 'spirit' of 1968 was folded back into TANU's nation-building attempts. One Tanzanian studying in London wrote to the *Nationalist* to argue that the country's youth should channel their energies towards the national revolution. 'Whereas students here [in Europe] feel frustrated because they do not have a chance to contribute to the betterment of humanity, in Tanzania the country is full of opportunities at all levels.'[79] The lessons of '1968' were inflected back onto national politics, in ways which both evoked the sense of possibility in the postcolonial state and warned against the threats it faced in pursuing its socialist ambitions.

This task was taken up enthusiastically by the TANU Youth League, as it turned its activism towards more conservative ends on the streets of Dar es Salaam. In October 1968, the TYL announced its plans for 'Operation Vijana', a campaign against 'indecent dress'. The wearing of miniskirts or tight trousers was deemed antithetical to Tanzania's 'national culture' – TANU's reclamation of an African heritage which had been trampled on by colonialism and risked corruption by a decadent cosmopolitan modernity. Lawi Sijaona, as the TYL's chairman, emphasised that the enforcement of the ban would be concentrated on Dar es Salaam, since 'the people whose minds have been enslaved by dehumanising practices are confined into the urban areas'. As Andrew Ivaska has argued, this move brought together official state policy towards promoting 'national culture' and anti-Westernism with masculine vulnerabilities bound up in shifting gender roles in a time of rapid urbanisation.[80] After the introduction of the ban in January 1969, TYL members patrolled the streets of the capital in search of any sartorial transgressions. Fearful that the TYL's vigilante-style approach might be counterproductive, Nyerere himself reined in the TYL during Operation Vijana, by ordering that cadres involved must carry identification cards and only carry out arrests with police assistance. These restrictive measures meant that the campaign soon fizzled out.[81]

---

[78] Extracts from report on Eppler's visit to Tanzania and Kenya, April 1970, enclosed in BA-K, B213/7673.
[79] M. L. N. Baregu, letter to the editor, *Nationalist*, 3 June 1968, 4–5.
[80] Ivaska, *Cultured States*, quotation at 62.
[81] Burns to State Dept, 31 March 1969, NARA, RG 59, CFPF 1967–69, Box 2513, POL 2 TANZAN.

Operation Vijana demonstrates how the image of a global moment of revolutionary activism might obscure the less cosmopolitan – indeed, anti-cosmopolitan – politics of local youth activists. Slightly paradoxically, the same youth activism that built internationalist bridges with the Vietcong and other Third World struggles had a more insidious, conservative manifestation in the realm of cultural politics. Tanzania's experience of the 'global 1968' encapsulated the sometimes-paradoxical nature of TANU's socialist project, which presented itself as a part of a pan-African and Third World revolutionary movement that stretched across borders while adopting a more intolerant, insular agenda within its own frontiers. Whereas much of the recent literature on 1968 presents youth activists as creating a transnational community beyond the state, Tanzanian youths were Third World nationalists who mobilised themselves through the structures of the ruling party.

The Limits to Activism

The alignment of the world views of the TANU leadership with the nation's youth did not give the latter unbridled freedom to pursue their political activism in attacking Tanzania's 'imperialist' enemies. There were limits to protest, in two main ways. First, such activities were expected to be carried out through the growing institutional apparatus of TANU, rather than autonomous grassroots movements. Second, there was a fine line between condemning instances of imperialism abroad and needlessly antagonising foreign powers, with the potential to upset Nyerere's carefully crafted foreign policy.

Critical to the government's endorsement and even encouragement of these protests was the condition that they took place under the party umbrella. The demonstrations at the American and Soviet embassies, as we have seen, were arranged through the TYL, while the anti-Banda protest was the work of NUTA. The relationship between the TYL's leadership, its university branch, and other student groups was complicated. Jenerali Ulimwengu, then a radical student, recalled that at times their positions overlapped. 'Sometimes they fused', he said. 'For instance, when the Prague Spring was crushed, both the TANU Youth League and the students' bodies condemned the Soviet Union.' Yet whereas the TYL was 'controlled and directed by the party', the students 'engaged on a broader line, with a freer spirit that engaged with the rest of the world in a more liberal manner'.[82] The party increasingly demanded a monopoly over youth politics. In December 1968, the University Students' Union tried to arrange a Pan-African Students Conference in Dar es Salaam. The *Nationalist* responded by accusing the students of challenging the TYL's 'exclusive right and power to speak for the entire youth of the country in both internal and international affairs. ... Those who oppose this fact are enemies of the Tanzanian Youth, and the youth will not hesitate to smash them.'[83]

The state-backed dominance of the TYL was confirmed by developments on campus. As Luke Melchiorre argues, the 1970s witnessed the institutionalisation of TANU control over the university, subsuming previously autonomous student organisations into the party and eliminating dissenting groups.[84] The case of the University Students' African Revolutionary Front (USARF) is instructive. USARF was founded in November 1967 by a small but vocal group of students.[85] They were ardent Marxists, possessing an intellectual edge that they were prepared to turn not only against imperialists and superpowers abroad, but also against the Tanzanian government. USARF set up a journal, *Cheche*. It invited leftist intellectuals from around the world to the campus, including Samir Amin, Angela Davies, and C. L. R. James. Although the basic causes of Third World revolution and African liberation were common to both movements, USARF's more internationalist Marxism was at odds with the TYL's nationalist commitment to *ujamaa*. Ulimwengu recalled that this 'dichotomy' always brought about a 'dynamic of tension' between these two youth groups.[86] When *Cheche* carried an extended Marxist critique of Arusha socialism written by Issa Shivji, Nyerere banned USARF. He reasoned that since the TYL was a 'revolutionary organisation' with a monopoly on political activity in all Tanzanian educational

---

[82] Interview with Jenerali Ulimwengu, Oyster Bay, Dar es Salaam, 18 August 2015.
[83] 'Youth Organisation', editorial, *Nationalist*, 18 December 1968, 4.
[84] Luke Melchiorre, '"Under the Thumb of the Party": The Limits of Tanzanian Socialism and the Decline of the Student Left', *Journal of Southern African Studies*, 46 (2020), 635–54.
[85] On USARF, see Ivaska, *Cultured States*, 147–62; Markle, *Motorcycle*, 75–103; Karim F. Hirji (ed.), *Cheche: Reminiscences of a Radical Magazine* (Dar es Salaam: Mkuki na Nyota, 2010).
[86] Interview with Jenerali Ulimwengu, Oyster Bay, Dar es Salaam, 18 August 2015.

institutions, USARF was redundant.[87] Youth movements and student groups were brought under the exclusive auspices of TANU. These trends intensified further following the TANU *Mwongozo* of 1971, as Chapter 7 explains.

A second brake on protest was Nyerere's concern that public vitriol would tarnish Tanzania's international image. Firstly, it risked undermining the credibility of the country's principled stance in the global arena, which Nyerere had cultivated with so much care and consistency. In the cases of the Vietnam war and the invasion of Czechoslovakia, Nyerere's behind-closed-doors diplomacy was marked by a tone of moderation. The foreign media was already awash with claims that Tanzania was under the thumb of the Chinese. Maoist outbursts about imperialism and its running dogs were only grist to the mill for Tanzania's critics. Second, there was little to be gained from needlessly antagonising potential aid donors. As we have seen, Nyerere and a number of more economically minded cabinet ministers stressed that Tanzania's commitment to self-reliance did not mean that it rejected foreign aid. If anything, external support was essential for driving forward its socialist revolution. The government was therefore aware that unbridled attacks on the West could be counterproductive. Finally, there were basic issues of international respectability: facing an ambassador soon after his embassy had been showered with the confetti of torn-up propaganda was not a particularly appealing task.

These concerns brought the TANU Youth League's leaders under the microscope. The antics of Sijaona and Mgonja, who had led protesters into the Soviet embassy grounds, embarrassed Nyerere. In the president's eyes, their behaviour was deemed hardly befitting of responsible adults, let alone government ministers. Nyerere told the American ambassador that he had been 'stunned' by Mgonja's and Sijaona's actions. 'We still have a lot of growing up to do', he remarked.[88] Soon after the Czechoslovakia demonstration, the pair were moved to less politically sensitive roles in more technocratic ministries. Sijaona became minister for health and housing; Mgonja, having previously been minister of state for foreign affairs, was appointed minister of

---

[87] Ivaska, 'Movement Youth', 726.
[88] Burns to State Dept, 13 December 1968, NARA, RG 59, CFPF 1967–69, Box 2517, POL US-TANZAN.

education. The following year, Mgonja's successor, Stephen Mhando, acknowledged to an American diplomat that there had been a change in approach. He admitted that while Tanzania still had its 'radicals and extremists', they were now 'buried bureaucratically but effectively' in new posts. Mhando stated that his government sought only friendly relations with the West. Tanzania was now 'less inclined to look for opportunities to antagonize countries which might wish to help them'.[89]

Nonetheless, the polemical tone of Tanzanian commentary on global affairs continued to attract complaints from foreign embassies. In July 1969, the United States protested to the Tanzanian Ministry of Foreign Affairs about various recent attacks on Washington made by Sijaona, who was still a cabinet minister, at TYL rallies. At one event, he proclaimed the inevitability of a North Vietnamese victory and described the United States as a 'rampant abomination inflicting death tears on humanity'.[90] At another rally, Sijaona shouted 'slaughter Nixon'.[91] This triggered the complaint from the American embassy. At an audience with American diplomats, a Tanzanian official at the Ministry of Foreign Affairs 'winced' at the mention of Sijaona's name and distanced the government from the TYL's activities. Attempting to placate the Americans, he mentioned that the organisation was 'specifically for children (*watoto*)' and so 'some of its actions were inclined to be childish (*utoto*) and had to be overlooked'. He added that the United States was not without its own problems with its youth.[92] Similar dynamics characterised the relationship between the government, diplomats, and the TANU press, as the following chapter shows.

His patience exhausted, Nyerere issued a pamphlet on foreign policy entitled *Argue Don't Shout*. It contained little new concerning Tanzania's actual foreign relations but represented Nyerere's attempt to rein in some of the ideologues in the media, the TYL, and even his own cabinet. Nyerere called for Tanzanians to show a more mature attitude towards foreign states and nationals. He opened by drawing an

---

[89] Leonhart to State Dept, 17 October 1969, NARA, RG 59, CFPF 1967–69, Box 2514, POL 7 TANZAN. Leonhart was the former American ambassador to Tanzania. For more on Mhando's appointment, see Chapter 3.
[90] 'Youths Hail Heroic Fight Against US Aggressors', *Nationalist*, 31 March 1969, 8.
[91] 'Hill Students Denounce U.S. Imperialism', *Nationalist*, 22 July 1969, 1.
[92] Memcon (Mfinanga, Tunze, Mwandaji, Pickering), 24 July 1969, NARA, RG 59, CFPF 1967–69, Box 2517, POL US-TANZAN.

analogy between a family, which must live and cooperate with its neighbours, to a state like Tanzania in an increasingly interdependent world.[93] 'Any word or action of ours which changes a potential friend or neutral into an active opponent of our policies is the word or action of a saboteur or a fool', he argued.[94] Nyerere encouraged Tanzanians to argue from the basis of their country's well-defined policy positions, rather than resorting to insults. 'Of course', he wrote,

> it is much more difficult to present a reasoned argument than to shout slogans like 'imperialism', 'communism', or 'racism', and there is sometimes less immediate emotional satisfaction. But temper tantrums are the reaction of children; adults who speak for their country should have better control over themselves.[95]

Nyerere noted that although Tanzania had always claimed a non-aligned position, 'our manner of expressing policies in the past has not always made this claim sound very convincing'.[96] This sort of behaviour was not just tarnishing Tanzania's image abroad but was also undermining its credentials to serve as a mediator in international crises. 'No country can help in this work if it has shown an unremitting hostility towards half of the world on the grounds that it disagrees with the internal policies of that half, or even if it has allowed its disagreements on particular issues of external policy to colour its whole approach to the countries concerned.'[97] Previously, Nyerere had called upon his critics abroad to judge Tanzania by what it did, rather than said in the international sphere. Now he acknowledged that words mattered, too. Whereas most of Nyerere's public foreign policy addresses were delivered to an external audience, this was intended for domestic consumption. Here, Nyerere embraced his role as *Mwalimu*, lecturing this local foreign affairs commentariat for its infantile disposition. His scolding words did not go down well with this target audience. One staff member at the TANU press privately described it as 'nonsense', which would sap Tanzania's 'revolutionary vitality'.[98] The gulf between the priorities of government leaders and party polemicists was clear.

---

[93] Julius K. Nyerere, *Argue Don't Shout: An Official Guide to Foreign Policy by the President* (Dar es Salaam: Government Printer, 1969), 1.
[94] Ibid., 2.   [95] Ibid., 11.   [96] Ibid., 14.   [97] Ibid., 15.
[98] Pickering to State Dept, 1 August 1969, NARA, RG 59, CFPF 1967–69, Box 2512, POL.

Sijaona's own demise demonstrated the degree to which youth protest, international affairs, and African liberation politics were all embedded within the power structures of the TANU party-state. Having been a key activist during Tanganyika's independence struggle, Sijaona's intemperate rhetoric now endangered the credibility of the government's foreign policy. In addition, Nyerere came to recognise that the TYL had become too powerful, in no small part because of its highly visible street presence, whether demonstrating against superpower imperialism or cracking down on improper attire. Sijaona's hostility towards Eduardo Mondlane became another mark on his card, especially after the assassination of the FRELIMO president in 1969, as we saw in the previous chapter. Sijaona was finally forced from his leadership position in the TYL in 1971, after the introduction of new age limitations for office holders, which Nyerere pushed through against opposition from the party membership.[99] Overall, the TYL's autonomy from central party organs declined over the 1970s.

The state's involvement in Tanzania's experience of '1968' meant that the protests were entwined with the *ujamaa* project, the tenets of the government's foreign policy, and the world view which tied them together, predicated on anti-imperialism and a defence of national sovereignty. There was therefore a direct relationship between the party-state's nation-building polices and its official international relations on the one hand, and the popular mobilisations and revolutionary rhetoric on the other. But TANU's increasingly monopolistic approach to political life meant that the latter were only permitted to take place under the aegis of party institutions, like the TANU Youth League. Even within the structures of the party, Nyerere in particular was sensitive to the danger of its polemicists discrediting Tanzania's position in the international sphere. In doing so, they risked damaging Tanzania's ability to speak out on the same questions of Third World liberation that inspired the protests in the first place, while hindering the country's chances of attracting donor aid.

Conclusion

The shift towards transnational or global approaches to the study of 1968 has been a fruitful one. But we should not overlook how such

---

[99] Brennan, 'Youth', 240–41; interview with Kingunge Ngombale-Mwiru, Victoria, Dar es Salaam, 26 August 2015.

dynamics could be subsumed into state-directed ideological projects that also offered little room for dissent. Experiences of the 'global 1968' all came with their own local dynamics. In Tanzania, youth activists, students, and journalists interpreted Cold War interventions abroad through the teachings of the likes of Fanon, Mao, and Ho Chi Minh, which they encountered through Dar es Salaam's propaganda-pumped public sphere. However, whereas their contemporaries in the global North challenged the political legitimacy of their government, in Tanzania party activists rallied to Nyerere's regime. The state – more precisely, TANU's party-state – was the solution, not the problem. Public attacks on 'imperialism' fed into a national discourse emphasising the need for vigilance and unity in order to fulfil the revolutionary goals set out in the Arusha Declaration. Africa's vulnerability to Cold War interventions and the dangers involved in supporting armed liberation movements, rendered all the more visceral by Banda's claims to Tanzanian territory, enabled the lessons from distant conflicts to be refracted back onto local affairs. The government encouraged youth activists to take to the streets and largely permitted a diet of anti-imperialist polemics in the party press as alternative voices of protest beyond formal diplomacy.

However, this same relationship between anti-imperialist protest and the party-state also defined the limits to the means and tone of the former's language. In common with other one-party states across the Third World, at an institutional level TANU set about seeking to create a monopoly over public life. On a level of content and tone, the engagement of protesters, journalists, party leaders, and even government ministers with international questions such as Vietnam or Czechoslovakia risked upsetting the carefully balanced foreign policy that Nyerere had constructed in Tanzania. Non-alignment was not just a question of 'official' foreign relations, but their everyday practice in Dar es Salaam's public sphere. Ransacking embassy grounds or penning gratuitous tirades, even if they overlapped with the ethos of Nyerere's clearly articulated world view, were deemed counterproductive. Similar dynamics were at play in Dar es Salaam's newspaper sector, as the next chapter shows.

6 | *Decolonising the Media: Press and Politics in Revolutionary Dar es Salaam*

Around the turn of 1966, there was a new addition to the radical literature available in Dar es Salaam's bookshops and bookstalls: a slim pamphlet entitled *The African Journalist*, authored by Kwame Nkrumah. Sam Kajunjumele, who we encountered in his failed attempt to stand for election in 1965 at the end of Chapter 1, wrote a short preface in his capacity as the president of the Tanganyika Institute of Journalists. He declared Nkrumah's work to be an 'inspiring message' not just to journalists, but 'to all African peoples, young and old, men and women, who are engaged in a struggle for Liberation, Defence and Reconstruction of Africa'. Kajunjumele concluded that the pamphlet would 'sharpen your vigilance and political consciousness and embolden you with courage to meet the challenges of international imperialist conspiracies which undermine our efforts to unite and create a Continental Union Government for Africa'.[1] Kajunjumele, as we saw, was closely associated with China's propaganda activities in Dar es Salaam, not least as the editor of *Vigilance Africa*. China likely funded the booklet's publication.[2]

The pamphlet reproduced Nkrumah's address to a Conference of African Journalists, held in Accra in 1963. His speech set out a radical blueprint for the role of the press in postcolonial Africa. A former journalist himself, Nkrumah first attacked the premise of a capitalist press. Journalists who worked for privately owned media houses, he argued, were beholden to the commercial interests of their employers. Then he moved on to what African newspapers *should* be. 'Just as in the capitalist countries the press represents and carries out the purpose of capitalism, so in Revolutionary Africa, our Revolutionary African

---

[1] B. Sam Kajunjumele, 'Preface' to Kwame Nkrumah, *The African Journalist* (Dar es Salaam: Tanzania Publishers, n.d. [1965–66]). I am grateful to James Brennan for sharing a copy of this pamphlet with me.
[2] In addition to Kajunjumele's role in its production, the pamphlet was issued as 'Vigilance Publications Booklet No.1', thereby resembling *Vigilance Africa*.

press must present and carry out our revolutionary purpose', Nkrumah exhorted. Channelling concepts of a socialist press first propounded by Lenin, he declared that the newspaper should be 'a collective organiser, a collective instrument of mobilisation and a collective educator – a weapon, first and foremost, to over-throw colonialism and imperialism, and to assist total African independence and unity'.[3]

What sort of press did an African socialist state require? How 'free' could it be? What did such 'freedom' even entail? These were questions which preoccupied journalists, intellectuals, and politicians in Dar es Salaam. Their responses are the subject of this chapter. As the interventions by Kajunjumele and Nkrumah indicate, the implications of these answers extended beyond the printed word. They spoke to the fundamental challenges of the struggle against 'neoimperialism', as Nkrumah put it. African stakeholders advocated a press which contributed to the building of nation-states and fostering continental unity. Nkrumah's words captured the feeling that independent Africa needed not simply to take control of its own press, but to comprehensively reconsider the role which the media played in society. However, some saw this rethinking as nothing more than an ideological gloss to justify the muzzling of the press. Nkrumah himself drew criticism for introducing repressive censorship laws, banning dissenting newspapers, and creating a state monopoly on the press.[4] In revolutionary Dar es Salaam, these questions were bound up in the international networks of the city's political economy of information, as the involvement of Kajunjumele and his Chinese associates in the publication of Nkrumah's speech demonstrated.

Social scientists at the time had much to say about these matters, too. But their analyses of the African press suffer from serious defects. Western communications specialists, operating through in-vogue modernisation paradigms, connected the growth of the Third World's media with socio-economic development. Inflected with Cold War liberalism, this literature held dear to concepts of the 'freedom of the press', associated with democratic government and the rise of a free-market capitalist

---

[3] Kwame Nkrumah, 'Africa's New Type of Journalists: The Torch Bearers', in W. M. Sulemana-Sibidow (ed.), *The African Journalist* (Winneba: Kwame Nkrumah Ideological Institute, 1964), 5, 7. I am grateful to Jeffrey Ahlman for sharing a copy of this book with me.

[4] Jennifer Hasty, *The Press and Political Culture in Ghana* (Bloomington: Indiana University Press, 2005), 34.

economy. It argued that this freedom had been extinguished in independent Africa, when an energetic late colonial press was inevitably brought into the repressive orbit of the one-party state and then put to work as an instrument of regime propaganda.[5] Many African intellectuals responded by arguing that the 'freedom of the press' was mere ideological camouflage for the dissemination of 'imperialist' propaganda via private newspapers. They advocated a state-owned press that would be able to bring about the genuine decolonisation of Africa's media and contribute to the nation-building cause. By the late 1970s, this had crystallised into a media ideology known as 'development' or 'developmental' journalism.[6] Yet both these positions failed to capture the nuanced realities of the politics of the African press after independence. They are better understood as normative world views regarding communications which framed debates, but were confounded by political realities, especially given the international circles in which the newspaper business operated in Dar es Salaam.

The recent boom in interest among historians in newspapers in Africa has tended towards a focus on the colonial era, rather than the press after independence.[7] This is despite historians frequently turning to newspapers as a key source in light of the spotty nature of the postcolonial archive in Africa.[8] Indeed, newspapers have already featured prominently in the footnotes of preceding chapters, providing transcripts of official speeches and snippets of information. But we have also heard a lot from newspapermen themselves, who shaped

[5] Rosalynde Ainslie, *The Press in Africa: Communications Past and Present* (London: Victor Gollancz, 1966); William A. Hachten, *Muffled Drums: The News Media in Africa* (Ames: Iowa State University Press, 1971); Dennis L. Wilcox, *Mass Media in Black Africa: Philosophy and Control* (New York: Praeger, 1975); Frank Barton, *The Press of Africa: Persecution and Perseverance* (New York: Africana, 1979); Gunilla L. Faringer, *Press Freedom in Africa* (New York: Praeger, 1991); Louise M. Bourgault, *Mass Media in Sub-Saharan Africa* (Bloomington: Indiana University Press, 1995); Festus Eribo and William Jong-Ebot (eds.), *Press Freedom and Communication in Africa* (Trenton, NJ: Africa World Press, 1997).
[6] For Tanzania, see Nkwabi Ng'wanakilala, *Mass Communication and Development of Socialism in Tanzania* (Dar es Salaam: Tanzania Publishing House, 1981); Haji Konde, *Press Freedom in Tanzania* (Arusha: East African Publications, 1984).
[7] See especially Derek R. Peterson, Emma Hunter, and Stephanie Newell (eds.), *African Print Cultures: Newspapers and Their Publics in the Twentieth Century* (Ann Arbor: University of Michigan Press, 2016).
[8] On newspapers as a source in Africa history, see Ellis, 'Writing Histories', 15–18.

debate about *ujamaa* at home and weighed in on the global stories of the day via editorial columns or feature articles. Newspapers did not simply reflect the opinion of the party or the government. Editors and writers were active participants in the city's revolutionary political landscape. They intervened on questions of international diplomacy and the affairs of liberation movements. Sometimes, as this chapter shows, these interventions impressed neither foreign officials in Dar es Salaam nor the top level of the Tanzanian government, including President Nyerere himself.

By the mid-1970s, Tanzania's media was essentially in the hands of the TANU party-state. Just as in the case of the youth movements explored in the previous chapter, the party came to monopolise a particular aspect of Tanzanian political life. Yet the path towards a pared-down newspaper sector under tight control of the party-state was not a straight one. After setting out the contours of Dar es Salaam's media landscape, this chapter turns to the running battle between the party-owned *Nationalist* and the independent *Standard*. This brought together disputes about foreign capital, Africanisation, and Cold War and anti-imperial agendas, which were all channelled into a debate about the 'freedom of the press'. Through a study of the short-lived, yet explosive experiment which followed the nationalisation of the *Standard*, the chapter then highlights how debate shifted towards the tension between the demands of the *ujamaa* revolution at home and a more cosmopolitan socialist internationalism.

Making News in a Cold War City

In the late 1960s, most residents of Dar es Salaam received news about the world over the airwaves. One survey found that three-quarters of the city's inhabitants listened to the radio on a daily basis.[9] Prior to independence, foreign services such as Radio Cairo had provided an alternative feed of news and political invective to the blanched offerings of the colonial Tanganyika Broadcasting Corporation (TBC). However, the nation-building spirit of the post-*uhuru* years encouraged a turn towards the TBC, as an 'African' voice. In 1965, the government formally conscripted national radio to its efforts. The

---

[9] Graham Mytton, 'The Role of the Mass Media in Nation-Building in Tanzania', PhD diss. (University of Manchester, 1971), 404.

TBC was nationalised, brought under the auspices of the Ministry of Information, and renamed Radio Tanzania Dar es Salaam.¹⁰ Even so, foreign broadcasts continued to provide an alternative source of news, opinion, and entertainment to state-controlled media. The BBC was highly regarded, especially among the elite: Nyerere half-joked that he listened to it himself in order to find out what was going on in Tanzania.¹¹ The Cold War powers responded to this appetite for radio in Africa by expanding their output. By the late 1960s, communist states were broadcasting fifty-seven hours of Swahili-language programming per week.¹²

Even as the radio became the main tool for accessing news, newspaper culture was an important marker of urban life in Dar es Salaam.¹³ The most popular newspaper at the time of the Arusha Declaration was the Swahili tabloid *Ngurumo*, meaning 'Roar' or 'Thunder'. The newspaper had been founded in 1959 by Randhir Thaker, the Asian owner of a local printworks. Around half of its estimated 14,000 daily copies circulated in Dar es Salaam.¹⁴ Consisting of just a single sheet folded into four pages and costing just ten cents, *Ngurumo* was a shoestring production, run by a small number of African journalists and printed on a slow, hand-driven letterpress. Its parlous financial situation meant it transcribed foreign news from radio broadcasts rather than use expensive wire services.¹⁵ *Ngurumo* augmented its meagre revenue by accepting paid content from foreign powers, particularly North Korea, which regularly took out jargon-heavy supplements that ran to a dozen or more pages long

---

[10] On the radio in Tanzania, see Graham Mytton, *Mass Communication in Africa* (London: Edward Arnold, 1983), 100–101; David Wakati, 'Radio Tanzania Dar es Salaam', in George Wedell (ed.), *Making Broadcasting Useful: The African Experience. The Development of Radio and Television in Africa in the 1980s* (Manchester: Manchester University Press, 1986), 212–30; Martin Sturmer, *The Media History of Tanzania* (Mtwara: Ndanda Mission Press, 1998), 112–17; James R. Brennan, 'Radio Cairo and the Decolonization of East Africa, 1953–1964', in Christopher J. Lee (ed.), *Making a World After Empire: The Bandung Moment and Its Political Afterlives* (Athens: Ohio University Press, 2010), 173–95. On the radio elsewhere in Africa, see Marissa J. Moorman, *Powerful Frequencies: Radio, State Power, and the Cold War in Angola, 1931–2002* (Athens: Ohio University Press, 2019).

[11] Kellas to Brinson, 30 February 1973, UKNA, FCO 26/1389/1.

[12] USIA, 'Country Programs – Africa', 2 February 1968, LBJL, Marks Papers, Box 18.

[13] Ivaska, *Cultured States*, 32–33.   [14] Mytton, 'Role of the Mass Media', 250.

[15] Ibid., 240–46; Konde, *Press Freedom*, 41–43.

(thus sometimes increasing the length of the newspaper fourfold). As Emily Callaci and Andrew Ivaska have shown, *Ngurumo*'s columnists and correspondents were participants in a print forum in which questions of public morality and urban society sat adjacent to Swahili poetry and gossip gleaned from the beat of Dar es Salaam's streets.[16] Although, as we have seen in previous chapters, *Ngurumo* was not afraid to weigh in on international stories, it was generally more oriented towards local issues of urban life than the high politics of the Cold War.

The emerging work on Dar es Salaam's postcolonial print media mainly focuses on its consumption at the level of the street. But newspaper stands and cafés were not the only important sites of news discussion. In government offices, at embassy desks, and on the terrace bars of upmarket hotels, Dar es Salaam's political elite also perused and debated the contents of the press. Their preference was for English, rather than Swahili newspapers. While complaints about potholes, noise, and dirtiness were still a perennial feature of readers' published letters to the editor, the English newspapers were strikingly outward-looking, engaging in the global questions of the day. Liberation movement leaders gave interviews to their journalists. Members of the Tanzanian intelligentsia wrote long treatises on socialism and imperialism as guest columnists. For the politics of the press, we must therefore turn to Tanzania's two English-language newspapers, the *Nationalist* and the *Standard*.

The *Nationalist* launched in April 1964. It was published by the Mwananchi News Company, which also produced *Uhuru*, the party's Swahili newspaper. 'This newspaper is the baby of the Tanganyika African National Union and for that matter of the Government', stated the *Nationalist*'s inaugural issue. 'We will speak authoritatively for Tanganyika, but that does not prevent us making constructive suggestions wherever we deem them necessary.'[17] The *Nationalist*'s primary purpose was the development of the postcolonial nation. On its first anniversary in April 1965, the newspaper congratulated itself for 'assisting in constructive nation building and wiping out imperialist and neo-colonialist propaganda'.[18] Yet at a time when the language of

---

[16] Ivaska, *Cultured States*; Callaci, *Street Archives*.
[17] Quoted in Sturmer, *Media History*, 108.
[18] 'We're 1 Year Old Tomorrow', *Nationalist*, 16 April 1965, 6.

Tanzanian high politics was beginning to shift away from the colonial medium and towards Swahili, the decision to publish an English newspaper also demonstrated the party's desire to reach beyond the local African population. Explaining the rationale behind the creation of the *Nationalist*, TANU's Publicity Department stated it would ensure that 'the truth about our country will be disseminated to various parts of the world'.[19] President Nyerere himself took a keen interest in the newspaper's activities and on occasion penned unattributed editorials when he sought to make a particular point, especially in the field of foreign affairs.

The *Standard* was founded in 1930 as a colonial newspaper of record. It was part of the Nairobi-based East African Standard Group, which was then bought by the Lonrho multinational in 1967. The *Standard*'s staff contained a large number of Europeans, including the editors Ken Ridley (1964–67) and Brendon Grimshaw (1967–70). The considerable space which the newspaper devoted to business affairs and international news, plus the advertisements for high-end hotels and foreign airlines, were indicative of its audience: an estimated 70 per cent of its readership was either Asian or European, primarily members of Dar es Salaam's business community.[20] The *Standard* had initially been opposed to TANU, but recognised the changing winds as *uhuru* became imminent and was then broadly supportive of the postcolonial government. Its criticism tended to be indirect, in calling for caution moving forwards, rather than outright opposition to state policy. As Ridley admitted, 'you cannot bang the table about the more sensitive issues'.[21] He recognised that, in a state committed to the Africanisation of its economy, an independent newspaper which was owned and edited by foreigners like the *Standard* could not speak entirely freely.

An outward-looking media required international sources of news. Tanzanian newspapers, like their counterparts across the Third World, could not support an expensive network of foreign correspondents. They therefore relied on words purchased from foreign news agencies. Tanzania's information officials and newspaper editors were not short for options, yet the choices were loaded with Cold War ideological and

---

[19] TANU Publicity Department, 11 January 1963, HIA, Bienen Papers, Box 1.
[20] Haji to Mytton, 31 July 1967, Mytton Papers, ICS 115/1/2.
[21] Mytton interview with K. J. N. Ridley, 26 September 1967, Mytton Papers, ICS 115/1/1.

geopolitical implications. Despite Tanzania's general suspicion of the Western media, Reuters, the British agency, emerged as the most popular international source. In 1965, Reuters' Dar es Salaam correspondent estimated that his firm provided up to 80 per cent of the foreign news material to the *Nationalist* and the *Standard*. Material from the communist agencies was less popular.[22] The *Standard* editor said that Reuters was essentially the only agency the newspaper used. Other press agencies sent 'a lot of bumf, but most of it goes in the wastepaper basket'.[23] This dependence on foreign agencies was routinely bemoaned in the Tanzanian media. In January 1966, a *Nationalist* editorial attacked Western news agencies for spreading 'pernicious propaganda' to make Africans 'the intellectual slaves of the Capitalist press'.[24] Meanwhile, the government's efforts to create its own Tanzanian news agency stalled.[25]

Just as news of distant developments arrived at Dar es Salaam's press offices via wire services, foreign journalists and agency stringers found the Tanzanian capital a fertile site for information gathering. They clustered around tables in offices on Nkrumah Street as Mondlane or Tambo gave updates on their struggles, packed out Nyerere's press conferences at State House, and spent long evenings at the bars of the Kilimanjaro and New Africa hotels. As journalists operated outside of the official protocol that governed the activity of diplomats, many served as informal or formal intelligence agents. Both the French and the Portuguese identified the representative of Četeka as a key intermediary between African liberation movement leaders and Eastern Bloc diplomats in Dar es Salaam.[26] We saw in Chapter 3 that the correspondent of the East German agency, the ADN, played a similar role with certain Tanzanian politicians. The Western powers had no such recourse to state-owned news agencies available, but they did utilise informal press connections. In 1973, the British high

[22] James R. Brennan, 'The Cold War Battle over Global News in East Africa: Decolonization, the Free Flow of Information and the Media Business, 1960–1980', *Journal of Global History*, 10 (2015), 342.
[23] Mytton interview with K. J. N. Ridley, 26 September 1967, Mytton Papers, ICS 115/1/1.
[24] 'Future of Our Press', editorial, *Nationalist*, 22 January 1966, 4.
[25] Brennan, 'Cold War Battle', 347.
[26] General Division of Political Affairs and International Administration, MNE, 18 August 1965, AHD, MNE, PAA 527; Naudy to Information and Press Department, MAE, 7 November 1967, CADN, 193PO/1/11 K1.

commissioner reported that the Reuters correspondent was 'cooperative and tries to get for us any material we require from the liberation movements'.[27] The insider knowledge provided by David Martin, a *Standard* journalist, was valued especially highly by Western diplomats. According to one British official, Martin had 'excellent access to State House' and often brought 'morsels of information'.[28]

Diplomats and foreign agents also attempted to influence the content and outlook of the local media. They took out articles extolling the virtues of their own societies and generous aid policies or besmirching the reputations of their rivals. Money could buy column inches: one Soviet correspondent remembered being instructed by the KGB *rezident* in Dar es Salaam to place an article in the Tanzanian press exposing United States' Peace Corps volunteers who were alleged CIA agents. An editor agreed to print the article without reference to the source for 1,000 shillings.[29] Foreign diplomats also sought to influence journalists directly, either at newspaper premises or in more informal locations on Dar es Salaam's social scene. Jenerali Ulimwengu recalled his experiences as a Tanzanian journalist in the 1970s:

> I would be approached by representatives of the Soviet Union, of China, of Vietnam, of the US. They would all give me their immediate views, hoping to influence me. ... Every time I met the American diplomats, they would tell me, 'no, no, you don't understand what we stand for.' ... If I wrote something that was against the Chinese, the Chinese would come and tell me, 'that's not true, it's not like that.' ... It was a Cold War setting.[30]

Whether advances of this type made much of a difference is difficult to assess. African journalists were generally less pliant than foreign observers expected. As Chapter 3 showed, the GDR's representatives had little to show for the time they invested in 'publicity work' in Dar es Salaam. A more productive approach, as shown here, was for diplomats to complain directly to the Tanzanian government about what they felt was misleading media coverage.

---

[27] Kellas to Brinson, 30 October 1973, UKNA, FCO 26/1389/1.
[28] Wilson to Dawbarn, 10 March 1972, UKNA, FCO 31/1312/3. See also Brennan, 'David Martin'.
[29] Ilya Dzhirkvelov, *Secret Servant: My Life with the KGB and the Soviet Elite* (London: Collins, 1987), 341.
[30] Interview with Jenerali Ulimwengu, Oyster Bay, Dar es Salaam, 18 August 2015.

As we have seen throughout previous chapters, the Tanzanian government was highly sensitive to its image in the international media. The Western press regularly carried articles that portrayed the country as being absorbed within the spheres of influence of the communist powers in Africa. The *Nationalist* regularly rebutted these accusations. But the government was also concerned at the aggressive tone of these refutations, which at times only seemed to illustrate the point that the jaundiced articles in the Western press were making about Tanzania's extremism. Voices within the Tanzanian state also drew attention to the need to make a positive impression on visiting journalists. In August 1965, an official at the Tanzanian high commission in London wrote to the Ministry of Information in Dar es Salaam. He conveyed complaints from British journalists that they no longer received the same levels of cooperation when they were in Tanzania as they previously received and were therefore being discouraged from visiting the country.[31] Once again, maintaining a balance between staying true to Tanzania's anti-imperialist credo and creating a positive international image was a difficult act to pull off.

Dar es Salaam's Newspaper Wars

The *Nationalist* was founded in part as a means of ensuring that TANU's message reached an audience beyond Tanzania. However, this message was not always to the president's tasting or deemed conducive to the country's diplomatic and development prospects. In April 1965, the British minister of overseas development, Barbara Castle, paid a visit to Tanzania to discuss foreign aid. She received a warm reception. But, in a private meeting with Nyerere, Castle complained about an article attacking British foreign policy which had appeared in the *Nationalist* on the day of her arrival in Tanzania. Nyerere told Castle that he was increasingly embarrassed by the *Nationalist*.[32] This was a sensitive period in Tanzania's relations with Britain, especially as the situation in Rhodesia continued to deteriorate. The Western press was already awash with claims that Tanzania was a springboard for communist penetration of Africa. As previous

---

[31] Mwanyika to Sozigwa, 6 August 1965, TNA, 593, IT/I/609, 23.
[32] 'Note of Conversations with President Nyerere', n.d. [1965], UKNA, DO 213/128.

chapters have shown, Nyerere recognised that aggressive anti-imperialist polemics risked tarnishing Tanzania's international respectability, the credibility of its non-alignment, and its chances of securing aid. The article's (British) author, Richard Kisch, was expelled from the country shortly after.[33]

The incident was embarrassing for Nyerere, but it was not an isolated case. After its foundation in 1964, the *Nationalist* quickly gained a reputation as a hotbed of radicalism. The newspaper's staff consisted of a cosmopolitan crowd of revolutionaries with ideological horizons that stretched from Havana to Hanoi. Its managing editor was Jimmy Markham, a Ghanaian who had worked at Nkrumah's *Evening News* in Accra and then for the Anti-Colonial Bureau of the Asian Socialist Conference in Rangoon.[34] At least two staff members worked for *Vigilance Africa*, the Chinese propaganda magazine: Sam Kajunjumele and Kabenga Nsa Kaisi. Kajunjumele was the *Nationalist*'s business manager. Nsa Kaisi had studied at a GDR trade union school, though he was closer to China than the Eastern Bloc. A. M. Babu, the government minister and former Chinese news agency correspondent in Zanzibar, wrote a weekly column under the pseudonym 'Pressman'. The Portuguese suspected that the *Nationalist* received financial help from the Chinese embassy: there is no evidence that this was the case, but the belief reflected just how pro-Beijing the newspaper was.[35] Finally, the *Nationalist* was closely associated with Oscar Kambona.[36] Together, these figures ensured a stream of anti-imperialist articles that attacked the United States, Britain, and their

---

[33] Emma Hunter, 'British Tanzaphilia, 1961–1972', MA diss. (University of Cambridge, 2004), 45–47. Babu told an American official that Kisch got in a heated argument about his bill in the Canton Restaurant, was taken to the police station, and then said that no-one could throw him out of Tanzania because he had influential friends. This proved the final straw for Nyerere. Memcon (Babu, Phillips), enclosed in Strong to State Dept, 22 June 1965, NARA, RG 59, SNF 1964–66, POL 1; Mytton interview with Belle Harris, 10 July 1968, Mytton Papers, ICS 115/1/4.

[34] Gerard McCann, 'Where Was the *Afro* in Afro-Asian Solidarity? Africa's "Bandung Moment" in 1950s Asia', *Journal of World History*, 30 (2019), 89–123.

[35] General Division of Political Affairs and International Administration, MNE, 18 March 1965, TT, PIDE, SC, SR, 856/61, NT 3078, 139.

[36] Bienen, *Tanzania*, 210.

allies and called out misleading reporting about Tanzania in Western newspapers.

By late 1965, Nyerere decided that the *Nationalist* needed reining in. He invited Benjamin Mkapa, a Makerere graduate and young civil servant at the Ministry of Foreign Affairs, to a meeting at the president's beachfront house. Nyerere explained that he was unhappy with the management of the *Nationalist* and wanted Mkapa to take over as editor. Mkapa protested that he had no experience in journalism. This would not be a problem, Nyerere responded: he would arrange an apprenticeship at the *Daily Mirror*, a left-leaning British tabloid – ironically via the help of Barbara Castle, whose complaints about the *Nationalist* had helped to trigger this reorientation. This allowed Mkapa to spend five months training in Britain in preparation for his new role.[37] Mkapa assured an American diplomat that he had ended 'the virulent, anti-Western hyperbole of his predecessor' and would 'pursue a more truly non-aligned policy less dependent on communist propaganda handouts'.[38] Nsa Kaisi, who remained at the newspaper, complained to the East Germans that these changes had been encouraged by conservative members of the government, who considered the newspaper 'more Vietnamese than the Vietnamese'.[39] Even so, an expatriate tutor at Kivukoni College told a researcher that Nyerere and other government ministers were still concerned about the *Nationalist*'s interventions on international matters and when it was 'rude to other countries'.[40] Mkapa himself privately wished for a 'leftist' newspaper in Tanzania, which would take away the charge that the *Nationalist* was too 'bourgeois', even as its politics continued to be more radical than the government.[41]

For all its criticism of Western neo-imperialism, the *Nationalist* reserved its sharpest invective for its direct competitor, the *Standard*. This took three interconnected lines of attack. First, the *Standard* was deemed a colonial relic, which had been hostile to TANU and the independence struggle until the late 1950s, when it finally

---

[37] Mkapa, *My Life*, 53–54.
[38] Burns to State Dept, 4 June 1966, NARA, RG 59, SNF 1964–66, Box 428, PPB TANZAN.
[39] Scholz, 23 August 1966, BA-B, SAPMO, DY 30/98139, 330–32.
[40] Mytton interview with Belle Harris, 10 July 1968, Mytton Papers, ICS 115/1/4.
[41] Mytton interview with Benjamin Mkapa, 3 November 1967, Mytton Papers, ICS 115/1/4.

acknowledged the changing winds. Second, the *Standard* was owned by foreign capitalists and therefore served as an expression of their vested class interests. Third, the *Standard* was the vehicle for imperialist intrigue, which relayed the subversive lies of Western newspapers about Tanzania to a local audience in order to stir up trouble. Babu's 'Pressman' column was originally conceived as a space for exposing, condemning, and dismantling such mendacious stories in the 'imperialist' press.[42] In June 1966, the *Nationalist* picked up on calls in parliament for legal action to be taken against the *Standard*, arguing that 'some newspapers selling in Tanzania remain in the throes of a colonial hangover. … They still think of news in the same way as they reported the sundowner gossip during colonial days.'[43] The *Nationalist* alleged that the *Standard* had failed to accept the changing responsibilities of a newspaper in independent Africa and instead continued to serve as a mouthpiece for its capitalist owners and their imperialist allies.

An example of this confrontation came in the aftermath of the appearance of a magazine entitled *Revolution in Africa* in Dar es Salaam in March 1965. It claimed to have been published in Albania and had an unmistakably pro-Chinese editorial line. 'If anyone should be in doubt about the extent of the Communist effort to subvert Africa', commented the *Standard*, 'we would recommend the first edition of a booklet entitled "Revolution in Africa"'.[44] But on closer inspection, something did not seem quite right. At a time when China was growing closer to Tanzania, the magazine's articles seemed intended to stir up discontent and uncertainty inside the country. It described African socialism as 'a clumsy attempt to rationalize the primitive mumbo-jumbo of a backward Africa that still dances to the colonialist tune'. Another article speculated that 'Babu and his enlightened cadres are now poised to capture control of the united front in Tanzania just as they did in Zanzibar.'[45] These were apparently efforts to stain China's reputation in Africa. The *Nationalist* therefore seized on the *Standard*'s decision to reprint extracts from the magazine as evidence of its imperialist sympathies. 'If anyone should be in doubt as to who the agents of

---

[42] [A. M. Babu], 'Pressman's Commentary', *Nationalist*, 19 November 1965, 4.
[43] 'The Press in Tanzania', editorial, *Nationalist*, 23 June 1966, 4.
[44] 'First Edition', editorial, *Standard*, 24 March 1965, 4.
[45] See copy of *Revolution Africa* at the CIA Electronic Reading Room, cia.gov/library/readingroom/docs/CIA-RDP78-02646R000500180002-2.pdf.

subversion in Africa, and in particular Tanzania, they can find out from those who reproduce and disseminate sedition under false colours', it stated, mimicking its rival's wording.[46] Meanwhile, the Chinese embassy stated that *Revolution in Africa* was an 'out-and-out forgery', attributed it to an imperialist plot, and praised the TANU press for its 'helpful' exposure.[47] The magazine's origins remained a mystery. Cold War 'black literature' thus became co-opted into Dar es Salaam's newspaper wars.

Politics aside, the *Nationalist*'s confrontational stance towards the *Standard* was sharpened by commercial rivalry. A survey carried out in 1967 found that the *Standard* sold 16,000 copies per day against the *Nationalist*'s claimed 7,000 copies.[48] In part, this was a consequence of the *Nationalist*'s editorial line. Both the *Standard* and the *Nationalist* were competing for a similar target market, the city's anglophone business community, which was unlikely to have taken kindly to the *Nationalist*'s daily harangues. The *Standard*, with its coverage of international commodity markets and European political affairs, was far more attractive. Indeed, the *Standard*'s editor, Ken Ridley, said that the *Nationalist* served as a 'kind of foil' for his newspaper. 'We'd like to see the *Nationalist* keep going; it is no competition, the reverse in fact.'[49] The *Nationalist*'s TANU ideologues gritted their teeth at their rival's comparative success. When an American journalist visiting Dar es Salaam in 1968 asked Nsa Kaisi about the newspaper's circulation figures, he received a cold response. 'If you insist on asking such questions you will no longer welcome in Tanzania', Nsa Kaisi said.[50]

Losing the competition with the Standard meant that the *Nationalist* was beset with financial difficulties. TANU had acknowledged that the expense of producing an English-language newspaper was beyond the party's own funds and placed the newspaper inside its commercial arm, the Mwananchi Development Corporation.[51] Even so, TANU had originally anticipated that the *Nationalist* would reach a circulation

---

[46] 'Seditious Publication', editorial, *Nationalist*, 26 March 1965, 4.
[47] 'Publication Is a Forgery – Envoy', *Nationalist*, 2 April 1965, 1.
[48] Mytton, 'Role of the Mass Media', 250.
[49] Mytton interview with K. J. N. Ridley, 26 September 1967, Mytton Papers, ICS 115/1/1.
[50] Robert Carl Cohen, *Black Crusader: A Biography of Robert Franklin Williams* (Oregon: Jorvik Press, 3rd ed., 2015), 6.
[51] TANU Publicity Department, 11 January 1963, HIA, Bienen Papers, Box 1.

of 30,000 copies per day.⁵² The issue of poor sales was noted at a meeting of TANU's National Executive Committee in 1966, which decided that government offices must prioritise buying the *Nationalist* ahead of other newspapers.⁵³ In 1968, the *Nationalist*'s printers demanded that the party newspapers pay off their significant debts, which essentially amounted to two-thirds of the company's annual revenue. Parliament hurried through extra funding to keep the TANU newspapers afloat.⁵⁴ They only survived through government subvention. According to one estimate, this amounted to 7 million shillings between 1965–66 and 1968–69, equivalent to one third of the entire grant to Radio Tanzania. The size of these subsidies demonstrated the significance which TANU's leadership placed on publishing an English-language newspaper, but at the same time represented an expensive drain on central government resources.⁵⁵

However, as Tanzania moved down a socialist path, the success of private businesses like the *Standard* became a problem rather than an asset. As TANU unleashed its strategy for socialist revolution in 1967, the *Standard*'s foreign ownership and less partisan editorial line came under renewed scrutiny. The Arusha Declaration included 'news media' in its definition of 'the major means of production and exchange in the nation' which were to be brought 'under the control of the workers and peasants'.⁵⁶ When Nyerere addressed a crowd in Dar es Salaam in February, a voice called for the *Standard* to be brought under public ownership. 'Can you edit it?', shouted back Nyerere, highlighting the shortage of experienced journalists in Tanzania at the time, but not challenging the principle that a major newspaper should be in Tanzanian hands.⁵⁷ Although the sweeping nationalisations spared the *Standard*, the new order made the newspaper stick out as a vestige of colonial rule. These arguments came to a head soon after, as the government tightened its control over the press.

---

⁵² Mytton thought that the real figure was much lower, at around 4,000: 'Role of the Mass Media', 234, 250.
⁵³ Minutes of the TANU NEC Meeting, Dar es Salaam, 6–9 June 1966, TNA, 589, BMC 11/02 C, 9.
⁵⁴ Mytton, 'Role of the Mass Media', 162–68.
⁵⁵ Mytton, *Mass Communication*, 275.
⁵⁶ 'The Arusha Declaration: Socialism and Self-Reliance', in Nyerere, *Freedom and Socialism*, 234.
⁵⁷ Sturmer, *Media History*, 120.

The 'Freedom of the Press'

As one African regime after another moved away from multiparty democracy towards single-party or military rule, the question of the 'freedom of the press' became increasingly fraught. Colonial regimes had not hesitated to ban publications which revealed uncomfortable truths. By the mid-1960s, many in Africa and the West feared that postcolonial states were exhibiting similar tendencies, outlawing newspapers that displeased their leaders, replacing independent newspapers with state- or party-owned titles, introducing restrictive legislation, and generally discouraging debate via self-censorship. A normative concept of the 'freedom of the press' became a yardstick by which especially Western observers judged the success or failure of the development of the media in Africa. This was often bound up in a Cold War theory of modernisation, whereby the 'freedom of the press' was seen as accompanying the success of capitalist development, following Euro-American experiences (and often overlooking the questionable degree of 'press freedom' in their own historical trajectories). State-owned newspapers, on the other hand, were believed to be little more than propaganda organs for authoritarian governments, with comparisons drawn with the situation in Eastern Europe.[58]

The Tanzanian government contended otherwise. Employing similar logic to that which justified 'one-party democracy', it argued that the press could not be allowed to disrupt the country's development by concentrating on divisive stories about political infighting. Instead, the press was tasked with acting as an integrating force, communicating the party's policies and soldering together a nation. In 1967, the director of Tanzania's Information Services, Abdulla Riyami, wrote that the job of African journalists as 'patriots' was to both inform and educate the reader. The journalist would 'contribute towards the nation's unity, economic and general progress', rather than 'create destructive propaganda'. He noted with alarm that 'some journalists have fallen into the snares of press freedom'.[59] Speaking in the heated parliamentary debates described shortly, Babu distinguished between the people's 'freedom to be informed' and the 'freedom to publish',

---

[58] See for example Hachten, *Muffled Drums*; Wilcox, *Mass Media*; Barton, *Press of Africa*.

[59] Abdulla Riyami, 'Role of the Press in Developing Nations', *Standard*, 11 September 1967, 4.

which was limited to just a handful of individuals with the requisite capital means.[60] The 'freedom' of the reader was to be prioritised over the 'freedom' of the writer or publisher. Whereas foreign- or privately owned newspapers were believed to be instruments for imperialist or capitalist manipulation, an Africanised, state-owned media would be 'free' to inform and educate. The approach taken by Tanzania later became known as 'development' or 'developmental' journalism.[61]

These debates had simmered in Tanzania since independence, but came to a boil in May 1968, when the government brought a Newspaper Ordinance (Amendment) Bill before parliament. This empowered the president to close down any newspaper when he or she considered it in the public interest to do so. The bill was prompted by the difficulties which the government had encountered in January in attempting to shut down *Ulimwengu*, which was published by Otini Kambona, the brother of Oscar. *Ulimwengu* had called for people who had been arrested under preventive detention measures to be brought to trial.[62] In the context of the detentions of Oscar Kambona's supporters which followed the Arusha Declaration, the government regarded this as an inappropriate, subversive intervention. Announcing the subsequent ban on *Ulimwengu*, the *Nationalist* stated that while constructive criticism of the government was welcome in Tanzania, unconstitutional attempts to change it were not.[63] However, the government possessed no legal instrument for closing the newspaper and therefore had banned it on a spurious technicality relating to its registration.

Introducing the Newspaper Ordinance Bill in parliament, the minister for information and tourism, Hasnu Makame, defended the new measures as vital for national security against foreign subversion. He argued that although freedom of speech was protected by the constitution, it could also be abused. 'Someone can also express subversive ideas with the intention of hindering the development of the country',

---

[60] 'Newspapers: Class Tools', *Nationalist*, 3 May 1968, 1, 4.
[61] Onuma O. Oreh, '"Developmental Journalism" and Press Freedom: An African View Point', *Gazette*, 24 (1978), 36–40.
[62] 'Bring the Detainees to Trial', *Ulimwengu*, 19 November 1967, quoted in Oscar S. Kambona, *Tanzania and the Rule of Law* (London: African News Service, n.d. [1970]), 13–15.
[63] 'Gov't Won't Tolerate Subversive Activities', *Nationalist*, 5 February 1968, 8.

Makame said. 'If such views are published and circulated in a newspaper they can bring danger in the country.' But parliament received the bill with unusual hostility. Concerned about its consequences for the trade union newspaper, *Mfanya Kazi*, Michael Kamaliza criticised the government for not making clear the grounds upon which the president would ban a publication.[64] Lady Marion Chesham, a European MP, told parliament that the bill 'smells of Fascism'. She feared for 'the future generations of Tanzania if the power to muzzle and kill the Press is in the hands of the Office of the President'.[65] Another MP worried that while Nyerere could be trusted with such powers, his successors might not be so responsible.[66]

When the house adjourned on the evening of 2 May, there was some doubt that the bill would pass. The next day, Rashidi Kawawa made a decisive intervention. Referring to the threat to the nation from its imperialist 'enemies', the second vice-president rounded on the *Standard* and its foreign owners. He noted erroneous reports recently published in the *Standard* that the TPDF had acquired missiles, which might incite a strike from Tanzania's Portuguese enemies. 'All [the imperialists] are trying to achieve with this type of propaganda against us is to justify their eventual aggression against our independence and sovereignty', Kawawa argued. 'Whose freedom [of the press] is this? Lonrho's?', he asked to laughter. 'The freedom to write that Tanzania is importing missiles? And we are expected to remain quiet and let them ruin our country, for Lonrho to say whatever it wishes about Tanzania on our own soil, and for the Portuguese to come and bomb us? Is that freedom?'[67] Kawawa's speech again demonstrated the extent to which Tanzania's support for the liberation movements and the fear of a backlash from the white minority states of southern Africa had become a touchstone in the shaping of domestic policy – in this case, towards the media. The speech rallied support for the bill, which passed by 107 votes to 19, with 6 abstentions and 51 members absent.[68]

The confrontation continued in the pages of Dar es Salaam's press. A *Standard* editorial stressed that it respected the rule of parliament and had never 'wittingly published anything which could be termed undesirable to the national interest', referring back to Makame's

[64] Mytton, *Mass Communication*, 104–109, quotation on 106.
[65] Quoted in Aminzade, *Race*, 168.   [66] Mytton, *Mass Communication*, 106.
[67] Quoted in Mytton, 'Role of the Mass Media', 211–12.
[68] 'Press Ban Bill Passed', *Standard*, 4 May 1968, 1, 3.

speech. It asked for clarification as to what the minister had meant. The newspaper likened the bill to 'a pistol pointed at the head'.[69] The government issued a scathing response through Riyami, who claimed that Makame had never used the word 'undesirable'. 'This appears to be your own invention', Riyami wrote, 'or, perhaps, you have been let down by a poor translation'. This was a not-so-thinly veiled reference to the disjunction between the English-language (read: foreign) *Standard* and the Swahili-speaking (read: Tanzanian) parliament. 'Any responsible newspaper would understand what is "subversive" material', Riyami added.[70] In the *Nationalist*, Babu's 'Pressman's Commentary' delved into the archives to quote several pre-independence articles in which the *Standard* had expressed its disapproval of TANU.[71]

These debates were not confined to parliamentary benches and newsprint in Dar es Salaam but formed part of an international conversation about the media in the decolonising world. A month after Tanzania's Newspaper Ordinance Act was passed, journalists, newspaper proprietors, and government representatives gathered in Nairobi for the annual conference of the International Press Institute (IPI). Funded by the Ford and Rockefeller foundations, the IPI ran seminars across the decolonising world, including a training school in Kenya which aimed to inculcate Western-style journalism practices.[72] The Nairobi meeting witnessed a collision between liberal ideas of 'press freedom' and voices from the Third World who argued that these Western principles were inappropriate in the context of developing nations. President Jomo Kenyatta and his Zambian counterpart, Kenneth Kaunda, both spoke in favour of the 'freedom of the press', but also reminded journalists that a duty to criticise governments had to be balanced with a responsibility to support their state-building efforts. Other African participants expressed their concerns at unrestricted government intervention. Hilary Ng'weno, a Kenyan journalist, warned that 'Governments cannot be left alone to decide how much freedom the Press can have. ... We must keep poking our necks out

---

[69] 'Comment', *Standard*, 4 May 1968, 1.
[70] 'Government Replies to Press Bill', *Standard*, 11 May 1968, 4.
[71] [A. M. Babu], 'Hypocrisy Exposed', *Nationalist*, 24 May 1968, 4.
[72] John Jenks, 'Crash Course: The International Press Institute and Journalism Training in Anglophone Africa, 1963–1975', *Media History*, 26 (2020), 508–21.

until we get chopped.'[73] Inevitably, several participants cited Tanzania's new press legislation as an example of the threat to the 'freedom of the press' in Africa. In his own address, Riyami defended his government's actions. 'Just as the Press is free to disagree with the Government, the Government, too, is free to disagree with the Press on any subject', he said.[74] Back in Dar es Salaam, the *Nationalist* reacted angrily to the 'audacity and arrogance' of the conference's participants. It drew attention to the lack of both black Africans and communists in Nairobi. The *Nationalist* renewed its calls for the total Africanisation of the continent's newspapers, 'manned by Africans, edited by Africans, managed by Africans, sold by Africans, read by Africans'.[75] In this ideological climate, the days of the Lonrho-owned *Standard* appeared numbered.

The shift in the Tanzanian government's treatment of the press was in evidence again in October, when it banned Kenya's Nation Group of newspapers. The decision was announced soon after the *Daily Nation* published a story about unrest in Tanzania's northern Kilimanjaro region. Like the Standard Group, the Nation Group was under non-African ownership – in this case the Ismaili leader, the Aga Khan. The *Daily Nation* responded indignantly. 'With newspapers censored, suppressed or muzzled in so many parts of the world (Czechoslovakia and South Africa are examples that spring easily to mind), it is sad indeed that the bright image recorded in Nairobi four months ago has been so quickly tarnished', it reflected. The editorial drew on analogies that were particularly galling for Tanzania, equating it with both its sworn enemy in Pretoria and Soviet imperialism in the Eastern Bloc, which had been the target of recent protests in Dar es Salaam.[76] In a tit-for-tat response, in January 1969 the Kenyan government banned the sale of the *Nationalist* after the newspaper published an 'extremely hostile' article about student protests in Nairobi. Taking a swipe at the *Nationalist*'s Marxist and Maoist revolutionaries, a Kenyan government statement declared that it was 'not prepared to accept lessons on democracy' from a newspaper 'whose pre-occupation is with clichés and slogans borrowed from foreign countries'.[77] Accusations of

[73] 'The Role of the Press in Africa', *Daily Nation*, 5 June 1968, 10.
[74] 'Our Press Is Free, Says Tanzania', *Daily Nation*, 6 June 1968, 9.
[75] 'The Press of Africa', editorial, *Nationalist*, 5 June 1968, 4.
[76] 'Tanzania's Ban', editorial, *Daily Nation*, 21 October 1968, 6.
[77] 'Kenya Bans TANU Paper', *Standard*, 1 February 1969, 1.

corrupting foreign influences, inflected with the politics of the Cold War, could be marshalled in multiple directions.

These tensions stretched beyond abstract principles and government interventions to the streets and newsprint of Dar es Salaam. The trigger for a fresh round of attacks on the *Standard* was an editorial in December 1968, in which the newspaper expressed its scepticism about the TANU Youth League's Operation Vijana campaign against 'indecent dress'.[78] This dissenting opinion was red rag to the newspaper's critics. In the *Nationalist*, Babu called the *Standard* editorial a 'blatant sermon in anti-Tanzanianism, racism and subversion'.[79] In January 1969, Youth League cadres marched to the *Standard* offices. They shouted 'slaughter! slaughter!' and lit a bonfire of copies of the newspaper. Drawing on Chinese motifs, the 'Green Guards' affirmed their 'determination to carry forward the cultural revolution right through to the end'.[80] *Uhuru* joined this attack, accusing the *Standard* of obtaining secret information about the government's next economic plan by talking to officials in upmarket establishments like the Kilimanjaro Hotel and the New Dar es Salaam Club.[81] This moment of especially acute anti-*Standard* militancy soon passed. But the underlying notion of a newspaper owned and staffed by Europeans in socialist Tanzania remained deeply problematic.

Frene Ginwala's *Standard*

On 5 February 1970, the third anniversary of the Arusha Declaration, the *Standard*'s front page announced that it was 'appearing for the first time as the official newspaper of the government of Tanzania'.[82] Its managing editor was to be directly responsible to the president alone. A statement from Nyerere set out that,

In accordance with the Arusha Declaration, it is clearly impossible for the largest daily newspaper in independent Tanzania to be left indefinitely in the hands of a foreign company. In a country committed to building socialism, it

---

[78] 'Take Care', editorial, *Standard*, 16 December 1968, 4.
[79] [A. M. Babu], '"Standard Tanzania" versus "Operation Vijana"', *Nationalist*, 20 December 1968, 4.
[80] 'Ban the "Standard"', *Nationalist*, 3 January 1969, 1, 8; 'T.Y.L. Members in Protest at "The Standard"', *Standard*, 3 January 1969, 1.
[81] 'Mpaka lini?', editorial, *Uhuru*, 8 January 1969, 2.
[82] 'Government Takes Over "The Standard"', *Standard*, 5 February 1970, 1.

is also impossible for such an influential medium to be left indefinitely in the control of non-socialist, capitalist owners. The reasons for [the] Government's decision to acquire the '"Standard"' are thus both nationalistic and socialistic; we want Tanzanians to have control of this newspaper, and we want those Tanzanians to be responsible for the people as a whole.

Nyerere stressed that although the *Standard* would be expected to support the government's policies, it would also be free to criticise their implementation. The newspaper would be 'guided by the principle that free debate is an essential statement of true socialism'. The *Standard*'s commitment was to the *res publica*, rather than to the government.[83]

Not everyone in Dar es Salaam's media world greeted the announcement with unqualified praise. *Ngurumo*, now the only privately owned Tanzanian daily, warned of the dangers to the free circulation of news. In an editorial that made no direct reference to the *Standard*'s nationalisation, *Ngurumo* complained about problems caused by the lack of knowledge about the scarcity of consumer essentials like beans or maize. Citizens needed reliable information to make such informed everyday choices. 'If the freedom to be informed equally about the news is not exercised, people will not be able to exercise their equal freedom to choose and act, and the result will be complaints about the government', it argued. In other words, citizens would not be able to make informed judgements about their leaders' decisions if alternative sources of news dried up.[84] Here, *Ngurumo* adopted the 'freedom to be informed' arguments which had become one plank of the TANU retort to accusations that Tanzania did not uphold the freedom of the press. Meanwhile, the government hinted that it was not trying to stifle all independent newspapers in Tanzania by simultaneously lifting the ban on the *Daily Nation*.[85]

Given the government's acquisition of the *Standard* was justified on 'nationalistic' grounds, Nyerere's choice of its new managing editor seemed odd. Frene Ginwala was a 38-year-old South African ANC member of Parsi-Indian descent. She possessed the CV of a Third World revolutionary par excellence but had a mixed history with the Tanzanian authorities. Following the Sharpeville massacre in 1960,

---

[83] Julius K. Nyerere, 'A Socialist Paper for the People', *Standard*, 5 February 1970, 1.
[84] 'Kujua', editorial, *Ngurumo*, 11 February 1970, 1.
[85] 'Ban Lifted on Kenyan Papers', *Standard*, 5 February 1970, 1.

Ginwala had joined Oliver Tambo in establishing the ANC's 'external mission' in exile. From Dar es Salaam, she had edited the movement's magazine, *Spearhead*. Ginwala had served on the editorial board of the Algiers-based journal *Révolution africaine* and worked as a stringer for London's *Guardian*. She was also rumoured to be a member of the South African Communist Party (SACP). However, in 1963 Ginwala was suddenly declared persona non grata in Tanganyika, for reasons which remain unclear.[86] Her expulsion may have been linked to a *Spearhead* editorial which condemned early initiatives to create a one-party state in Tanganyika as the work of a self-entrenching 'privileged élite'.[87] By the time she returned to Dar es Salaam in 1970, her identity as an Asian in a position of authority was even more problematic in the eyes of the TANU radicals than it had been at the time of her departure. Moreover, the ANC's relationship with the Tanzanian government was in ruins due to its alleged connections with Oscar Kambona's failed coup plot, as explained in the next chapter. Ginwala was, in her own words, 'an identikit picture of who should NOT be the editor of a Tanganyikan [sic] newspaper'.[88]

The appointment of Ginwala was therefore a surprising move from Nyerere, particularly given the eclectic editorial team which she then assembled using her contacts among the international socialist world. In London, she recruited Richard Gott, a British national who had written on revolutionary movements in Latin America, to the position of foreign editor. Other members of staff included Iain Christie, who developed a close relationship with FRELIMO's leadership; Tony Hall, another ANC supporter; Rod Prince, the former editor of the British pacifist magazine *Peace News*; and Philip Ochieng, a talented and outspoken young Kenyan columnist.[89] The international composition of the staff reflected Dar es Salaam's reputation as a mecca of revolution. Yet it was also at odds with the nationalist vein that ran through Tanzanian politics at the time. In parliament, one MP complained that

---

[86] Sturmer, *Media History*, 120–22; Ginwala's testimony in Hilda Bernstein, *The Rift: The Exile Experience of South Africans* (London: Jonathan Cape, 1994), 9–11.
[87] Frene Ginwala, 'No Party State?', *Spearhead*, February 1963, 3. I am grateful to Chambi Chachage for bringing this article to my attention.
[88] Bernstein, *Rift*, 11.
[89] Trevor Grundy, 'Frene Ginwala, the Lenin Supplement, and the Storm Drains of History', 15 August 2017, politicsweb.co.za/opinion/frene-ginwala-the-lenin-supplement-and-the-storm-d.

Ginwala had overlooked the local 'youth' in composing her team and questioned whether 'this woman has a Tanzanian heart'.[90] But, as Nyerere had previously pointed out, there remained a serious shortage of trained manpower in the journalism sector in Tanzania.

Ginwala immediately signalled her intention to meet Nyerere's call for the *Standard* to be critical of his government where it failed to meet its own standards. On 13 February, it broke the alarming story about the detention of Cornelius Ogunsanwo, a Nigerian doctoral student at the London School of Economics. Ogunsanwo had been conducting research on Chinese activity in Tanzania when he was imprisoned without trial for thirty-nine days. After his release, Ogunsanwo gave an interview to the *Standard*, in which he described the 'animalistic and inhumane' conditions inside the prison and gave details of a number of other inmates detained for political reasons, including many foreign nationals.[91] The *Standard*'s sister paper, the *Sunday News*, presented this incident as indicative of a broader malaise. 'There is today an atmosphere of fear and intimidation which prevents people from raising and exposing illegal actions', it remarked. It also instructed people to draw attention to such abuses of power when they encountered them. 'If the people allow themselves to be intimidated, and by their silence act as if they are living in a police state, they will run the danger of creating one.'[92] Another *Standard* editorial was explicitly supportive of China, but criticised the 'air of secrecy' which surrounded its activities in Tanzania.[93] The incident showed Ginwala's willingness to speak out on particularly controversial issues, such as the detention of political prisoners and Tanzania's relationship with China. The latter point was particularly sensitive, given Ginwala shared the ANC and SACP's preferences for Moscow over Beijing.

The *Standard*'s critique of imperialism was apiece with the line taken in TANU's newspapers. Both Ginwala's *Standard* and Mkapa's *Nationalist* were engaged with global affairs and ideological debates about socialism. Yet the *Nationalist*'s priority, as its name suggested, was nation-building. In contrast, many of the *Standard*'s foreign staff considered themselves as international revolutionaries. The newspaper's

[90] Bwenda, 29 July 1970, *Hansard* (Tanzania), 21st meeting, col. 2425.
[91] 'Political Prisoners' Row', *Standard*, 13 February 1970, 1.
[92] 'Abuse of Power', editorial, *Sunday News*, 15 February 1970, 4.
[93] Alan Hutchison, *China's African Revolution* (London: Hutchinson, 1975), 186–87.

offices were cluttered with Marxist texts and propaganda. Andy Chande, a Tanzanian Asian businessman who remained on the board of the newspaper after its nationalisation, recalled that to celebrate the centenary of Lenin's birth in April 1970, the *Standard* published a supplement so bulky that it was 'jettisoned into the gutters of the city' by delivery boys struggling under the weight of paper, causing a blockage in Dar es Salaam's storm drains.[94] Ginwala and Gott immediately sought to diversify the *Standard*'s news sources, in spite of financial constraints.[95] Ginwala took communist news from the New China News Agency and the Soviet Union's Tass, while Gott made use of Cuba's Prensa Latina and the Liberation News Service, a Harlem-based underground agency which connected the American New Left into global circuits of counterculture and revolution.[96]

The *Standard*'s sharp, anti-Western tone predictably caused confrontations with diplomatic representations in Dar es Salaam. It was a government, rather than a party newspaper, even if the distinction between the two institutions was increasingly blurred. For this reason, it was much harder for state officials to distance themselves from arguments made in the *Standard* than comments emanating from TANU organs like the Youth League or *Nationalist*. In November 1970, the *Standard* published two articles by Walter Rodney, a lecturer at UDSM, in which the Guyanese academic extolled the kidnapping of diplomats and the hijacking of civilian aircraft as a form of revolutionary violence.[97] The British high commissioner, Horace Phillips, responded by asking the Ministry of Foreign Affairs what place such articles had in a government newspaper.[98] His note was leaked to Ginwala, who replied through an editorial in the *Sunday News*. This accused Phillips of 'gross interference' in Tanzania's internal affairs and suggested that the letter was part of a British

---

[94] J. K. Chande, *A Knight in Africa: Journey from Bukene* (Manotick: Penumbra, 2005), 141–42.
[95] Riyami to Ginwala, 27 February 1970, TNA, 593, IS/P/120/6.
[96] Sturmer, *Media History*, 124; Blake Slonecker, *A New Dawn for the New Left: Liberation News Service, Montague Farm, and the Long Sixties* (New York: Palgrave Macmillan, 2012).
[97] Walter Rodney, 'Revolutionary Violence: An Answer to Oppression', *Standard*, 5 November 1970, 4; 'Revolutionary Action – Way to Justice', *Standard*, 6 November 1970, 4, 9.
[98] Phillips to Katikaza, 5 and 6 November 1970, enclosed in Phillips to FCO, 9 November 1970, UKNA, FCO 31/700/12.

attempt to distract attention from London's plans to sell arms to South Africa.[99] At a diplomatic reception, she told Phillips that the editorial was an attempt to establish her right to publish as she wished. Phillips then raised this conversation with Nyerere himself. The president, he noted, 'raised his eyebrows in incredulity' and stressed that the matter would have no impact on Tanzania's relations with Britain.[100] Other Western states lodged complaints with the Tanzanian government. The West German embassy identified that a number of articles were essentially identical to the GDR's propaganda handouts.[101] The American ambassador described editorials in the *Standard* as 'indistinguishable in tone, content, and general animus from what might have appeared in Moscow and Peking'.[102]

Just as Nyerere had previously warned the TANU Youth League and the *Nationalist* journalists against unnecessary provocation, he now moved to clamp down on the *Standard*'s editorial line. In June 1971, Nyerere summoned local newspaper and radio editors to State House, where he lectured them over their 'inaccurate' reporting. In a tone which recalled his *Argue Don't Shout* pamphlet, discussed in the previous chapter, the president ridiculed the media's excessive use of terms like 'imperialism', 'stooge', and 'puppet'. This 'nonsense', he said, was 'becoming something of a disease in Tanzania', so much so that he was getting 'afraid to use the word "imperialism" once in a two hour question and answer session, because it will be presented with such headlines that the people will imagine I talk about nothing else'.[103] The American ambassador noted that this intervention came after a *Standard* editorial had misrepresented Nyerere's views on ongoing negotiations over peace in Vietnam, by describing the talks as Washington's 'search for an honourable, but cowardly, retreat'. According to Joan Wicken, Nyerere's personal assistant and occasional source of information for the American embassy, the president had rebuked Ginwala the day after the story's publication.[104] Again, where

---

[99] 'Interference', editorial, *Sunday News*, 8 November 1970, 4.
[100] Phillips to FCO, 14 November 1970, UKNA, FCO 31/700/32.
[101] Roberts, 'Press', 164.
[102] Ross to State Dept, 30 March 1971, NARA, RG 59, SNF 1970–73, Box 2619, POL TANZAN-US.
[103] 'Weigh Your Words – Nyerere', *Nationalist*, 14 June 1971, 1, 5.
[104] Ross to State Dept, 13 May 1971, NARA, RG 59, SNF 1970–73, Box 2619, POL TANZAN-US.

Tanzania's anti-imperialism strayed into antagonistic territory, Nyerere prioritised good relations with foreign powers.

The pressure on Ginwala from above was accompanied by discontent from within her newspaper's staff. The editorial staff were divided by their own squabbles as much as united by their revolutionary socialism – 'packed with political and ideological nitroglycerine', as Chande put it.[105] Trevor Grundy, another expatriate journalist, described Ginwala herself as 'a pin-less hand grenade in a *sari*'. The Sino-Soviet split played out in microcosm in the *Standard* newsroom. Ginwala, a member of the ANC, which had close relations with Moscow, clashed with Gott, who sided with the Third World radicalism of Mao and Castro. One heated confrontation ended with Ginwala allegedly shouting at Gott, '[y]ou get your politics from Peking and your arrogance from Winchester', referring to his somewhat unproletarian private education in Britain.[106] Ginwala's ANC membership also caused rifts in Dar es Salaam's world of revolutionary politics. The PAC, the ANC's rival in the South African liberation struggle, protested about the lack of coverage they received in the *Standard*. This followed complaints from Potlako Leballo, the PAC's leader and the chief state witness in the treason trial in 1970, that Ginwala had sought to 'destroy him' by supplying evidence to the defence lawyers.[107] These tensions were entwined with racial friction between Ginwala's predominantly non-black editorial board and the *Standard*'s African journalists. A group of staff members found Ginwala's attitude towards African employees patronising. They called for the full Tanzanianisation of the newspaper.[108]

The radical 'Guidelines' issued by TANU in February 1971 provided a political framework through which these grievances gained expression. As explained in the following chapter, the Guidelines (*Mwongozo*) encouraged workers to challenge managers who abused their power, which unintentionally led to a series of strikes and lockouts. These developments were not confined to factory floors. At the *Standard*, the staff formed a 'Worker's Council' and accused Ginwala of various charges, including racialism. The workers aired these complaints during

---

[105] Chande, *Knight in Africa*, 141.   [106] Grundy, 'Frene Ginwala'.
[107] 'Leballo a Key to State Case', *Standard*, 29 December 1970, 1, 5; Ross to State Dept, 18 August 1970, NARA, RG 59, SNF 1970–73, Box 2618, POL 23 TANZAN. For more on the trial, see Chapter 7.
[108] Konde, *Press Freedom*, 60.

a marathon meeting, which lasted three days, including the whole of a weekday night. Reuters' correspondent in Dar es Salaam reported that Gott sided with the Africans present, while brandishing a copy of Mao's *Little Red Book*.[109] The *Standard* ran an editorial about these 'sometimes acrimonious and bitter' internal debates. 'Newspapers do not normally publicise their internal activities', it noted. 'But we are not living in normal times.' Ginwala was not mentioned by name and the debate was spun in a positive light, as an example of *Mwongozo* in action.[110] Nonetheless, the episode demonstrated how Ginwala no longer commanded the confidence of her own workers. In particular, the tension between Ginwala and Gott reached breaking point. Both appear to have approached Nyerere to complain about the other. Nyerere responded by informing Gott, Hall, and Prince that they would have to leave the country within a month.[111]

Having already lost the respect of her team, Ginwala finally exhausted Nyerere's confidence. The breaking point came when the *Standard* imperilled Tanzania's attempts to build international solidarities against Idi Amin, who seized power in Uganda in January 1971. Among Nyerere's few allies in this situation was Gaafar Nimeiry, the president of Sudan, whose own rule was in a precarious state. On 19 July, Nimeiry's government was briefly toppled from power in Sudan in a left-wing coup. After being relieved by loyal troops, Nimeiry carried out a violent purge of the Sudanese Communist Party. Shortly afterwards, a *Standard* editorial accused Nimeiry of a 'senseless witch hunt of people whose only crime is to share an ideology with countries like the Soviet Union and China'. It condemned him for practicing 'a form of ideological intolerance which in Africa has been hitherto the preserve of Mr. Vorster and Mr. Houphouet-Boigny', the Ivorian leader who had entered into a diplomatic 'dialogue' with South Africa.[112] Unbeknown to Ginwala, the editorial was published shortly before Nimeiry was scheduled to visit Tanzania. While Nyerere could not have approved of the bloody purges in Sudan, geopolitical circumstances meant that he turned a blind eye. The new government in

---

[109] Moore to general manager, 14 March 1971, Reuters Archive, CRF, Box 157.
[110] Editorial, *Standard*, 14 March 1971, 1; see also Konde, *Press Freedom*, 60–62.
[111] Barton, *Press of Africa*, 122; Philip Ochieng, *I Accuse the Press: An Insider's View of Media and Politics in Africa* (Nairobi: Initiatives, 1992), 129–31.
[112] Editorial, *Standard*, 29 July 1971, 1.

Uganda threatened both Sudan and Tanzania, which were among the few African states not to recognise Amin's regime.[113] Ginwala, Gott, and the other foreign editorial staff were immediately relieved of their jobs. Sammy Mdee, a Tanzanian who had led the anti-Ginwala faction among the *Standard* staff, was appointed as the new editor.[114] Once again, Nyerere showed that foreign policy was a delicate matter. He had previously intervened directly in the press when he deemed its attacks on the West counterproductive. When Ginwala and Gott unwittingly placed their ideological solidarities ahead of questions of national security, Nyerere concluded that the experiment could go on no longer.[115]

Ginwala's turn at the helm of the *Standard* lasted less than eighteen months but serves as a window onto dynamics in Tanzanian political society which stretched beyond the media sphere. Nyerere sought to harness Dar es Salaam's cosmopolitan revolutionary energy to the decolonisation of the Tanzanian media, but the plan backfired. The socialist credentials of Ginwala and her fellow expatriates could not be questioned, yet they remained outsiders in the eyes of Tanzanians who prioritised the accelerated Africanisation of institutions like a state-owned newspaper. The paradox of a nationalised newspaper run by foreigners, whose interests did not necessarily line up with those of the state, collapsed under the weight of its contradictions. Inside the newsroom, racial, personal, and ideological tensions created rifts among the staff. Outside of it, the *Standard*'s internationalist Marxism rubbed up against Tanzania's geopolitical priorities, as the *ujamaa* revolution took on a more defensive outlook.

Inward Turns

The end of Ginwala's reign at the *Standard* marked a decisive moment in the inward turn of the Tanzanian media. Less than a year after she lost her job, the newspaper ceased to exist. As party and state became

---

[113] David Martin, 'Nyerere Dismisses an Editor', *Guardian*, 2 August 1971, 3.
[114] 'Tanzanian Editor Takes Over at "The Standard"', *Sunday News*, 1 August 1971, 1.
[115] David Martin, long a Nyerere confidant, was himself deported in March 1974 after a series of articles and broadcast appearances in which he criticised Amin, during a short-lived window when Nyerere was trying to build bridges with Kampala. Moore to managing director, 1 April 1974, Reuters Archive, CRF, Box 157B.

more closely aligned, the duplication of news in the *Nationalist* and the *Standard* was deemed a waste of resources. In April 1972, the government merged the two newspapers to form the *Daily News*, which became the sole English-language newspaper published in Tanzania. Benjamin Mkapa was named as the new managing editor. A party-based Press Council, headed by TANU's director of information, oversaw this reconfigured media arrangement. Echoing both Lenin's conception of the press and Nkrumah's speech from 1965, the first edition of the *Daily News* set out that in a socialist country, the press must act as a 'collective mobiliser, collective educator, collective inspirer and an instrument for the dissemination of socialist ideas. ... Like all true revolutionary activities, such a task for the press begs of no liberalism.'[116]

But the 'dissemination of socialist ideas' increasingly meant the dissemination of a particular *type* of socialist ideas: *ujamaa*. The revolutionary Marxism of some of those Africans who remained on the staff of the government newspaper after the departure of Ginwala and the creation of the *Daily News* jarred with the regime's ideological message. Philip Ochieng's radicalism proved too much for this new order. After he made a wholesale defence of Marxist-Leninist 'vanguardism' in the *Daily News*, Mkapa and the Press Council made clear that Ochieng's presence was no longer welcome at the newspaper. He resigned in January 1973 and then went to study in the GDR.[117] Another young journalist, Jenerali Ulimwengu, joined the *Daily News* shortly after graduating from UDSM and initially shared a column with Ochieng. Two years later, he was also pushed out. 'The reason I was removed was because I was perceived as not being totally compliant with the party line, maybe seen to be a bit too radical', Ulimwengu reflected. 'I was working with people who criticised the government too much, too often. It was quite tense.'[118]

Over time, the party line came to predominate, aggravated by the potential for instability brought about by external danger and then economic crisis. Local news about *ujamaa* villages or regional commissioners took priority over international stories.[119] Mkapa acknowledged

---

[116] Editorial, *Daily News*, 26 April 1972, 4.
[117] Ochieng, *I Accuse the Press*, 162; see his 'Why Karl Marx Is Relevant', *Sunday News*, 14 January 1973, 4, 12.
[118] Interview with Jenerali Ulimwengu, Oyster Bay, Dar es Salaam, 18 August 2015.
[119] Phillips to Brinson, 21 July 1972, UKNA, FCO 26/1042/1.

that the *Daily News* contained 'less controversial coverage regarding the implementation of policy'. Instead, criticism came by way of highlighting the mistakes of individuals.[120] That is not to say that the *Daily News* was devoid of any kind of debate about government policy, but the critique that remained tended towards the same limitations as those found among social scientists at the university: increasingly abstract discussions reflective of a rarefied political atmosphere. The radical journalists who had been attracted by the sense of possibilities in the Tanzanian revolution were disappointed by the post-Ginwala media. Ochieng lamented that 'as the party became more stymied and the government hardened', the 'good *apparatchiks*' who edited the *Daily News* sought 'more and more to conform'.[121]

These more doctrinaire positions held that the media's principal role was to assist in the goal of socialist development and nation-building. Taking a Marxist perspective, they argued that the idea of the 'freedom of the press' was a mirage. According to one Tanzanian communications scholar, it was 'utterly impossible anywhere in our world today' for newspapers to be 'free from ideological ties and control' since the press 'not only promotes ideology but it is also to be part of it'.[122] These Tanzanian debates and practices prefigured broader arguments about the role and nature of the media in the Third World in the 1970s. The New World Information and Communications Order (NWICO), the media's corollary of the better known New International Economic Order, represented a fightback from the Third World against what they considered to be the 'imperialism' of global communications networks. The NWICO's advocates rejected the hegemonic influence of international media houses, especially Western news agencies, which inculcated the developing world with neocolonial mentalities. It called for an end to unrestricted 'flows' of information, which, much like free markets, perpetuated the dependency of the Third World. In their place, the NWICO proposed a more equitable system which revolved around regional coordination bodies and nationally sourced information.[123]

Tanzania was an active participant in these conversations, which represented an internationalisation of attitudes to the media that had

---

[120] Mkapa, *My Life*, 68.   [121] Ochieng, *I Accuse the Press*, 146.
[122] Ng'wanakilala, *Mass Communication*, 19.
[123] Vanessa Freije, '"The Emancipation of Media": Latin American Advocacy for a New International Information Order in the 1970s', *Journal of Global History*, 14 (2019), 301–20.

gestated in the country since independence. In 1976, Mkapa became the first director of SHIHATA (*Shirika la Habari la Tanzania*, News Agency of Tanzania), putting into practice plans which had been called for regularly in the Tanzanian media since independence. SHIHATA was legally empowered with a monopoly on the collection of local and foreign news, though financial difficulties proved insurmountable obstacles to fulfilling this goal. Much like the broader agenda of the Third World fightback against cultural imperialism through the media, Tanzania's attempts to break its dependency ties to powerful Western news agencies failed to meet their ambitions.[124] More broadly, among the various criticisms levelled at the NWICO was that its true motivation was to insulate repressive regimes against media criticism. International collaboration between Third World states over the media paradoxically cemented state sovereignty and introspective politics over transnational cooperation.

The decline of the independent media in Tanzania was not solely a function of a changing ideological landscape, as the financial collapse of *Ngurumo* shows. Its circulation plummeted to just 2,000, as it struggled to compete with *Uhuru*, the TANU Swahili newspaper. In a period of economic crisis, the party- and state-owned newspapers were able to fall back on the economic infrastructure of parastatals for access to credit and the supply of essential materials such as newsprint in a time of shortage. *Ngurumo* had no such security. While the *Daily News* and *Uhuru* benefited from investment in efficient, modern presses that produced a relatively slick final copy, *Ngurumo* remained stuck with primitive colonial-era technology. In 1976, the last issue of *Ngurumo* rolled over the newspaper's creaking press.[125] That left Tanzania's mass media in the hands of the party-state, in the form of the *Daily News*, *Uhuru*, and the radio. This situation continued until the economic liberalisation measures of the late 1980s.

At the same time as the Tanzanian state monopolised the local news media, international journalists found their own room for manoeuvre limited. Dar es Salaam's foreign press pack (or, more specifically, Western journalists) attested to a shift in the attitude of the Tanzanian state towards their activities. In November 1973, the Reuters correspondent noted that there was a worrying tendency for foreign reporters to be excluded from press conferences in Dar es

[124] Sturmer, *Media History*, 157–63.   [125] Konde, *Press Freedom*, 42–43.

Salaam.¹²⁶ In the same month as the establishment of the *Daily News*, the Reuters teleprinter was temporarily removed from the Kilimanjaro Hotel, denying journalists of a critical source of information. Reuters thought that the Kilimanjaro's unreliable payments for its services were only partly responsible for the decision. More significant, its correspondent believed, was that at a time when the government appeared to be offering greater direction as to what news should be printed in Tanzanian newspapers, 'it struck them as a bit odd to give everyone access to such stories in the foyer of the city's leading hotel'.¹²⁷ Yet this only made journalists more reliant on the rumour networks which the government deplored: shortly after the removal of the teleprinter, a reporter for *Jeune Afrique* reflected that the best way of knowing what was going on in the city was to 'go for a pint in the pub'.¹²⁸

Conclusion

Making news in Dar es Salaam was an international affair. In striking contrast to today's press in Tanzania, where international stories seldom make the front page or editorial columns, the newspapers of the early socialist era had broad horizons. In part, this reflected the intellectual climate of revolutionary Dar es Salaam. The *Nationalist* and *Standard* drew ideological inspiration from the diverse strands of anticolonial political thought and action that coalesced in the Tanzanian capital. The Cold War, the struggle against minority rule, and Tanzania's socialist state-making project fuelled friction between newspapers and also within them, as Ginwala's turbulent experience demonstrates. But a commitment to Third World revolution also became problematic when it clashed with both the momentum towards Africanisation and the regime's foreign policy priorities, especially Nyerere's non-aligned position. In such circumstances, the president moved to replace editors and shore up top-down control over newspaper content. Meanwhile, the state's control over the economic levers of production meant it was increasingly difficult for independent ventures to survive.

---

¹²⁶ Parsons to general manager, September 1973, Reuters Archive, CRF, Box 157A.
¹²⁷ Fox to general manager, 4 April 1972, Reuters Archive, CRF, Box 157C.
¹²⁸ Bruno Crimi, 'Nyerere à l'épreuve', *Jeune Afrique*, 24 February 1973, 10–12.

At first glance, the state's de facto monopolisation of the media in Tanzania might seem to be a classic case of an authoritarian regime shutting down the possibilities for dissent. That would be too simplistic a verdict. Dar es Salaam's newspaper wars were part of a broader ideological landscape in which independent Third World regimes grappled with the challenge of managing a postcolonial media sector. For journalists like Ochieng, government or party ownership did not necessarily preclude a vibrant, critical media, provided the state respected a certain degree of editorial independence. He reflected on his time in Dar es Salaam as 'years of freedom of expression', which 'few other African and Third World countries have ever enjoyed'.[129] The debates which emerged from these developments reveal just how shallow concepts of the 'freedom of the press' are for analysing the politics of the media in Africa, which persist in contemporary studies, often taking the form of a crude opposition between the 'state' and 'civil society'. As Emma Hunter argues, via her analysis of state-owned newspapers in the colonial era, the monolithic concept of 'civil society' masks complex entanglements that resist such easy separation.[130] Similar lessons for today's African press can be taken from the present study of the contingent politics of revolutionary Dar es Salaam's newspapers, whose trajectories only make sense once we break down these relationships and address the nature of the tensions – economic, ideological, political, and personal – that defined them.[131] The path to a nationalised, largely toothless press owned by the party-state was not straight, but marked by moments of tension and experimentation. A similar story characterised the radicalisation of Tanzanian socialism through the TANU 'Guidelines' of 1971, which form the focus of the final chapter.

---

[129] Ibid., 125.

[130] Emma Hunter, '"Our Common Humanity": Print, Power, and the Colonial Press in Interwar Tanganyika and French Cameroun', *Journal of Global History*, 7 (2012), 300–301.

[131] For more nuanced assessments of these contemporary relationships, see Francis B. Nyamnjoh, *Africa's Media: Democracy and the Politics of Belonging* (London: Zed, 2005); Wale Adebanwi, 'The Radical Press and Security Agencies in Nigeria: Beyond Hegemonic Polarities', *African Studies Review*, 54 (2011), 45–69.

7 Mwongozo: *The African Revolution, Reloaded*

It was like Arusha all over again. On 21 February 1971, a week-long meeting of the TANU National Executive Committee came to an end in Dar es Salaam. President Nyerere stepped into the late afternoon sunshine and addressed the crowd that had gathered outside the party headquarters at Lumumba Street, Kariakoo. His purpose was to introduce a new party document – the 'TANU Guidelines' or *Mwongozo*. To cheers and applause, Nyerere narrated a history of Africa which emphasised the catastrophic impact of centuries of European domination, from the slave trade through colonial occupation to the neo-imperial support provided to the white minority regimes. He argued that *Mwongozo* was a means of finally breaking with these legacies. TANU's task was 'to wipe out oppression in our country, to wipe out the exploitation of man by man in Tanzania, and to create a new African, an African who utterly refuses to be exploited, oppressed, and humiliated'.[1]

This chapter tells the story of TANU's attempt to reload Tanzania's socialist revolution and revive Africa's flagging liberation struggles in the early 1970s. In contrast to the Arusha Declaration, *Mwongozo* has received little attention from historians. Yet it was a key turning point in the course of the *ujamaa* project. *Mwongozo* emerged from a moment of acute domestic and continental crisis. The development path set out in Arusha was failing to yield the anticipated economic growth. Tanzania seemed no closer to fulfilling its goal of national self-reliance. The elite continued to be divided as to the way forward. The uneasy union with Zanzibar was creating a headache for the mainland government. Meanwhile, the forces of Tanzania's white minority enemies and their allies had regrouped. To Tanzanian eyes, they appeared to be on the counteroffensive. A failed attempt to topple the government in Guinea was followed by a successful coup in Uganda,

---

[1] Enclosed in Ewans to Holmes, 1 March 1971, UKNA, FCO 31/970/4.

which Tanzanians attributed to outside interference by 'imperialists', including Britain and Israel, rather than the Cold War superpowers.

In these circumstances, TANU's radical wing gained an upper hand over the government's moderates. Having previously resisted certain popular economic interventions on the basis that they would be too disruptive and divisive, Nyerere now relented. But the outcome of *Mwongozo* was a situation in which TANU's dominance and the ideological doxa of *ujamaa* precluded serious discussions about political economy. We have seen in previous chapters how the party-state increasingly exercised greater top-down control over youth politics and the press in Dar es Salaam, justified by the language of unity and vigilance against the imperialist threat. This chapter takes these conversations into the sphere of high politics, picking up the story which we left off in Chapter 2. Social scientists working on the magnetic topic of villagisation have identified the source of Tanzanian authoritarianism in the modernising visions of bureaucrats and TANU officials.[2] Yet, as Priya Lal argues, there is a teleological element to these arguments, which attribute the failure of Tanzanian socialism to 'fundamental flaws in the *ujamaa* experiment'.[3] Moving from the village to the seat of state power, this chapter understands the authoritarian turn in Tanzanian politics via a context which is simultaneously local and global, rooted in Dar es Salaam but stretching beyond the country's frontiers.

The Strains of Self-Reliance

At the start of the new decade, the Nyerere government was strained by the pressures of implementing the Arusha programme while snuffing out internal threats and managing the unsteady relationship with Zanzibar. First, fulfilling the promises of the Arusha Declaration tested the capacity of the government to build a democratic socialist state. The pursuit of self-reliance stretched the sinews of the economy. Debates

---

[2] See especially Schneider, *Government of Development*; James C. Scott, *Seeing Like a State: How Certain Schemes to Improve the Human Condition Have Failed* (New Haven, CT: Yale University Press, 1998). There are substantial differences between these two accounts: Scott's perception of villagisation as a 'high modernist' attempt to reorder rural society has been perceptively criticised by Schneider, who draws attention to bureaucratic process and agency.
[3] Lal, *African Socialism*, 13–14.

over the future direction of economic policy and the role of TANU in a one-party democracy proved divisive. Meanwhile, the uncovering of a coup plot against the government showed the residual threat posed by high-profile dissenters, as well as the dangers Tanzania assumed by hosting exiled revolutionaries. The hastily devised union with Zanzibar was increasingly unstable. Nyerere looked on with embarrassment from Dar es Salaam as the excesses of the Karume regime attracted negative international attention.

Following a burst of activity after the Arusha Declaration, economic growth had plateaued out by 1970. These years witnessed the rapid expansion of the parastatal sector, despite senior voices within government warning that they were placing dangerous stress on Tanzania's underdeveloped manpower resources. As Amir Jamal, the minister for finance, told parliament, the parastatals and nationalised banks were mutually dependent upon each other. The failure of one would trigger a chain reaction that affected the others, spilling over into the entire economy.[4] This strain was increased by the Second Five-Year Plan of 1969–74, which was funded by overseas borrowing, contra the Arusha Declaration's warnings. The State Trading Corporation (STC) responded to shortages of consumer goods by importing them in large quantities, draining precious foreign exchange. A trade surplus of 135 million shillings in 1967 became a deficit of 519 million shillings by 1970. The balance of payments crisis was aggravated by the decision taken in early 1970 to nationalise import-export houses and wholesale trade, against the counsel of the government's expatriate advisors.[5] This was something Nyerere had previously warned against. Among the reasons for the decision was the need to purchase around 250 million shillings' worth of goods from China in each of the five years which it would take to build the railway to Zambia. The contradictions of the search for self-reliance were becoming sharper.[6]

Different politicians and economists offered different solutions to the difficulties of implementing socialism. Nyerere continued to prioritise development through rural transformation and accelerated efforts to roll out *ujamaa* villagisation. A. M. Babu, the minister of commerce, shared the view that socialist development could not come about while Tanzania remained dependent on unequal relationships of foreign

---

[4] Hartmann, 'Development Policy-Making', 264. [5] Aminzade, *Race*, 221–23.
[6] Coulson, *Tanzania*, 229, 339–40, 348–49.

trade. However, as we saw in Chapter 2, Babu differed from the president in calling for intensive industrialisation rather than agricultural revolution. The pair clashed over the contents of the Second Five-Year Plan. Nyerere also objected to Babu's Marxism. He reportedly threw one of Babu's cabinet papers out three times for being too theoretically esoteric.[7] Yet despite his reputation as an 'extremist' abroad, Babu demonstrated a strong pragmatic streak. In 1970, Nyerere instructed Babu to draw up plans for nationalising Tanzania's wholesale trade by the end of the year. Babu refused to carry out these instructions. He believed that the current system of internal commerce, while not necessarily congruent with socialist ideals, was cost effective. Babu argued that the state should not be 'a seller of bread and butter'.[8] Nyerere reacted angrily. He established a separate task force on the issue, which bypassed Babu's own ministry.[9] After November's general election, Babu was shifted from the ministry of commerce to the ministry for economic affairs and development. Much later, as Tanzania's socialist project became an indisputable economic disaster, Babu declared himself vindicated. 'The Tanzanian example has shown that indiscriminate nationalisation of the private sector ... may turn into a destructive move which hampers rather than accelerates development', he reflected.[10]

Just as they had done at the time of the Arusha Declaration, more moderate ministers and bureaucrats also urged for caution in moving forwards.[11] They included the likes of Amir Jamal and the governor of the national bank, Edwin Mtei, as well as a number of European expatriate advisors. While still committed to the goals of Arusha socialism, their technocratic education and cosmopolitan experience led them to prioritise accepted economic logic above political exhortation or rigid Marxist categorisations in setting out a development strategy.[12] For example, they advised Nyerere against pushing ahead with a 'frontal' approach to *ujamaa* villagisation, arguing that working

---

[7] Shivji et al., *Development as Rebellion*, vol. 3, 276.
[8] Wilson, *US Foreign Policy*, 135.   [9] Babu, 'Entrepreneurs', 349.
[10] A. M. Babu, 'Memoirs: An Outline', in Othman (ed.), *I Saw the Future*, 44.
[11] This section draws heavily on Hartmann, 'Development Policy-Making', 228–71.
[12] See the frustrations with the 'radical' social scientists expressed by one former economic advisor: Gerry Helleiner, *Toward a Better World: Memoirs of a Life in International and Development Economics* (Toronto: University of Toronto Press, 2018), 56–57.

within the existing structures of small-scale peasant farming would be far more effective.[13] They maintained that Tanzania must continue to export goods in order to sustain foreign exchange reserves in an interconnected global economy. 'We shall not pretend that self-reliance and self-sufficiency are one and the same thing', Jamal told parliament in 1969. 'We recognise that they are not, and we know we are increasingly part of an interdependent world.'[14] Mtei similarly used the press to explain why Tanzania had to preserve its foreign currency reserves if it was to succeed in implementing socialism.[15]

At the opposite end of the scale to these economists were many TANU leaders and members of parliament, who eschewed conventional strategies of development through *economics* and instead advocated for development through *politics*. That is not to say that the former lacked a political basis or the latter economic justification. Rather, the TANU radicals came to emphasise that development could only be achieved through popular mobilisation under the banner of the party. Their interventions were driven by political principle, especially regarding complete Africanisation, rather than economic calculation. They thus called for not just the nationalisation of internal trade (to which Nyerere eventually acceded), but also housing. These calls also came with a racial edge, as many Tanzanians continued to resent the prominence of Asians in the retail sector and their role as a property-owning rentier class. At the radical tip of TANU, Youth League leaders agitated for party cadres to serve as a 'vanguard' in order to mobilise the workers and peasants in pursuit of the goals of *ujamaa*, much as had occurred in Mao's China. The TYL declared that Tanzania's most pressing task was to transform TANU into 'an ideological streamlined nerve centre of the revolution'.[16] Debate about development policy was therefore not just a case of alternative strategies, but also a question of whether political mobilisation rather than economic calculation offered Tanzania the best route forwards.

Meanwhile, the TANU leadership constricted space for dissent among the party's ranks. In October 1968, the National Executive

---

[13] Cranford Pratt, 'Democracy and Socialism in Tanzania', *Canadian Journal of African Studies*, 12 (1978), 424.
[14] Quoted in Hartmann, 'Development Policy-Making', 254.
[15] Edwin Mtei, 'Foreign Exchange Vital to Development', *Standard*, 29 December 1970, 4.
[16] 'Nation Faces Three Major Tasks – TYL', *Nationalist*, 7 November 1970, 1.

Committee expelled nine members from TANU. They included the exiled Oscar Kambona, as well as Eli Anangisye, who was under preventive detention after his failed attempt to subvert the armed forces in July 1967.[17] This disgraced pair were joined by seven MPs. The reasons for their expulsion all differed slightly and, in some cases, remain murky. But several had questioned party policy, especially regarding the state of democracy in Tanzania. F. K. Chogga, the MP for Iringa South, had criticised Tanzania's foreign policy and called for democratic elections to be held in Zanzibar. Fortunatus Masha, the former TANU publicity secretary and Kambona associate, had long been among the more critical voices in parliament. He alleged that the party press and Radio Tanzania were vilifying dissenters like himself.[18] This mass expulsion served as a warning to any would-be dissenters that criticism of fundamental policy would no longer be tolerated. The *Nationalist* asserted that the nine were not expelled from TANU for being 'vocal and outspoken', but rather because they were opposed to the party and 'contemptuous' of its principles and ideology.[19] Nyerere's own message was clear. 'A leader who disagrees with the policy of Tanu and destroys people's unity cannot be our friend; he is our enemy and we must take necessary steps', he warned.[20] At the NEC meeting, he described the dissenters as being 'in league' with 'imperialists' in undermining the Arusha Declaration. The incident served as further confirmation of the increasing concentration of power in the hands of the party leadership, rather than in parliament (or, for that matter, in central government).

Further evidence of the subversive threat facing Tanzania came via a high-profile treason trial case the following year. In September 1969, the government announced that it had unearthed a plot against it, orchestrated by Kambona in London and involving several army officers, plus former TANU heavyweights Bibi Titi Mohammed and Michael Kamaliza. Both held grievances with Nyerere. From Chapter 2, we will recall that Bibi Titi, a long-time Kambona ally, had resigned from her role as head of TANU's women's movement in 1967 due to 'back trouble', which many took as a coded rejection of the

---

[17] See Chapter 2.
[18] H. U. E. Thoden van Velzen and J. J. Sterkenburg, 'The Party Supreme', *Kroniek van Afrika*, 1 (1969), 65–88.
[19] 'Party Expulsion', editorial, *Nationalist*, 21 October 1968, 4.
[20] 'Trouble Makers to Be Dealt With', *Nationalist*, 18 October 1968, 1, 8.

leadership conditions attached to the Arusha Declaration. Bibi Titi was also embittered by the marginalisation of the East African Muslim Welfare Society, of which she was vice-president, as the government sought to extend its control into religious life in Tanzania.[21] Kamaliza had been dropped as minister for labour in the post-Arusha fallout of 1967 and then was replaced as secretary-general of NUTA in 1969. The arrests followed rumours of discontent among the armed forces. The dramas of the subsequent treason trial captivated Dar es Salaam's public throughout 1970. It exposed secretive meetings held between conspirators in upmarket hotels like the Twiga and Palm Beach, as well as letters smuggled between Kambona and his associates in Eastern Africa. It culminated in four defendants, including Bibi Titi, being found guilty of treason in January 1971. While the trial was further grist to the mill of those in Tanzania advocating for greater national vigilance, it was an uncomfortable affair for Nyerere. One defendant accused him of presiding over a dictatorship, with no freedom of the press.[22]

While rumours about the roles of various Cold War powers fluttered around the trial, it was more closely tied up with the politics of Dar es Salaam's African liberation movements. The prosecution's case depended on the testimony of Potlako Leballo, the acting president of the Pan-Africanist Congress of Azania (PAC), a rival South African movement to the ANC. Leballo claimed that he had been approached by one of the plotters, who requested the PAC's cooperation in a coup, in return for a more favourable relationship with a post-Nyerere government. Leballo had much to gain from the success of a plot. His leadership had been divisive within the PAC, which was a particularly fractious organisation even by the standards of the liberation movements. The PAC lacked an international profile, especially after the coup in Ghana in 1966 deprived the movement of its main sponsor in Africa. The support it received from China was meagre in comparison to the ANC's strong connections with Moscow. But rather than siding with Kambona and his conspirators, Leballo instead sensed an

---

[21] Mohammed Said, *The Life and Time of Abdulwahid Sykes (1924–1968): The Untold Story of the Muslim Struggle Against British Colonialism in Tanganyika* (London: Minerva Press, 1998), 270–315.

[22] On the trial, see George Roberts, 'Politics, Decolonization, and the Cold War in Dar es Salaam, c.1965–72', PhD diss. (University of Warwick, 2016), 169–74; Geiger, *TANU Women*, 182–83.

opportunity to ingratiate himself with the present regime. He reported the approach to the Tanzanian authorities, who instructed him to act as a mole within the movement. Despite concerns over his credibility as a witness being raised in the trial, Leballo subsequently drew on the government's support to suppress resistance within the PAC.[23]

More generally, the trial exposed the dangers that were inherent in providing the liberation movements with a support base in exile and the extent to which they had become enmeshed in Tanzania's domestic affairs. As outlined in Chapter 4, the Tanzanian government was concerned about the presence of armed and often idle guerrilla cadres in the country. Politicking between the movements – in this case, the South African contenders – plus their dire financial situation were believed to increase their sense of venality. An array of liberation movement leaders became dragged into rumours surrounding the plot. They included Oliver Tambo, who allegedly failed to report an effort to recruit the ANC into the conspiracy to the Tanzanian authorities. He then refused to testify at the trial, on the grounds that the ANC should remain neutral vis-à-vis Tanzania's internal affairs. Tambo's association with the plot may have triggered a sudden Tanzanian decision to close down the ANC's training camp at Kongwa in July 1969, ostensibly on the grounds of national security.[24] To complicate matters further, there were reports that Frene Ginwala, editor of the recently nationalised *Standard* and an ANC supporter, was supplying evidence to the defence lawyers, which they redeployed in court to besmirch Leballo's character. An employee of a government newspaper was thus seeking to undermine a state prosecution of a treason trial.[25] However unlikely it was to have succeeded, Kambona's plot supplied the government with an illustration of the serious threats which it faced from conspirators. It therefore provided justification for clamping down on dissent in its calls for unity and vigilance. But it also

---

[23] Ahlman, 'Road to Ghana'; Tom Lodge, *Black Politics in South Africa since 1945* (London: Longman, 1983), 306–314; Kwandiwe Kondlo, *In the Twilight of the Revolution: The Pan-Africanist Congress of Azania (South Africa), 1959–1994* (Basel: Basler Afrika Bibliographien, 2009).

[24] Stephen Ellis and Tsepo Sechaba, *Comrades Against Apartheid: The ANC and the South African Communist Party in Exile* (London: James Currey, 1992), 59; Stephen Ellis, *External Mission: The ANC in Exile, 1960–1990* (London: Hurst, 2012), 83–84.

[25] See Chapter 6.

underlined the degree to which disaffection among the liberation movements provided a source of potential support for opponents to the regime.

Meanwhile, Zanzibar continued to pose a headache for Nyerere's government. By 1968, four years after the revolution and union with Tanganyika, Zanzibar had sunk into an economic and political malaise. Whereas the mainland embraced the flexible concept of 'self-reliance', Karume's regime pursued economic autarky. Ill-conceived policies led to food shortages. The racial persecution of Zanzibaris of Arab, Indian, and Comorian descent continued. Africans were scarcely better off. They may have benefited from the land redistribution scheme which followed the revolution, but their everyday freedoms were significantly curbed. The government restricted travel to the mainland. The Stasi-trained security services clamped down on any signs of dissent. Power became concentrated in a cabal of hardliners, who could call on support bases inside the government, the armed forces, and the Afro-Shirazi Party's youth wing. Nestled within the structure of the union, this situation in Zanzibar was largely shielded from the gaze of the rest of the world.[26]

However, the 'disappearance' of two high-profile Zanzibari politicians in 1969 could not simply be brushed aside by the mainland government. In August, Karume asked Nyerere to approve the extradition of Kassim Hanga and Othman Shariff to Zanzibar. After initially refusing to grant this request, Nyerere acquiesced when Karume returned with firm 'evidence' of a plot. Hanga and Shariff had both played key roles within the Afro-Shirazi Party prior to independence but had subsequently fallen out with Karume. Hanga, as we saw in Chapter 2, had joined Kambona in London in the political turbulence which followed the Arusha Declaration and was then imprisoned almost immediately after his ill-considered return to Tanzania in late 1967. Since his release from detention in December 1968, Hanga had been living quietly in Dar es Salaam. Shariff had served as Tanzania's first ambassador to Washington, but at the time of his arrest he was working as a veterinary officer in Iringa. Both men were unlikely conspirators; no evidence surfaced that a coup was being planned. In

[26] George W. Triplett, 'Zanzibar: The Politics of Revolutionary Inequality', *Journal of Modern African Studies*, 9 (1971), 612–17; Toibibou Ali Mohamed, 'Les Comoriens de Zanzibar durant la "Révolution Okello" (1964–1972)', *Journal des africanistes*, 76 (2006), 137–54.

October, Zanzibar's armed forces explained that a plot had been uncovered, naming a number of conspirators and stating that four of them had been sentenced to death. Although the names of those who were executed were not given, Hanga and Shariff were never seen again. Nyerere was reportedly furious. At a time when Tanzania routinely condemned the execution of political activists in Rhodesia and South Africa, the executions left Nyerere open to charges of hypocrisy. In response, Nyerere and several union ministers held meetings with Karume. They told him that he was embarrassing Tanzania in the eyes of the world.[27]

Relations between Zanzibar and the mainland became increasingly fractious. In the economic sphere, Zanzibar declined to provide the Bank of Tanzania with details of foreign exchange reserves held in the archipelago, despite the mainland government having constitutional control over currency matters. Jamal observed to Nyerere that, short of 'actually printing their own currency', Zanzibar could have done little more to declare its 'monetary independence'.[28] The Karume regime's behaviour continued to create public embarrassment. In September 1970, four teenage girls of Iranian descent were forced into marriages with senior ASP figures, attracting international press coverage and widespread revulsion.[29] Nairobi's *East African Journal* asked readers to 'consider how many Africans (including Zanzibaris) would support the idea of abducting Joshua Nkomo's teenage daughter and forcing her to marry Ian Smith on the grounds of national unity?'[30] This was precisely the sort of embarrassment that piqued Nyerere's anger and exposed him to accusations of double standards. When he condemned apartheid at the UN General Assembly in November, Nyerere acknowledged that he could not 'claim that Tanzania is faultless, or that offenses against human rights never take place in my country'.[31] Despite the routine fanfare about the pan-African spirit of the union, Zanzibar appeared more and more as a millstone around the

---

[27] Roberts, 'Politics', 164–69.
[28] Jamal to Nyerere, 1 December 1969, Jamal Papers, AR/MISR/157/6.
[29] Shivji et al., *Development as Rebellion*, vol. 2, 192–94.
[30] Iconoclastes, 'How Not to Create National Unity', *East African Journal*, September 1970, 5.
[31] 'At the United Nations General Assembly', in Nyerere, *Freedom and Development*, 212.

Tanzanian government's neck, endangering its claim to the moral high ground in the struggle against minority rule in Africa.

The Imperialist Offensive

Africa's 1960s had begun with high hopes: independence had arrived across most of the continent; armed struggles were soon launched to liberate those territories where colonial rule remained resilient. By the end of the decade, much of this optimism had evaporated. The liberation movements were riven with internal divisions, as the assassination of Mondlane had all too tragically shown. The 'frontline states' also seemed to have become pessimistic about the potential of anticolonial war. The Lusaka Manifesto of 1969, which revived the prospect of peaceful negotiations with the white minority regimes, was decried by the liberation movement leaders. African leaders were increasingly at odds over their tactics towards the anticolonial struggle. South Africa attempted to capitalise on this disunity by cultivating diplomatic relationships with independent governments. But alongside these olive branches came more violent warnings of the threat posed to progressive African states from the white minority regimes and their supporters.

In June 1970, Edward Heath's Conservatives swept to power in the British general election. The new administration immediately signalled its intention to reconsider the policy of its Labour predecessors to refuse to sell arms to South Africa. It drew attention to the Simonstown Agreement of 1955, which provided Britain with access to naval facilities in South Africa, although it contained no obligation for the supply of arms in return. The rationale for renewing the export of military hardware to Pretoria was couched in the terms of the Cold War. When the British foreign secretary, Alec Douglas-Home, was challenged on the strategic logic for his government's stance, he emphasised the expanding communist influence in the Indian Ocean region, including Tanzania's recent decision to receive arms exclusively from China. In response, Labour's shadow secretary for defence, Denis Healey, argued that the Conservative decision would fuel a 'pitiful arms race' in Africa, with China and the Soviet Union acting as the major suppliers. 'Can we blame the countries of black Africa if in this matter they take the line that their enemy's enemy is their friend?', asked another Labour MP.[32]

---

[32] See *Hansard* (UK), 22 July 1970, vol. 804, cols. 596–97, 613, 658.

However, the more significant opposition to Heath's decision came not from within parliament, but from within Africa. In particular, he misjudged Nyerere's resolve. On 18 July, the British high commissioner, Horace Phillips, met the president in Dodoma. Nyerere stated that should Britain resume arms sales to South Africa, he would feel obliged to withdraw Tanzania from the Commonwealth. Phillips urged London to reconsider its stance. He said that it was a sign of the strength of the Commonwealth that Tanzania had remained a member, despite the previous rupture with Britain over Rhodesia's UDI.[33] 'None of the eager-beaver communist governments represented here who have assiduously wooed Nyerere have managed to break the link', Phillips wrote. 'It grieves me that they may soon be able incredulously to rejoice that we ourselves have taken the step that breaks it.'[34] Nyerere's objections forced the British government into backtracking on their initial plans. No immediate decision was to be announced on the matter of arms sales. Instead, Heath committed only to respecting the terms of the Simonstown Agreement. But this postponement did not put an end to African concern. At the request of Milton Obote, the Ugandan president, the leaders of the so-called Mulungushi Club, which also comprised the leaders of Tanzania and Zambia, met in Dar es Salaam on 22 July. They told Phillips that they believed that Britain was free to identify its own defence interests, but also thought Heath had come to the wrong conclusions regarding Soviet activity in the Indian Ocean.[35]

Recognising that they were not going to drop the issue, Heath consulted further with the Mulungushi leaders. He invited Nyerere to his country residence in October, when the Tanzanian leader passed through London en route to the UN General Assembly in New York. The talks ended in deadlock. Nyerere rejected Britain's assessment of its own defence interests in southern Africa and the Indian Ocean. He was resistant to the Heath government's Cold War logic. In exchanges with Heath's special advisor on African affairs in Dar es Salaam in September, Nyerere had already argued that – whatever the scaremongers in the British press wrote about China – Tanzania had no 'big brother'.[36] Now he pointed out to Heath himself that Britain's Cold

[33] Phillips to FCO, 18 July 1970, UKNA, PREM 15/186.
[34] Phillips to Johnston, 18 July 1970, UKNA, PREM 15/186.
[35] Phillips to FCO (two telegrams), 22 July 1970, UKNA, PREM 15/186.
[36] Phillips to FCO, 25 September 1970, UKNA, PREM 15/187.

War policy in Africa had yielded little success. 'If the West really believed that Communism was a danger', Nyerere said, 'they should re-examine their policies in the light of the results they had achieved', rather than 'act in a way which encouraged the spread of Communism'.[37]

Shortly after Nyerere returned from New York, events in Guinea reminded Tanzania of the visceral threat that came with supporting African liberation movements. On the night of 22–23 October, a force of Portuguese officers, colonial troops, and exiled opponents of Sékou Touré's regime invaded Guinea-Conakry by sea. The failed attack sought to free Portuguese prisoners of war and destroy the assets of Amílcar Cabral's PAIGC (*Partido Africano da Independência da Guiné e Cabo Verde*, African Party for the Independence of Guinea and Cape Verde), which had been given shelter in Conakry while it waged guerrilla war against Portugal in neighbouring Guinea-Bissau. The invaders also unsuccessfully tried to overthrow Touré. Although Portugal denied any involvement, the invasion sparked international outrage. In Africa, it was received as another white imperialist intrigue against the continent's independent states.[38]

Ever since FRELIMO launched its guerrilla war in Mozambique in 1964, the Tanzanian government had warned of the risk of a Portuguese invasion. The dangers which Tanzania voluntarily assumed by housing the guerrillas were fresh in the memory after the assassination of Mondlane, which was followed by another parcel-bombing at the FRELIMO offices in July 1970.[39] Events in Guinea redoubled the authorities' warnings to remain vigilant against neo-imperialism. The relationship between Nyerere and Touré, once strong, had soured somewhat after the latter hosted the disgraced Kambona and Hanga in Guinea in late 1967. But the threat to the African revolution overrode such misgivings. The Tanzanian government pledged 10 million shillings in assistance to Guinea.[40] Rashidi Kawawa, as second vice-president, addressed a demonstration by the

---

[37] 'Record of a Meeting Held at Chequers', 11 October 1970, UKNA, PREM 15/197.
[38] Norrie MacQueen, 'Portugal's First Domino: "Pluricontinentalism" and Colonial War in Guiné-Bissau, 1963–1974', *Contemporary European History*, 8 (1999), 216–17.
[39] 'Bomb Shatters FRELIMO Office', *Standard*, 24 July 1970, 1.
[40] Reginald Mhange, 'Tanzania Sends Aid', *Standard*, 24 November 1970, 1.

TANU Youth League from the balcony of the Guinean embassy. In a defiant speech, he warned Portugal from perpetrating similar acts against Tanzania. 'Let them cross the [River] Ruvuma into Tanzania and they will see', he said. 'Let them land in Dar es Salaam and they will see.'[41]

In Dar es Salaam, there was a sense that the African revolution was facing an all-out assault of unprecedented danger. This consisted not just of the sort of violence witnessed in Guinea, but also attempts by South Africa to cultivate diplomatic and economic relationships with independent African states. It was not just Hastings Banda's Malawi which was now deliberating a modus vivendi with Pretoria. The Ivorian president, Félix Houphouët-Boigny, declared his interest in entering into a dialogue with Pretoria.[42] Ghana made similar noises. These developments elicited words of caution in Dar es Salaam. The Tanzanian executive secretary of the OAU Liberation Committee, George Magombe, warned that leaders who grasped South Africa's poisoned olive branch would 'be walking into a Boer trap'.[43] Nyerere himself remained resolute. Addressing the UN, he dismissed any possibility of Tanzania signing a non-aggression treaty with South Africa. An 'African Munich', he declared, 'would no more bring peace than did that of Europe in 1938'.[44]

In this spirit, Nyerere went with Kaunda and Obote to the Commonwealth Heads of State Conference in Singapore in January 1971. The summit had been identified as a crunch meeting ever since Heath had decided to delay finalising his government's position on arms to South Africa in July. Writing in London's *Times* ahead of the conference, Nyerere set out Tanzania's position. 'The sale of arms to South Africa means support for the enemies of the African people', he stated.[45] Obote travelled reluctantly, fearing for the security of his regime at the hands of a disgruntled military; he made the trip

---

[41] '"The War Is Also Ours" – Kawawa', *Standard*, 25 November 1970, 1; 'We Are Ready to Die and to Kill for Freedom – Kawawa', *Nationalist*, 25 November 1970, 1, 8.
[42] Abou B. Bamba, 'An Unconventional Challenge to Apartheid: The Ivorian Dialogue Diplomacy with South Africa, 1960–1978', *International Journal of African Historical Studies*, 47 (2014), 77–99.
[43] 'Dialogue a Boer Trap – Magombe', *Nationalist*, 11 November 1970, 1.
[44] 'At the United Nations General Assembly', in Nyerere, *Freedom and Development*, 209.
[45] Julius K. Nyerere, 'Arming Apartheid', *Times*, 16 January 1971, 17.

only under the persuasion of Kaunda and Nyerere. Obote was right to be concerned. On 25 January, word reached Singapore from Kampala that General Idi Amin had seized power in a military coup.

—

The news from Kampala sent shockwaves through political circles in Dar es Salaam. For all the fury that had accompanied the Portuguese intervention in Conakry, Guinea was a distant state in West Africa. Uganda, on the other hand, shared a common border with Tanzania and was a member of the East African Community. The *Nationalist* condemned the 'rightest, reactionary coup' as 'the saddest and most shameful thing that could befall Uganda, East Africa, and Africa as a whole'.[46] Obote immediately flew back from Singapore to East Africa, with the intention of crushing the coup. He first stopped in Nairobi but found the Kenyan government unreceptive. Invited to Tanzania, Obote arrived at the airport in Dar es Salaam on 26 January with all the trappings of a state visit. At a press conference at State House, Obote insisted that he would return home, denied that Amin commanded popular support in Uganda, and accused Israel of engineering the coup. Nyerere himself cut short a visit to India, arriving back in Dar es Salaam on 28 January to a rapturous reception which betrayed local anxieties.[47]

The Tanzanian response to the Ugandan crisis was defined by the close relationship between Nyerere and Obote. The Ugandan president was only the latest in a litany of African heads of state to be overthrown in a coup. Despite much hand-wringing in the press, the Tanzanian government had hitherto followed other African states in recognising usurping juntas rather than risk splitting the front of continental unity. But Obote was different. He was Nyerere's ally and friend. Nyerere had supported Obote's 'Move to the Left', under which the Ugandan government proposed the nationalisation of key sectors of the economy, following the course of the Arusha Declaration. Nyerere was also wracked with guilt, having persuaded Obote to travel to Singapore in spite of his own – evidently justified – fears.[48] Nyerere therefore

[46] 'Uganda Coup', editorial, *Nationalist*, 26 January 1971, 4.
[47] 'Obote Accuses Israel of Coup', *Nationalist*, 27 January 1971, 1, 8; David Martin, *General Amin* (London: Faber and Faber, 1974), 49–53; Kenneth Ingram, *Obote: A Political Biography* (London: Routledge, 1994), 138.
[48] Nyerere later privately admitted his remorse, telling the Canadian Prime Minister Pierre Trudeau that 'Ken [Kaunda] and I feel slightly guilty ... Milton

asserted that Tanzania continued to regard Obote as the president of Uganda. 'We do not recognise the authority of those who have killed their fellow citizens in an attempt to overthrow the established government of a sister republic', read a Tanzanian government statement, in contradiction to its usual position.[49] The matter of non-recognition was complicated by Uganda's and Tanzania's common membership of the EAC. But Nyerere declared that he would not work with Amin. 'How can I sit at the same table with a killer?', he told a mass rally at the Jangwani grounds. 'Jomo [Kenyatta] is speaking for the people who elected him. I am speaking for you. Whom will Amin be representing? I cannot sit with murderers.'[50] Nyerere's decision to reject Amin and provide shelter for Obote was motivated by a personal relationship instead of political calculation. In the long run, it had costly consequences.

Britain's swift recognition of the military regime in Kampala, together with rumours of Israeli involvement in the coup itself, fuelled allegations in Tanzania that Amin's seizure of power was a neocolonial conspiracy intended to smash anti-imperialism in Africa. Britain had quietly welcomed the coup: London's relationship with Obote had soured as a result of his attitude towards arms sales to South Africa and his 'Move to the Left', which threatened the nationalisation of British business assets in Uganda.[51] A TANU Youth League statement declared that the coup had been 'engineered by imperialism and international Zionism in collaboration with servile internal reactionary forces'.[52] Press commentary portrayed the putsch as an imperialist plot to break 'an axis of progressive states that runs right from Cairo through Khartoum to Dar es Salaam and Lusaka'.[53] This talk

didn't want to come to Singapore. We made him because we were then all fighting on South Africa and Simonstown'. Memcon (Nyerere, Trudeau), 13 August 1981, Jamal Papers, AR/MISR/157/8.
[49] 'Uganda People Back Obote', *Standard*, 29 January 1971, 1.
[50] Kusai Kamisa and Juma Penza, 'Our Stand Is Firm – Nyerere', *Standard*, 31 January 1971, 1.
[51] Mark Curtis, *Unpeople: Britain's Secret Human Rights Abuses* (London: Vintage, 2004), 245–61. However, as Harriet Aldrich argues, we should not overstate British influence in these events: 'Uganda, Southern Sudan and the Idi Amin Coup', *Journal of Imperial and Commonwealth History*, 48 (2020), 1109–39.
[52] 'Coup Attempt is the Work of Imperialism – TYL', *Nationalist*, 27 January 1971, 1.
[53] 'We Recognise Obote', editorial, *Nationalist*, 29 January 1971, 4.

of a pan-continental imperialist assault reflected a pervasive atmosphere of anxiety in Dar es Salaam. 'The commotion produced by the Ugandan rebellion is of exceptional gravity', remarked the French ambassador.[54] 'We are all concerned', reflected a sober *Standard* editorial. 'For if a gun toting soldier in Kampala is allowed to get away with undermining everything we are trying to build up – is there any security for any one of us?'[55]

By early 1971, a concatenation of events elsewhere in Africa created a sense of crisis in political circles in Dar es Salaam. The forces of white minority rule seemed to be on the offensive. As South Africa made diplomatic inroads with independent African regimes, it also appeared to be consolidating its military strength via the new government in London. Pressure from progressive African leaders had stalled these developments. But in taking the fight to Britain at the Commonwealth meeting, Nyerere had assisted in propping open the door for Amin's coup in Uganda. In tackling one threat, he inadvertently helped to precipitate another. Meanwhile, events in Guinea remained fresh in the mind and reminded Tanzania of a more direct military threat from across its southern frontier. Nyerere remained bullish. 'I can be assassinated, but there will never be a coup d'état', he told the Jangwani rally. 'This [an assassination] is possible because it can be done by any maniac, but not a coup d'état in Tanzania.'[56] His hubris echoed Obote, who had once stated, 'I am perhaps the only African leader who is not afraid of a military takeover.'[57] Against the background of domestic economic strife, this international crisis propelled TANU into a major intervention – *Mwongozo*.

Creating the 'Guidelines'

In December 1970, Kingunge Ngombale-Mwiru led a TANU Youth League delegation to a meeting of the Pan-African Youth Movement (PAYM) in Dakar. Ngombale-Mwiru was the TYL's secretary-general and a rising intellectual influence within the party. His politics were

---

[54] Desparmet to MAE-DAL, 9 March 1971, CADN, 193PO/1/1 A1.
[55] Editorial, *Standard*, 1 February 1971, 1.
[56] Kusai Kamisa and Juma Penza, 'Our Stand Is Firm – Nyerere', *Standard*, 31 January 1971, 1.
[57] Milton A. Obote, *Myths and Realities: Letter to a London Friend* (Kampala: Consolidated Printers, 1968), 30.

informed by his exposure to key Marxist texts and association with leading African radicals. He was well-travelled, having studied in Monrovia, Dakar, and Paris, where he met African luminaries including Amílcar Cabral. Ngombale-Mwiru then taught at Kivukoni College, TANU's training school in Dar es Salaam. All these formative experiences left their mark on *Mwongozo*, as did Ngombale-Mwiru's trip to West Africa for the PAYM meeting.

Like many pan-African meetings at the time, the PAYM conference was a stormy affair. More radical participants believed that its Senegalese hosts were not committed enough to the anticolonial struggle and too close to the former colonial occupier, France. In the build-up to the conference, the hosts became embroiled in a diplomatic spat with Guinea, which had broadcast allegations that Portuguese troops and mercenaries were planning an invasion from Senegalese territory. In the end, the Guinean delegation declined to show up. Those which did, including Tanzania and representatives of various liberation movements, sided against Senegal. Rather than follow precedent and offer the chair of the PAYM to the hosts, the conference voted to give it to the absent Guineans. En route home, Ngombale-Mwiru stopped off in Conakry to hand over the reins of the movement. There, he was impressed by stories of the defence of Guinea by its celebrated 'people's militia'. These thoughts remained with him as he flew back to Dar es Salaam.[58]

Shortly after the coup in Uganda, Ngombale-Mwiru was summoned to a meeting with Rashidi Kawawa. The second vice-president explained to Ngombale-Mwiru that he had been charged by President Nyerere to lead a group of TYL cadres on a training mission to the Ugandan frontier, where they would provide security for the local population. However, with his Guinean experience fresh in his mind, Ngombale-Mwiru also drew attention to the threat posed by the Portuguese from Mozambique in the south. Tanzania faced imperialist encirclement. Ngombale-Mwiru therefore talked up his impression of the civil defence arrangements which he had encountered in Conakry. In response to these recommendations and in a general atmosphere of crisis, Nyerere called an emergency meeting of the TANU National

---

[58] Interview with Kingunge Ngombale-Mwiru, Victoria, Dar es Salaam, 26 August 2015; 'Mazungumzo kati ya Kingunge Ngombale-Mwiru na Issa Shivji', *Chemchemi*, 2 (2009), 68–69.

Creating the 'Guidelines'

Executive Committee, which convened in Dar es Salaam on 13 February.[59]

The NEC meeting was unusually long, lasting a whole week. It was also particularly turbulent. Paul Bomani, the minister of commerce, told the British high commissioner that he and others had criticised Nyerere's handling of the Ugandan situation, on the basis that it was endangering the EAC. Other NEC members argued for a more radical approach, calling for Tanzania to leave the Commonwealth and sever its ties with Britain again.[60] Amid these disagreements, the NEC discussed the text of a landmark party document, which had been drafted by a committee comprising Kawawa, Ngombale-Mwiru, Babu, General Mrisho Sarakikya of the TPDF, and Hashim Mbita, the TANU executive secretary. This team brought together revolutionary socialist thought, the military top brass, and the key leaders of an increasingly assertive party. *Mwongozo* discarded the lengthy economic rationale of the Arusha Declaration in favour of thirty-five punchy clauses that spoke directly to the people.[61] Four years earlier in Arusha, the party had recognised the challenges posed to development by an unfavourable global economic environment; now *Mwongozo* presented revolutionary Africa as facing an existential assault from the forces of imperialism.

The imprint of events in Conakry and Kampala on *Mwongozo* was clear. Both Obote and the Guinean ambassador addressed the NEC meeting.[62] One section of *Mwongozo* was dedicated to the Guinea invasion, another to the Uganda coup. The 'big lesson' of Guinea was the threat to progressive African regimes which supported the liberation movements. 'For similar reasons the imperialists may attempt to attack Tanzania one day.'[63] Regarding Uganda, *Mwongozo* said that the coup

---

[59] Kingunge Ngombale-Mwiru, 'Utangulizi: Ujio na Uzito wa Miongozo Miwili', in Bashiru Ally, Saida Yahya-Othman, and Issa Shivji (eds.), *Miongozo Miwili na Kutunguliwa kwa Azimio la Arusha* (Dar es Salaam: Chuo Kikuu cha Dar es Salaam, 2013), 12–26.

[60] Phillips to FCO, 22 February 1971, UKNA, FCO 31/1031/250.

[61] The quotations here follow the translation in TANU, *Tanzania: Party Guidelines. Mwongozo wa TANU* (Richmond, BC: LSM Information Center, 1973). Relatively little has been written on *Mwongozo*, but see Shivji, *Class Struggles*, 123–26; James R. Brennan, 'Debating the Guidelines: Literacy, Text, and Socratic Socialism in 1970s Tanzania', unpublished paper presented at the African Studies Workshop, University of Chicago (2014).

[62] 'Mwalimu Will Announce N.E.C. Decisions Tomorrow', *Standard*, 20 February 1971, 1.

[63] *Mwongozo*, clause 8.

showed how, instead of bringing down revolutionary governments by direct invasion, imperialism preferred to employ local stooges to achieve its goals. 'The people must learn from the events in Uganda and from those in Guinea that although imperialism is still strong, its ability to topple a revolutionary government greatly depends on the possibility of getting domestic counter-revolutionary puppets to help them thwart the revolution', the section concluded.[64] In his speech introducing *Mwongozo*, Nyerere referred to a story from Guinea, where a server in a café had reported a suspicious individual to the authorities. When the security services turned up, they found it was a man for whom they had been searching. This example of the virtuous, vigilant citizen again underlined the government's fears of foreign subversion in Dar es Salaam's public spaces.[65]

In response to these external threats, *Mwongozo* sought to mobilise and politicise the Tanzanian population through the vehicle of TANU. This involved a renewed emphasis on the role of the party's leadership. *Mwongozo* stated that '[t]he responsibility of the party is to lead the masses, together with their institutions, in their efforts to safeguard national independence and advance the liberation of the African'.[66] Through this leadership, the party would 'arouse political consciousness' to 'make the people aware of our national enemies and the strategies they employ to subvert our policies, our independence, our economy and our culture'.[67] Finally, since the masses were 'the nation's shield', *Mwongozo* provided for the creation of an armed 'people's militia', modelled on the forces by which Ngombale-Mwiru had been impressed in Guinea.[68] This satisfied the TYL's request for the nation's youth to be armed, which had become a refrain over recent years – calls to which Nyerere had previously been opposed.

Mwongozo was a nationalist call to arms, but it was also intended to rejuvenate Africa's fight against the forces of colonialism and neo-imperialism. 'Today, our African continent is a hot-bed of the liberation struggle', the document opened.[69] Yet this 'hot-bed' was rife with tension. Pan-African gatherings, like the PAYM conference in Dakar, were marked more by division than unity. There was a loss of

[64] *Mwongozo*, clause 4.
[65] Enclosure in Ewans to Holmes, 1 March 1971, UKNA, FCO 31/970/4.
[66] *Mwongozo*, clause 11.   [67] *Mwongozo*, clauses 24 and 25.
[68] *Mwongozo*, clause 26. See Lal, *African Socialism*, 83–102.
[69] *Mwongozo*, clause 1.

confidence in the prospects of armed liberation struggles. Certain African states were responding positively to South African overtures. *Mwongozo* was very much a document born of this particular moment. FRELIMO described it as 'exactly what African countries need at this stage'.[70] Juma Mwapachu, who held a string of senior positions within the Tanzanian state apparatus in the 1970s, recalled that *Mwongozo* was a 'rebirth' of TANU's original principles: 'Africa is one, Africans are all the same.'[71] TANU, as an African liberation movement itself, took the Tanzanian revolution onto the international stage. In the same spirit, Tanzania led its regional neighbours away from the softer position which they had assumed through the Lusaka Manifesto. In October, a summit of East and Central African states issued the Mogadishu Declaration, which reaffirmed their 'unflinching support for the armed struggles being waged by African peoples against colonialism'.[72] *Mwongozo* was simultaneously a powerful nationalist statement that sought to radicalise Tanzania's socialist project, while situating it within a continental landscape of liberation struggles. It showed how domestic nation-building and international revolution were deeply entwined.

Mwongozo was the first major party document that did not bear the stamp of Nyerere himself. Moreover, the principles and policies it advocated contrasted with much of his previous approach. Before *Mwongozo*, Nyerere had previously expressed his reluctance to create an armed popular militia. Now, acting on the advice of Ngombale-Mwiru, he decided otherwise. More controversially, *Mwongozo* cast TANU as a vanguard party in all but name. 'The time has now come for the Party to take the reins and lead all mass activities', it stated.[73] The idea was celebrated by the more radical sections of Tanzanian political society. 'For the first time in the history of our glorious Party, its vanguard role has been given new, definite and concrete expression', enthused the *Nationalist*. 'The Party and the Party alone shall exercise the vanguard role of leading Tanzania's revolution.'[74]

[70] 'TANU Guidelines Get Wide Okay', *Nationalist*, 23 February 1971, 1, 8.
[71] Interview with Juma Mwapachu, Oyster Bay, Dar es Salaam, 29 May 2018.
[72] Quoted in *Africa Contemporary Record: Annual Survey and Documents, 1971–1972* (Rex Collings: London, 1972), C16–17.
[73] *Mwongozo*, clause 11.
[74] 'Revolutionary Preparedness', editorial, *Nationalist*, 22 February 1971, 4.

The idea of the 'vanguard party' had been subject to heated debate in Tanzania. First introduced to Marxist theory by Lenin, the concept was frequently employed by African politicians, though often in ambiguous ways. Among the Tanzanian political elite, vanguardism found support among at least two of the architects of *Mwongozo*, Babu and Ngombale-Mwiru. The constitution of Babu's Umma Party in Zanzibar had declared that it would be 'the dynamic vanguard for removing all forms of oppression, exploitation of man by man and for the establishment of a socialist society'.[75] But the term 'vanguard' was used with little precision in Tanzania; it functioned as a signifier for a more militant TANU, not a fleshed-out strategy for socialist transformation. Moreover, support for vanguardism was far from universally shared. In 1965, the presidential commission on the creation of a single-party state emphasised that TANU must remain a 'mass' rather than 'elite' party. The report asserted that '[t]o insist on narrow ideological conformity would clearly be inconsistent with the mass participation in the affairs of the Party which we regard as essential'.[76] Among these sceptics was Nyerere. Even as he affirmed TANU's preeminent role in the struggle to build a socialist state, the president was uneasy about its radicalisation into a vanguard party. He had used the term in a more general sense when speaking to the TYL, whom he considered to be 'the vanguards' of 'socialist construction in Tanzania'.[77] Yet in debates about the Arusha Declaration, he had rejected calls for the creation of a vanguard party.[78] Despite the clear shift in the party's self-conceptualisation in *Mwongozo*, Nyerere remained sceptical. 'A vanguard party would need to be a party of angels', he told an interviewer in 1974, 'and we are not angels'.[79]

The language of *Mwongozo* led foreigners to draw parallels with Maoism. By the early 1970s, as we have seen, observers in both the Eastern Bloc and especially the West had developed the habit of reading Chinese influence into any socialist initiative in Tanzania. According to the GDR's Stasi, the central purpose of *Mwongozo* 'was to give people the impression that Tanzania had taken a Great Leap Forwards [*großen Sprung nach vorn*]'.[80] Certainly, Maoist ideas were popular among party circles, especially in the TANU Youth League. But the

[75] Wilson, *Threat of Liberation*, 139–48.   [76] Quoted in Bienen, *Tanzania*, 242.
[77] 'Be Vigilant Call to Green Guards', *Nationalist*, 8 February 1967, 1, 5.
[78] See Chapter 2.   [79] Pratt, *Critical Phase*, 26.
[80] MfS, 8 September 1971, BStU, MfS, HV A, no. 391, 105–109.

document's ideological origins were much more cosmopolitan than that. Babu and Ngombale-Mwiru drew their influences not only from Lenin and Mao, but also their experiences travelling and studying more widely. *Mwongozo* drew on the ideology and praxis of revolutionary movements from across Africa, as well as elsewhere in the Third World. It was a nationalist manifesto, based around the mobilisation of the Tanzanian people in the building of socialism, yet it framed its thirty-five clauses in the context of an international struggle against imperialism.

Firecracker Socialism

The tocsin of *Mwongozo* echoed across the nation but did little to settle nerves in Dar es Salaam. A public surge of enthusiasm for the new measures masked private unease among government circles at this gear-shift within TANU and its implications for government policy. The threat from abroad, especially the sabre-rattling in Uganda, had not disappeared. The capital swirled with rumours once again. One held that Nyerere had suffered a mental breakdown and was going to Switzerland for treatment.[81] In an attempt to calm this foment, Nyerere convened another meeting of the NEC, at which the party leadership would translate the aims of *Mwongozo* into practice. He tactically chose to hold it in Kigoma, near the border with Burundi, between 16 and 20 March. This was, as the British high commissioner recognised, 'to put it about as far away from the capital – and cocktail gossip – as possible'.[82]

In Kigoma, the NEC discussed the problems surrounding the implementation of the *ujamaa* villagisation programme and sketched out arrangements for the creation of the people's militia. It also discussed the so-called *karadha* system, which allowed for civil servants to take out low interest loans to pay for luxury goods, such as cars. The NEC determined that 'our country cannot tolerate playing with our foreign currency for the enjoyment of some individuals'.[83] More significantly, it agreed on the nationalisation of all houses worth over 100,000 shillings and not primarily occupied by their owner. This was

---

[81] Hintjens to Harmel, 10 April 1971, ADB, 16.248.
[82] Phillips to Le Tocq, 5 May 1971, UKNA, FCO 31/968/9.
[83] Shivji et al., *Development as Rebellion*, vol. 1, 256–57.

a popular move since it largely affected Asian landlords. According to Issa Shivji, a clause about housing had initially featured on the draft of *Mwongozo*, but Nyerere had removed it since the nationalisation of buildings was a one-time measure rather than a political principle. Government lawyers raised objections to it. They suggested that a better, less confrontational measure would be to tax landlords. Nyerere replied that some actions were political and so had to be taken regardless of their rationality.[84] The policy was hurried through, with little scrutiny in parliament and apparently no discussion at all in cabinet. Nyerere had been resistant to acting on the housing matter before; now he gave way to the radicals in the party. This drastic measure propelled another exodus of Tanzania's Asian population and capital, at a time when foreign exchange resources were scarce.[85]

The ultra-radical path taken by TANU was difficult for the 'moderate' members of cabinet to stomach. Much like the case of the nationalisations after the Arusha Declaration, they had been given no opportunity to discuss the Buildings Act. Reports reached the diplomatic community that Derek Bryceson and Amir Jamal had both tendered their resignations from cabinet.[86] Paul Bomani told a representative of the British business lobby in East Africa that he was 'absolutely against' the nationalisation of buildings. Bomani recommended that the British government should warn Nyerere of the dangerous consequences which it could have on foreign confidence in Tanzania.[87] *Mwongozo* did not represent a sudden power shift in itself: the cabinet's strength vis-à-vis the party elite had long been in decline. Still, the loss of faith in the direction of Tanzanian socialism which Bomani, Bryceson, and Jamal apparently experienced was problematic for Nyerere. These ministers were not just experts at running technocratic departments, but also faces of Tanzania's economic diplomacy who commanded respect from foreign partners. East German intelligence understood that Jamal had only withdrawn his resignation after Nyerere persuaded him that it would have disastrous effects on Western investment in Tanzania.[88]

---

[84] Ibid., vol. 3, 149–50.   [85] Brennan, *Taifa*, 190–92; Aminzade, *Race*, 225–27.
[86] Hintjens to Harmel, 10 April 1971, ADB, 16.248.
[87] Rose to Holmes, 18 May 1971, UKNA, FCO 31/998/76. I am grateful to Julia Held for bringing this document to my attention.
[88] MfS, 8 September 1971, BStU, MfS, HV A, no. 391, 105–109.

Just as the issue of speed had been a major point of contention in debates about Tanzanian political economy before the Arusha Declaration, *Mwongozo* emphasised the need to quicken the pace of development. Clause two of *Mwongozo* asserted that 'revolution means the rapid transformation of society'. John Malecela, a Tanzanian representative to the East African Community, argued that *Mwongozo*'s commitment to involve the people in development through the party machinery meant that the speed of transformation could now be quickened. Opening a conference of East African administrators and planners in Arusha in September, Malecela accepted that there was a need to avoid the extremes of either 'over-zealous' or 'over-cautious' policies. But he believed the time was ripe for an acceleration of the *ujamaa* programme. 'As long as people know that change will be in their interest the speed of change can be as revolutionary as one may wish', Malecela argued. 'Already we have lost a lot of time in the process of speeding up development', he concluded. 'The people's impatience can everywhere be seen.'[89]

Not everyone agreed. At the same conference, Knud Erik Svendsen, a Danish economist and a personal assistant to Nyerere, reminded participants that the president himself had warned against turning *ujamaa* into doctrine and stressed the need to learn from experiences of other countries. This, Svendsen said, was 'an internationalist credo of non-alignment *vis-à-vis* ideological schools'.[90] In private, he was far more critical of TANU's new approach. In November, Svendsen conveyed his fears about the acceleration of the Tanzanian revolution in an extraordinary letter to Nyerere. He warned that the pursuit of socialism was becoming dogmatic. 'A policy of socialization is not just a matter of principle. If it is handled as such, it turns into doctrine.' He felt that there had been no proper deliberation by cabinet or parliament on major initiatives, such as the expansion of the STC's activities or planned new decentralisation policies. 'The jumping of issues has in a way become your special style of presidential leadership', Svendsen wrote. *Mwongozo* claimed to empower the Tanzanian people

---

[89] J. S. Malecela, 'Some Issues of Development Planning', in Anthony H. Rweyemamu and Bismarck U. Mwansasu (eds.), *Planning in Tanzania: Background to Decentralisation* (Nairobi: East African Literature Bureau, 1974), 18, 19, 21.

[90] K. E. Svendsen, 'Development Administration and Socialist Strategy: Tanzania after Mwongozo', in ibid., 43.

by bringing them into the decision-making process, but Svendsen felt that current practice risked alienating senior bureaucrats and cabinet ministers.

Svendsen stated that Tanzania was 'faced with serious problems of speed'. Like Babu, he called for the private sector to continue to play a role in a gradual transformation to socialism. Svendsen wrote that the economic consequences of the 'rushed' acquisition of buildings had not been properly considered and that 'references to this problem' had been 'carefully deleted' from a government economic survey. 'There has emerged here and there a wrong sense of urgency, as if everything will be lost if we do not push ahead on all fronts at the same time, trying to change the whole structure of the economy in a matter of years. More and more people feel that this is the problem at the top.' He feared that rash development of policy and its reckless implementation would sap popular confidence in *ujamaa*. 'I sometimes ask myself: why this dangerous hurry, this socialist brinksmanship?', Svendsen asked. 'Are we faced with mounting enemies abroad and inside, strong enough to stop a socialist policy which moves ahead steadily, so that we must rush with the risk of losing everything?' As we have seen, Nyerere and especially the TANU ideologues *did* believe that the country faced powerful enemies from within and without. Svendsen did not share this view. He warned against the celebration of the upcoming tenth anniversary of independence with 'firecracker' policies. 'Would it be better to celebrate with some cautioning words about not rushing ahead with little regard for realistic implementation?' The letter was an astonishing critique of Nyerere's leadership style and policy.[91] Perhaps the rift proved impossible to bridge, as Svendsen left Tanzania the following year.

Mwongozo was a disruptive document. Its aftermath is usually associated with a period of labour unrest in Dar es Salaam, in which workers appropriated *Mwongozo*'s language to challenge the exploitative behaviour of their superiors in the workplace. This triggered a wave of wildcat strikes, which the government only brought under control through heavy-handed measures, including the dismissal of workers and their 'repatriation' to the countryside.[92] However,

---

[91] Svendsen to Nyerere, 12 November 1971, Jamal Papers, AR/MISR/157/2.
[92] Shivji, *Class Struggles*, 134–45; Juma Volter Mwapachu, 'Industrial Labour Protest in Tanzania: An Analysis of Influential Variables', *African Review*, 3 (1973), 383–401; Pascal Mihyo, 'The Struggle for Workers' Control in Tanzania', *Review of African Political Economy*, 4 (1975), 62–84.

Mwongozo also marked an important turning point in elite politics in Tanzania. The Arusha Declaration had been a compromise package designed by Nyerere to bring about a socialist transition without provoking major political rupture. Like Arusha, *Mwongozo* electrified the masses. But its revolutionary rhetoric and the dramatic economic interventions which followed raised serious concerns inside government circles. *Mwongozo*, as Jeannette Hartmann argues, represented the subordination of Tanzanian development policy to the instruments of political activism rather than more studious economic reasoning.[93] As *Mwongozo* set out 'it is not correct for leaders and experts to usurp the people's right to decide on an issue just because they have the expertise'.[94] Whereas previously radical clamour had been moderated by the trust placed in cabinet ministers and trained economists to formulate economic plans, now faith was placed in the political mobilisation of the masses.

Shuffling the Pack

In September 1971, TANU's National Conference unanimously approved *Mwongozo*. More radical members of government sensed an opportunity for sweeping economic revolution. The document said relatively little about specific policies but noted the shortcomings of the Second Five-Year Plan and the danger of spending foreign exchange on importing manufactured goods. In December, Babu wrote optimistically in London's *Financial Times* that recent events marked a 'decisive shift' in Tanzania's development strategy. The country, Babu thought, was beginning to loosen its ties of dependence on the international community. It had accepted 'the basic premise of the new school of thought – that development stems from within and not from outside'.[95] The moderates were unhappy. In an interview with the *Sunday News*, Jamal urged Tanzanians to avoid 'emotional and doctrinaire statements and arguments'. In a clear barb towards Babu, he stated that it was 'not necessary for a man to be a hermit to be self-reliant nor for a country to cut itself off from international economic relations'.[96]

---

[93] Hartmann, 'Development Policy-Making', 228ff. [94] *Mwongozo*, clause 28.
[95] A. M. Babu, 'A New Strategy for Development', *Financial Times*, 9 December 1971, 29. Extracts appeared in the *Standard*, 11 December 1971, 5.
[96] 'Treasury's Role in Post-Uhuru Bid for Progress', *Sunday News*, 23 January 1972, 9.

Nyerere's response, as during the period of tension which followed the Arusha Declaration, was a major reshuffle of central government. Announcing the news in a radio broadcast on 17 February 1972, he acknowledged the stir which it would provoke. 'Some of the changes are on a familiar pattern, but others – especially as regards Ministers – are more unusual for Tanzania', Nyerere said.[97] His prediction was correct: the *Sunday News* described the news as a 'bombshell', which 'quickly became an over-heated talking-point', triggering 'an uncheckable flurry of gossip and speculation ... newspapers were sold out as soon as they hit the streets'.[98] Five ministers were moved out of the cabinet to become regional commissioners – presidential appointments who acted as the executive's arm in the provinces. More significantly, three senior figures who had held cabinet portfolios since the inception of the union government were dropped altogether: Babu, Bryceson, and Bomani. Jamal remained in cabinet, but was transferred to the Ministry of Commerce and Industries, where he was tasked with cleaning up the situation at the STC.

The relocation of senior ministers to regional commissioners was expected. The government was committed to decentralising administration in order to implement the socialist programme more effectively, especially villagisation. Nyerere emphasised that increasing the powers of regional commissioners, who were also members of TANU's National Executive Committee, was intended to strengthen the party vis-à-vis the cabinet.[99] The 'massive shake-up', observed the Indian High Commission, 'was a measure to inject new vigour into the old body-politic and specifically to make the decentralization programme more effective'.[100] Nyerere's choice of the new regional commissioners, who included Chediel Mgonja and Lawi Sijaona, was carefully calculated. They had proved their value as party activists since independence through the TANU Youth League and their militancy was deemed important in mobilising the provinces in the drive towards socialism. Simultaneously, Nyerere isolated these radicals from the entanglements

---

[97] 'Govt Reshuffle to Give More Power to the People', *Standard*, 18 February 1972, 1; 'Mwalimu's Speech', *Standard*, 18 February 1972, 1, 5.
[98] Robert Rweyemamu, 'It's a Tough Leadership Shake-Up', *Sunday News*, 20 February 1972, 4.
[99] 'Mwalimu's Speech', *Standard*, 18 February 1972, 1, 5.
[100] Mehta, 'Annual Political Report for the Year 1972', 26 March 1973, INA, HI/1011(73)/73, 2.

of politics in Dar es Salaam which had caused the president concern, particularly when they weighed in on issues of foreign policy.

The departures of Bomani and Bryceson came as little surprise. Both men, as we have seen, had profound disagreements with Nyerere about the direction of socialist strategy in Tanzania. Pro-business and friendly to the West, Bomani's longevity in cabinet had often seemed anomalous. He appeared, as *Africa Confidential* put it, 'like a Kenyan Minister on safari in Tanzania'.[101] Nyerere had entrusted Bomani with vital economic portfolios in cabinet and valued his role in smoothing the country's economic diplomacy abroad – something no better demonstrated than by his new appointment as Tanzania's ambassador to the United States. As a European, Bryceson's continued presence in government had also been unusual, especially as the racial edge of populist politics sharpened in the post-Arusha years. He became director of Tanzania's national parks.

Nyerere's decision to drop Babu was more complicated. When the reshuffle was announced, Babu was leading a delegation to the OAU Council of Ministers in Addis Ababa. To learn about his dismissal in such a manner, Babu later recalled, was 'embarrassing and humiliating'.[102] It can only be understood against the backdrop of events in Zanzibar. At the time, the union was under severe strain. Karume's regime chafed for greater autonomy within the union, including in the sphere of foreign policy. Karume openly attacked the principles of the Arusha Declaration and resisted attempts by senior ministers in the mainland government to exercise greater control of Zanzibar's financial affairs.[103] In April 1971, the Revolutionary Council travelled en masse to Dar es Salaam, where they asked Nyerere to cease all intervention in Zanzibari affairs and assume a purely ceremonial role as union president. Nyerere refused.[104] The economic situation in the archipelago deteriorated further still, drawing criticism in the mainland press. Philip Ochieng wrote in the *Standard* about Zanzibar's empty markets, soaring prices, and bread

---

[101] 'Tanzania: No More Than Meets the Eye', *Africa Confidential*, 17 March 1972, 3–6.
[102] Babu, 'Memoirs', 21.
[103] Shivji et al., *Development as Rebellion*, vol. 2, 188–92.
[104] Biesel to Desparmet, 25 May 1971, CADN, 193PO/1/13 Z3. See also Ghassany, *Kwaheri Ukoloni*, 325–26, as well as comments by Salim Rashid, the former chief secretary to the Zanzibari government: Peter Nyanje, 'Mze: Karume Was Jittery over Union Before His Death', *Citizen*, 27 April 2014, 11.

queues which formed from the middle of the night. Ochieng advised both the Zanzibari and union authorities 'that we are dealing with human beings, and we cannot sacrifice humans at the altar of political considerations and narrow minds'.[105] By 1972, the future of the union seemed more precarious than at any point since 1964.

When Nyerere came under pressure from Karume to axe Babu from cabinet, he therefore recognised the chance to make a relatively minor concession to Zanzibar. Babu's Umma networks, officially banned, remained at large in Zanzibar, where the level of paranoia about anti-government activity outstripped even that in evidence in Dar es Salaam. Babu was critical of the self-enriching behaviour of members of the Revolutionary Council.[106] Further evidence of a Karume-driven crackdown on potential rivals came the day after Nyerere's reshuffle of the union government, when Ali Sultan Issa and Badawi Qullatein, two former Umma comrades, were sacked from the Zanzibari government. Babu later claimed that Nyerere had caved into Karume's long-standing demands for his removal from cabinet.[107] But there was a second factor: the simmering tensions between Babu and Nyerere. They had disagreed on the matter of price controls, the post-Arusha nationalisations, and the nationalisation of wholesale trade. On all three occasions, Babu, the notorious 'communist' of the Zanzibar Revolution, had supported what might seem the *less* radical option, emphasising the danger of overstretching the limited capacity of the state. Indeed, and contrary to what he later stated in public, Babu told an acquaintance in Dar es Salaam that he believed that his downfall was due to political differences with Nyerere, rather than pressure from Karume.[108]

The February 1972 reshuffle was a clinical political move which confidently asserted Nyerere's authority after the wobbles of the previous year. In one fell swoop, Nyerere removed three discontented ministers from the upper echelons of power and dispersed their radical colleagues to the provinces, where they could zealously enforce the policies of *ujamaa* far from the febrile politics of the capital. 'In our

---

[105] Philip Ochieng, 'The Plenty and the Empty on Clove Islands', *Standard*, 3 September 1971, 4.
[106] Interview with Ashura Babu, Mikocheni, Dar es Salaam, 2 April 2019.
[107] Babu, 'Memoirs', 48–49.
[108] Interview with Jenerali Ulimwengu, Oyster Bay, Dar es Salaam, 18 August 2015.

place were appointed some very junior and inexperienced technocrats', wrote Babu in his memoirs, 'whose only qualification for such senior appointments was their total and uncritical loyalty to Nyerere personally'.[109] The Polish embassy concurred: those who remained inside a weakened cabinet and central bureaucracy comprised 'specialists and people hitherto unengaged with political games'.[110] Meanwhile, Babu sought to put a positive gloss on his fall from power. In a letter to the *Standard*, he argued that the relegation of senior ministers to the backbenches would allow greater scrutiny of the government in parliament. But this public expression of support suggested insecurity as much as loyalty. 'It is curious that he thought this was necessary', mused the French ambassador.[111] Similarly, Babu wrote in his memoirs that he initially told Nyerere that he was pleased to have been dropped from government, since he could now talk freely about the situation in Zanzibar. 'That's very positive', Nyerere responded 'but if you criticise me, I will lock you up'.[112]

Two months later, Nyerere did place Babu behind bars. On the evening of 7 April 1972, Karume was assassinated at the ASP headquarters in Zanzibar. That night, the Zanzibari government began to round up men with Umma connections. Scores were shot dead; hundreds more were detained over subsequent days. On the mainland, the union government sought to keep news of the assassination to a bare minimum. Dar es Salaam was rife with rumour. Some speculated as to whether a foreign hand had been involved – perhaps the Soviet Union, concerned about mounting Chinese influence in Zanzibar? Others suggested that the plot may have had Nyerere's blessing. There is no evidence for any of these external interventions. The assassination itself was the work of disaffected members of Zanzibar's armed forces, led by Humud Mohammed, a TPDF lieutenant whose father had been killed in detention by the revolutionary regime. The precise details of a broader, aborted coup plot remain unclear.[113]

The involvement of Umma cadres in the assassination naturally meant that suspicion fell on Babu. On 14 April, Babu was arrested and placed in detention in Dar es Salaam, along with several other former Umma comrades. Tried in absentia in Zanzibar, Babu was

---

[109] Babu, 'Memoirs', 20–21.
[110] Witek to Wilski, 20 February 1972, MSZ, DV 1972, 44/75 W-1.
[111] Desparmet to MAE-DAM, 29 February 1972, CADN, 193PO/1/2 A5.
[112] Babu, 'Memoirs', 48.   [113] Roberts, 'Politics', 187–93.

found guilty of being the ringleader of a botched coup plot against Karume and sentenced to death, alongside forty-three other defendants.[114] However, Nyerere refused to allow his extradition to Zanzibar. Immediately after Babu's imprisonment, Nyerere called Ngombale-Mwiru. 'He explained what had happened to my friends', Ngombale-Mwiru recalled. 'He said, "they will be safe here". It was better than risking other consequences.'[115] The president also told the African-American activist Amiri Baraka that, although he believed Babu was not guilty, he would not hand him over to the Zanzibaris out of fears for his safety.[116] Mindful of the fate which had met Hanga and Shariff, Nyerere resisted requests for Babu and his former Umma colleagues to be extradited to stand trial in Zanzibar. In terms of international reputation, Babu was probably Tanzania's most high-profile politician after the president himself. Should he have been executed, Nyerere would have been confronted with a public relations disaster and pressure to either break the union or seize control of Zanzibar's affairs. At the same time, letting Babu walk free would have put further, perhaps unbearable strain on the mainland's relationship with the islands. Nyerere therefore determined Babu's continued detention a necessary compromise, if an ugly one. While Babu languished behind bars, Nyerere assisted his wife, Ashura, in finding work. Yet Babu and his comrades suffered from appalling physical treatment during their imprisonment. They were not released until 1978.[117]

By the mid-1970s, TANU totally dominated Tanzania's political landscape. It fortified its institutional authority, fleshing out the expanding structures of the one-party state. Opening the party's biennial meeting in Dar es Salaam in 1973, Nyerere insisted that TANU was 'supreme', with power flowing from the cell meeting to the national conference.[118] While other African states continued to succumb to military coups, Nyerere's position seemed secure. Just as Kambona's efforts to enlist officers in a plot in 1969 had never materialised into a serious threat to the regime, so signs of unrest in the armed forces in

---

[114] Later reduced to twenty-four death sentences on appeal.
[115] Interview with Kingunge Ngombale-Mwiru, Victoria, Dar es Salaam, 26 August 2015.
[116] Amiri Baraka, *The Autobiography of LeRoi Jones* (New York: Freundlich, 1984), 441. I am grateful to Andrew Ivaska for bringing this reference to my attention.
[117] Interview with Ashura Babu, Mikocheni, Dar es Salaam, 2 April 2019.
[118] 'Tanu Is Supreme, Says Nyerere', *Daily News*, 1 October 1973, 1.

early 1974 were quickly snuffed out.[119] Meanwhile, the situation in Zanzibar stabilised after the assassination of Karume. His successor as president, Aboud Jumbe, arrested the slide in living conditions on the islands. The relationship between the mainland and Zanzibar was consolidated in 1977 by a new constitution, which provided for the merger of the ASP and TANU to form the *Chama cha Mapinduzi* (Party of the Revolution, CCM).[120] Humud's bullet proved no panacea for tensions over the union, but ultimately strengthened Nyerere's political hand.

Ideologically, *ujamaa* went virtually unchallenged in Tanzania. In an interview in 1973, Nyerere noted that it was 'very difficult to get a Tanzanian now to attack publicly the ideology of the Arusha Declaration.... One criticises the implementation – not the ideology itself. I think this is important.'[121] Ironically, just as Babu lost his place in cabinet, the government embraced the sort of development strategy he had advocated, as the Harvard-trained economist Justinian Rweyemamu experimented with internal growth through industrialisation.[122] Jamal continued to argue against a blinkered approach to development. He stressed the continued need for maintaining strong foreign exchange reserves through exports, rather than focusing on internal development alone. But, amid the increasingly insular world of Tanzanian politics, Jamal found himself a lone voice shouting into the winds of *ujamaa*.[123] This consensus only came into question under challenging economic circumstances in the early 1980s, as donor states began withdrawing their support and reform-minded technocrats called for change.

Conclusion

At 2.10a.m. on 12 June 1972, residents of Dar es Salaam's upmarket neighbourhoods of Upanga and Oyster Bay were rudely awoken by the

---

[119] Desparmet to MAE, 25 February 1974, CADN, 193PO/1/1 A1; Kellas to Callaghan, 27 March 1974, UKNA, FCO 31/1754/3.
[120] Shivji, *Pan-Africanism*, 144–80.
[121] David Martin, interview with Julius Nyerere, *New Internationalist*, May 1973, 6–10.
[122] Justinian Rweyemamu, *Underdevelopment and Industrialization in Tanzania: A Study of Perverse Capitalist Industrial Development* (Nairobi: Oxford University Press, 1973).
[123] Hartmann, 'Development Policy-Making', 255–56, and passim.

sound of an explosion. A second blast followed fifteen minutes later. Dawn revealed damage to the supporting pillars of the Selander Bridge, the main route into the city from the northern suburbs. Further explosions punctuated the day. Two bombs wrecked cars owned by a Swiss national and a junior employee at the British high commission.[124] Another caused panic among shoppers on Independence Avenue, the city's commercial thoroughfare. A further seven bombs were reportedly found attached to the Selander Bridge, with fuses primed for a two-week delay.[125] The *Daily News* decried the bombings as an attempt 'to deflect us from our chosen path of revolution, of total liberation of the African in Tanzania and on the Continent. They aim to create an atmosphere of wariness, of fear, of panic.'[126] If this was the case, the bombings seem to have succeeded. Although there were no casualties, their scattergun nature heightened anxieties across the capital. The militia created by *Mwongozo* was deployed to guard industrial premises and residential areas. Observers testified to an increased suspicion about the activities of foreigners in Dar es Salaam. Two Israeli tourists were shot dead by guards after entering an exclusion zone around an unmarked ammunitions depot.[127] After the end of apartheid, South African special forces claimed responsibility for the June bombings. The intention, it seems, was not to cause significant loss of life, but to remind the Tanzanian government of the powerful enemies it had made in choosing to support Africa's liberation movements.[128]

The bombings took place against a background of murky stories about Kambona's plotting abroad, in conjunction with both the Portuguese and the Ugandans.[129] However, the real threat to Tanzania's sovereignty did not emanate from this scheming, but rather from Amin's own army. After the coup, there had been repeated reports of minor skirmishing in the border area. In September 1972, around one thousand armed supporters of Obote crossed from Tanzania into Uganda, with the secret backing of Nyerere. Amin responded by

---

[124] 'Five Bomb Blasts in Dar', *Daily News*, 13 June 1972; Savage to Holmes, 14 June 1972, UKNA, FCO 31/1285/21.
[125] Hart to Holmes, 9 August 1972, UKNA, FCO 31/1285/32.
[126] Editorial, *Daily News*, 13 June 1972, 1.
[127] Desparmet to MAE-DAM, 24 July 1972, CADN, 193PO/1/1 A1.
[128] Peter Stiff, *The Silent War: South African Recce Operations, 1969–1994* (Alberton: Galago, 1999), 46–52.
[129] José Freire Antunes, *Jorge Jardim: Agente secreto* (Venda Nova: Bertrand Editora, 1996), 359–99.

bombing Tanzanian cities near the border. As the situation developed into a regional crisis, the Somali president, Siad Barre, brokered a peace settlement.[130] Although both Amin and Nyerere agreed to cease supporting forces hostile to the other's regime, their relations remained acrimonious. Whereas in the mid-1960s, the subversive threat to Tanzania seemed to come from Cold War agents, a decade later it was Ugandan spies who had become a danger to national security in Dar es Salaam. In 1973, the Tanzanian security services arrested forty-eight people and announced that they had broken up a Ugandan 'spy ring' in the capital.[131] All of these developments provided further justification for the TANU party-state to impress upon the local population the messages of vigilance and unity.

If the Arusha Declaration was a response to the structural dilemmas facing the postcolonial state, then *Mwongozo* was a manifesto for a crisis. Its introduction was stimulated by events in Uganda, which brought an enemy to the gates in the form of Amin, as Nyerere broke with precedent in refusing to recognise the new regime in Kampala. The coup in Uganda came at a time when Africa's anticolonial front felt particularly fragile and exposed to violent interventions from their enemies, like the invasion of Guinea. If the Arusha Declaration was informed by the fallout from Tanzania's Cold War aid entanglements, *Mwongozo* was aimed squarely at the forces of imperialism, which the TANU leadership presented as being arrayed against the nation. Tanzania was now wracked less by the fears of Cold War subversion which had characterised the mid-1960s and more by an often-unspecified threat from 'imperialism' and its 'stooges' within the country.

Mwongozo was also representative of a trend in Tanzanian affairs whereby major decisions were taken in the name of political principle rather than economic planning, as demonstrated by the nationalisations of wholesale trade and buildings. Nyerere had been previously resistant to these measures. But, against the advice of senior advisors, he opted for the more radical path. However politically justified TANU's advocates felt these decisions were, the consequences were economically deleterious. The flight of capital and the inward turn in development strategy drained foreign exchange reserves and made

---

[130] Martin, *General Amin*, 170–210, 242–43.
[131] 'Dar Smashes Spy Ring: 48 Ugandans Arrested', *Daily News*, 7 March 1973, 1.

Tanzania even more reliant on external aid. A lack of trained manpower contributed to the mismanagement of an overstretched parastatal sector.[132] Power flowed from the hands of more moderate socialists within the government to party radicals who offered political solutions to economic problems. The path to TANU's supremacy was not the inevitable consequence of some centralised state despotism, but a response to the challenges of governing and building a socialist state in a tumultuous international environment.

[132] Aminzade, *Race*, 224–25.

Conclusion

Willy Gamba did not appreciate being awoken by a ringing telephone at five o'clock in the morning. Especially not on a Sunday. Especially not after returning home from a night out in Dar es Salaam just a few hours earlier.

But when Gamba lifted the receiver, his ears pricked up. On the other end of the line was his boss, the head of Tanzanian intelligence. Gamba was told to report to the office immediately. Leaving the clutches of his latest girlfriend, Gamba left his Upanga apartment and headed for the intelligence headquarters. Driving through the city's deserted streets, Gamba noticed that he was being followed. When Gamba arrived, he found his boss shaken. There had been an armed break-in at a liberation movement office on Nkrumah Street: a guard was dead; more seriously, secret papers outlining the guerrillas' plans had been stolen. The intruders had reportedly escaped to Kenya, where they aimed to sell the documents to Portuguese agents. Tasked with saving the African revolution and granted a license to kill, Gamba jetted off for Nairobi in hot pursuit.[1]

Willy Gamba belonged to the same Dar es Salaam as Julius Nyerere and Eduardo Mondlane, as A. M. Babu and Frene Ginwala, and all the other characters who have populated the pages of this book. The only difference was that Willy Gamba did not actually exist. He was the fictional star of Elvis Musiba's series of spy thrillers – in this instance, *Kufa na Kupona* ('Life and Death'). Yet the urban landscape painted by Musiba would have been instantly recognisable to his readers: spies, guerrillas, secret papers, rumour, and the risks shouldered by Tanzania in supporting the liberation of southern Africa. The conspiratorial tropes of the Cold War and anticolonial struggle suffused not just the reality, but also the fiction of Dar es

---

[1] A. E. Musiba, *Kufa na Kupona* (Dar es Salaam: Mkuki na Nyota, 2018 [1974]).

Salaam – though, as this book has shown, the two were often difficult to separate.[2]

However, just as Musiba's novel hit the bookstalls of Dar es Salaam in 1974, the world was changing, and fast. The spark was a military coup in Lisbon. In April, a group of Portuguese officers overthrew the creaking *Estado Novo*. Among the new regime's priorities was to negotiate an exit from Portugal's expensive and unpopular colonial wars in Africa. The following year, Angola and Mozambique became independent. With the collapse of the Portuguese Empire, the frontiers of liberation in Africa shifted further south. Lusaka and Luanda replaced Dar es Salaam as staging-posts for the struggle against the surviving white minority governments in Rhodesia and South Africa. Although Tanzania continued to host the OAU Liberation Committee until the end of apartheid, Dar es Salaam's moment in the global spotlight came to an end.

Over the course of the 1970s, the Cold War paranoias of foreign powers in Tanzania also faded away. As other postcolonial states succumbed to cycles of military coups, Tanzania appeared a model of sturdiness in Africa. This image of political calm, as well as *ujamaa*'s grassroots-focused development schemes, encouraged donors to swing behind Tanzanian socialism. In 1973, the World Bank praised Nyerere's government for being 'seriously committed to development in a climate of political and social stability'.[3] Britain and the United States came to regard Nyerere as a known quantity: a reliable if stubborn negotiating partner on the endgames in southern Africa. After the end of the war in Vietnam, the United States experienced an upturn in its relations with Tanzania. China's retreat from the Third World in the mid-1970s eased not only Western fears, but also those of Moscow. While the Soviet Union's approach to Africa became increasingly interventionist, it concentrated on supporting the Marxist regimes in Angola and Ethiopia. Nonetheless, its relationship with Tanzania

---

[2] On 'briefcase fiction' in Dar es Salaam, see Emily Callaci, 'Street Textuality: Socialism, Masculinity, and Urban Belonging in Tanzania's Pulp Fiction Publishing Industry, 1975–1985', *Comparative Studies in Society and History*, 59 (2017), 183–210.

[3] Quoted in Duncan Holtom, 'Reconsidering the Power of the IFIs: Tanzania and the World Bank, 1978–1985', *Review of African Political Economy*, 32 (2005), 552. See also Sean Delehanty, 'From Modernization to Villagization: The World Bank and Ujamaa', *Diplomatic History*, 44 (2020), 289–314.

also improved: when the TPDF entered Uganda in 1979, it did so with Soviet arms.

This local détente in Dar es Salaam was encouraged by Tanzania's foreign policy. After the 'crises' of 1964–65, Nyerere sought not only to diversify Tanzania's sources of aid, but also to disconnect political disputes from economic agreements. Take the example of the 'German Cold War': irritated by the GDR and recognising the potential of West German aid, Nyerere looked to rebuild Tanzania's donor relationship with Bonn, despite the latter's ties with Lisbon and Pretoria. Conscious of the negative implications in some quarters of Tanzania's close relationship with Beijing, Nyerere continually emphasised his non-aligned credentials. Although cognisant of the domestic propaganda value to be reaped from attacking superpower imperialism abroad, he refrained from allowing issues like Vietnam or Czechoslovakia from affecting his own diplomatic endeavours. Members of government recognised that unbridled polemic risked undermining the credibility of Tanzania's international stance, deterring potential aid partners, and placing members of a cosmopolitan elite in awkward situations with aggrieved diplomats.

This approach worked. By the mid-1970s, Western reporters travelling to Dar es Salaam no longer reported the same nightmarish image of communist encroachment that had prevailed a decade earlier. 'Chinese "influence", never strong, is if anything on the wane in Tanzania', reflected *Africa Confidential* in 1973.[4] In the same year, browsing the notorious, Chinese-owned Tanganyika Bookshop, the South African writer Nadine Gordimer noted that there was 'only the voice of the muezzin of the street to disturb the solitary peace in which I contemplated the mounds of the Little Red Book curling at the edges'. Elsewhere, she reported, it was Nyerere and Nkrumah that filled bookshelves, rather than Lenin, Marx, or Mao.[5] Western diplomats came to accept that Tanzania was not about to become a Chinese client state or a bastion for communism in Eastern Africa. They were joined by their Indian colleagues, who observed that 'relations with China are no longer quite as euphoric as they appear on the surface', citing tensions over the implementation of the railway loan arrangements.[6]

---

[4] 'Tanzania: Contradictions', *Africa Confidential*, 16 November 1973, 5–7.
[5] Nadine Gordimer, 'Tanzania', *Atlantic*, May 1973, 8–18.
[6] Mehta, 'Annual Political Report for the Year 1972', 26 March 1973, INA, HI/1011(73)/73, 2.

Over time, Nyerere's experience of Cold War politics and Tanzania's development struggle led him to recognise the limits of political self-determination and to view non-alignment in primarily economic terms. Nyerere realised that genuine *uhuru* was impossible without economic 'self-reliance', as the Arusha lexicon put it. 'The real and urgent threat to the independence of almost all the non-aligned states thus comes not from the military but from the economic power of the big states', Nyerere told a non-aligned meeting in Dar es Salaam in 1970. 'It is poverty which constitutes our greatest danger, and to a greater or lesser extent we are all poor.'[7] He recognised that Tanzania's project of national self-reliance was swimming against the powerful currents of the global economy, dominated by capital from the North. In the 1970s Nyerere was therefore at the forefront of calls for a 'New International Economic Order', which sought to redress the needs of the developing world by restructuring global trade relations.[8]

Tanzania's internationalism, based on the ideas of non-alignment and Third World solidarity, helped it to diversify its aid arrangements over the course of the 1970s. *Ujamaa* was an attractive development agenda for European social democratic countries, as the example of Brandt's West Germany demonstrated in Chapter 3. Scandinavian states became major aid partners. The poorer states of the Third World had less to offer in terms of material aid, but emerging economies still represented new outlets for Tanzanian trade, as well as technical cooperation. An agreement between the National Development Corporation, Tanzania's largest parastatal, and its Indian counterpart noted that the former sought to 'learn from the experience of other developing countries which have faced problems to those facing Tanzania'.[9] Similarly, an NDC delegation travelling to Pakistan presented itself as a 'younger brother' asking for assistance from its 'elder brother'.[10] Tanzania cultivated stronger trade

---

[7] 'Developing Tasks of Non-Alignment', in Nyerere, *Freedom and Development*, 164.

[8] Getachew, *Worldmaking After Empire*; Priya Lal, 'African Socialism and the Limits of Global Familyhood: Tanzania and the New International Economic Order in Sub-Saharan Africa', *Humanity*, 6 (2015), 17–31.

[9] 'Agreement between the National Development Corporation (Tanzania) and National Industrial Development Corporation Limited (India)', 24 February 1973, TNA, 596, Box 3, D/1000/6.3.

[10] 'Report on the Official Visit of NDC Delegation to Pakistan, 23 to 25 May 1973', TNA, 596, Box 3, D/1000/6.1.

connections with the Third World, extending the idea of self-reliance beyond its own borders. 'This kind of reorientation of trade is an advantage to the Third World as a whole as well as to ourselves, for it makes the poor countries less dependent on the rich states', stated Nyerere.[11] These relationships all helped to disentangle Tanzania from the Cold War imbroglios which had characterised the early years of independence.

But just as the Third World rallied to the cause of the New International Economic Order and built 'South-South' relationships, the global economic climate took a turn for the worse. Alongside the Portuguese revolution, the other seismic shock from abroad that hit Tanzania in 1974 was the impact of oil price increases introduced by the Organisation of the Petroleum Exporting Countries. The cost of petrol in Tanzania soared and there were widespread shortages of goods, aggravated by drought. The oil crisis exposed the fragile state of the Tanzanian economy, particularly the unwieldy parastatals which had mushroomed after the Arusha Declaration. The villagisation policy, which was enforced sometimes violently from 1973 onwards, proved an economic disaster. The government struggled through on a drip of foreign aid. However, the donors' embrace of the socialist project cooled as the situation deteriorated and Nyerere resisted pressure for economic reform. 'Dar es Salaam stood rooted in a morality that warmed many a revolutionary heart', a Nigerian journalist reflected, 'but broke the hearts of international bankers'.[12]

This collapse was not simply the result of misguided policy or the harsh realities of the global economic order – though these were certainly key factors. It was exacerbated by political choices. First, during the period after the Arusha Declaration and especially after *Mwongozo*, Tanzanian socialism became more and more dogmatic in conceptualisation and authoritarian in implementation. The development agenda was increasingly put in the hands of party mobilisation. Once the regime began the coercive resettlement of the rural population, TANU found itself at war with the same peasantry which it idealised as the inspiration behind its socialist project. The doctrine of party supremacy replaced the dynamic debates about development

---

[11] Julius K. Nyerere, *The Arusha Declaration: Ten Years After* (Dar es Salaam: Government Printer, 1977), 26.
[12] Peter Enahoro, 'Dar Revisited', *Africa Now*, April 1986, 4.

of the pre-Arusha years with an unbending loyalty towards Nyerere and *ujamaa*. As Issa Shivji reflected during the democratisation debates that accompanied the end of the Cold War, the idea of 'national unity' was 'an ideological euphemism for imposed unanimity'. TANU and its successor, CCM, had 'managed successfully to suppress any organised expression of diversity and differences'.[13]

Second, Nyerere's decision not to recognise the regime of Idi Amin culminated in a fatal blow to the Tanzanian economy. In 1971, Nyerere broke with his well-established policy of accepting military usurpers, even as he lamented the rash of coups. By offering shelter and support for Milton Obote, Nyerere initiated a feud with Amin that rumbled on throughout the 1970s. On a regional level, these tensions fuelled an expensive arms race. Nyerere's refusal to compromise with Amin hastened the demise of the EAC, which collapsed in 1977. When a Ugandan barracks mutiny in the following year spilt over into a haphazard invasion of northwest Tanzania, Nyerere took the opportunity to unleash a counteroffensive. This drove Amin into exile in April 1979. However, Tanzania enjoyed only a pyrrhic victory, as the crippling financial cost of the war further depleted its scarce foreign exchange reserves.[14] After resisting the structural adjustment reforms demanded by the International Monetary Fund and World Bank for so long, Nyerere finally acknowledged there was no alternative. Rather than swallow the bitter pill himself, he stepped aside as president in 1985. The socialist dream was over.

The demise of *ujamaa* socialism sketched out here is very much a state-centred narrative. However, as this book has shown, the politics of the *ujamaa* era cannot be fully appreciated when confined to the framework of the Tanzanian nation-state. Equally, histories of Tanzanian foreign relations or liberation movements like FRELIMO overlap not just with one another, but innumerable other transnational, international, global, and local dynamics, which converged and collided in Dar es Salaam. 'The problem with historical events which are

[13] Issa G. Shivji, 'The Democracy Debate in Africa: Tanzania', *Review of African Political Economy*, 18 (1991), 87.
[14] George Roberts, 'The Uganda-Tanzania War, the Fall of Idi Amin, and the Failure of African Diplomacy', *Journal of Eastern African Studies*, 8 (2014), 692–709.

inextricably interwoven is that, the better to understand their constituent elements, we have to pull them apart', remarked Tony Judt. 'But in order to see the story in its plenitude, you have to interweave those elements back together. ... Separatism falsifies one party of the story; its absence has a comparably distorting impact on something else.'[15] Although this book has merely dipped its toes into the many historical currents which winded through Dar es Salaam in the time of *ujamaa*, by analysing them through the lens of the city, it has sought to offer a partial answer to Judt's dilemma.

Dar es Salaam's emergence as an epicentre of Cold War politics and revolutionary anticolonial struggle was the consequence of the provocative foreign policy of Nyerere's government. Tanzania's support for African liberation led to exiled movements setting up offices in the city. This attracted the interest of the Cold War powers, who turned the city into a propaganda and intelligence-gathering battleground. Nyerere signalled the depth of Tanzania's commitment to African liberation by snapping its relations with Britain in the aftermath of Rhodesia's UDI. At the same time, the government confronted local and regional upheavals. The mutiny of January 1964 laid bare the fragility of the postcolonial state and informed subsequent responses to domestic dissent. The Zanzibar Revolution simultaneously propelled East Africa into global headlines and brought the Cold War uncomfortably close to Nyerere's doorstep. His response – the act of union – was a qualified success. However, it also saddled the mainland government with the troublesome Karume regime.

At the heart of Dar es Salaam's revolutionary networks were the liberation movement leaders, who operated in the city's diplomatic margins but were central to its political life. Disaggregating a movement like FRELIMO and locating its politics in cosmopolitan Dar es Salaam renders visible all sorts of intersecting divisions and alliances. In the years preceding Mondlane's assassination in 1969, FRELIMO fractured along multiple fault lines: ideology, ethnicity, race, class, personality. A study of the city's numerous other movements would have exposed similar dynamics. Rival liberation movements – and rivals *within* liberation movements – jostled for support from the Cold War powers, as well as the Tanzanian government and

---

[15] Tony Judt with Timothy Snyder, *Thinking the Twentieth Century* (New York: Penguin, 2012), 43.

the OAU Liberation Committee. They exploited the city's international media networks to spread their messages of resistance. But Dar es Salaam also provided cover for agents of white minority rule to disrupt anticolonial solidarities. Once the experience of the guerrilla leaders is viewed through the perspective of exile in the Tanzanian capital, the usual nationalist narratives appear particularly misleading.

The presence of the liberation movements brought the Cold War powers running to Dar es Salaam. By the mid-1960s, the city was a focal point of diplomatic activity in Africa south of the Sahara. Among the Cold War subplots which played out in the Tanzanian capital was the bitter, shadowy rivalry between the two German states. By shifting between the perspective of presidential diplomacy and everyday iterations of this rivalry in Dar es Salaam's political life, we see how propaganda wars and interference in local affairs played an important role in shaping the perceptions and responses of state actors. Ideological positions – non-alignment, *Ostpolitik*, and competing concepts of socialism – informed these relationships. The global politics of Willy Brandt's turn away from Cold War confrontation to a constructive position, which blended détente in Europe with a more sensitive commitment to Third World development, improved the Federal Republic's relations with Tanzania. To further the *ujamaa* project, Nyerere responded positively to these endeavours, even as West Germany retained dubious arrangements with Tanzania's white-minority enemies. Meanwhile, the GDR's support for Africa's liberation movements was not enough to dispel Nyerere's belief in its fundamental illegitimacy. This was aggravated by the GDR's track record of clumsy, ideologically misinformed interventions in Tanzanian politics. Hence Tanzania, with the liberation of Africa as the cornerstone of its foreign policy, refused to recognise a state which supported this goal. The Cold War in Africa was rife with such contradictions.

Seen from a Tanzanian perspective, the Cold War looked very different altogether to the zero-sum game of East-West politics. Relationships with the superpowers and their allies came with significant baggage, whether in the forms of strings attached to material aid or smears from rival powers that Tanzania was too close to a particular state. From the vantage point of the Third World, the Cold War order appeared to many observers as the wolf of imperialism dressed in the sheepskins of modernisation. Tanzanian commentators and politicians tended to interpret global affairs not through East-West dichotomies, but via a Manichean

Conclusion

scheme that pitted the forces of imperialism against those of Third World anticolonialism. This increasingly mapped onto an alternative hemispheric geography of 'North' and 'South'. Tanzanian politics defied simplistic interpretations that classified ideological positions along a Cold War left-to-right spectrum. The dynamics of the Cold War were certainly a significant influence on post-independence developments in Dar es Salaam. But they cannot – and did not – make an effective guide for understanding them.

The Arusha Declaration was among the Third World's most powerful ripostes to the Cold War order. *Ujamaa* socialism was an original and innovative attempt to pursue a non-aligned path to development. In contrast to studies that analyse the Arusha Declaration through a narrow Tanzanian framework, this book has set its genealogy and aftermath in a transnational and international context. Like TANU's *Mwongozo* of 1971, the Arusha Declaration was a response to not just domestic socio-economic strife, but also the fate of progressive independent governments elsewhere in Africa. The downfall of Lumumba in Congo and Nkrumah in Ghana demonstrated the vulnerability of postcolonial elites to local opponents who claimed support from powerful interests outside of the continent. The presence of the liberation movements in Dar es Salaam enhanced the Nyerere government's sense of insecurity, especially after the failed Portuguese attack on Guinea in 1970. Tanzania's socialist revolution was a political and economic rejoinder to these mounting pressures from outside the country, as well as internal state-building challenges. At the same time, more economically minded members of the Tanzanian government argued that the country could not simply isolate itself from the global economy to pursue 'development from within'. They also recognised that Tanzania paradoxically still required foreign aid to attain its goal of 'self-reliance'.

The book has argued that a fresh analysis of Tanzanian politics in the time of *ujamaa* requires us to look beyond the figure of Julius Nyerere. This political scene was marked by ideological diversity. For all that, Nyerere still retains a prominent, even central place in this history of revolutionary state-making. How can he not? It remains difficult not to write about Nyerere 'saying this' or 'doing that'. This becomes particularly clear in the field of formal foreign policy, where Nyerere maintained a strong hand until his departure from power. He was happy to use the ideological proclivities and international connections of his government ministers – A. M. Babu with China, Stephen Mhando with the Eastern Bloc, Paul Bomani with the West, Amir Jamal with just about anyone – but that did not translate into their influence over the direction of Tanzania's foreign policy. Nyerere's subordinates claimed that they needed little guidance. Ibrahim Kaduma, who became foreign minister in 1975, recalled that Nyerere rarely provided instructions on policy, since the principles were so well established that even a student could have represented Tanzania at the OAU.[16] To a large extent, this was true. The cardinal principles of anticolonial liberation, non-alignment, and pan-Africanism were made clear from an early stage, even if their application changed in subtle fashion over time. However, non-alignment in particular was a slippery concept involving many moving parts and therefore tricky balancing acts, which were often upset by more junior ministers, party spokespersons, and journalists.

In other spheres of government, Nyerere's authority requires greater qualification. Liberation movement leaders, operating in the grey areas of informal diplomacy and entangled in local power struggles, continually resisted control from above. More generally, Nyerere's concept of *ujamaa* may have provided the underlying ethos of Tanzanian politics, but its actual elaboration as policy was the product of conflict and concession. Twice, through the Arusha Declaration and *Mwongozo*, Nyerere compromised with an increasingly assertive radical wing of TANU to take steps against which he had previously advised. On both occasions, Nyerere eschewed the advice of more cautious government ministers. On both occasions, this brought about splits in the elite, which Nyerere redressed through a mixture of political guile, like ministerial reshuffles, and the use of repressive tools, like preventive detention or party expulsions. The minimisation of political space which these processes involved closed off avenues for fresh ideas to revive the flagging *ujamaa* project.

The problems of snuffing out dissent were most acute in Dar es Salaam, where a kaleidoscopic mixture of local and foreign actors came together. This gave rise to concerns at the potentially destabilising entanglements of discontented Tanzanian elites, Cold War diplomats, guerrilla leaders, and a host of other intermediaries who joined together the city's internationalised political networks. As the mutiny of 1964 made clear, if a strike at the state was to occur, it would come in

---

[16] Interview with Ibrahim Kaduma, Makongo, Dar es Salaam, 23 July 2015.

the capital. Bar gossip and anonymous flyers unsettled a party-state bent on setting the terms of political discourse. In an era where externally-backed coups and conspiracies seemed ubiquitous, this public sphere assumed a subversive character – the hallmark of the 'Cold War city', or, as Nyerere had it, 'Rumourville'. In this light, Nyerere's announcement in 1972 that the capital would be moved to Dodoma, a dusty provincial town, was unsurprising. This was a pragmatic decision, which resituated the seat of power in the centre of the country in order to be more accessible for all Tanzanians. It was a cultural intervention, too, since it sought to replace a cosmopolitan capital associated with a history of foreign domination with an authentically 'African' city. Yet it was also consistent with Nyerere's anxieties about external subversion in Dar es Salaam.[17]

This 'inward turn' was exemplified by the politics of the press in postcolonial Dar es Salaam. From the perspective of the party-state, the media was a significant element in its socialist state-building project. It was an international space, in which radical TANU ideologues and expatriate journalists engaged with the global issues of the day. However, the press was also beset with tensions. The *Standard* was unable to shake off its colonial associations, especially given the pressure for the Africanisation and nationalisation of foreign-staffed and foreign-owned assets. Amid a debate about what the 'freedom of the press' might actually mean in the Third World, the government took control of the *Standard*. The new expatriate editorial team reflected Tanzania's commitment to Third World liberation, but also exposed the limits to it. Frene Ginwala's *Standard* could reconcile its revolutionary politics with neither the foreign policy priorities of an embattled Tanzanian state nor the task of full Africanisation. The idea of 'developmental journalism', which informed the government's approach to the press in the 1970s, typified the tensions in the Third World project, in which an anti-imperialist ethos went hand in hand with an insular politics founded on the nation-state.

Tanzania was not alone in taking this inward turn. Other Third World states exhibited similar tendencies. Based on his study of Algeria, Jeffrey Byrne argues that, faced with external and internal threats to their sovereignty, Africa's postcolonial elites chose to calcify

[17] Emily Callaci, '"Chief Village in a Nation of Villages": History, Race and Authority in Tanzania's Dodoma Plan', *Urban History*, 43 (2016), 96–116.

national borders and abandon much of the radical Third Worldism and pan-Africanism of earlier anticolonial struggles.[18] Tanzania fits into this mould. Even as Nyerere began to question the OAU's commitment to inherited colonial borders and national sovereignty, the vision he shared of a New International Economic Order was built on the bedrock of the nation-state. Similar dynamics emerged when Dar es Salaam hosted the Sixth Pan-African Congress in June 1974. This witnessed the decision to structure the congress' organisation around representatives of nation-states, to the exclusion of radicals from the African diaspora who had travelled in large numbers from the Caribbean and North America, as Seth Markle has shown.[19] Moreover, nationalist state-making was not just about the consolidation of external frontiers. The Tanzanian example demonstrates in particularly stark terms how the firming up of borders was often accompanied by the constriction of domestic politics. TANU's militant nationalism was presented as to counter the threat posed by imperialism from without the country and its 'lackeys' from within. Studying the transnational movement of people and ideas might ask us to reconsider the normative adoption of the nation-state as a frame of analytical reference, but these dynamics were not necessarily at odds with the entrenchment of state power. As Chapter 5 demonstrated, the global languages of 1968 were appropriated by the party-state to channel transnational anticolonialism into a more defensive Tanzanian nationalism.

It is tempting, as Miles Larmer does in the case of Zambia, to conclude that the threat from imperialism was 'frequently distorted or overstated' to justify the oppression of internal opposition and shore up the power of the ruling party.[20] There is certainly some truth in that idea. By the 1970s, the official organs of the Tanzanian state were presenting any kind of internal challenge as an imperialist conspiracy. But any interpretation of the rise of authoritarianism must also appreciate the burden which Tanzania assumed in hosting the liberation movements, while simultaneously fending off Cold War challenges, and maintaining a non-aligned foreign policy. Tanzania's authoritarianism was shaped by choices by Tanzanian elites which emerged from

---

[18] Byrne, *Mecca of Liberation*. [19] Markle, *Motorcycle*, 141–76.
[20] Miles Larmer, *Rethinking African Politics: A History of Opposition in Zambia* (Farnham: Ashgate, 2011), 224.

the interwoven challenges of building a socialist state while unselfishly supporting anticolonial revolution across Africa and beyond. These circumstances opened opportunities for the accumulation of power in the hands of a party elite, which justified their decisions by reference to continental and global developments. Ten years after Tanganyika gained independence, the president was asked by a journalist as to what he considered his greatest achievement. 'We have survived', Nyerere answered, grimly.[21] This might seem a low bar to clear, but it was nevertheless a tough challenge, as the fate of other aspirational postcolonial regimes demonstrated.

Dar es Salaam was one revolutionary city among many – a city, moreover, connected to many others. The struggle against imperialism transcended borders, even as African states became increasingly defensive about guarding them. To return to the vignette which opened this conclusion, although Willy Gamba's mission begins in Dar es Salaam, the majority of *Kufa na Kupona* is set in Nairobi. Writing a more extensive exile history of a movement like FRELIMO would involve a multi-sited study that grounds anticolonial politics in cities such as Algiers, Cairo, and Lusaka plus metropolitan and Cold War capitals, like Paris, Beijing, and Moscow. These urban locales, as well as the transnational or international connections which joined them together, constituted a networked geography of Third World liberation.[22] If the findings of this book are anything to go by, the history such approaches should reveal will be messy: at times confusing, in places contradictory.

—

A visiting journalist arriving in Dar es Salaam today would encounter a very different city to 'Rumourville'. The sprawling metropolis is emblematic of Africa's post-socialist urban landscape. The city centre has been transformed, architecturally and politically. The OAU Liberation Committee headquarters on Garden Avenue, surrounded

---

[21] Quoted in Issa G. Shivji, 'The Rule of Law and *Ujamaa* in the Ideological Formation of Tanzania', *Social and Legal Studies*, 4 (1995), 158–59. Asked the same question by the same journalist ten years later, Nyerere gave the same response.

[22] See Byrne, *Mecca of Liberation;* Chamberlin, *Global Offensive;* Anne Garland Mahler, *From the Tricontinental to the Global South: Race, Radicalism, and Transnational Solidarity* (Durham, NC: Duke University Press, 2018).

by securitised embassy compounds, stands dilapidated against a gleaming skyline. The bar at the rebuilt New Africa Hotel is no longer propped up by guerrilla leaders or Cold War diplomats, but businessmen working for multinationals and the 'experts' of an expanding number of NGOs, which jostle for influence in a congested development sector.

Look closer, and traces of Dar es Salaam's revolutionary past remain. As the threat posed to the city's architectural heritage by the voracious construction of skyscrapers becomes clear, groups are organising to alert residents to the imminent material loss of a rich urban history. African liberation struggles feature prominently in these campaigns. Outside the New Zahir Restaurant on Mosque Street, a small plaque commemorates that, in another time, the freedom fighters took their meals under the same canopied veranda. Beyond the city centre, on the Msasani peninsula, a larger memorial marks the former home of Eduardo Mondlane. Mejah Mbuya, a social activist and co-founder of the Afriroots tour company, runs guided visits of revolutionary Dar es Salaam. He aims to engage not only tourists, but also the local population. 'I want Tanzanians to know their history', he says. 'It's something that they should know and be proud of.'[23]

Yet politically, the Tanzanian state is moving in the opposite direction. Despite these attempts to reclaim the country's revolutionary past from below, the government has broken with the commitment to Third World liberation that was the paramount feature of *ujamaa*-era foreign policy. In 2017, Tanzania's fifth president, John Magufuli, addressed students at the University of Dar es Salaam. Where once liberation movement leaders and visiting radical academics had emphasised their commitment to a global struggle against imperialism, now Magufuli signalled a new approach. 'We have carried the burdens of other peoples' conflicts for too long', he said. 'Our goal is to focus on the interests of our country – Tanzania first.'[24] This came against the backdrop of Tanzania strengthening its relationship with Morocco, a long-time African pariah due to its continued occupation of Western Sahara. Magufuli's speech was also interpreted as a response to criticism over Tanzania's decision to open an embassy in Israel.

---

[23] Chris Oke, 'Lost Legacy: Untold Story of D'Salaam', *Citizen*, 30 April 2014.
[24] 'JPM "Echoes" Trump, Says Tanzania First', *Guardian on Sunday*, 16 April 2017, 2.

Nyerere had been a supporter of both Sahrawi liberation and the Palestine Liberation Organisation, which had operated an office in Dar es Salaam.[25] In both cases, the government's about-turn was based on the calculations of attracting foreign aid.

For some commentators, the Tanzanian government's new stance was a betrayal of Nyerere's legacy. Amid a massacre in Gaza in 2018, one MP drew attention to Tanzania's past role in the non-aligned movement and support for the cause of African liberation and contrasted it with present policy towards Israel and Morocco. 'I am certain that *Mwalimu* Nyerere, the "Father of the Nation", must be turning in his grave.'[26] Another opposition politician, Zitto Kabwe, noted that 'yesterday, the people whom we liberated in South Africa withdrew their ambassador after the massacre in Gaza, while our Foreign Minister sipped wine with Netanyahu, the butcher of the Palestinians'.[27] In the press, Kabwe declared that '[w]e are no longer Tanzania, which stands with the oppressed. We are being driven by economic gains instead of human rights and dignity.'[28] One journalist perceived the shifting policy as nothing less than the surrender of Tanzania's raison d'être. 'We brought a torch to the top of Mount Kilimanjaro, for the purpose of bringing light to darkness, to bring hope to the desperate around the world', he wrote. 'If we no longer have this faith, what meaning do we have as a nation?'[29] Such charges might be read as yet another example of the ubiquitous invocation of Nyerere's memory for political capital or simply dismissed as the fringe views of the intelligentsia. But they also speak of a lost past: a recognition of the fading place of Tanzania – and Dar es Salaam – as the revolutionary heartbeat of Africa.

---

[25] 'Palestine Movement to Open Dar Office', *Daily News*, 22 May 1974, 1.
[26] Mbilinyi, 23 May 2018, *Hansard* (Tanzania), 35th meeting, 145.
[27] Kabwe, 23 May 2018, *Hansard* (Tanzania), 35th meeting, 164.
[28] Zitto Kabwe, 'Looking at Israel-Palestine Conflict, Tanzania Has Abandoned the Oppressed', *Citizen*, 30 May 2018, 13.
[29] Ndahani Mwenda, 'Je, Nyerere angempokea Joseph Kasavubu', *Rai*, 25 October 2018, 15.

Bibliography

Archives

Australia

National Archives of Australia, Canberra (NAA) [accessed online, naa.gov.au]
   A8138 – Department of External Affairs

Belgium

Archives diplomatiques, Brussels (ADB)

Ethiopia

African Union Common Repository [accessed online, archives.au.int]

Federal Republic of Germany

Bundesarchiv, Koblenz (BA-K)
Friedrich Ebert Stiftung – Archiv der sozialen Demokratie (AdsD), Bonn
   Sammlung Personalia (SP) – Erhard Eppler
Politisches Archiv des Auswärtiges Amt, Berlin (PAAA)
   Neues Amt (NA)

France

Centre des Archives diplomatiques, Nantes (CADN)
   193PO – French embassy, Dar es Salaam
Archive Nationales, Paris (AN)
   19850665– Centre d'études et de documentation d'Afrique et d'Outre-mer

German Democratic Republic

Bundesarchiv, Berlin (BA-B)
   Stiftung Archiv der Parteien und Massenorganisationen der DDR (SAPMO)
   DY 30 – Zentralkomitee der SED
   DZ 8 – Solidaritätskomitee der DDR
Bundesbeauftragte für die Unterlagen des Staatsicherheitsdienstes der ehemaligen DDR, Berlin (BStU)
   Ministerium für Staatsicherheit (MfS) – 'Stasi'
Politisches Archiv des Auswärtiges Amt, Berlin (PAAA)
   Ministerium für Auswärtige Angelegenheiten (MfAA)

India

Indian National Archives, New Delhi (INA)
   Ministry of External Affairs

Netherlands

Nationaal Archief, The Hague (NAN)
   2.05.253 – Dutch embassy, Dar es Salaam

Poland

Archiwum Ministerstwa Spraw Zagraniczynch, Warsaw (MSZ)
   Department V (DV)

Portugal

Arquivo-Histórico e Diplomático, Ministério dos Négocios Estrangeiros, Lisbon (AHD)
   Minstério dos Négocios Estrangeiros (MNE)
   Ministério do Ultramar (MU)
Arquivo Nacional, Torre do Tombo, Lisbon (TT)
   Polícia Internacional e do Defesa do Estado (PIDE)
   Serviços de Centralização da Informação de Moçambique (SCCIM)
Fundação Mário Soares, Lisbon (FMS) [accessed online, casacomum.org]
   Arquivo Mário Pinto de Andrade

South Africa

South African Defence Force Archives, Pretoria (SADF)

Tanzania

Tanzania National Archives, Dar es Salaam (TNA)
589– Papers of I. Bhoke Munanka
593– Idara ya Habari (Information Services)
596– National Development Corporation
National Records Centre, Dodoma (NRC)
Prime Minister's Office (PMO)
Zanzibar National Archives (ZNA)
AK – Provincial Administration

Uganda

Makerere Institute of Social Research, Kampala (MISR)
Papers of Amir Jamal

United Kingdom

Bodleian Library, Oxford (BL)
Papers of George Ivan Smith
Institute for Commonwealth Studies, London (ICS)
Papers of Graham Mytton
Reuters Archive, London
The National Archives, London (UKNA)
Dominion Office (DO)
Foreign and Commonwealth Office (FCO)
Foreign Office (FO)
Prime Minister's Office (PREM)

United States

CIA Electronic Reading Room [accessed online, cia.gov/library/readingroom]
Cold War International History Project, Wilson Center (CWIHP)
[accessed online, wilsoncenter.org/program/cold-war-international-history-project]
Frontline Diplomacy: The Foreign Affairs Oral History Collection of the Association for Diplomatic Studies and Training (FAOHC) [accessed online, loc.gov/collections/foreign-affairs-oral-history]
Hoover Institute Archives, Stanford, California (HIA)

Papers of Henry Bienen
Lyndon Baines Johnson Presidential Library, Austin, Texas (LBJL)
   National Security Files (NSF)
      Special Head of State Correspondence (SHSC)
   Papers of Leonhard H. Marks
National Archives and Records Administration II, College Park, Maryland (NARA)
   Record Group 59 – Department of State (RG 59)
      Bureau of African Affairs (BAA)
         Office of East African Affairs (OEAA)
      Central Foreign Policy Files (CFPF), 1967–69
      Czechoslovakian Crisis Microfilm
      Subject Numeric Files (SNF), 1964–66, 1970–73
Oberlin College Archives, Ohio (OCA)
   Herbert Shore Collection in Honor of Eduardo C. Mondlane (HSC)
Richard Nixon Presidential Library, Yorba Linda, California (RNL)
   National Security Council Files (NSCF)

Newspapers and Periodicals

Africa Confidential (UK; published as *Africa* plus the year number before 1967, e.g., *Africa 1966*)
Africa Contemporary Record (UK)
Africa Now (UK)
Atlantic (United States)
Citizen (Tanzania)
Daily Nation (Kenya)
Daily News (Tanzania)
Daily Telegraph (UK)
Die Zeit (FRG)
East African Journal (Kenya)
Financial Times (UK)
Foreign Affairs Bulletin: An Official Record of Foreign Policy of the United Republic of Tanzania (Tanzania)
Frankfurter Allgemeine Zeitung (FRG)
Guardian (UK)
Guardian on Sunday (Tanzania)
Index on Censorship (UK)
Jeune Afrique (Tunisia)
Mfanya Kazi (Tanzania)
Nationalist (Tanzania)
New Internationalist (UK)
New York Times (United States)
Ngurumo (Tanzania)

Observer (UK)
Peking Review (China)
Rai (Tanzania)
Raia Mwema (Tanzania)
Reporter (Kenya)
Revolution in Africa ('Albania'; real provenance unknown)
Spearhead (Tanzania)
Standard (Tanzania)
Sunday News (Tanzania)
Sunday Telegraph (UK)
Sunday Times (UK)
Times (UK)
Uhuru (Tanzania)
Vigilance Africa (China/Tanzania)
Wall Street Journal (United States)
Washington Post (United States)
Weekly News (Kenya)

Interviews

Babu, Ashura. Mikocheni, Dar es Salaam, 2 April 2019 (untaped).
Kaduma, Ibrahim. Makongo, Dar es Salaam, 23 July 2015 (untaped).
Msoma, Salim. Oyster Bay, Dar es Salaam, 2 July 2015 (untaped).
Mwapachu, Juma. Oyster Bay, Dar es Salaam, 12 June 2015 (taped), 29 May 2018 (untaped).
Ngombale-Mwiru, Kingunge. Victoria, Dar es Salaam, 26 August 2015 (taped).
Nyakyi, Anthony. Masaki, Dar es Salaam, 28 July 2015 (taped).
Rupia, Paul. Central Dar es Salaam, 3 August 2015 (untaped).
Said, Mohamed. Magomeni Mapipa, Dar es Salaam, 8 July 2015 (untaped).
Salim, Salim Ahmed. Masaki, Dar es Salaam. 29 August 2015 (taped).
Ulimwengu, Jenerali. Oyster Bay, Dar es Salaam, 18 August 2015 (taped).

Personal Correspondence

Eppler, Erhard. 31 December 2016 (by email).

Published Primary Sources

Foreign Broadcasting Information Services [FBIS] Daily Report
Foreign Relations of the United States [FRUS], 1964-1968, vol. 24 – Africa
Hansard (Tanzania)
Hansard (UK)

Multimedia Resources

British Pathé and Reuters Historical Collection (BPRHC). britishpathe. com.
CBS 'Face the Nation' interview with Julius Nyerere, 2 January 1966, Herkovits Library of African Studies Audio Collection.
Furtado, Joaquim (dir.), *A Guerra* (RTP, 2012), episode 13 – 'Morte de Eduardo Mondlane'.

Secondary Sources

Aalen, Lovise. 'Ethiopian State Support to Insurgency in Southern Sudan from 1962 to 1983: Local, Regional and Global Connections', *Journal of Eastern African Studies*, 8 (2014), 626–41.
Adebanwi, Wale. 'The Radical Press and Security Agencies in Nigeria: Beyond Hegemonic Polarities', *African Studies Review*, 54 (2011), 45–69.
Ahlman, Jeffrey S. 'Road to Ghana: Nkrumah, Southern Africa, and the Eclipse of a Decolonizing Africa', *Kronos*, 37 (2011), 23–40.
Ahlman, Jeffrey S. *Living with Nkrumahism: Nation, State, and Pan-Africanism in Ghana* (Athens: Ohio University Press, 2017).
Ainslie, Rosalynde. *The Press in Africa: Communications Past and Present* (London: Victor Gollancz, 1966).
Aldrich, Harriet. 'Uganda, Southern Sudan and the Idi Amin Coup', *Journal of Imperial and Commonwealth History*, 48 (2020), 1109–39.
Alexander, Jocelyn, JoAnn McGregor, and Blessing-Miles Tendi. 'The Transnational Histories of Southern African Liberation Movements: An Introduction', *Journal of Southern African Studies*, 43 (2017), 1–12.
Alexander, Jocelyn, Paolo Israel, Miles Larmer, and Ricardo Soares de Oliveira. 'Liberation Beyond the Nation: An Introduction', *Journal of Southern African Studies*, 46 (2020), 821–28.
Allman, Jean. 'Phantoms of the Archive: Kwame Nkrumah, a Nazi Pilot Named Hanna, and the Contingencies of Post-Colonial History-Writing', *American Historical Review*, 118 (2013), 104–29.
Allman, Jean. 'The Fate of All of Us: African Counterrevolutions and the Ends of 1968', *American Historical Review*, 123 (2018), 728–32.
Amate, C. O. C. *Inside the OAU: Pan-Africanism in Practice* (London: Macmillan, 1986).
Aminzade, Ronald. *Race, Nation, and Citizenship in Post-Colonial Africa: The Case of Tanzania* (New York: Cambridge University Press, 2013).

Anderson, David M. 'Mau Mau in the High Court and the "Lost" British Empire Archives: Colonial Conspiracy or Bureaucratic Bungle?', *Journal of Imperial and Commonwealth History*, 39 (2011), 699–716.

Antunes, José Freire. *Jorge Jardim: Agente secreto* (Venda Nova: Bertrand Editora, 1996).

Ashekee, Toivo. 'Black Power and Armed Decolonization in Southern Africa: Stokely Carmichael, the African National Congress, and the African Liberation Movements, November 1967–December 1973', *Journal of African American History*, 104 (2019), 415–44.

Babu, A. M. 'The 1964 Revolution: Lumpen or Vanguard?', in Abdul Sheriff and Ed Ferguson (eds.), *Zanzibar under Colonial Rule* (London: James Currey, 1991), 220–47.

Babu, A. M. 'Entrepreneurs in Tanzania: A Minister's Story', in Stephen Ellis and Yves-A. Fauré (eds.), *Entreprises et entrepreneurs africains* (Paris: Éditions Karthala, 1995), 347–53.

Babu, A. M. 'Memoirs: An Outline', in Haroub Othman (ed.), *Babu: I Saw the Future and It Works. Essays Celebrating the Life of Comrade Abdulrahman Mohamed Babu* (Dar es Salaam: E&D, 2001), 11–58.

Babu, A. M. 'The Tanzania That Might Have Been', in Salma Babu and Amrit Wilson (eds.), *The Future That Works: Select Writings of A. M. Babu* (Trenton, NJ: Africa World Press, 2002), 16–23.

Baker, Colin. *Revolt of the Ministers: The Malawi Cabinet Crisis, 1964–1965* (London: IB Tauris, 2001).

Bamba, Abou B. 'An Unconventional Challenge to Apartheid: The Ivorian Dialogue Diplomacy with South Africa, 1960–1978', *International Journal of African Historical Studies*, 47 (2014), 77–99.

Bamba, Abou B. *African Miracle, African Mirage: Transnational Politics and the Paradox of Modernization in Ivory Coast* (Athens: Ohio University Press, 2016).

Baraka, Amiri. *The Autobiography of LeRoi Jones* (New York: Freundlich, 1984).

Barton, Frank. *The Press of Africa: Persecution and Perseverance* (New York: Africana, 1979).

Bayart, Jean-François. *The State in Africa: The Politics of the Belly* (London: Longman, 1993 [1989]).

Bedasse, Monique A. *Jah Kingdom: Rastafarians, Tanzania, and Pan-Africanism in the Age of Decolonization* (Chapel Hill: North Carolina University Press, 2017).

Bernstein, Hilda. *The Rift: The Exile Experience of South Africans* (London: Jonathan Cape, 1994).

Bgoya, Walter. 'From Tanzania to Kansas and Back Again', in William Minter, Gail Hovey, and Charles Cobb, Jr (eds.), *No Easy*

Victories: African Liberation and American Activists over a Half Century, 1950–2000 (Trenton, NJ: Africa World Press, 2007), 103–106.

Bienen, Henry. *Tanzania: Party Transformation and Economic Development* (Princeton, NJ: Princeton University Press, 1970).

Bjerk, Paul. 'Postcolonial Realism: Tanganyika's Foreign Policy Under Nyerere, 1960–1963', *International Journal of African Historical Studies*, 44 (2011), 216–47.

Bjerk, Paul. 'Bomani, Paul', in Emmanuel A. Akyeampong and Henry Louis Gates, Jr (eds.), *Dictionary of African Biography*, vol. 1 (Oxford: Oxford University Press, 2012), 484–85.

Bjerk, Paul. *Building a Peaceful Nation: Julius Nyerere and the Establishment of Sovereignty in Tanzania* (Rochester, NY: University of Rochester Press, 2015).

Blum, Françoise, Pierre Guidi, and Ophélie Rillon (eds.). *Étudiants africains en mouvements: Contribution à une histoire des années 1968* (Paris: Publications de la Sorbonne, 2016).

Boittin, Jennifer Anne. *Colonial Metropolis: The Urban Grounds of Anti-Imperialism and Feminism in Interwar Paris* (Lincoln: University of Nebraska Press, 2010).

Bonate, Liazzat J. K. 'Muslims of Northern Mozambique and the Liberation Movements', *Social Dynamics*, 35 (2009), 280–94.

Bourgault, Louise M. *Mass Media in Sub-Saharan Africa* (Bloomington: Indiana University Press, 1995).

Bragança, Aquino de, and Immanuel Wallerstein (eds.). *The African Liberation Reader, vol. 2: The National Liberation Movements* (London: Zed, 1982).

Brandt, Willy. 'Problems of the Second Development Decade', *Intereconomics*, 4 (1969), 242–44.

Brazinsky, Gregg A. *Winning the Third World: Sino-American Rivalry During the Cold War* (Chapel Hill: University of North Carolina Press, 2017).

Brennan, James R. 'Democratizing Cinema and Censorship in Tanzania, 1920–1980', *International Journal of African Historical Studies*, 38 (2005), 481–511.

Brennan, James R. 'Youth, the TANU Youth League, and Managed Vigilantism in Dar es Salaam, 1925–73', *Africa*, 76 (2006), 221–46.

Brennan, James R. 'The Short History of Political Opposition and Multi-Party Democracy in Tanganyika, 1958–64', in Gregory H. Maddox and James L. Giblin (eds.), *In Search of a Nation: Histories of Authority and Dissidence in Tanzania* (Oxford: James Currey, 2007), 250–76.

Brennan, James R. 'Destroying Mumiani: Cause, Context, and Violence in Late Colonial Dar es Salaam', *Journal of Eastern African Studies*, 2 (2008), 95–111.

Brennan, James R. 'Radio Cairo and the Decolonization of East Africa, 1953–1964', in Christopher J. Lee (ed.), *Making a World After Empire: The Bandung Moment and Its Political Afterlives* (Athens: Ohio University Press, 2010), 173–95.

Brennan, James R. *Taifa: Making Nation and Race in Urban Tanzania* (Athens: Ohio University Press, 2012).

Brennan, James R. '*Julius Rex*: Nyerere Through the Eyes of His Critics', *Journal of Eastern African Studies*, 8 (2014), 459–77.

Brennan, James R. 'The Cold War Battle over Global News in East Africa: Decolonization, the Free Flow of Information and the Media Business, 1960–1980', *Journal of Global History*, 10 (2015), 333–56.

Brennan, James R. 'David Martin: Tracking the 1969 Killing of Mozambique's Independence Fighter, Eduardo Mondlane', in Anya Schiffrin and George Lugalambi (eds.), *African Muckraking: 100 Years of African Investigative Journalism* (Johannesburg: Jacana, 2017), 11–19.

Brennan, James R. 'The Secret Lives of Dennis Phombeah: Decolonization, the Cold War, and African Political Intelligence, 1953–1974', *International History Review*, 43 (2021), 153–69.

Brennan, James R., and Andrew Burton. 'The Emerging Metropolis: A History of Dar es Salaam, circa 1862–2000', in James R. Brennan, Andrew Burton, and Yusuf Lawi (eds.), *Dar es Salaam: Histories from an Emerging African Metropolis* (Dar es Salaam: Mkuki na Nyota, 2007), 13–76.

Brennan, James R., Andrew Burton, and Yusuf Lawi (eds.). *Dar es Salaam: Histories from an Emerging African Metropolis* (Dar es Salaam: Mkuki na Nyota, 2007).

Brownell, Emily. *Gone to Ground: A History of Environment and Infrastructure in Dar es Salaam* (Pittsburgh, PA: University of Pittsburgh Press, 2020).

Burgess, G. Thomas. 'The Young Pioneers and the Rituals of Citizenship in Revolutionary Africa', *Africa Today*, 51 (2005), 3–29.

Burgess, G. Thomas. 'An Imagined Generation: Umma Youth in Nationalist Zanzibar', in Gregory H. Maddox and James L. Giblin (eds.), *In Search of a Nation: Histories of Authority and Dissidence in Tanzania* (Oxford: James Currey, 2007), 216–49.

Burgess, G. Thomas. 'A Socialist Diaspora: Ali Sultan Issa, the Soviet Union, and the Zanzibari Revolution', in Maxim Matusevich (ed.), *Africa in Russia, Russia in Africa: Three Centuries of Encounter* (Trenton, NJ: Africa World Press, 2007), 263–91.

Burton, Andrew. *African Underclass: Urbanisation, Crime and Colonial Order in Dar es Salaam* (London: British Institute in Eastern Africa, 2005).

Burton, Eric. 'Diverging Visions in Revolutionary Spaces: East German Advisers and Revolution from Above in Zanzibar, 1964–1970', in Anna Calori, Anne-Kristin Hartmetz, Bence Kocsev, James Mark, and Jan Zofka (eds.), *Between East and South: Spaces of Interaction in the Globalizing Economy of the Cold War* (Oldenbourg: De Gruyter, 2019), 85–115.

Byrne, Jeffrey James. 'Beyond Continents, Colours, and the Cold War: Yugoslavia, Algeria, and the Struggle for Non-Alignment', *International History Review*, 37 (2015), 912–32.

Byrne, Jeffrey James. *Mecca of Revolution: Algeria, Decolonization and the Third World Order* (Oxford: Oxford University Press, 2016).

Cabrita, João M. *Mozambique: The Torturous Road to Democracy* (Basingstoke: Palgrave, 2000).

Cahen, Michel. 'The Mueda Case and Maconde Political Ethnicity: Some Notes on a Work in Progress', *Africana Studia*, 2 (1999), 29–46.

Cahen, Michel. 'Nationalism and Ethnicities: Lessons from Mozambique', in Einar Braathen, Morten Bøås, and Gjermund Sæther (eds.), *Ethnicity Kills? The Politics of War, Peace and Ethnicity in SubSaharan Africa* (Basingstoke: Macmillan, 2000), 163–87.

Cahen, Michel. 'Lutte d'émancipation anticoloniale ou mouvement de libération nationale?', *Revue Historique*, 637 (2006), 113–38.

Cahen, Michel. 'La "fin de l'histoire…unique": Trajectoires des anticolonialismes au Mozambique', *Portuguese Studies Review*, 16 (2008), 171–237.

Callaci, Emily. '"Chief Village in a Nation of Villages": History, Race and Authority in Tanzania's Dodoma Plan', *Urban History*, 43 (2016), 96–116.

Callaci, Emily. *Street Archives and City Life: Popular Intellectuals in Postcolonial Tanzania* (Durham, NC: Duke University Press, 2017).

Callaci, Emily. 'Street Textuality: Socialism, Masculinity, and Urban Belonging in Tanzania's Pulp Fiction Publishing Industry, 1975–1985', *Comparative Studies in Society and History*, 59 (2017), 183–210.

Carpenter, Nathan Riley, and Benjamin N. Lawrance (eds.). *Africans in Exile: Mobility, Law, and Identity* (Bloomington: Indiana University Press, 2018).

Červenka, Zdenek. *The Unfinished Quest for Unity: Africa and the OAU* (London: Julian Friedmann, 1977).

Chamberlin, Paul Thomas. *The Global Offensive: The United States, the Palestine Liberation Organisation, and the Making of the Post-Cold War Order* (Oxford: Oxford University Press, 2012).

Chande, J. K. *A Knight in Africa: Journey from Bukene* (Manotick: Penumbra, 2005).

Chaves, Rita. 'Autobiografias em Moçambique: A escrita como monument (2001–2013)', *Revista de História*, 178 (2019), 1–22.
Chiume, Kanyama. *Autobiography of Kanyama Chiume* (London: Panaf, 1982).
Chiume, Kanyama. *Banda's Malawi: An African Tragedy* (Lusaka: Multimedia Publications, 1992).
Christiansen, Samantha, and Zachary A. Scarlett (eds.). *The Third World in the Global 1960s* (New York: Berghahn, 2013).
Clayton, Anthony. *The Zanzibar Revolution and Its Aftermath* (London: Hurst, 1981).
Cliffe, Lionel. 'Review of Henry Bienen, *Tanzania: Party Transformation and Economic Development*', *Africa Review*, 1 (1971), 119–35.
Cliffe, Lionel. 'Political Struggles Around the Adoption and Implementation of the Arusha Declaration', in Jeanette Hartmann (ed.), *Re-Thinking the Arusha Declaration* (Copenhagen: Centre for Development Research, 1991), 105–12.
Cohen, Robert Carl. *Black Crusader: A Biography of Robert Franklin Williams* (Secaucus, NJ: Lyle Stuart, 1st ed., 1972).
Cohen, Robert Carl. *Black Crusader: A Biography of Robert Franklin Williams* (Oregon: Jorvik Press, 3rd ed., 2015).
Cook, Alexander C. 'Introduction: The Spiritual Atom Bomb and Its Global Fallout', in Alexander C. Cook (ed.), *Mao's Little Red Book: A Global History* (Cambridge: Cambridge University Press, 2014), 1–22.
Cooper, Frederick. 'Possibility and Constraint: African Independence in Historical Perspective', *Journal of African History*, 49 (2008), 167–96.
Cooper, Frederick. *Citizenship Between Empire and Nation: Remaking France and French Africa, 1945–1960* (Princeton, NJ: Princeton University Press, 2014).
Coulson, Andrew. *Tanzania: A Political Economy* (Oxford: Oxford University Press, 2013).
Curtis, Mark. *Unpeople: Britain's Secret Human Rights Abuses* (London: Vintage, 2004).
Dallywater, Lena, Chris Saunders, and Helder Adegar Fonseca (eds.). *Southern African Liberation Movements and the Global Cold War "East": Transnational Activism, 1960–1990* (Oldenbourg: De Gruyter, 2019).
Daly, Samuel Fury Childs. 'Archival Research in Africa', *African Affairs*, 116 (2017), 311–20.
Das Gupta, Amit. 'The Non-Aligned and the German Question', in Nataša Mišković, Harald Fischer-Tiné, and Nada Boškovska (eds.), *The Non-Aligned Movement and the Cold War: Delhi-Bandung-Belgrade* (Oxford: Routledge, 2014), 143–60.

Das Neves Tembe, Joel. '*Uhuru na Kazi*: Recapturing MANU Nationalism Through the Archive', *Kronos*, 39 (2013), 257–79.

Das Neves Tembe, Joel (ed.). *História da luta de libertação nacional* (Maputo: Ministerio dos Combatentes – Direcçao Nacional de Historia, 2014).

Davidson, Basil. *The Black Man's Burden: Africa and the Crisis of the Nation-State* (Oxford: James Currey, 1992).

Dedering, Tilman. '*Ostpolitik* and the Relations Between West Germany and South Africa', in Carole Fink and Bernd Schaefer (eds.), *Ostpolitik, 1969–1974: European and Global Responses* (New York: Cambridge University Press, 2009), 206–31.

Delehanty, Sean. 'From Modernization to Villagization: The World Bank and Ujamaa', *Diplomatic History*, 44 (2020), 289–314.

Derluguian, Georgi. 'The Social Origins of Good and Bad Governance: Re-Interpreting the 1968 Schism in FRELIMO', in Éric Morier-Genoud (ed.), *Sure Road? Nations and Nationalisms in Angola, Guinea-Bissau and Mozambique* (Leiden: Brill, 2012), 79–101.

DeRoche, Andy. *Kenneth Kaunda, the United States and Southern Africa* (London: Bloomsbury, 2016).

Dietrich, Christopher R. W. *Oil Revolution: Anticolonial Elites, Sovereign Rights, and the Economic Culture of Decolonization* (Cambridge: Cambridge University Press, 2017).

Dinani, Husseina. 'Gendering Villagization: Women and Kinship Networks in Colonial and Socialist Lindi', *International Journal of African Historical Studies*, 50 (2017), 275–99.

Dinerman, Alice. *Revolution, Counter-Revolution and Revisionism in Post-Colonial Africa: The Case of FRELIMO, 1975–1994* (London: Routledge, 2006).

Dinkel, Jürgen. *The Non-Aligned Movement: Genesis, Organization and Politics (1927–1992)*, trans. Alex Skinner (Leiden: Brill, 2019).

Dube, Emmanuel M. 'Relations Between Liberation Movements and the OAU', in N. M. Shamuyarira (ed.), *Essays on the Liberation of Southern Africa* (Dar es Salaam: Tanzania Publishing House, 1971), 25–68.

Dzhirkvelov, Ilya. *Secret Servant: My Life with the KGB and the Soviet Elite* (London: Collins, 1987).

Eckert, Andreas. '"We Must Run While Others Walk": African Civil Servants, State Ideologies and Bureaucratic Practices in Tanzania, from the 1950s to the 1970s', in Thomas Bierschenk and Jean-Pierre Olivier de Sardan (eds.), *States at Work: Dynamics of African Bureaucracies* (Boston: Brill, 2014), 205–19.

Elkins, Caroline. 'Looking Beyond Mau Mau: Archiving Violence in the Era of Decolonization', *American Historical Review*, 120 (2015), 852–68.

Ellis, Stephen. 'Writing Histories of Contemporary Africa', *Journal of African History*, 43 (2002), 1–26.

Ellis, Stephen. *External Mission: The ANC in Exile, 1960–1990* (London: Hurst, 2012).

Ellis, Stephen, and Tsepo Sechaba. *Comrades Against Apartheid: The ANC and the South African Communist Party in Exile* (London: James Currey, 1992).

El Shakry, Omnia. '"History Without Documents": The Vexed Archives of Decolonization in the Middle East', *American Historical Review*, 120 (2015), 920–34.

Engel, Ulf. '"I will not recognise East Germany just because Bonn is stupid". Anerkennungsdiplomatie in Tansania, 1964 bis 1965', in Ulrich van der Heyden and Franziska Benger (eds.), *Kalter Krieg in Ostafrika: Die Beziehungen der DDR zu Sansibar und Tansania* (Berlin: Lit Verlag, 2009), 9–30.

Eppler, Erhard. *Not Much Time for the Third World* (London: Oswald Wolff, 1972).

Eppler, Erhard. *Komplettes Stückwerk: Erfahrungen aus fünfzig Jahren Politik* (Frankfurt: Insel Verlag, 1996).

Eppler, Erhard. *Links Leben: Erinnerungen eines Weltkonservativen* (Berlin: Prophyläen, 2015).

Eribo, Festus, and William Jong-Ebot (eds.). *Press Freedom and Communication in Africa* (Trenton, NJ: Africa World Press, 1997).

Fair, Laura. *Reel Pleasures: Cinema Audiences and Entrepreneurs in Twentieth-Century Urban Tanzania* (Athens: Ohio University Press, 2018).

Faringer, Gunilla L. *Press Freedom in Africa* (New York: Praeger, 1991).

Fink, Carole, and Bernd Schaefer (eds.). *Ostpolitik, 1969–1974: European and Global Responses* (New York: Cambridge University Press, 2009).

Fouéré, Marie-Aude. 'Recasting Julius Nyerere in Zanzibar: The Revolution, the Union, and the Enemy of the Nation', *Journal of Eastern African Studies*, 8 (2014), 478–92.

Freije, Vanessa. '"The Emancipation of Media": Latin American Advocacy for a New International Information Order in the 1970s', *Journal of Global History*, 14 (2019), 301–20.

Friedman, Jeremy. *Shadow Cold War: The Sino-Soviet Competition for the Third World* (Chapel Hill: University of North Carolina Press, 2015).

Ganser, Daniele. *NATO's Secret Armies: Operation GLADIO and Terrorism in Western Europe* (London: Frank Cass, 2005).

Garland Mahler, Anne. *From the Tricontinental to the Global South: Race, Radicalism, and Transnational Solidarity* (Durham, NC: Duke University Press, 2018).

Gehrig, Sebastian. 'Reaching Out to the Third World: East Germany's Anti-Apartheid and Socialist Human Rights Campaign', *German History*, 36 (2018), 574–97.
Geiger, Susan. *TANU Women: Gender and the Making of Tanganyikan Nationalism* (Portsmouth, NH: Heinemann, 1997).
Gerits, Frank. '"When the Bull Elephants Fight": Kwame Nkrumah, Non-Alignment, and Pan-Africanism as an Interventionist Ideology in the Global Cold War (1957–66)', *International History Review*, 37 (2015), 951–69.
Getachew, Adom. *Worldmaking After Empire: The Rise and Fall of Self-Determination* (Princeton, NJ: Princeton University Press, 2019).
Ghassany, Harith. *Kwaheri Ukoloni, Kwaheri Uhuru!* (n.p.: self-published, 2010).
Glassman, Jonathon. *War of Words, War of Stones: Racial Thought and Violence in Colonial Zanzibar* (Bloomington: Indiana University Press, 2011).
Gleijeses, Piero. *Conflicting Missions: Havana, Washington and Africa, 1959–1976* (Chapel Hill: University of North Carolina Press, 2002).
Gleijeses, Piero. *Visions of Freedom: Havana, Washington, Pretoria and the Struggle for Southern Africa, 1976–1991* (Chapel Hill: University of North Carolina Press, 2013).
Glukhov, Arkadi. 'The Fateful August of 1968: Hot Summer in Dar es Salaam', in Russian Academy of Sciences Institute of African Studies, *Julius Nyerere: Humanist, Politician, Thinker*, trans. B. G. Petruk (Dar es Salaam: Mkuki na Nyota, 2005), 42–49.
Goebel, Michael. *Anti-Imperial Metropolis: Interwar Paris and the Seeds of Third World Nationalism* (New York: Cambridge University Press, 2015).
Goyens, Tom. *Beer and Revolution: The German Anarchist Movement in New York City, 1880–1914* (Urbana: University of Illinois Press, 2007).
Gray, William Glenn. *Germany's Cold War: The Global Campaign to Isolate East Germany, 1949–1969* (Chapel Hill: University of North Carolina Press, 2003).
Grilli, Matteo. *Nkrumaism and African Nationalism: Ghana's Pan-African Foreign Policy in the Age of Decolonization* (Cham: Palgrave Macmillan, 2017).
Grovogui, Siba N'Zatioula. *Sovereigns, Quasi Sovereigns and Africans: Race and Self-Determination in International Law* (Minneapolis: University of Minnesota Press, 1996).
Gruffydd Jones, Branwen. 'Comradeship, Committed, and Conscious: The Anticolonial Archive Speaks to Our Times', in Shiera El-Malik and Isaac A. Kamola (eds.), *Politics of African Anticolonial Archive* (London: Rowman and Littlefield, 2017), 57–82.

Grundy, Trevor. 'Frene Ginwala, the Lenin Supplement, and the Storm Drains of History', Politics Web, 15 August 2017. politicsweb.co.za/opinion/frene-ginwala-the-lenin-supplement-and-the-storm-d.

Guevara, Ernesto 'Che'. *The African Dream: The Diaries of the Revolutionary War in the Congo*, trans. Patrick Camillier (London: Harvill, 2001).

Hachten, William A. *Muffled Drums: The News Media in Africa* (Ames: Iowa State University Press, 1971).

Harper, Tim. 'Singapore, 1915, and the Birth of the Asian Underground', in Tim Harper and Sunil Amrith (eds.), *Sites of Asian Interaction: Ideas, Networks, and Mobility* (Delhi: Cambridge University Press, 2014), 10–37.

Harper, Tim, and Sunil Amrith (eds.). *Sites of Asian Interaction: Ideas, Networks, and Mobility* (Delhi: Cambridge University Press, 2014).

Hashil, Hashil Seif. *Mimi, Umma Party na Mapinduzi ya Zanzibar* (Paris: DL2A Buluu, 2018).

Hasty, Jennifer. *The Press and Political Culture in Ghana* (Bloomington: Indiana University Press, 2005).

Helleiner, Gerry. *Toward a Better World: Memoirs of a Life in International and Development Economics* (Toronto: University of Toronto Press, 2018).

Hirji, Karim F. (ed.). *Cheche: Reminiscences of a Radical Magazine* (Dar es Salaam: Mkuki na Nyota, 2010).

Holtom, Duncan. 'Reconsidering the Power of the IFIs: Tanzania and the World Bank, 1978–1985', *Review of African Political Economy*, 32 (2005), 549–67.

Hong, Young-Sun. *Cold War Germany, the Third World, and the Global Humanitarian Regime* (New York: Cambridge University Press, 2015).

Hopkins, Raymond F. *Political Roles in a New State: Tanzania's First Decade* (New Haven, CT: Yale University Press, 1971).

Hunter, Emma. 'Jamal, Amir Habib', in Emmanuel A. Akyeampong and Henry Louis Gates, Jr (eds.), *Dictionary of African Biography*, vol. 3 (Oxford: Oxford University Press, 2012), 190–191.

Hunter, Emma. '"Our Common Humanity": Print, Power, and the Colonial Press in Interwar Tanganyika and French Cameroun', *Journal of Global History*, 7 (2012), 279–301.

Hunter, Emma. 'Julius Nyerere', in Steven Casey and Jonathon Wright (eds.), *Mental Maps in the Era of Détente and the End of the Cold War, 1968–91* (Basingstoke: Palgrave Macmillan, 2015), 81–96.

Hunter, Emma. 'Julius Nyerere, the Arusha Declaration, and the Deep Roots of a Contemporary Political Metaphor', in Marie-Aude Fouéré (ed.),

Remembering Julius Nyerere in Tanzania: History, Memory, Legacy (Dar es Salaam: Mkuki na Nyota, 2015), 73–94.

Hunter, Emma. *Political Thought and the Public Sphere in Tanzania: Freedom, Democracy and Citizenship in the Era of Decolonization* (New York: Cambridge University Press, 2015).

Hutchison, Alan. *China's African Revolution* (London: Hutchinson, 1975).

Igreja, Victor. 'Politics of Memory, Decentralisation and Recentralisation in Mozambique', *Journal of Southern African Studies*, 39 (2013), 313–55.

Ingram, Kenneth. *Obote: A Political Biography* (London: Routledge, 1994).

Ivaska, Andrew. *Cultured States: Youth, Gender, and Modern Style in 1960s Dar es Salaam* (Durham, NC: Duke University Press, 2011).

Ivaska, Andrew. 'Movement Youth in a Global Sixties Hub: The Everyday Lives of Transnational Activists in Postcolonial Dar es Salaam', in Richard Ivan Jobs and David M. Pomfret (eds.), *Transnational Histories of Youth in the Twentieth Century* (Basingstoke: Palgrave Macmillan, 2015), 188–210.

Ivaska, Andrew. 'Liberation in Transit: Eduardo Mondlane and Che Guevara in Dar es Salaam', in Martin Klimke, Masha Kirasirova, Mary Nolan, Marilyn Young, and Joanna Waley-Cohen (eds.), *The Routledge Handbook of the Global Sixties: Between Protest and Nation-Building* (London: Routledge, 2018), 27–38.

Jackson, Stephen R. 'China's Third World Policy: The Case of Angola and Mozambique', *China Quarterly*, 142 (1997), 388–422.

Jenks, John. 'Crash Course: The International Press Institute and Journalism Training in Anglophone Africa, 1963–1975', *Media History*, 26 (2020), 508–21.

Jesus, José Manuel Duarte de. *Eduardo Mondlane: Um homem a abater* (Coimbra: Almedina, 2010).

Jesus, José Manuel Duarte de. *A guerra secreta de Salazar em África. Aginter Press: Um rede internacional de contra-subversão e espionagem em Lisboa* (Algragide: Dom Quixote, 2012).

Johnson, Phyllis, and David Martin. *Apartheid Terrorism: The Destabilization Report* (London: Commonwealth Secretariat, 1989).

Judt, Tony, with Timothy Snyder. *Thinking the Twentieth Century* (New York: Penguin, 2012).

Kaiser, Daniel. '"Makers of Bonds and Ties": Transnational Socialisation and National Liberation in Mozambique', *Journal of Southern African Studies*, 43 (2017), 29–48.

Kambona, Oscar S. *Tanzania and the Rule of Law* (London: African News Service, n.d. [1970?]).

Kapuściński, Ryszard. *The Shadow of the Sun: My African Life*, trans. Klara Glowczewska (London: Allen Lane, 2001).

Kasrils, Ronnie. *Armed and Dangerous: From Undercover Struggle to Freedom* (Johannesburg: Jonathan Ball, 1998).

Kassum, Al Noor. *Africa's Winds of Change: Memoirs of an International Tanzanian* (London: IB Tauris, 2007).

Keller, Renata. *Mexico's Cold War: Cuba, the United States, and the Legacy of the Mexican Revolution* (New York: Cambridge University Press, 2015).

Keese, Alexander. 'Just Like in Colonial Times? Administrative Practice and Local Reflections on "Grassroots Neocolonialism" in Autonomous and Postcolonial Dahomey, 1958–65', *Journal of African History*, 60 (2019), 257–76.

Khuri-Makdisi, Ilham. *The Eastern Mediterranean and the Making of Global Radicalism, 1860–1914* (Berkeley: University of California Press, 2010).

Kilian, Werner. *Die Hallstein-Doktrin: Der Diplomatische Krieg zwischen der BRD und der DDR, 1955–1973* (Berlin: Duncker und Humblot, 2001).

Konde, Hadji S. *Press Freedom in Tanzania* (Arusha: Eastern Africa Publications, 1984).

Kondlo, Kwandiwe. *In the Twilight of the Revolution: The Pan-Africanist Congress of Azania (South Africa), 1959–1994* (Basel: Basler Afrika Bibliographien, 2009).

Lal, Priya. 'Self-Reliance and the State: The Multiple Meanings of Development in Early Post-Colonial Tanzania', *Africa*, 82 (2012), 212–34.

Lal, Priya. 'Maoism in Tanzania: Material Connections and Shared Imaginaries', in Alexander C. Cook (ed.), *Mao's Little Red Book: A Global History* (Cambridge: Cambridge University Press, 2014), 96–116.

Lal, Priya. *African Socialism in Postcolonial Tanzania: Between the Village and the World* (New York: Cambridge University Press, 2015).

Lal, Priya. 'African Socialism and the Limits of Global Familyhood: Tanzania and the New International Economic Order in Sub-Saharan Africa', *Humanity*, 6 (2015), 17–31.

Lal, Priya. 'Tanzanian *Ujamaa* in a World of Peripheral Socialisms', in Martin Klimke, Masha Kirasirova, Mary Nolan, Marilyn Young, and Joanna Waley-Cohen (eds.), *The Routledge Handbook of the Global Sixties: Between Protest and Nation-Building* (London: Routledge, 2018), 367–80.

Langland, Victoria. *Speaking of Flowers: Student Movements and the Making and Remembering of 1968 in Military Brazil* (Durham, NC: Duke University Press, 2013).

Larmer, Miles. *Rethinking African Politics: A History of Opposition in Zambia* (Farnham: Ashgate, 2011).

Larmer, Miles. 'Nation-Making at the Border: Zambian Diplomacy in the Democratic Republic of Congo', *Comparative Studies in Society and History*, 61 (2019), 145–75.

Larmer, Miles, and Erik Kennes. 'Rethinking the Katangese Secession', *Journal of Imperial and Commonwealth History*, 42 (2014), 741–61.

Laweki, Lawe. *Mateus Pinho Gwenjere: A Revolutionary Priest* (Wandsbeck: Reach, 2019).

Lawi, Yusufu Qwaray. 'Tanzania's Operation *Vijiji* and Local Ecological Consciousness: The Case of Eastern Iraqwland, 1974–1976', *Journal of African History*, 48 (2007), 69–93.

Laurent, Frederic, and Nina Sutton. *L'Orchestre noir* (Paris: Éditions Stock, 1978).

Levine, Katherine. 'The TANU Ten-House Cell System', in Lionel Cliffe and John Saul (eds.), *Socialism in Tanzania: An Interdisciplinary Reader. Vol 1.: Politics* (Dar es Salaam: East African Publishing House, 1972), 329–37.

Lewis, Su Lin. *Cities in Motion: Urban Life and Cosmopolitanism in Southeast Asia, 1920–1940* (Cambridge: Cambridge University Press, 2016).

Lewis, Su Lin, and Carolien Stolte. 'Other Bandungs: Afro-Asian Internationalisms in the Early Cold War', *Journal of World History*, 30 (2019), 1–19.

Lodge, Tom. *Black Politics in South Africa Since 1945* (London: Longman, 1983).

Lofchie, Michael F. *Zanzibar: Background to Revolution* (Princeton, NJ: Princeton University Press, 1965).

Lopes, Rui. *West Germany and the Portuguese Dictatorship, 1968–1974: Between Cold War and Colonialism* (Basingstoke: Palgrave Macmillan, 2014).

Lorenzini, Sara. 'Globalising Ostpolitik', *Cold War History*, 9 (2009), 223–42.

Lüthi, Lorenz M. 'Non-Alignment, 1946–1965: Its Establishment and Struggle Against Afro-Asianism', *Humanity*, 7 (2016), 201–23.

Lüthi, Lorenz M. 'The Non-Aligned Movement and the Cold War, 1961–1973', *Journal of Cold War Studies*, 18 (2016), 98–147.

MacQueen, Norrie. 'Portugal's First Domino: "Pluricontinentalism" and Colonial War in Guiné-Bissau, 1963–1974', *Contemporary European History*, 8 (1999), 209–30.

Malecela, J. S. 'Some Issues of Development Planning', in Anthony H. Rweyemamu and Bismarck U. Mwansasu (eds.), *Planning in*

Tanzania: Background to Decentralisation (Nairobi: East African Literature Bureau, 1974), 13–21.

Maluwa, Tiyanjana. 'Some Aspects of the Boundary Dispute Between Malawi and Tanzania over Lake Malawi', *Michigan Journal of International Law*, 37 (2016), 351–420.

Mamdani, Mahmood. *Citizen and Subject: Contemporary Africa and the Legacy of Late Colonialism* (Princeton, NJ: Princeton University Press, 1996).

Manghezi, Nadja. *O meu coração está nas mãos de um negro: uma história da vida de Janet Mondlane*, trans. Machado da Graça (Maputo: Imprensa Universitária, 2nd ed., 2001).

Manghezi, Nadja. *The Maputo Connection: The ANC in the World of FRELIMO* (Auckland Park: Jacana, 2009).

Marchesi, Aldo. *Latin America's Radical Left: Rebellion and Cold War in the Global 1960s*, trans. Laura Pérez Carrara (New York: Cambridge University Press, 2018).

Marcum, John A. *Conceiving Mozambique* (Cham: Palgrave Macmillan, 2018).

Mark, James, Péter Apor, Radina Vučetić, and Piotr Osęka. '"We are with you Vietnam": Transnational Solidarities in Socialist Hungary, Poland and Yugoslavia', *Journal of Contemporary History*, 50 (2015), 439–64.

Markle, Seth M. *A Motorcycle on Hell Run: Tanzania, Black Power, and the Uncertain Future of Pan-Africanism, 1964–1974* (East Lansing: Michigan State University Press, 2017).

Martin, David. *General Amin* (London: Faber and Faber, 1974).

Martín Luque, Alba. 'International Shaping of a Nationalist Imagery? Robert van Lierop, Eduardo Mondlane and *A luta continua*', *Afriche e Orienti*, 19 (2017), 115–38.

Martins, Helder. *Porqué Sakrani? Mémorias dum medico duma guerrilha esquecida* (Maputo: Editorial Terceiro Milénio, 2001).

Masha, F. Lwanyantika. *The Story of the Arusha Declaration (1967)* (Mwanza: self-published, 2011).

Matera, Marc. *Black London: The Imperial Metropolis and Decolonization in the Twentieth Century* (Berkeley: University of California Press, 2015).

Mateus, Dalila Cabrita. *PIDE/DGS na guerra colonial, 1961–1974* (Lisbon: Terramar, 2004).

Matthes, Helmut. 'Zur Entwicklung außenpolitischer Grundlagen der Beziehungen zwischen der Deutschen Demokratischen Republik und der Vereinigten Republik Tansania bis Mitte der siebziger Jahre', in Ulrich van der Heyden and Franziska Benger (eds.), *Kalter Krieg in Ostafrika: Die Beziehungen der DDR zu Sansibar und Tansania* (Berlin: Lit Verlag, 2009), 55–97.

Maundi, Mohammed Omar. 'The Role of the Organisation of African Unity in the Liberation Struggle of Southern Africa', in A. J. Temu and Joel das Neves Tembe (eds.), *Southern African Liberation Struggles: Contemporaneous Documents, 1964–1994*, vol. 9 (Dar es Salaam: Mkuki na Nyota, 2014), 381–430.

Mayall, James. 'The Malawi-Tanzania Boundary Dispute', *Journal of Modern African Studies*, 11 (1973), 611–28.

Mazov, Sergey. *A Distant Front in the Cold War: The USSR in West Africa and the Congo, 1956–1964* (Washington, DC: Woodrow Wilson Center Press, 2010).

Mazrui, Ali A. 'Tanzaphilia', *Transition*, 31 (1967), 20–26.

'Mazungumzo kati ya Kingunge Ngombale-Mwiru na Issa Shivji', *Chemchemi*, 2 (2009), 64–77.

Mbembe, Achille. 'The Power of the Archive and Its Limits', in Carolyn Hamilton, Verne Harris, Michèle Pickover, Graeme Reid, Razia Saleh, and Jane Taylor (eds.), *Refiguring the Archive* (Dordrecht: Kluwer, 2002), 19–27.

McCann, Gerard. 'Where was the Afro in Afro-Asian Solidarity? Africa's "Bandung Moment" in 1950s Asia', *Journal of World History*, 30 (2019), 89–123.

McKeon, Nora. 'The African States and the OAU', *International Affairs*, 42 (1966), 390–409.

McMaster, Carolyn. *Malawi: Foreign Policy and Development* (London: Julian Friedman, 1974).

Mëhilli, Elidor. *From Stalin to Mao: Albania and the Socialist World* (Ithaca, NY: Cornell University Press, 2017).

Melchiorre, Luke. '"Under the Thumb of the Party": The Limits of Tanzanian Socialism and the Decline of the Student Left', *Journal of Southern African Studies*, 46 (2020), 635–54.

Mkapa, Benjamin William. *My Life, My Purpose: A Tanzanian President Remembers* (Dar es Salaam: Mkuki na Nyota, 2019).

Mihyo, Pascal. 'The Struggle for Workers' Control in Tanzania', *Review of African Political Economy*, 4 (1975), 62–84.

Milford, Ismay. 'Federation, Partnership, and the Chronologies of Space in 1950s East and Central Africa', *Historical Journal*, 63 (2020), 1325–48.

Miller, Jamie. *An African Volk: The Apartheid States and Its Struggle for Survival* (Oxford: Oxford University Press, 2016).

Miller, Robert A. 'Elite Formation in Africa: Class, Culture, and Coherence', *Journal of Modern African Studies*, 12 (1974), 521–42.

Mills, Sean. *The Empire Within: Postcolonial Thought and Political Activism in Sixties Montreal* (Montreal: McGill-Queen's University Press, 2010).

Mišković, Nataša, Harald Fischer-Tiné, and Nada Boškovska (eds.). *The Non-Aligned Movement and the Cold War: Delhi-Bandung-Belgrade* (Oxford: Routledge, 2014).

Mitchell, Nancy. *Jimmy Carter in Africa: Race and the Cold War* (Washington, DC: Woodrow Wilson Center Press, 2016).

Mohamed, Toibibou Ali. 'Les Comoriens de Zanzibar durant la "Révolution Okello" (1964–1972)', *Journal des africanistes*, 76 (2006), 137–54.

Mohiddin, Ahmed. 'Ujamaa na Kujitegemea', *Mawazo* (December 1967), 24–38.

Mokhtefi, Elaine. *Algiers, Third World Capital: Freedom Fighters, Revolutionaries, Black Panthers* (London: Verso, 2018).

Molony, Thomas. *Nyerere: The Early Years* (Woodbridge: James Currey, 2014).

Mondlane, Eduardo. *The Struggle for Mozambique* (Baltimore, MD: Penguin, 1969).

Monson, Jamie. *Africa's Freedom Railway: How a Chinese Development Project Changed Lives and Livelihoods in Tanzania* (Bloomington: Indiana University Press, 2009).

Moorman, Marissa J. *Powerful Frequencies: Radio, State Power, and the Cold War in Angola, 1931–2002* (Athens: Ohio University Press, 2019).

Morier-Genoud, Éric. *Catholicism and the Making of Politics in Central Mozambique, 1940–1986* (Rochester, NY: University of Rochester Press, 2019).

Moskowitz, Kara. *Seeing Like a Citizen: Decolonization, Development, and the Making of Kenya, 1945–1980* (Athens: Ohio University Press, 2019).

Mtei, Edwin. *From Goatherd to Governor: The Autobiography of Edwin Mtei* (Dar es Salaam: Mkuki na Nyota, 2009).

Müller-Enbergs, Helmut, Jan Wielgohs, and Dieter Hoffmann (eds.). *Wer war wer in der DDR? Ein biographisches Lexikon* (Berlin: Ch. Links Verlag, 2000).

Musiba, A. E. *Kufa na Kupona* (Dar es Salaam: Mkuki na Nyota, 2018 [1974]).

Mwakawago, Daudi. 'Dar es Salaam: Two Urban Campaigns', in Lionel Cliffe (ed.), *One-Party Democracy: The 1965 Tanzania General Elections* (Nairobi: East African Publishing House, 1967).

Mwakikagile, Godfrey. *The Union of Tanganyika and Zanzibar: Product of the Cold War?* (Pretoria: New Africa Press, 2008).

Mwapachu, Juma Volter. 'Industrial Labour Protest in Tanzania: An Analysis of Influential Variables', *African Review*, 3 (1973), 383–401.

Mytton, Graham. *Mass Communication in Africa* (London: Edward Arnold, 1983).

Namikas, Lise. *Battleground Africa: Cold War in the Congo, 1961–1965* (Washington, DC: Woodrow Wilson Center Press, 2013).
National Union of Mozambican Students. 'The Mozambican Revolution Betrayed', *African Historical Studies*, 3 (1970), 169–80.
Ncomo, Barnabé Lucas. *Uria Simango: um homem, uma causa* (Maputo: Edições Novafrica, 2004).
Ndelana, Lopes Tembe. *From UDENAMO to FRELIMO and Mozambican Diplomacy* (Terra Alta, WV: Headline Books, 2016).
Ndlovu, Sifiso Mxolisi. 'The ANC's Diplomacy and International Relations', in SADET, *The Road to Democracy in South Africa, vol. 2 (1970–1980)* (Cape Town: UNISA Press, 2006), 615–67.
Ngombale-Mwiru, Kingunge. 'Utangulizi: Ujio na Uzito wa Miongozo Miwili', in Bashiru Ally, Saida Yahya-Othman, and Issa Shivji (eds.), *Miongozo Miwili na Kutunguliwa kwa Azimio la Arusha* (Dar es Salaam: Chuo Kikuu cha Dar es Salaam, 2013), 12–26.
Ng'wanakilala, Nkwabi. *Mass Communication and Development of Socialism in Tanzania* (Dar es Salaam: Tanzania Publishing House, 1981).
Nicholas, Claire. 'Des corps connectés: les Ghana Young Pioneers, tête de proue de la mondialisation de Nkrumahisme (1960–1966)', *Politique africaine*, 147 (2017), 87–107.
Nkrumah, Kwame. *The African Journalist* (Dar es Salaam: Tanzania Publishers, n.d. [1965–66]).
Nkulunguila, Josefina Daniel. 'Frente de Cabo Delgado', in Joel das Neves Tembe (ed.), *História da luta de libertação nacional* (Maputo: Ministerio dos Combatentes – Direcçao Nacional de Historia, 2014), 211–448.
Niedhart, Gottfried. 'Ostpolitik: Transformation Through Communication and the Quest for Peaceful Change', *Journal of Cold War Studies*, 18 (2016), 14–59.
Nyamnjoh, Francis B. *Africa's Media: Democracy and the Politics of Belonging* (London: Zed, 2005).
Nyerere, Julius K. *Freedom and Unity: A Selection from Writings and Speeches, 1952–65* (Dar es Salaam: Oxford University Press, 1966).
Nyerere, Julius K. *Freedom and Socialism: A Selection from Writings and Speeches, 1965–1967* (Dar es Salaam: Oxford University Press, 1968).
Nyerere, Julius K. *Argue Don't Shout: An Official Guide to Foreign Policy by the President* (Dar es Salaam: Government Printer, 1969).
Nyerere, Julius K. *Freedom and Development: A Selection from Writings and Speeches, 1968–1973* (Dar es Salaam: Oxford University Press, 1973).
Nyerere, Julius K. *The Arusha Declaration: Ten Years After* (Dar es Salaam: Government Printer, 1977).

Obote, Milton A. *Myths and Realities: Letter to a London Friend* (Kampala: Consolidated Printers, 1968).

Ochieng, Philip. *I Accuse the Press: An Insider's View of Media and Politics in Africa* (Nairobi: Initiatives, 1992).

Ochonu, Moses E. 'Elusive History: Fractured Archives, Politicized Orality, and Sensing the Postcolonial Past', *History in Africa*, 42 (2015), 287–98.

Onah, Emmanuel, Chinwe Okoyeuzu, and Chibuike Uche. 'The Nationalisation of British Banks in Post-Colonial Tanzania', *Business History* (forthcoming).

Opello Jr, Walter C. 'Pluralism and Elite Conflict in an Independence Movement: FRELIMO in the 1960s', *Journal of Southern African Studies*, 2 (1975), 66–82.

Oreh, Onuma O. '"Developmental Journalism" and Press Freedom: An African View Point', *Gazette*, 24 (1978), 36–40.

Osei-Opare, Nana. 'Uneasy Comrades: Postcolonial Statecraft, Race, and Citizenship. Ghana-Soviet Relations, 1957–1966', *Journal of West African History*, 5 (2019), 85–111.

Othman, Haroub (ed.). *Babu: I Saw the Future and It Works. Essays Celebrating the Life of Comrade Abdulrahman Mohamed Babu* (Dar es Salaam: E&D, 2001).

Pallotti, Arrigo. 'Post-Colonial Nation-Building and Southern African Liberation: Tanzania and the Break of Diplomatic Relations with the United Kingdom, 1965–1968', *African Historical Review*, 41 (2009), 60–84.

Panzer, Michael G. 'The Pedagogy of Revolution: Youth, Generational Conflict, and Education in the Development of Mozambican Nationalism and the State, 1962–1970', *Journal of Southern African Studies*, 35 (2009), 803–20.

Parsons, Timothy H. *The 1964 Army Mutinies and the Making of Modern East Africa* (Westport, CT: Praeger, 2003).

Pearce, Justin. 'Global Ideologies, Local Politics: The Cold War as Seen from Central Africa', *Journal of Southern African Studies*, 43 (2017), 13–27.

Peterson, Derek R., Emma Hunter, and Stephanie Newell (eds.). *African Print Cultures: Newspapers and Their Publics in the Twentieth Century* (Ann Arbor: University of Michigan Press, 2016).

Piccini, Jon. *Transnational Protest, Australia and the 1960s: Global Radicals* (London: Palgrave Macmillan, 2016).

Pratt, Cranford. *The Critical Phase in Tanzania, 1945–1968* (Cambridge: Cambridge University Press, 1976).

Pratt, Cranford. 'Democracy and Socialism in Tanzania', *Canadian Journal of African Studies*, 12 (1978), 407–28.

Putnam, Lara. 'The Transnational and the Text-Searchable: Digitized Sources and the Shadows They Cast', *American Historical Review*, 121 (2016), 377–402.

Roberts, George. 'The Uganda-Tanzania War, the Fall of Idi Amin, and the Failure of African Diplomacy, 1978–1979', *Journal of Eastern African Studies*, 8 (2014), 692–709.

Roberts, George. 'Press, Propaganda and the German Democratic Republic's Search for Recognition in Tanzania, 1964–72', in Philip Muehlenbeck and Natalia Telepneva (eds.), *Warsaw Pact Intervention in the Third World: Aid and Influence in the Cold War* (London: IB Tauris, 2018), 148–72.

Roberts, Priscilla, and John M. Carroll (eds.). *Hong Kong in the Cold War* (Hong Kong: Hong Kong University Press, 2016).

Rweyemamu, Justinian. *Underdevelopment and Industrialization in Tanzania: A Study of Perverse Capitalist Industrial Development* (Nairobi: Oxford University Press, 1973).

Sackeyfio-Lenoch, Naarborko. 'The Ghana Trades Union Congress and the Politics of International Labor Alliances, 1957–1971', *International Review of Social History*, 62 (2017), 191–213.

Said, Mohammed. *The Life and Time of Abdulwahid Sykes (1924–1968): The Untold Story of the Muslim Struggle Against British Colonialism in Tanganyika* (London: Minerva Press, 1998).

Sanders, Ethan R. 'Conceiving the Tanganyika-Zanzibar Union in the Midst of the Cold War', *African Review*, 41 (2014), 35–70.

Saul, John S. *The State and Revolution in East Africa* (London: Heinemann, 1979).

Saunders, Chris. 'SWAPO, Namibia's Liberation Struggle and the Organisation of African Unity's Liberation Committee', *South African Historical Journal*, 70 (2018), 152–67.

Schilling, Britta. *Postcolonial Germany: Memories of Empire in a Decolonized Nation* (Oxford: Oxford University Press, 2014).

Schler, Lynn. 'Dilemmas of Postcolonial Diplomacy: Zambia, Kenneth Kaunda, and the Middle East Crisis', *Journal of African History*, 59 (2018), 97–119.

Schmidt, Elizabeth. *Cold War and Decolonization in Guinea, 1946–1958* (Athens: Ohio University Press, 2007).

Schmidt, Heide-Irene. 'Pushed to the Front: The Foreign Assistance Policy of the Federal Republic of Germany, 1958–1971', *Contemporary European History*, 12 (2003), 473–507.

Schneider, Leander. *Government of Development: Peasants and Politicians in Postcolonial Tanzania* (Bloomington: Indiana University Press, 2014).
Schneidman, Witney W. *Engaging Africa: Washington and the Fall of Portugal's Colonial Empire* (Lanham, MD: University of America Press, 2004).
Schrafstetter, Susanna. 'A Nazi Diplomat Turned Apologist for Apartheid: Gustav Sonnenhol, *Vergangenheitsbewältigung* and West German Foreign Policy Towards South Africa', *German History*, 28 (2010), 44–66.
Scott, James C. *Seeing Like a State: How Certain Schemes to Improve the Human Condition Have Failed* (New Haven, CT: Yale University Press, 1998).
Shamuyarira, N. M. 'The Lusaka Manifesto on Southern Africa', *African Review*, 1 (1971), 67–78.
Shipanga, Andreas, with Sue Armstrong. *In Search of Freedom* (Gibraltar: Ashanti, 1989).
Shityuwete, Helao. *Never Follow the Wolf: The Autobiography of a Namibian Freedom Fighter* (London: Kliptown, 1990).
Shivji, Issa G. *Class Struggles in Tanzania* (London: Heinemann, 1976).
Shivji, Issa G. 'The Democracy Debate in Africa: Tanzania', *Review of African Political Economy*, 18 (1991), 79–91.
Shivji, Issa G. 'The Rule of Law and *Ujamaa* in the Ideological Formation of Tanzania', *Social and Legal Studies*, 4 (1995), 147–74.
Shivji, Issa G. *Pan-Africanism or Pragmatism? Lessons of the Tanganyika-Zanzibar Union* (Dar es Salaam: Mkuki na Nyota, 2008).
Shivji, Issa G., Saida-Yahya Othman, and Ng'wanza Kamata. *Development as Rebellion – Julius Nyerere: A Biography* (Dar es Salaam: Mkuki na Nyota, 2020).
Short, Philip. *Banda* (London: Routledge, 1974).
Skinner, Kate. 'West Africa's First Coup: Neo-Colonial and Pan-African Projects in Togo's "Shadow Archives"', *African Studies Review*, 63 (2020), 375–98.
Slobodian, Quinn. *Foreign Front: Third World Politics in Sixties West Germany* (Durham, NC: Duke University Press, 2012).
Slonecker, Blake. *A New Dawn for the New Left: Liberation News Service, Montague Farm, and the Long Sixties* (New York: Palgrave Macmillan, 2012).
Smith, William Edgett. *Nyerere of Tanzania* (London: Victor Gollancz, 1973).
Souto, Amélia Neves de. 'Memory and Identity in the History of Frelimo: Some Research Themes', *Kronos*, 39 (2013), 280–96.

Spacek, Peter. 'Die Anfänge in Sansibar und Dar es Salaam', in Ulrich van der Heyden and Franziska Benger (eds.), *Kalter Krieg in Ostafrika: Die Beziehungen der DDR zu Sansibar und Tansania* (Berlin: Lit Verlag, 2009), 169–83.

Speich, Daniel. 'The Kenyan Style of "African Socialism": Developmental Knowledge Claims and the Explanatory Limits of the Cold War', *Diplomatic History*, 33 (2009), 449–66.

Speller, Ian. 'An African Cuba? Britain and the Zanzibar Revolution, 1964', *Journal of Imperial and Commonwealth History*, 35 (2007), 283–302.

Stiff, Peter. *The Silent War: South African Recce Operations, 1969–1994* (Alberton: Galago, 1999).

Straker, Jay. *Youth, Nationalism, and the Guinean Revolution* (Bloomington: Indiana University Press, 2009).

Stur, Heather Marie. *Saigon at War: South Vietnam and the Global Sixties* (Cambridge: Cambridge University Press, 2020).

Sturmer, Martin. *The Media History of Tanzania* (Mtwara: Ndanda Mission Press, 1998).

Sun, Jodie Yuzhou. '"Now the Cry Was Communism": The Cold War and Kenya's Relations with China, 1964–70', *Cold War History*, 20 (2020), 39–58.

Suri, Jeremi. 'The Promises and Failure of "Developed Socialism": The Soviet "Thaw" and the Crucible of the Prague Spring, 1964–1972', *Contemporary European History*, 15 (2006), 133–58.

Suriano, Maria. 'Transnational Music Collaborations, Affective Networks and Everyday Practices of Convivial Solidarity in *Ujamaa* Dar es Salaam', *Journal of Southern African Studies*, 46 (2020), 985–1008.

Svendsen, K. E. 'Development Administration and Socialist Strategy: Tanzania After Mwongozo', in Anthony H. Rweyemamu and Bismarck U. Mwansasu (eds.), *Planning in Tanzania: Background to Decentralisation* (Nairobi: East African Literature Bureau, 1974) 23–44.

Swift, Charles R. *Dar Days: The Early Years in Tanzania* (Lanham, MD: University of America Press, 2002).

Tague, Joanna T. *Displaced Mozambicans in Postcolonial Tanzania: Refugee Power, Mobility, Education, and Rural Development* (London: Routledge 2018).

Tanganyika African National Union. *Tanzania: Party Guidelines. Mwongozo wa TANU* (Richmond, BC: LSM Information Center, 1973).

'Tanzania: Soviet Views on the Arusha Programme', *Mizan*, 9 (1967), 197–201.

Tarimo, Elias C. J., and Neville Z. Reuben. 'Tanzania's Solidarity with South Africa's Liberation', in SADET, *The Road to Democracy in South*

Africa, vol. 5: African Solidarity, Part 1 (Pretoria: UNISA Press, 2013), 201–46.

Telepneva, Natalia. 'Mediators of Liberation: Eastern-Bloc Officials, Mozambican Diplomacy and the Origins of Soviet Support for FRELIMO, 1958–1965', *Journal of Southern African Studies*, 43 (2017), 67–81.

Terretta, Meredith. 'Cameroonian Nationalists Go Global: From Forest *Maquis* to a Pan-African Accra', *Journal of African History*, 51 (2010), 189–212.

Thoden van Velzen, H. U. E. , and J. J. Sterkenburg. 'The Party Supreme', *Kroniek van Afrika*, 1 (1969), 65–88.

Thomson, J. B. *Words of Passage: A Journalist Looks Back* (n.p.: Xlibris, 2012).

Tordoff, William. *Government and Politics in Tanzania* (Nairobi: East African Publishing House, 1967).

Tordoff, William, and Ali A. Mazrui. 'The Left and the Super-Left in Tanzania', *Journal of Modern African Studies*, 10 (1972), 427–45.

Triplett, George W. 'Zanzibar: The Politics of Revolutionary Inequality', *Journal of Modern African Studies*, 9 (1971), 612–17.

Tripp, Aili Mari. *Changing the Rules: The Politics of Liberalization and the Urban Informal Economy in Tanzania* (Berkeley: University of California Press, 1997).

Turok, Ben. *Nothing but the Truth: Behind the ANC's Struggle Politics* (Johannesburg: Jonathan Ball, 2003).

United Republic of Tanzania. *Arusha Declaration: Answers to Questions* (Dar es Salaam: Government Printer, 1967).

Vaughan, Chris. 'The Politics of Regionalism and Federation in East Africa, 1958–1964', *Historical Journal*, 62 (2019), 519–40.

Vieira, Sérgio. *Participei, por isso testemunho* (Maputo: Editorial Ndijira, 2010).

Vitalis, Robert. 'The Midnight Ride of Kwame Nkrumah and Other Fables of Bandung (Ban-Doong)', *Humanity*, 4 (2013), 261–88.

Vu, Tuong. *Vietnam's Communist Revolution: The Power and Limits of Ideology* (New York: Cambridge University Press, 2017).

Wakati, David. 'Radio Tanzania Dar es Salaam', in George Wedell (ed.), *Making Broadcasting Useful: The African Experience. The Development of Radio and Television in Africa in the 1980s* (Manchester: Manchester University Press, 1986), 212–30.

Wallerstein, Immanuel. 'Left and Right in Africa', *Journal of Modern African Studies*, 9 (1971), 1–10.

Westad, Odd Arne. *The Global Cold War: Third World Interventions and the Making of Our Times* (Cambridge: Cambridge University Press, 2005).

White, Luise. *Speaking with Vampires: Rumor and History in Colonial Africa* (Berkeley: University of California Press, 2000).
White, Luise. *The Assassination of Herbert Chitepo: Texts and Politics in Zimbabwe* (Bloomington: Indiana University Press, 2003).
White, Luise. 'Hodgepodge Historiography: Documents, Itineraries, and the Absence of Archives', *History in Africa*, 42 (2015), 309–18.
White, Luise, and Miles Larmer. 'Introduction: Mobile Soldiers and the Un-National Liberation of Southern Africa', *Journal of Southern African Studies*, 40 (2014), 1271–74.
Wilcox, Dennis L. *Mass Media in Black Africa: Philosophy and Control* (New York: Praeger, 1975).
Wilder, Gary. *Freedom Time: Negritude, Decolonization and the Future of the World* (Durham, NC: Duke University Press, 2015).
Williams, Christian. *National Liberation in Post-Colonial Southern Africa: An Ethnographic History of SWAPO's Exile Camps* (Cambridge: Cambridge University Press, 2015).
Wilson, Amrit. *US Foreign Policy and Revolution: The Creation of Tanzania* (London: Pluto, 1989).
Wilson, Amrit. *The Threat of Liberation: Imperialism and Revolution in Zanzibar* (London: Pluto, 2013).
Wolfers, Michael. *Politics in the Organization of African Unity* (London: Methuen, 1976).
Yihun, Belete Belachew. 'Ethiopian Foreign Policy and the Ogaden War: The Shift from "Containment" to "Destabilization", 1977–1991', *Journal of Eastern African Studies*, 8 (2014), 677–91.
Yihun, Belete Belachew. 'Ethiopia's Troubled Relations with the Sudan, 1956–1983', *International Journal of Ethiopian Studies*, 10 (2016), 67–88.
Yordanov, Radoslav A. *The Soviet Union and the Horn of Africa During the Cold War* (Lexington, MD: Lexington, 2016).
Young, Alden. *Transforming Sudan: Decolonization, Economic Development, and State Formation* (Cambridge: Cambridge University Press, 2018).
Young, Crawford. *The Postcolonial State in Africa: Fifty Years of Independence, 1960–2010* (Madison: University of Wisconsin Press, 2012).
Zolov, Eric. *The Last Good Neighbor: Mexico in the Global Sixties* (Durham, NC: Duke University Press, 2020).

Unpublished Theses and Papers

Altorfer-Ong, Alicia N. 'Old Comrades and New Brothers: A Historical Re-Examination of the Sino-Zanzibari and Sino-Tanzania Bilateral Relationships', PhD diss. (London School of Economics, 2014).

Bodie, George. 'Global GDR? Sovereignty, Legitimacy and Decolonization in the German Democratic Republic, 1960–1989', PhD diss. (University College London, 2019).

Brennan, James R. 'Intelligence and Security: Revolution, Espionage, and the Cold War in Tanzania', unpublished paper in author's possession.

Brennan, James R. 'Debating the Guidelines: Literacy, Text, and Socratic Socialism in 1970s Tanzania', unpublished paper presented at the African Studies Workshop, University of Chicago (2014).

Chachage, Chambi. 'A Capitalizing City: Dar es Salaam and the Emergence of an Entrepreneurial Elite (c.1862–2015)', PhD diss. (Harvard University, 2018).

Hartmann, Jeannette. 'Development Policy-Making in Tanzania: A Critique of Sociological Interpretations', PhD diss. (University of Hull, 1983).

Hunter, Emma. 'British Tanzaphilia, 1961–1972', MA diss. (University of Cambridge, 2004).

LeBlanc, Zoe. 'Circulating Anti-Colonial Cairo: Decolonizing News Media and the Making of the Third World in Egypt, 1952–78', PhD diss. (Vanderbilt University, 2019).

Lissoni, Arianna. 'The South African Liberation Movements in Exile, c.1945–1970', PhD diss. (School of Oriental and African Studies, London, 2008).

Mytton, Graham. 'The Role of the Mass Media in Nation-Building in Tanzania', PhD diss. (University of Manchester, 1971).

Niblock, Timothy. 'Aid and Foreign Policy in Tanzania, 1961–68', PhD diss. (University of Sussex, 1971).

Rajab, Ahmed. 'Maisha na nyakati za Abdulla Kassim Hanga', unpublished paper presented at the Zanzibar Institute for Research and Public Policy (2016).

Roberts, George. 'Politics, Decolonization, and the Cold War in Dar es Salaam, c.1965–72', PhD diss. (University of Warwick, 2016).

Swagler, Matthew. 'Youth Radicalism in Senegal and Congo-Brazzaville, 1958–1974', PhD diss. (Columbia University, 2017).

Telepneva, Natalia. 'Our Sacred Duty: The Soviet Union, the Liberation Movements in the Portuguese Colonies, and the Cold War, 1961–1975', PhD diss. (London School of Economics, 2015).

Index

ADN (*Allgemeiner Deutscher Nachrichtendienst, General German News Agency*), 123, 210
African Bookshop, 178
African National Congress (ANC)
 condemns Hastings Banda, 190
 criticises Lusaka Manifesto, 171
 criticises Stokely Carmichael, 142
 Frene Ginwala, 224, 229
 Morogoro Conference, 170
 office in Dar es Salaam, 141, 156
 relations with GDR, 103
 relocates headquarters, 39
 treason trial in Tanzania, 243–44
African socialism. *See ujamaa*
African-American Institute, 149
Africanisation, 37, 74–75, 81, 91, 93, 209, 222, 231, 241
Afriroots, 286
Afro-Shirazi Party (ASP)
 creation of CCM, 269
 relations with TANU, 41–42
 rivalry with ZNP, 35
 youth wing, 245
 Zanzibar Revolution, 33, 36
Aga Khan, 222
Aginter Press, 166
Aldridge, Leo Clinton. *See* Milas, Leo
Algeria, 5, 38, 53, 78, 283
American Committee on Africa, 156
Amin, Idi, 230, 251, 252, 270–71, 278
Amin, Samir, 197
Anangisye, Eli, 91, 96, 242
archives, 16–20, 104
Arusha Declaration
 announcement of, 66
 comparison with *Mwongozo*, 271
 consequences for press, 217
 criticised by Abeid Karume, 265
 Eastern Bloc views on, 110–11
 leadership code, 85, 92–94
 nationalisations, 86–88
 preparation of, 82–86
 scholarship on, 66–67
 Western views on, 89
Asian Association, 71
Asian Socialist Conference, 213
Asians, 37, 75, 143–44, 159, 241, 260
Australia, 52

Babu, Abdulrahman Mohammed
 'Pressman's Commentary' column in *Nationalist*, 76, 78, 81, 173, 186, 193, 213, 215, 221, 223
 and Julius Nyerere, 90–91, 239–40, 266–68
 arrest and imprisonment, 267–68
 Arusha Declaration, 88, 89–91
 as minister for lands, settler, and water development, 94
 as minister of health, 90
 at Palm Beach Hotel, 53
 background, 34
 dismissed from cabinet, 264, 265
 in Directorate of Development and Planning, 41, 72
 Mwongozo, 255
 relations with China, 34, 49–50, 282
 relations with Eastern Bloc, 76
 relations with GDR, 36, 48, 77, 90, 104, 105, 108, 111
 relations with Soviet Union, 48
 rumour, 59, 81
 Tanganyika-Zanzibar union, 42, 48
 Umma Party, 258
 views on economic policy, 75–76, 89–91, 239–40, 263
 views on press freedom, 218
 Zanzibar Revolution, 35, 42
Babu, Ashura, 268

318

Index

Bahr, Egon, 115
Banda, Hastings, 187–92, 250
Bank of Tanzania, 71, 86, 87
Baraka, Amiri, 268
Barongo, Edward, 83
Barre, Siad, 124, 271
Beira, Pamela, 152
Belgium, 44, 61
Ben Bella, Ahmed, 28, 78, 82, 173
Bgoya, Walter, 144
Biafra, 185–86, 193
Bomani, Paul
   and Julius Nyerere, 72
   as minister for economic affairs and planning, 72, 94
   as minister of commerce and cooperatives, 90
   background and education, 71
   dismissed from cabinet, 264, 265
   in parliament, 95
   Mwongozo, 255
   relations with West, 282
   views on 'German question', 105
   views on Arusha Declaration, 88
   views on nationalisation of buildings, 260
Brandt, Willy
   and Julius Nyerere, 127–28, 129, 131
   as foreign minister, 115
   criticism in Tanzania, 129, 130
   Ostpolitik, 115, 129
   Third World development, 126–27
Britain
   break in relations with Tanzania, 47, 84
   complaints about rumour, 60
   concerns about China, 50
   intervention in Tanganyikan mutiny, 38
   involvement in coup in Uganda, 252
   propaganda,
   response to Arusha Declaration, 89
   sale of arms to South Africa, 247–49
   Tanganyika-Zanzibar union, 42
British Broadcasting Corporation (BBC), 207
British Council, 55
Bryceson, Derek, 64, 71
   as minister for agriculture and cooperatives, 94
   background and education, 71
   dismissed from cabinet, 264, 265
   rumoured resignation from cabinet, 260
   views on Arusha Declaration, 88
buildings, nationalisation of, 259–60, 262
Bulgaria, 119
Burma, 4
Burns, John F., 179, 181
Butzke, Eric, 124, 132

Cabral, Amílcar, 249, 254
Cambodia, 124
Canada, 52, 122
Canton Restaurant, 54, 147, 178, 213
Carlucci, Frank, 45
Carmichael, Stokely, 142
Castle, Barbara, 212, 214
Castro, Fidel, 85, 153, 229
Central African Republic, 78
Central Intelligence Agency (CIA), 34, 60–61, 79, 80, 149, 162, 211
Četeka, 210
Chama cha Mapinduzi (Party of the Revolution, CCM), 17, 170, 269
Chande, Andy, 227, 229
Chesham, Marion, 95, 220
China
   activities in Dar es Salaam, 54, 64
   connections to *Nationalist*, 213
   influence on Tanzanian politics, 241, 258
   influence on TYL, 176–77
   propaganda, 55, 100, 107, 120, 178, 179–80, 215–16
   relations with COREMO, 148
   relations with FRELIMO, 147–48, 154
   relations with Kenya, 178–79
   relations with Malawi, 189
   relations with Tanzania, 49–50, 122, 226, 275
   relations with Third World, 49
   relations with Zanzibar, 36
   support for liberation movements, 141
   Tanganyika-Zanzibar union, 48
   TAZARA railway, 50, 239, 275
   Western concerns about, 50–51, 117

Index

Chipembere, Henry, 188, 191, 192
Chisiza, Yatuta, 187, 188, 189, 192
Chitepo, Herbert, 140, 163
Chiume, Kanyama, 187, 188, 191, 192
Chogga, F. K., 242
Christian Democratic Union (*Christlich Demokratische Union*, CDU), 115
Christie, Iain, 225
cities, 3–10, 285
Cold War
 in Dar es Salaam, 6–7
 political culture, 8–9, 45–46
 problem of geopolitical and ideological labels, 19
 propaganda, 55–57
 Tanzanian perspectives of, 280–81
Commonwealth, 46, 180, 248, 250–51, 255
Congo-Brazzaville, 194
Congo-Leopoldville, 8, 29, 43–44, 45, 61, 281
COREMO *(Comité Revolucionário de Moçambique*, Mozambique Revolutionary Committee), 148, 168
Criminal Investigation Department (CID), 164, 167, 170
Cuba, 34, 44, 53, 85, 178, 227
Czechoslovakia
 letter plot, 44
 relations with Dennis Phombeah, 111
 relations with FRELIMO, 148
 relations with FRG, 119
 relations with Tanzania, 49
 Warsaw Pact invasion, 183–87

Daily Nation, 222, 224
Daily News, 232–33
Dar es Salaam, 6
 bars and restaurants in, 53–54
 bombings in, 269–70
 capital relocated to Dodoma, 283
 contemporary perspectives, 285–86
 demonstrations in, 44, 46–47, 82, 184, 187, 249
 elections in, 64
 embassies in, 52–53, 178
 espionage in, 60–64, 271
 historiography, 9–10
 hosts Sixth Pan-African Congress, 284
 liberation movements in, 7, 137–45
 newspapers in, 208
 official receptions, 53
 population, 9
 propaganda in, 55–57, 215–16
 radical literature in, 177–78
 rumour in, 2, 57–60, 259, 267
Davies, Angela, 197
decentralisation, 264
decolonisation, 11
demonstrations
 invasion of Czechoslovakia, 184
 invasion of Guinea, 249
 Rhodesia's UDI, 46–47
 threats from Malawi, 187
 war in Vietnam, 182–83
 Western intervention in Congo-Leopoldville, 44
Dodoma, 248, 283
dos Santos, Marcelino, 148, 150, 152, 158, 164, 168
Douglas-Home, Alec, 247
Dubček, Alexander, 183

East African Common Services Organisation, 71
East African Community (EAC), 29–30, 252, 255, 278
East African Federation, 29, 42
East African Standard Group, 209
East Germany. *See* German Democratic Republic (GDR)
Edinburgh, University of, 69
Egypt, 5, 62, 76, 124
elite, 13–14
embassies, 52–53, 62
Eppler, Erhard, 127, 129, 130–31, 194
espionage, 60–64, 271

Fanon, Frantz, 177
Federal Republic of Germany (FRG)
 Anerkennungsdiplomatie in Tanzania, 105–7
 complaints about GDR propaganda, 109
 complaints about Tanzanian press, 228
 embassy in Dar es Salaam, 52
 global rivalry with GDR, 102–4
 Ostpolitik, 115–18, 126–27, 129

(FRG) (cont.)
  relations with Tanzania, 84, 128, 129–31
  Third World development policy, 126–27
film, 56, 179
Ford Foundation, 149, 162, 221
France, 52, 254
Fredericks, Wayne, 146, 162
FRELIMO (*Frente de Libertação de Moçambique*, Mozambique Liberation Front)
  bombing of offices, 249
  historiography, 154, 169
  Mozambique Institute, 146, 149, 155, 160, 162, 168
  OAU Liberation Committee, 139
  origins, 146
  relations with China, 147–48
  relations with Czechoslovakia, 148
  relations with FRG, 130
  relations with GDR, 103, 125, 148
  relations with Malawi, 189, 190
  relations with Soviet Union, 147–48
  relations with United States, 148–49
  Special Congress (1968), 157–58
  splits inside, 150–54
  students, 152–53, 155
  views on *Mwongozo*, 257
  violence at offices, 156
  war against Portugal, 44
Friendship Textile Factory, 154

Gamba, Willy, 273, 285
German Democratic Republic (GDR)
  'publicity work', 107–8, 111
  All-African Initiative Committee, 123
  Anerkennungsdiplomatie in Tanzania, 105–7
  global rivalry with FRG, 102–4
  interventions in Tanzanian politics, 111–14
  propaganda, 100, 125
  relations with FRELIMO, 148
  relations with Oscar Kambona, 95
  relations with Tanzania, 109–10, 120, 124–25, 131
  relations with Zanzibar, 36, 104–5, 106, 125
  response to Arusha Declaration, 110–11
  response to *Ostpolitik* in Tanzania, 120
  Tanganyika-Zanzibar union, 48
German Social Democratic Party (*Sozialdemocratische Partei Deutschlands*, SPD), 115, 126, 132
Ghana, 5, 63, 79–80, 113, 139, 146, 281
Ginwala, Frene
  appointed *Standard* editor, 224–25
  background, 140, 224–25
  clashes with diplomats, 227
  criticism of, 226, 229
  dismissed as *Standard* editor, 230–31
  rebuked by Nyerere, 228
  treason trial, 244
Goethe Institute, 55
Gordimer, Nadine, 275
Gordon, Robert, 45
Gott, Richard, 225, 227, 229, 230, 231
Grimshaw, Brendon, 209
Grundy, Trevor, 229
Guevara, Ernesto 'Che', 44, 141, 177
Guinea, 112, 249–50, 254, 255
Gwenjere, Mateus, 155, 156–57, 159, 163, 168–69

Hall, Tony, 225, 230
Hallstein Doctrine, 102, 107, 115, 116, 120
Hanga, Kassim
  and Oscar Kambona, 73, 95, 97
  and Sékou Touré, 249
  as minister of industries, mines, and power, 41
  background, 34
  death of, 245–46
  dismissed from cabinet, 94, 112
  relations with GDR, 48, 105, 108, 111, 112
  relations with Soviet Union, 48, 49
  return to Tanzania and arrest, 97–98, 112
  Tanganyika-Zanzibar union, 43, 48
  views on economic policy, 72
  Zanzibar Revolution, 36, 42
Healey, Denis, 247
Heath, Edward, 247

Index

Hebich, Norbert, 116–17, 118, 119, 120, 128, 131
Ho Chi Minh, 177, 179, 182
Ho Lin, 54
Hong Kong, 4
Houphouët-Boigny, Félix, 230, 250
Houser, George, 156, 162
Hungary, 119

ideology, 14–15
India, 84, 85, 276
Indonesia, 53
International Monetary Fund, 71, 278
International Press Institute (IPI), 221–22
Interpol, 164
Iraq, 124
Israel, 252, 286, 287
Issa, Ali Sultan, 266
Ivory Coast, 116, 171, 250

Jamal, Amir
and Erhard Eppler, 130, 131
and Julius Nyerere, 71–72
as minister of commerce and industries, 264
as minister of finance, 94, 246
background and education, 71
economic diplomacy, 282
in Directorate of Development and Planning, 72
nationalisations, 88
papers of, 17
relations with FRG, 128
relations with Yugoslavia, 118
rumoured resignation from cabinet, 260
views on economic policy, 75, 87–88, 239, 240–41, 263, 269
James, C. L. R., 197
Jardim, Jorge, 166
Johnson, Lyndon B., 84, 180–81
Johnson, Phyllis, 143
Jumbe, Aboud, 269

Kabwe, Zitto, 287
Kaduma, Ibrahim, 282
Kajunjumele, Sam, 64, 203–4, 213
Kamaliza, Michael
as NUTA secretary-general, 76, 91
dismissed from cabinet, 94
Newspaper Ordinance (Amendment) Act, 220
treason trial, 242–43
Kambona, Mattiya, 97
Kambona, Oscar
and Julius Nyerere, 79, 80, 96–97, 112
and Kassim Hanga, 73
and Sékou Touré, 249
Arusha Declaration, 86, 93–94
as foreign minister, 80, 106, 123
as OAU Liberation Committee chairman, 143
as TANU secretary-general, 77
background and education, 72–73
expelled from TANU, 242
flight into exile, 96
mutiny, 37
Nationalist, 213
OAU Liberation Committee chairman, 28, 73, 138
plotting with Portugal, 270
relations with FRELIMO, 159
relations with GDR, 90, 108, 111–14
relations with Malawian dissidents, 188, 192
relations with United States, 43, 57
resigns from government, 95
rumours about, 39
Tanganyika-Zanzibar union, 42
treason trial, 143, 242–45
Kambona, Otini, 97, 112, 219
Kankhomba, Paulo, 163
Kapuściński, Ryszard, 140
karadha system, 259
Karume, Abeid
and A. M. Babu, 266
and Julius Nyerere, 265, 266
and Kassim Hanga, 94
assassination of, 267
deaths of Kassim Hanga and Othman Shariff, 245–46
relations with GDR, 105, 106
Tanganyika-Zanzibar union, 42
Zanzibar Revolution, 33
Kasella-Bantu, Joseph, 91
Kaunda, Kenneth, 221, 250, 251
Kavandame, Lazaro, 151–52, 157, 158, 159, 163, 167, 169

Kawawa, Rashidi
  addresses Malawi demonstration, 187, 193
  as second vice-president, 254
  invasion of Guinea, 249
  Mwongozo, 255
  Newspaper Ordinance (Amendment) Act, 220
  relations with China, 49
  relations with Eastern Bloc, 49
  relations with FRELIMO, 155, 159, 160
  relations with FRG and GDR, 118
Kenya
  ban on *Nationalist*, 222
  cabinet crisis, 78
  coup in Uganda, 251
  East African Federation, 29, 42
  mutiny in, 37
  relations with China, 178–79
Kenyatta, Jomo, 29, 162, 178, 221
KGB, 48, 60, 211
Kiesinger, Kurt Georg, 115, 128
Kilimanjaro Hotel, 1, 8, 53, 147, 210, 223, 235
Kisch, Richard, 213
Kivukoni College, 188, 214, 254

Leballo, Potlako, 229, 243–44
Leonhart, William, 43, 45, 149
Lessing, Gottfried, 109, 120
Lewis, Ida, 26
liberation movements
  concerns about security, 38–39
  criticism of, 141–43, 156, 161
  historiography, 136–37
  in Dar es Salaam, 28, 53, 137–45
  media, 140
  relations with communist world, 141
  subversion of, 143–44
  treason trial, 243–45
Liberation News Service, 227
Life magazine, 26
Little Red Book, 55, 177, 178, 230
Lonrho, 209
Lumumba University (Moscow), 34
Lumumba, Patrice, 8, 173, 281
Lusaka Manifesto, 171, 247, 257
Lusinde, Job, 62, 79, 93

Machel, Samora, 148, 153, 155, 168
Magaia, Filipe, 153
Magombe, George, 155, 171, 250
Magufuli, John, 286
Makame, Hasnu, 219–21
Makerere College, 69, 71, 122, 214
Makonde, 140, 150–52, 153, 154, 156, 158
Malawi, 187–92, 250
Malecela, John, 261
Manikam, Gerald, 167, 169
Mao Tse-tung, 49, 177
Maoism, 176–77, 258
Markham, Jimmy, 213
Markow, Walter, 100
Martin, David, 143, 164, 211
Martins, Helder, 168, 169
Masha, Fortunatus, 86, 242
Mbita, Hashim, 138, 255
Mbuya, Mejah, 286
Mdee, Sammy, 231
Mexico, 4
Mezhdunarodnaya Kniga, 178
Mfanya Kazi, 160, 220
Mgonja, Chediel
  as regional commissioner, 264
  protest at Soviet embassy, 184, 198–99
Mhando, Stephen
  relations with Eastern Bloc, 282
  relations with GDR, 100, 122–25, 132
  relations with West, 199
  views on liberation movements, 162, 171
Milas, Leo, 152
Mkapa, Benjamin
  at Ministry of Foreign Affairs, 32
  director of SHIHATA, 234
  editor of *Daily News*, 232
  editor of *Nationalist*, 182, 214
Mogadishu Declaration, 257
Mohammed, Bibi Titi, 92, 242–43
Mohammed, Humud, 267
Mondlane, Eduardo
  and Henry Chipembere, 192
  and Julius Nyerere, 158
  and Lawi Sijaona, 160–61, 201
  and Mateus Gwenjere, 156–57
  assassination, 135, 163–70

Index

background and education, 145–46, 150
criticism of, 152–53, 161–62
establishment of FRELIMO, 146
ideological outlook, 151
media, 146
memorial in Dar es Salaam, 286
relations with Britain, 155
relations with China, 147–48
relations with GDR, 148
relations with Soviet Union, 147–48
relations with Tanzanian leadership, 158, 163
relations with United States, 148–49
Second FRELIMO Congress, 157, 158
views on splits inside FRELIMO, 154
Mondlane, Janet, 145, 146, 152, 169–70
Mongolia, 185
Monteiro, Casimiro, 166
Morocco, 286, 287
Mozambique
   Cahora Bassa hydroelectric scheme, 129
   emigration from, 150
   memory politics in, 166–67, 169
Mtaki, Ali Saidi, 93
Mtei, Edwin
   Arusha Declaration, 86
   background and education, 71, 72
   views on economic policy, 87, 240–41
Mulungushi Club, 248
Musiba, Elvis, 273
mutiny, 37–38
Mwananchi Development Corporation, 216
Mwananchi News Company, 208
Mwapachu, Juma, 182, 194, 257
Mwongozo
   African liberation, 256
   announcement of, 237
   approved by TANU National Conference, 263
   comparison with Arusha Declaration, 271
   consequences of, 262
   contents of, 255–59
   Standard, 229–30
   vanguardism, 257–58

Nasser, Gamal Abdel, 5, 35, 62, 76, 98
Nation Group, 222
National Development Corporation (NDC), 276
National Union of Tanganyika Workers (NUTA)
   calls off Czechoslovakia demonstration, 186
   creation of, 39
   criticism of, 76
   liberation fund, 144
   organises Malawi demonstrations, 190, 196
   views on economic policy, 76, 91
nationalisation
   Arusha Declaration, 85–88
   buildings, 259–60, 262
   debate about, 76
   Standard, 223–24
Nationalist
   banned in Kenya, 222
   criticises Eduardo Mondlane, 161
   criticises foreign news agencies, 210
   criticises FRG, 108
   editorial staff, 213
   establishment, 208–9
   financial problems, 216–17
   merger with *Standard*, 232
   reputation, 212–14
   rivalry with *Standard*, 214–16
Naudy, André, 63
Netanyahu, Benjamin, 287
Netherlands, 80, 91
New Africa Hotel, 1, 8, 53, 140, 142, 210, 286
New China News Agency, 34, 227
New Dar es Salaam Club, 223
New International Economic Order, 233, 276, 284
New World Information and Communications Order (NWICO), 233, 234
New Zahir Restaurant, 54, 286
news agencies, 209–11
newspapers. *See* press, *Nationalist*, *Ngurumo*, *Standard*, *Uhuru*
Ng'weno, Hilary, 221
Ngombale-Mwiru, Kingunge
   background and education, 253–54
   creation of militas, 254

Ngombale-Mwiru, Kingunge (cont.)
  informed of Babu's imprisonment, 268
  Mwongozo, 255, 257
  relations with North Vietnam, 182
  vanguardism, 258
Ngurumo, 207–8, 224, 234
Nigeria, 38, 78, 185–86
Nimeiry, Gaafar, 230
Nkomo, Joshua, 246
Nkrumah, Kwame
  African liberation, 5, 139, 146
  decolonisation, 11
  overthrown in coup, 79, 82, 173, 281
  pan-Africanism, 29
  views on German question, 103
  views on press, 203–4
non-alignment, 30–31, 101–2, 202
  'German question', 103–4
  China, 122
North Atlantic Treaty Organization (NATO), 149, 166
North Korea, 178, 207
Northwestern University, 145
Nsa Kaisi, Kabenga, 213, 214, 216
Nungu, Silvério, 167, 168
Nyakyi, Anthony, 129
Nyerere, Julius
  1965 elections, 64
  African liberation, 2, 28, 172
  and A. M. Babu, 90–91, 239–40, 266–68
  and Amir Jamal, 71–72, 87, 260
  and Eduardo Mondlane, 145
  and Hastings Banda, 189, 190, 191
  and Kassim Hanga, 97
  and Milton Obote, 251–52
  and Oscar Kambona, 73, 80, 93, 96–97, 112
  and Paul Bomani, 72, 265
  and Sékou Touré, 249
  and Willy Brandt, 127–28, 129, 131
  Argue Don't Shout, 228
  Arusha Declaration, 66, 82–86
  as TANU chairman, 73
  assessment of Tanzania's achievements, 285
  background and education, 69
  bans USARF, 197
  cabinet reshuffles, 72, 90, 94–95, 161, 264–66
  Commonwealth, 250–51
  concerns about subversion, 2, 8, 45, 61, 78–79, 96, 98, 256
  criticises liberation movements, 142
  criticism of leadership style, 261–62
  deaths of Kassim Hanga and Othman Shariff, 245–46
  East African integration, 29
  economic diplomacy, 48, 260, 281–82
  engagement with international media, 51, 128, 207
  expulsion of TANU members, 241–42
  foreign policy, 27–32, 281
  human rights, 246
  international respectability, 198, 199
  interventions in Tanzanian press, 162, 186, 209, 212, 214, 228–29, 230–31
  leadership code, 92
  limits to power in Tanzania, 282
  mutiny, 37–38
  Mwongozo, 237, 256
  nationalisation of buildings, 260
  nationalisation of internal trade, 241
  nationalisation of *Standard*, 217, 223–24
  nationalisations after Arusha Declaration, 86
  New International Economic Order,
  non-alignment, 30–31, 101–2, 122
  opposition to arms sales to South Africa, 248–49
  orders demonstrations against invasion of Czechoslovakia, 184, 194
  pan-Africanism, 29
  recognition of Biafra, 185
  relations with Britain, 212, 228, 248–49
  relations with China, 50, 185
  relations with Commonwealth, 180
  relations with Eastern Bloc, 123
  relations with FRELIMO, 158, 159
  relations with FRG, 105–7, 128–29, 130

relations with GDR, 105–7, 112–13, 120–21, 124–25
relations with Netherlands, 91
relations with Soviet Union, 186
relations with TYL, 195, 198, 201, 254
relations with Uganda, 270–71, 278
relations with United States, 43, 180–81
relations with Zanzibar, 245–46, 265, 268
relocates capital to Dodoma, 283
response to coup in Ghana, 79
response to coup in Uganda, 251–52
response to student demonstrations, 46, 82
rumours about, 259, 267
self-reliance, 11, 83–85, 88, 114
stands down as president, 278
Tanganyika-Zanzibar union, 40–42
treason trial, 243
ujamaa, 69–70, 89
views on 1968 revolutions, 194
views on decolonisation, 11
views on democracy, 40
views on foreign propaganda, 56, 109
views on *Mwongozo*, 257
views on nationalisation, 76, 85–86
views on propaganda, 120, 180
views on relations with South Africa, 250
views on rumour, 57–59, 81
views on vanguardism, 91, 257–58
views on war in Vietnam, 180–81
views on youth politics, 176

Oberlin College, 145
Obote, Milton
  addresses TANU NEC meeting, 255
  and Julius Nyerere, 251–52
  Commonwealth, 250
  dismisses fears of coup, 253
  East African Federation, 29
  opposition to arms sales to South Africa, 248
  overthrown in coup, 250–51
  relations with Britain, 252
Ochieng, Philip, 225, 232, 233, 236, 265–66
Odinga, Oginga, 96, 178
Ogunsanwo, Cornelius, 226
Okello, John, 33
Operation GLADIO, 166
Organisation of African Unity (OAU)
  charter, 29, 79, 185
  emergency meeting after mutiny, 38
  foundation of, 28
  Liberation Committee, 28, 38, 62, 129, 138–39, 143, 170, 171, 189, 285
  politics following coup in Ghana, 80
  response to Rhodesia's UDI, 47
  Tanzania, 29
Organisation of the Petroleum Exporting Countries, 277

PAIGC (*Partido Africano da Independência da Guiné e Cabo Verde*, African Party for the Independence of Guinea and Cape Verde), 139, 249
Pakistan, 276
Palestine Liberation Organisation, 287
Palm Beach Hotel, 53, 108, 112, 243
Pan-African Congress, 284
Panafrican Democratic Party (PDP), 188
Pan-African Freedom Movement of Eastern and Central Africa (PAFMECA), 28
Pan-African Youth Movement (PAYM), 176, 253–54
pan-Africanism, 29, 41
Pan-Africanist Congress of Azania (PAC), 229, 243
Peace Corps, 182, 211
Peace News, 225
Phillips, Horace, 227–28, 248
Phombeah, Dennis, 90, 97, 111–12, 114
PIDE, 154, 165–66, 168
Plekhanov, Georgi, 135, 164
Poland, 49, 119
Portugal
  assassination of Eduardo Mondlane, 165–66
  coup in, 274
  intelligence activities in Dar es Salaam, 54, 143–44, 154, 210

Portugal (cont.)
  invasion of Guinea, 249
  letter plot, 44
  NATO member, 149
  relations with FRG, 103, 108, 125, 129
  relations with Malawi, 189
  resistance to colonial rule in Mozambique, 150
  response to coup in Ghana, 79
  threat to Tanzania, 44, 118, 190, 220, 250
Prensa Latina, 227
press
  'developmental journalism', 218
  ban on *Daily Nation*, 222
  concepts of, 204–5, 236, 283
  creation of Press Council, 232
  foreign journalists' complaints, 234–35
  freedom of the press, 218–22, 224
  liberation movements, 140–41
  Newspaper Ordinance (Amendment) Act, 219–20
Prince, Rod, 225, 230
propaganda, 55–57, 100, 120, 177–78

Qullatein, Badawi, 266

radio, 138, 140–41, 206–7
Radio Cairo, 206
Radio Tanzania Dar es Salaam, 138, 140, 217
Reuters, 210, 211, 230, 234–35
Rhodesia
  expulsion of spies from Dar es Salaam, 61
  threat to Tanzania, 118
  Unilateral Declaration of Independence (UDI), 46–47, 50
Ridley, Ken, 209, 216
Riyami, Abdulla, 218, 221, 222
Rockefeller Foundation, 221
Rodney, Walter, 227
Romania, 115, 119
rumour, 57–60, 80–81, 259, 267
Rupia, Paul, 28, 32
Rweyemamu, Justinian, 269

Salazar, António de Oliveira, 149, 166
Salim, Salim Ahmed, 60
Salumu, Hamisi, 96
Sarakikya, Mrisho, 39, 255
Schlegel, Horst, 123
Schroeder, Herbert, 105
Scotland Yard, 164
self-reliance, 83–85, 88, 114, 241
Senegal, 194, 254
Shaba, Austin, 105, 113
Shariff, Othman, 245–46
SHIHATA (*Shirika la Habari la Tanzania*, News Agency of Tanzania), 234
Shipanga, Andreas, 142
Shivji, Issa, 83, 197, 278
Sijaona, Lawi
  as regional commissioner, 264
  protest at Soviet embassy, 184, 198–99
  relations with FRELIMO, 159–61, 163, 169
  relations with FRG, 131
  TANU Youth League, 195, 199, 201
  views on Vietnam war, 193
Simango, Uria, 147, 155, 158, 159, 164, 168, 169
Simonstown Agreement, 247, 248
Smith, Ian, 46, 246
socialism, 76–77
Somalia, 124, 271
South Africa
  arms sales from Britain, 228, 247–49, 250–51
  bombings in Dar es Salaam, 270
  expulsion of spies from Dar es Salaam, 61
  intelligence on Tanzania, 26, 165
  post-apartheid diplomacy, 287
  relations with African states, 171, 250
  relations with FRG, 103, 108, 125, 130
  relations with Malawi, 189
South West Africa People's Organisation (SWAPO), 139, 142, 170

Index

Soviet Union, 55
  Afro-Asian People's Solidarity
    Organisation, 148
  intelligence activities in Dar es
    Salaam, 63
  interventions in Tanzanian press, 211
  invasion of Czechoslovakia, 183–87
  propaganda, 178
  relations with FRELIMO, 147–48
  relations with Oscar Kambona, 95
  relations with Tanzania, 48–49,
    183–87, 274
  relations with Zanzibar, 36
  response to Arusha Declaration, 110
  response to *Ostpolitik*, 119
  support for liberation movements,
    141
  Tanganyika-Zanzibar union, 48
Standard
  background, 209
  consequences of *Mwongozo*, 229–30
  criticism of, 223, 227–28
  implications of Arusha Declaration,
    217
  internationalism, 226–27
  merger with *Nationalist*, 232
  nationalisation, 217, 223–24
  news agencies, 210, 227
  Newspaper Ordinance (Amendment)
    Act, 220–21
  report on preventative detention, 226
  rivalry with the *Nationalist*, 214–16
  staff politics, 225–26, 229
Stanleyville, 44
Stasi, 45, 48, 104, 109, 110, 113, 245,
  258
State Trading Corporation (STC), 239,
  261, 264
state, scholarship on, 11–13
students
  as liberation movement members,
    141, 152–53, 155
  decolonisation and, 175
  demonstration against invasion of
    Czechoslovakia, 184, 194
  demonstration against national
    service, 82, 176
  demonstration against war in
    Vietnam, 182–83
  reading radical literature, 178

relations with TYL, 196–98
views on 1968 revolutions, 194
Sudan, 124, 230–31
Svendsen, Knud Erik, 261–62
Swai, Nsilo, 71, 72, 90
Sweden, 152
Syracuse University, 146

Tabora Boys School, 69, 71, 73
Tambo, Oliver, 225, 244
Tanganyika
  mutiny in, 37–38
  union with Zanzibar, 40–43
Tanganyika African Association, 69
Tanganyika African National Union
    (TANU)
  cell system, 39–40
  Central Committee, 73, 93
  creation of CCM, 269
  establishment of, 69
  expulsion of critics, 241–42
  ideology, 73
  institutional structure, 73
  National Conference, 73, 180,
    263
  National Executive Committee
    (NEC), 40, 64, 73, 83, 84, 92, 217,
    237, 241–42, 254–55, 259–60
  newspapers, 208–9, 216–17
  one-party state, 40
  Press Council, 232
  relations with ASP, 41–42
  special conference after Arusha
    Declaration, 91, 92
Tanganyika Bookshop, 54, 55, 64, 178,
  275
Tanganyika Broadcasting Corporation
  (TBC), 56, 138, 206
Tanganyika Federation of Labour, 39
Tanganyika Rifles, 37, 39, 176
Tanganyika Sisal Marketing
  Association, 123
Tanganyika Women's Union, 93
Tanganyika-Zanzibar union, 40–43
TANU Youth League (TYL)
  'Operation Vijana' campaign, 195,
    223
  criticises *Standard*, 223
  demonstration against invasion of
    Czechoslovakia,

TANU Youth League (TYL) (cont.)
  demonstration against invasion of Guinea, 250
  demonstration against war in Vietnam, 182–83
  establishment and role, 175–77
  Nyerere's views on, 198, 201
  Pan-African Youth Movement and, 253–54
  relations with student movements, 196–98
  response to Arusha Declaration, 91
  response to coup in Uganda, 252
  support for North Vietnam, 182–83
  vanguardism, 241
Tanzania
  cabinet reshuffles in, 72, 90, 94–95, 122, 161, 264–67
  creation of, 40–43
  economic performance, 81, 239–41, 277, 278
  elections, 64, 72, 74, 92
  elite in, 13–14
  one-party state, 40
  parliament, 95
  relations with United States, 180–81
  response to coup in Uganda, 251–53
  sensitivity to critical media coverage, 212
  treason trial, 242–45
Tanzania People's Defence Force (TPDF), 39, 78, 97, 138, 158, 176, 220, 255, 267, 275
Tanzanian economic policy
  First Five-Year Plan (1964–69), 72, 75, 81
  Second Five-Year Plan (1969–74), 130, 239, 240
Tanzanian foreign policy
  African liberation, 28–29
  contemporary perspectives, 286–87
  core principles, 27–32
  international respectability, 15, 198
  Ministry of Foreign Affairs, 32
  New International Economic Order, non-alignment, 30–31, 118, 200
  pan-Africanism, 29
  recognition of Biafra, 185
  relations with Britain, 47, 212, 248–49
  relations with China, 49–50, 122, 185, 275
  relations with FRG, 106–7, 117–18, 128–31
  relations with GDR, 109–10, 124–25, 131
  relations with India, 276
  relations with Malawi, 187–92
  relations with Pakistan, 276
  relations with Soviet Union, 48–49, 183–87, 274
  relations with Uganda, 270, 278
  relations with United States, 43–44, 274
Tass, 227
TAZARA railway, 50, 114, 122, 239
television, 56
Thaker, Randhir, 207
Tito, Josip Broz, 131
Touré, Sékou, 97, 249
transnational history, 3
treason trial, 242–45
Tshombe, Moïse, 43, 98
Turok, Ben, 53, 140
Twiga Hotel, 53, 243

Uganda
  cabinet crisis, 78
  East African Federation, 29, 42
  espionage in Dar es Salaam, 271
  influence of coup on *Mwongozo*, 255
  mutiny in, 37
  relations with Tanzania, 278
  Tanzanian response to coup, 251–53
Uhuru, 208, 234
ujamaa, 10–11, 58, 69–70, 77, 89, 98–99, 232, 261, 269
Ulimwengu, 219
Ulimwengu, Jenerali, 196, 197, 211, 232
Umma Party, 34, 35, 36, 258, 266, 267
United Nations (UN), 27, 30, 71, 145, 155, 184, 186, 246, 250
United States
  'letter plot', 43–44
  'phone tap' controversy, 45
  aid conditionality, 84
  complaints about TANU Youth League, 199

complaints about Tanzanian press, 228
concerns about China, 50–51
embassy in Dar es Salaam, 52
relations with FRELIMO, 148–49
relations with Tanzania, 43–44, 180–81, 274
response to Zanzibar Revolution, 33–34
Tanganyika-Zanzibar union, 42
war in Vietnam, 179–83
United States Information Service, 55
University College, Dar es Salaam, 54, 82
University of Dar es Salaam (UDSM), 227, 232, 286, *See* University College, Dar es Salaam
University Students African Revolutionary Front (USARF), 197–98
Upper Volta, 78

van Eeghen, Ernest, 96
vanguardism, 91, 93, 158, 232, 258
Verwoerd, Hendrik, 26
Vieira, Sérgio, 168–69
Vietnam, 5, 84, 179–83
Vigilance Africa, 55, 64, 213
villagisation, 11, 66, 238, 239, 240, 259, 264, 277
von Hassel, Kai-Uwe, 117, 121, 128
Vorster, John, 230

West Germany. *See* Federal Republic of Germany (FRG)
Western Sahara, 286–87

Willi Stoph, 129
Williams, G. Mennen, 45
Wilson, Harold, 46
Winzer, Otto, 124–25
World Bank, 274, 278

youth, 175–76
Yugoslavia, 103, 115, 116, 118, 120, 131

Zambia, 50, 114, 148, 168, 171, 190, 239, 284
Zanzibar
 economic situation in, 265–66
 FRELIMO in, 151
 racial politics in, 35, 245
 relations with China, 36
 relations with GDR, 36, 104–5, 106, 125
 relations with mainland, 246–47, 265
 relations with Soviet Union, 36
 Revolutionary Council, 36
 situation under Karume regime, 245
 teenage brides controversy, 246
 union with Tanganyika, 40–43
Zanzibar and Pemba People's Party (ZPPP), 33, 35
Zanzibar Nationalist Party (ZNP), 33, 34, 35
Zanzibar Revolution, 33–37
Zhou Enlai, 50, 185
Zimbabwe African National Union (ZANU), 46, 140, 142, 190
Zimbabwe African People's Union (ZAPU), 46, 61, 142, 190

African Studies Series

1 *City Politics: A Study of Leopoldville, 1962–63*, J. S. La Fontaine
2 *Studies in Rural Capitalism in West Africa*, Polly Hill
3 *Land Policy in Buganda*, Henry W. West
4 *The Nigerian Military: A Sociological Analysis of Authority and Revolt, 1960–67*, Robin Luckham
5 *The Ghanaian Factory Worker: Industrial Man in Africa*, Margaret Peil
6 *Labour in the South African Gold Mines*, Francis Wilson
7 *The Price of Liberty: Personality and Politics in Colonial Nigeria*, Kenneth W. J. Post and George D. Jenkins
8 *Subsistence to Commercial Farming in Present-Day Buganda: An Economic and Anthropological Survey*, Audrey I. Richards, Fort Sturrock, and Jean M. Fortt (eds.)
9 *Dependence and Opportunity: Political Change in Ahafo*, John Dunn and A. F. Robertson
10 *African Railwaymen: Solidarity and Opposition in an East African Labour Force*, R. D. Grillo
11 *Islam and Tribal Art in West Africa*, René A. Bravmann
12 *Modern and Traditional Elites in the Politics of Lagos*, P. D. Cole
13 *Asante in the Nineteenth Century: The Structure and Evaluation of a Political Order*, Ivor Wilks
14 *Culture, Tradition and Society in the West African Novel*, Emmanuel Obiechina
15 *Saints and Politicians*, Donal B. Cruise O'Brien
16 *The Lions of Dagbon: Political Change in Northern Ghana*, Martin Staniland
17 *Politics of Decolonization: Kenya Europeans and the Land Issue 1960–1965*, Gary B. Wasserman
18 *Muslim Brotherhoods in the Nineteenth-Century Africa*, B. G. Martin
19 *Warfare in the Sokoto Caliphate: Historical and Sociological Perspectives*, Joseph P. Smaldone
20 *Liberia and Sierra Leone: An Essay in Comparative Politics*, Christopher Clapham
21 *Adam Kok's Griquas: A Study in the Development of Stratification in South Africa*, Robert Ross
22 *Class, Power and Ideology in Ghana: The Railwaymen of Sekondi*, Richard Jeffries
23 *West African States: Failure and Promise*, John Dunn (ed.)
24 *Afrikaaners of the Kalahari: White Minority in a Black State*, Margo Russell and Martin Russell
25 *A Modern History of Tanganyika*, John Iliffe

26 *A History of African Christianity 1950–1975*, Adrian Hastings
27 *Slaves, Peasants and Capitalists in Southern Angola, 1840–1926*, W. G. Clarence-Smith
28 *The Hidden Hippopotamus: Reappraised in African History: The Early Colonial Experience in Western Zambia*, Gwyn Prins
29 *Families Divided: The Impact of Migrant Labour in Lesotho*, Colin Murray
30 *Slavery, Colonialism and Economic Growth in Dahomey, 1640–1960*, Patrick Manning
31 *Kings, Commoners and Concessionaries: The Evolution of Dissolution of the Nineteenth-Century Swazi State*, Philip Bonner
32 *Oral Poetry and Somali Nationalism: The Case of Sayid Mahammad 'Abdille Hasan*, Said S. Samatar
33 *The Political Economy of Pondoland 1860–1930*, William Beinart
34 *Volkskapitalisme: Class, Capitals and Ideology in the Development of Afrikaner Nationalism, 1934–1948*, Dan O'Meara
35 *The Settler Economies: Studies in the Economic History of Kenya and Rhodesia 1900–1963*, Paul Mosely
36 *Transformations in Slavery: A History of Slavery in Africa, 1st edition*, Paul Lovejoy
37 *Amilcar Cabral: Revolutionary Leadership and People's War*, Patrick Chabal
38 *Essays on the Political Economy of Rural Africa*, Robert H. Bates
39 *Ijeshas and Nigerians: The Incorporation of a Yoruba Kingdom, 1890s–1970s*, J. D. Y. Peel
40 *Black People and the South African War, 1899–1902*, Peter Warwick
41 *A History of Niger 1850–1960*, Finn Fuglestad
42 *Industrialisation and Trade Union Organization in South Africa, 1924–1955*, Stephen Ellis
43 *The Rising of the Red Shawls: A Revolt in Madagascar 1895–1899*, Stephen Ellis
44 *Slavery in Dutch South Africa*, Nigel Worden
45 *Law, Custom and Social Order: The Colonial Experience in Malawi and Zambia*, Martin Chanock
46 *Salt of the Desert Sun: A History of Salt Production and Trade in the Central Sudan*, Paul E. Lovejoy
47 *Marrying Well: Marriage, Status and Social Change Among the Educated Elite in Colonial Lagos*, Kristin Mann
48 *Language and Colonial Power: The Appropriation of Swahili in the Former Belgian Congo, 1880–1938*, Johannes Fabian
49 *The Shell Money of the Slave Trade*, Jan Hogendorn and Marion Johnson

50 *Political Domination in Africa*, Patrick Chabal
51 *The Southern Marches of Imperial Ethiopia: Essays in History and Social Anthropology*, Donald Donham and Wendy James
52 *Islam and Urban Labor in Northern Nigeria: The Making of a Muslim Working Class*, Paul M. Lubeck
53 *Horn and Crescent: Cultural Change and Traditional Islam on the East African Coast, 800–1900*, Randall L. Pouwels
54 *Capital and Labour on the Kimberley Diamond Fields, 1871–1890*, Robert Vicat Turrell
55 *National and Class Conflict in the Horn of Africa*, John Markakis
56 *Democracy and Prebendal Politics in Nigeria: The Rise and Fall of the Second Republic*, Richard A. Joseph
57 *Entrepreneurs and Parasites: The Struggle for Indigenous Capitalism in Zaire*, Janet MacGaffey
58 *The African Poor: A History*, John Iliffe
59 *Palm Oil and Protest: An Economic History of the Ngwa Region, South-Eastern Nigeria, 1800–1980*, Susan M. Martin
60 *France and Islam in West Africa, 1860–1960*, Christopher Harrison
61 *Transformation and Continuity in Revolutionary Ethiopia*, Christopher Clapham
62 *Prelude to the Mahdiyya: Peasants and Traders in the Shendi Region, 1821–1885*, Anders Bjorkelo
63 *Wa and the Wala: Islam and Polity in Northwestern Ghana*, Ivor Wilks
64 *H.C. Bankole-Bright and Politics in Colonial Sierra Leone, 1919–1958*, Akintola Wyse
65 *Contemporary West African States*, Donal Cruise O'Brien, John Dunn, and Richard Rathbone (eds.)
66 *The Oromo of Ethiopia: A History, 1570–1860*, Mohammed Hassen
67 *Slavery and African Life: Occidental, Oriental, and African Slave Trades*, Patrick Manning
68 *Abraham Esau's War: A Black South African War in the Cape, 1899–1902*, Bill Nasson
69 *The Politics of Harmony: Land Dispute Strategies in Swaziland*, Laurel L. Rose
70 *Zimbabwe's Guerrilla War: Peasant Voices*, Norma J. Kriger
71 *Ethiopia: Power and Protest: Peasant Revolts in the Twentieth-Century*, Gebru Tareke
72 *White Supremacy and Black Resistance in Pre-Industrial South Africa: The Making of the Colonial Order in the Eastern Cape, 1770–1865*, Clifton C. Crais
73 *The Elusive Granary: Herder, Farmer, and State in Northern Kenya*, Peter D. Little

74 *The Kanyok of Zaire: An Institutional and Ideological History to 1895*, John C. Yoder
75 *Pragmatism in the Age of Jihad: The Precolonial State of Bundu*, Michael A. Gomez
76 *Slow Death for Slavery: The Course of Abolition in Northern Nigeria, 1897–1936*, Paul E. Lovejoy and Jan S. Hogendorn
77 *West African Slavery and Atlantic Commerce: The Senegal River Valley, 1700–1860*, James F. Searing
78 *A South African Kingdom: The Pursuit of Security in the Nineteenth-Century Lesotho*, Elizabeth A. Elredge
79 *State and Society in Pre-Colonial Asante*, T. C. McCaskie
80 *Islamic Society and State Power in Senegal: Disciples and Citizens in Fatick*, Leonardo A. Villalon
81 *Ethnic Pride and Racial Prejudice in Victorian Cape Town: Group Identity and Social Practice*, Vivian Bickford-Smith
82 *The Eritrean Struggle for Independence: Domination, Resistance and Nationalism, 1941–1993*, Ruth Iyob
83 *Corruption and State Politics in Sierra Leone*, William Reno
84 *The Culture of Politics in Modern Kenya*, Angelique Haugerud
85 *Africans: The History of a Continent, 1st edition*, John Iliffe
86 *From Slave Trade to 'Legitimate' Commerce: The Commercial Transition in Nineteenth-Century West Africa*, Robin Law (ed.)
87 *Leisure and Society in Colonial Brazzaville*, Phyllis Martin
88 *Kingship and State: The Buganda Dynasty*, Christopher Wrigley
89 *Decolonialization and African Life: The Labour Question in French and British Africa*, Frederick Cooper
90 *Misreading the African Landscape: Society and Ecology in an African Forest-Savannah Mosaic*, James Fairhead, and Melissa Leach
91 *Peasant Revolution in Ethiopia: The Tigray People's Liberation Front, 1975–1991*, John Young
92 *Senegambia and the Atlantic Slave Trade*, Boubacar Barry
93 *Commerce and Economic Change in West Africa: The Oil Trade in the Nineteenth Century*, Martin Lynn
94 *Slavery and French Colonial Rule in West Africa: Senegal, Guinea and Mali*, Martin A. Klein
95 *East African Doctors: A History of the Modern Profession*, John Iliffe
96 *Middlemen of the Cameroons Rivers: The Duala and Their Hinterland, c.1600–1960*, Ralph Derrick, Ralph A. Austen, and Jonathan Derrick
97 *Masters and Servants on the Cape Eastern Frontier, 1760–1803*, Susan Newton-King
98 *Status and Respectability in the Cape Colony, 1750–1870: A Tragedy of Manners*, Robert Ross

99 *Slaves, Freedmen and Indentured Laborers in Colonial Mauritius*, Richard B. Allen
100 *Transformations in Slavery: A History of Slavery in Africa, 2nd edition*, Paul E. Lovejoy
101 *The Peasant Cotton Revolution in West Africa: Cote d'Ivoire, 1880–1995*, Thomas E. Basset
102 *Re-imagining Rwanda: Conflict, Survival and Disinformation in the Late Twentieth Century*, Johan Pottier
103 *The Politics of Evil: Magic, State Power and the Political Imagination in South Africa*, Clifton Crais
104 *Transforming Mozambique: The Politics of Privatization, 1975–2000*, M. Anne Pitcher
105 *Guerrilla Veterans in Post-War Zimbabwe: Symbolic and Violent Politics, 1980–1987*, Norma J. Kriger
106 *An Economic History of Imperial Madagascar, 1750–1895: The Rise and Fall of an Island Empire*, Gwyn Campbell
107 *Honour in African History*, John Iliffe
108 *Africans: A History of a Continent, 2nd edition*, John Iliffe
109 *Guns, Race, and Power in Colonial South Africa*, William Kelleher Storey
110 *Islam and Social Change in French West Africa: History of an Emancipatory Community*, Sean Hanretta
111 *Defeating Mau Mau, Creating Kenya: Counterinsurgency, Civil War and Decolonization*, Daniel Branch
112 *Christianity and Genocide in Rwanda*, Timothy Longman
113 *From Africa to Brazil: Culture, Identity, and an African Slave Trade, 1600–1830*, Walter Hawthorne
114 *Africa in the Time of Cholera: A History of Pandemics from 1817 to the Present*, Myron Echenberg
115 *A History of Race in Muslim West Africa, 1600–1960*, Bruce S. Hall
116 *Witchcraft and Colonial Rule in Kenya, 1900–1955*, Katherine Luongo
117 *Transformations in Slavery: A History of Slavery in Africa, 3rd edition*, Paul E. Lovejoy
118 *The Rise of the Trans-Atlantic Slave Trade in Western Africa, 1300–1589*, Toby Green
119 *Party Politics and Economic Reform in Africa's Democracies*, M. Anne Pitcher
120 *Smugglers and Saints of the Sahara: Regional Connectivity in the Twentieth Century*, Judith Scheele
121 *Cross-Cultural Exchange in the Atlantic World: Angola and Brazil During the Era of the Slave Trade*, Roquinaldo Ferreira

122 *Ethnic Patriotism and the East African Revival*, Derek Peterson
123 *Black Morocco: A History of Slavery and Islam*, Chouki El Hamel
124 *An African Slaving Port and the Atlantic World: Benguela and Its Hinterland*, Mariana Candido
125 *Making Citizens in Africa: Ethnicity, Gender, and National Identity in Ethiopia*, Lahra Smith
126 *Slavery and Emancipation in Islamic East Africa: From Honor to Respectability*, Elisabeth McMahon
127 *A History of African Motherhood: The Case of Uganda, 700–1900*, Rhiannon Stephens
128 *The Borders of Race in Colonial South Africa: The Kat River Settlement, 1829–1856*, Robert Ross
129 *From Empires to NGOs in the West African Sahel: The Road to Nongovernmentality*, Gregory Mann
130 *Dictators and Democracy in African Development: The Political Economy of Good Governance in Nigeria*, A. Carl LeVan
131 *Water, Civilization and Power in Sudan: The Political Economy of Military-Islamist State Building*, Harry Verhoeven
132 *The Fruits of Freedom in British Togoland: Literacy, Politics and Nationalism, 1914–2014*, Kate Skinner
133 *Political Thought and the Public Sphere in Tanzania: Freedom, Democracy and Citizenship in the Era of Decolonization*, Emma Hunter
134 *Political Identity and Conflict in Central Angola, 1975–2002*, Justin Pearce
135 *From Slavery to Aid: Politics, Labour, and Ecology in the Nigerian Sahel, 1800–2000*, Benedetta Rossi
136 *National Liberation in Postcolonial Southern Africa: A Historical Ethnography of SWAPO's Exile Camps*, Christian A. Williams
137 *Africans: A History of a Continent, 3rd edition*, John Iliffe
138 *Colonial Buganda and the End of Empire: Political Thought and Historical Imagination in Africa*, Jonathon L. Earle
139 *The Struggle over State Power in Zimbabwe: Law and Politics since 1950*, George Karekwaivanane
140 *Transforming Sudan: Decolonisation, Economic Development and State Formation*, Alden Young
141 *Colonizing Consent: Rape and Governance in South Africa's Eastern Cape*, Elizabeth Thornberry
142 *The Value of Disorder: Autonomy, Prosperity and Plunder in the Chadian Sahara*, Julien Brachet and Judith Scheele
143 *The Politics of Poverty: Policy-Making and Development in Rural Tanzania*, Felicitas Becker

144 *Boundaries, Communities, and State-Making in West Africa: The Centrality of the Margins*, Paul Nugent
145 *Politics and Violence in Burundi: The Language of Truth in an Emerging State*, Aidan Russell
146 *Power and the Presidency in Kenya: The Jomo Kenyatta Years*, Anaïs Angelo
147 *East Africa after Liberation: Conflict, Security and the State Since the 1980s*, Jonathan Fisher
148 *Sultan, Caliph, and the Renewer of the Faith: Ahmad Lobbo, the Tārīkh al-fattāsh and the Making of an Islamic State in West Africa*, Mauro Nobili
149 *Shaping the African Savannah: From Capitalist Frontier to Arid Eden in Namibia*, Michael Bollig
150 *France's Wars in Chad: Military Intervention and Decolonization in Africa*, Nathaniel K. Powell
151 *Islam, Ethnicity, and Conflict in Ethiopia: The Bale Insurgency, 1963–1970*, Terje Østebø
152 *The Path to Genocide in Rwanda: Security, Opportunity, and Authority in an Ethnocratic State*, Omar Shahabudin McDoom
153 *Development, (Dual) Citizenship and Its Discontents in Africa: The Political Economy of Belonging to Liberia*, Robtel Neajai Pailey
154 *Salafism and Political Order in Africa*, Sebastian Elischer
155 *Performing Power in Zimbabwe: Politics, Law and the Courts Since 2000*, Susanne Verheul
156 *Revolutionary State-Making in Dar es Salaam: African Liberation and the Global Cold War, 1961–1974*, George Roberts

For EU product safety concerns, contact us at Calle de José Abascal, 56–1°,
28003 Madrid, Spain or eugpsr@cambridge.org.

www.ingramcontent.com/pod-product-compliance
Ingram Content Group UK Ltd.
Pitfield, Milton Keynes, MK11 3LW, UK
UKHW020050040426
469672UK00019B/391